TANTRIC BUDDHISM

CENTENNIAL TRIBUTE TO
DR. BENOYTOSH BHATTACHARYYA

TANTRIC BUDDHISM

Centennial Tribute to Dr. Benoytosh Bhattacharyya

Edited by

N.N. BHATTACHARYYA

Associate Editor

AMARTYA GHOSH

MANOHAR

2005

First published 1999
Reprinted 2005

ISBN 81-7304-191-1 (Hb)
ISBN 81-7304-649-2 (Pb)

Published by
Ajay Kumar Jain for
Manohar Publishers & Distributors
4753/23 Ansari Road, Daryaganj
New Delhi 110 002

Typeset by
A J Software Publishing Co. Pvt. Ltd.
New Delhi 110 005

Printed at
Lordson Publishers Pvt Ltd
Delhi 110 007

Distributed in South Asia by
FOUNDATION BOOKS
4381/4, Ansari Road
Daryaganj, New Delhi 110 002
and its branches at Mumbai, Hyderabad,
Bangalore, Chennai, Kolkata

Contents

Preface

This is a centennial tribute to an outstanding pioneer in the field of Tantric-Buddhist studies, Dr. Benoytosh Bhattacharyya (1897-1964). The volume contains papers by a generation of scholars on different aspects of Tantric Buddhism and Tantrism in general. We are grateful to all who have contributed to this volume out of their genuine respect to the scholarship of Dr. Benoytosh Bhattacharyya.

In the preparation of the volume we have been immensely assisted by Dr. (Mrs.) Kalpakam Sankarnarayan, Director, Somaiya Centre of Buddhist Studies, Bombay, who has not only shown great interest in the project, but also made contact with scholars and persuaded them to contribute to this volume. In a similar way we have been assisted by Prof Suniti Kumar Pathak, formerly of the Visva-bharati University. Here we like to put on record the constant support and encouragement of Dr. Amiya Kumar Bhattacharyya of Naihati, the son of Dr. Benoytosh and convener of the Benoytosh Centenary Committee, who was the driving force behind this project. Finally we thank Ramesh Jain and Ajay Jain of Manohar Publishers & Distributors, New Delhi, for bringing out this volume as a fitting tribute to Dr. Benoytosh Bhattacharyya.

Benoytosh Bhattacharyya

Dr. Benoytosh Bhattacharyya (1897-1964)

Dr. Benoytosh Bhattacharyya, one of the greatest pioneers of Tantric and iconographical studies, was born on 6 January 1897 at Deasin in Burdwan District, West Bengal. His father was the celebrated Indologist, Mahāmahopādhyāya Haraprasād Sāstrī, whose contributions to Buddhism, Sanskrit literature, ancient Indian history and civilization, Bengali literature, as well as manuscriptology were proverbial. His mother was Hemantakumārī Devī. His family background was unique. It was an ancient family of Brāhmaṇa Paṇḍits of Bengal with a genealogical record of a few centuries. Māṇikya Tarkabhuṣaṇa, one of his illustrious ancestors, settled in Naihati (about 38 km north of Calcutta) and established a *catuṣpaṭhī* or *ṭol* for imparting Sanskrit knowledge. (In such *ṭols* students were fed, clothed, housed and taught for several years free of charge. The British government was careful to support and maintain this tradition, but after Independence successive governments allowed the *ṭols* to perish.)

Māṇikya, who was patronised by Mahāraja Krishna Chandra of Nadia, settled in Naihati on the fall of Nawab Siraj-ud-daullah after the battle of Plassey in 1757. His son Śrīnath Tarkālaṅkāra continued his father's vocation of teaching Sanskrit. Śrīnāth's son Rāmkamal, an erudite scholar in Nyāya philosophy, was respected all over Bengal for his knowledge and dedication to the cause of Sanskrit teaching. Rāmkamal passed away in 1860. Among his sons Nandakumār Nyāyacuñcu was a lecturer of the Sanskrit College. His untimely death in 1862 was a great loss to the world of scholarship. His brother Haraprasād who was the fifth son of Rāmkamal and a favourite of Paṇḍit Iswar Chandra Vidyasagar and Bankim Chandra Chatterjee, obtained an M.A. degree from Calcutta University, and the title Śāstrī for his proficiency in Sanskrit. His contributions to

Indological and Buddhological research and also to the field of Bengali literature made his fame spread far and wide, even over the seas. He taught at Calcutta University, and later joined the newly founded Dacca University which conferred on him the title D. Litt. *honoris causa.* He was president of the Vaṅgīya Sāhitya Pariṣad and the Asiatic Society. The Government of India honoured him twice, once with a Mahāmahopādhyaya and the second time with a C.I.E.

Benoytosh was the fourth son of Haraprasād Śāstrī. He was educated at the Scottish Churches College, Calcutta. He obtained his B.A. in 1917 and M.A. (with a Gold Medal for having stood first) in 1919 in Sanskrit. He obtained Ph.D. degree from the Dacca University (incidentally, he was the first Ph.D. of that University), the title of his doctorate thesis being 'Elements of Indian Buddhist Iconography'. It was first published by the Oxford University Press in 1924 under the title *Buddhist Iconography.* It should be stated in this connection that for his research Benoytosh had chosen a subject that was almost virgin ground. The usefulness of iconic studies in the Indian context had been first clearly understood by Edward Moor who in his *Hindu Pantheon* (1810) presented numerous pictures of bewildering variety of Indian gods and goddesses. Alfred Foucher's *Etude sur Iconographie de l'Inde* (in two parts, published respectively in 1900 and 1905) was the pioneering standard work on Buddhist iconography. This was followed by Alice Getty's *Gods of Northern Buddhism* (1914) in which, apart from identification, the conceptional bagkground of various Buddhist deities from Tibetan, Chinese and Japanese pantheons had been covered. The first comprehensive work on Hindu iconography was T.A. Gopinatha Rao's *Elements of Hindu Iconography* which was originally published in two volumes under the patronage of Travancore State in 1914 and 1916 respectively.

The work of Benoytosh (1924) is the next most important in this series. It laid more emphasis on the deities of Tantric Buddhism and their iconographical characteristics as found in the Indian texts. This was followed by N.K. Bhattasali's *Iconography of Buddhist and Brahmanical Images in the Dacca Museum* (1929), B.C. Bhattacharya's *Jaina Iconography* (1939) and J.N. Banerjea's *Development of Hindu Iconography* (1914) which have all attained the status of classics in this field of study. In the work of Benoytosh, passages from the *Sādhanamālā* and *Niṣpannayogāvalī* relating to the description of the deities of Vajrayāna Buddhism were quoted and translated into English, along with illustrations from extant Indian, Tibetan and Chinese specimens and also from Nepalese drawing. It dealt with the images of the Dhyānī and Mortal Buddhas; the Bodisattvas; Mañjuśrī and Avalokiteśvara; emanations of Amitābha, Akṣobhya, Vairocana, Amoghasiddhi and Ratnasambhava; the gods and goddesses of direction; the Uṣṇīṣa gods; the protectresses; Tārās of various groups; gods associated with dance, musical instruments, door, light, etc.; animal-faced deities; Hindu gods in Vajrayāna; the Dikpālas; the nine planets; the Balabhadras; the Yakṣas and the abstract deities. This *magnum opus* from which subsequent scholars have drawn heavily was revised in 1958.

Benoytosh entered Baroda State Service in 1924 as General Editor of the Gaekwad's Oriental Series and introduced the modern technique of editing old and rare books. This technique is manifested in his masterly edition of the *Sādhanamālā*, the first volume of which appeared in 1925 and the second in 1928 (GOS, Nos. 26 and 41). Among other texts edited by him are the *Jñānasiddhi* of Indrabhūti and *Prajñopāyaviniścayasiddhi* of Anaṅgavajra, both of which appeared in 1929 under the general title *Two Vajrayāna Works* (GOS, No. 44). His celebrated edition of the *Guhyasamājatantra* or *Tathāgataguhyaka* came out in 1931 (GOS, No. 53). It was followed by the edition of the *Śaktisaṅgamatantra* in three volumes—(1932, 1941 and 1947 (GOS, Nos. 61, 91 and 114). His edition of the *Niṣpannayogāvalī* was published in 1949 (GOS, No. 109).

He was in charge of the Sanskrit Library. Benoytosh persuaded Mahāraja Sayājirao III Gaekwad of Baroda to turn the Sanskrit Library into the Oriental Institute, which was founded in 1927. It has become one of the most celebrated Indological institutions of India and Benoytosh was its Director until his retirement in 1952. In admiration of his services His Highness Sayājirāo conferred on him the titles of *rājyaratna* and *jñānajyoti*. He was put in charge of the Marathi and Gujarati publications of the State, especially the Sayāji Sāhityamālā, Bālajñānamālā and the Grāmavikāśamālā. He organised the Seventh All India Oriental Conference which met in Baroda in 1933. Being the Secretary of the Central Committee of reception and the various committees he laboured sincerely and guided the proceedings, transactions and publication of the same in 1935 in a volume of 1200 pages. He was intimately associated with the Asiatic Society of Bengal, Bhandarkar Oriental Research Institute of Pune, Bihar and Orissa Research Society, Vaṅgīya Sāhitya Pariṣat,

International Psychic Research Congress of London and Kern Institute of Leiden, Holland.

Side by side Benoytosh made several original contributions to Indology. He published more than a hundred articles on epigraphy, iconography, history, literature, religion, rhetoric and sociology. Apart from his celebrated *Indian Buddhist Iconography* which was published in 1958 as the revised edition of his earlier work (1924), *Introduction to Buddhist Esoterism* (1932), a pioneering and fundamental work on Tantric Buddhism, was also originally published in 1924.

Although Benoytosh was not the first man to work on this subject (Tantric Buddhism had been studied since the inception of modern Buddhist studies in the West) there was a great confusion in this field due to various brands of Tantric Buddhism pertaining to different Asian countries, in which various theories and practices, mutually irreconcilable, were involved. It was hard to make out what they all meant in space and time and what their roots were. Benoytosh presented the most difficult and complicated aspects of Tantric Buddhism in an intelligible way and specified the roots from which its various forms were sprouted in countries outside India. This was the theoretical culmination of years of research on Buddhist texts, in which Bhattacharyya had laid down the basic principles of Tantric Buddhism. According to him in outward appearance the Buddhist Tantras resemble the Hindu Tantras to a marked degree, but in reality there is very little similarity between them, either in subject-matter, philosophical doctrines, or religious principles.

Benoytosh further found that the Buddhists were the first to introduce the Tantras in their religion and that Hindus had borrowed these in later times. He gave an account of the Tantric Buddhist texts and their authors, mainly from the Tibetan sources, as well as a superlative description of the deities of the Tantric pantheon. Two other books also deserve mention: *Sanskrit Culture in a Changing World* (1950) and *Bauddhader Devadevī* (in Bengali 1954). He planned a *Dictionary of Indian Iconography* for which purpose he collected thousands of *dhyānas* from Brahmanical, Buddhist and Jain texts, a project which unfortunately remained unfinished.

The talent of Benoytosh found another medium of expression. He was the founder of what is now known as alternative medicine. In Baroda he was popular as a Homeopath: his success in this field was proverbial and this led him to put forward a holistic view of healing. He wrote numerous articles on this approach to medical treatment and published on this subject *The Science of Tridoṣa* (1951), *Science of Cosmic Ray Therapy* (1957), *Āyur-Homoeo Samanvaya* (in Gujarati 1957), *Gem Therapy* (1958), *Ratna Cikitsā* (in Hindi 1959), *Magnet Dowsing* (1958), *Tridosa and Homoeopathy* (1960) and *Sepetenate Mixtures* (1962). Some of these have been translated into French and German. Apart from medicine he had a great interest in astrology. He was an efficient horoscope-maker and could correctly interpret the contents of any horoscope. In 1938 he sent a note to the Baroda Government informing them of a planetary combination that portended a famine. Mahāraja Sayājirāo was convinced and took precautionary measures and the calamity was averted Benoytosh made investments in the share market, where also he was successful. Many persons came to him for guidance in the share market. He used to guide them on the basis of planetary positions.

Benoytosh was a man of charismatic personality though he had many idyosyncracies which made him different from ordinary peoples. In his younger days he was a very good sportsman. In his later life he used to play billiards in Śrī Sayāji Vihār Club. Mahāraja Sayājirāo also used to come and play there. It should be noted in this connection that Benoytosh never took any advantage of his intimacy with the Mahārāja. He had interest in the finer aspects of life as well. He was fond of painting, music and dance. He was a good harmonium player. Though in views and ideas he was progressive, he preferred to maintain the traditional Brahmanical pattern of life. Notwithstanding numerous invitations from abroad, he did not cross the seas. He was very discriminatory in his food habits. In family life he was a strict disciplinarian and maintained all the norms of Brahmanical aristocracy.

Benoytosh passed away in his paternal home, the Sastri Villa at Naihati, after a brief illness on 22 June 1964. His son Dr. Amiya Kumar Bhattacharyya has inherited the tradition of alternative medicine and is whole-heartedly engaged in developing a holistic approach to medical treatment, but the tradition of the Sastri Villa in the field of Sanskrit scholarship, which evolved over generations, has not been continued, as none of his inheritors have taken to scholarly pursuits. And this is our great loss.

1

The Introduction to Jayākhya Saṃhitā by Benoytosh Bhattacharyya and Indological Chronology

PRABHAKAR APTE

The critical edition of the *Jayākhya Saṃhitā,* one of the three gems or *Ratnatrya* of the Pāñcarātra Āgama, published by the Oriental Institute, Baroda[1] has been enriched by an introduction by the General Editor, Benoytosh Bhattacharyya. This was an original contribution useful for interdisciplinary scholarship.

The *Jayākhya Saṃhitā* is an encyclopaedic work covering philosophy, yoga based Sādhanā, the formation of Mantras based on code-syllables, paleo-calligraphy, form and colour-schemes of mystic Tantric diagrams and so on. Bhattacharyya laid the guidelines for future research by giving able treatment to the import of the *Jayākhya Saṃhitā* for scholars trained in western research methods.

Bhattacharyya placed the *Jayākhya Saṃhitā* roughly at AD 450. To establish this he made a content analysis of the text. The chronological framework of the classical and post-classical Saṃhitās of the Pāñcarātra Āgama ranging from the *Sātvata-Pauṣkara Saṃhitās* to the *Pādma Saṃhitā* furnished by F. Otto Schrader[2] was before him. The date AD 450 for the *Jayākhya Saṃhitā* fit well in that framework. However, the paleographical evidence adduced by Bhattacharyya to ascertain the date of the *Jayākhya Saṃhitā* is not only his original contribution, it opened out an inter-disciplinary area of Tantric calligraphy coming forward to the aid of chronology in general. The main thrust of Bhattacharyya's argument is the changing shape of the Brahmi letter 'e' (Δ) in the course of the few centuries preceding and succeeding the Christian era. Thus the name given in the code language of the *Jayākhya Saṃhitā*: *tryaśra* (triangle) fits into the chronological table of inscriptional script furnished by Bhattacharyya.

The present author developed the theme and wrote an article on paleocalligraphy of the Tantras.[3] It was possible because there are many more shapes indicating epithets conferred to various syllables by the Tantric code contained in the *Jayākhya Saṃhitā* (Ch. 6). If all those shape-indicating letters are put to the test of chronological paleographic tables, that exercise may help us determine, alter or ascertain the dates of many important Sanskrit texts. This exercise may further lead to comparative and relative chronology of ancient texts and the historical personalities and events described in those texts. Thus the community of Indological researchers are indebted to Bhattacharyya for his pioneering work in chronology. The *Jayākhya Saṃhitā* in particular and the Pāñcarātra Saṃhitās in general have been benefited by the all-comprehensive scholarship of Bhattacharyya which happened to be his paternal heritage. The present head of the Rāmānuja Maṭha at Melkote near Mysore has preserved his cherished memory of his visit, alongwith his Guru H.H. Yadugiri Yatirāja Sampatkumāra Rāmānuja Muni (AD 1921-43) when they had the privilege of having fruitful discussion on the Āgamas with late Hara Prasad Shastri at Calcutta about seventy years ago. Consequently, the scholarly relation of Bhattacharyya to Vaiṣṇava Āgamas is well-justified.

One more contribution of the *Jayākhya Saṃhitā*, Baroda edition, is the inclusion of the chapter entitled '*Hastiśaila-Māhātmya*' incorporated as additional reading (*Adhikaḥ pāṭhaḥ*). F. Otto Schrader, in his 'Introduction to Pāñcarātra and Ahirbudhnya Saṃhitā (Adyar 1916)' established the pioneering chronological range, AD 300 to 800 for the Pāñcarātra Saṃhitās. That range has been revised by the present author by placing *Sātvata Saṃhitā* prior to the *Pauṣkara Saṃhitā* (vide *Pauṣkara Saṃhitā*, Tirupati 1991) instead of the reverse, relying on internal evidence (Ch. 34) of the *Pauṣkara Saṃhitā*. The assertion of the date of the *Jayākhya Saṃhitā* by Bhattacharyya was of great help to the present author. The three classical Saṃhitās are thus placed in the order of Sātvata, Pauṣkara, Jayākhya (*c.* third, fourth and fifth century AD). The three commentarial Saṃhitās, *Īśvara, Parameśvara* and *Padma,* which can be termed post-classical texts, are by nature more temple-oriented and the first two of these contain respectively the *Yādavādri-Māhātmya* (Īśvara Saṃhitā, Ch. 20) and *Śrīranga Māhātmya* (Parameśvara Saṃhitā, Ch. 10). By natural corollary there should have been a chapter on Hastigiri Mahātmya in the *Padma Saṃhitā,* the commentarial text on the *Jayākhya Saṃhitā,* but it is conspicuous by its absence; and somehow the additional chapter of the *Jayākhya Saṃhitā* contains the culminating account of the temple affiliation of the three post-classical Saṃhitās which cannot form part of one of the classical Saṃhitās. Here is a clear case of anachronism. The text of *Jayākhya Saṃhitā* cannot be said to have knowledge of any of the commentary texts, Īśvara, Parameśvara or Padma. Hence the rational conclusion would be to treat the additional chapter of the *Jayākhya Saṃhitā* as an integral part of *Padma Saṃhitā*. Thus the date of that chapter has to be pushed by at least 300 years. This done, the whole scheme of the placement of the classical and post-classical Saṃhitās of the Pāñcarātra Āgama as well as the continuing temple affiliation of the three post-classical Saṃhitās, the Īśvara, Parameśvara and Padma respectively to Yādavādri or Yadugiri (Nārāyaṇādri, i.e. present day Melkote near Mysore), Śrīraṅgam near Trichinapalli in Tamilnadu, and Haatiśaila or Viṣṇukāñci also in Tamilnadu, stands justified. The insertion of the *Adhikaḥ pāṭhaḥ* in the *Jayākhya Saṃhitā* by Bhattacharyya inspired the researcher in the present author to take up the investigation of the temple-text affiliation through content analysis and survey of the temple tradition and helped him reach the conclusion that the said chapter should be detached from the classical *Jayākhya Saṃhitā* and attached to the post-classical *Padma Saṃhitā*.[4]

The Baroda edition contains many more editorial merits useful to research scholars. The present author was benefited by the illustration (in colour in the first edition) of the Navapadma Maṇḍala diagram. Inspired by the editorial treatment to the artistic aspect of the mystic diagram, could carry out further research and succeeded in revising the diagram on the basis of textual content analysis. To cite one example, the verse *saisakta-navapadmāṇām eṣa eva vidhiḥ smṛtaḥ* means 'this is the mode of the sketching of nine closely attached lotuses'. The illustration in the Baroda edition, however depicts them in a detached position. The rectification was done by the present author in his article *Maṇḍalārādhanā* published in the *Journal of the Oriental Institute* (1973).[5] That article is appended with several illustrations detailing the sketching, colouring, motivation as well as the Mantra inscriptions over various parts of the Maṇḍala and the lotus-petals drawn therein.

The chapter of the *Jayākhya Saṃhitā* on external worship (*Bahyayāga*) incorporating Maṇḍala worship has also its own contribution in the total scheme of Maṇḍalas. While *Sātvata Saṃhitā* provides only few specimens of Maṇḍalas, the *Pauṣkara Saṃhitā* expends over twenty chapters in detailing Maṇḍalas and their components; and it further categorizes Maṇḍalas into four groups: Padmodara or lotus-centric, Aneka-kaja-garbha with multiple lotuses at the centre, Cakrājba with encircled lotus at the centre, and Miśracakrābhidhāna with complex wheels at the centre. The *Jayākhya Saṃhitā*[6] meticulously provides illustrations for Aneka-kaja-garbha pattern and further complements it by the addition of embellishing the diagram with calligraphical inscriptions. This I call paleo-calligraphy.

Another research achievement piloted by Bhattacharyya was the exercise of reconstructing Maṇḍala designs. Inspired by the Baroda edition, I continued the exercise for over a decade and succeeded in reconstructing those coloured illustrations which were hitherto concealed under a literary textual veil. The *Pauṣkara* and *Jayākhya Saṃhitās* proved to be mutually complementary. The whole exercise culminated in a coloured album enthusiastically refined by Kīrti Trivedi of IIT Bombay, who certified the *Pauṣkara Saṃhitā* scheme to be an example of artistic and design perfection and thought it to have the potential for a four-year course in art and geometrical design. The coloured plates of the Maṇḍala designs have been recently published by the Indira Gandhi National Centre for Art in *Prakṛti,* volume III, 1995. These illustrations are unique in that they are present-day reconstructions of age-old designs conceived and practised by ancient Tantric seers.

Hidden in the *Jayākhya Saṃhitā* Sanskrit text, and brought to light by the Baroda edition, is the tantric code of the alphabet. The tantras required secrecy for formation and application of Mantras which were artificially constructed on the basis of mystic convention. Thus all the vowels and consonants have their code names used in the Tantric tradition for the formation of Mantras. The combination of some names of gods or kings and animate or inanimate objects are meant to mislead outsiders. Other texts like the *Lakṣmī Tantra* which follow the Jayākhya pattern also serve the same purpose. A late lexicon, the *Tantrābhidhāna Kośa,* followed by the *Uddhāra Kośa* have done a good service to researchers in this field. However, *Jayākhya Saṃhitā* is a pioneering treatise. The tabulation and illustrations of Mantras indicating their purpose, employment, etc., is well documented in the Baroda edition.

Another aspect brought out in those illustrations is the scriptic sanctity and efficacy of Mantras: like phonetic potency, Mantras have scriptic potency as well. The table of Mantras appended to the Baroda edition contains some curious combinations of phonemes which are actually a phonetic impossibility. However, as graphems, these can be depicted on paper. Theoretically, if each syllabic element is taken to carry some tantric potency, then such clusters would carry a bundle of those potencies alongwith them. On the phonetic level, repeated chanting of Mantras carries the summation of the individual potencies of the constituent phonemes; so also inscribing mantras in a particular calligraphic style imbibes some mystic potency which is preserved for long by encashing those in seals or amulets. And for that purpose, such clusters need not be put to the phonetic test (pronouncing or muttering or chanting). This point struck the author after glancing at the appendices. It was found that clusters like '*t, j, r, a, u, au, m*', are a phonetic impossibility. In other words it is possible to go on clustering vowels, consonants and nasals as instructed by the verses in the Mantroddhāra chapter of the *Jayākhya Saṃhitā*; at the same time a research scholar cannot help but stumble at such clusters and then realise that they cannot be pronounced. This special aspect of calligraphy has come to the hands of inter-disciplinary researchers because of the multipurpose contribution of the Baroda edition.

On the ritual plane, the *Jayākhya Saṃhitā* and its Baroda edition have contributed much to that field of tantric worship based on mystic diagrams as its substratum. The diagrams appended to the Baroda edition make the otherwise obscure and secretive topic of Maṇḍala worship transparently clear, at least to scholars.[7] Even though it is believed that some of the tantric areas dominated by subjectivity are not to be conveyed to persons of inadequate authority or non-believers, the fact that the author of the *Jayākhya Saṃhitā* has revealed the secrets of Maṇḍala worship to disciples cum-devotees who were supposed to transmit the same to posterity by writing the text and copying it further, it would be justified to pay attention to its research potential.

In the field of Pāñcarātra research, the tradition of critical edition of Saṃhitā texts began with Rev. Banerjee who edited the *Nārada Pāñcarātra* in Calcutta in the 1870s. The real scholarly research and critical editorship, however, began with P.B. Anantacharya's *Sātvata Saṃhitā* (Kanchi,1902), then F. Otto Schrader who critically edited the *Ahirbudhnya Saṃhitā* with his pioneering *Introduction to Pāñcarātra and Ahirbudhnya Saṃhitā* in 1916. This was a unique exercise since he was doing the job from a long distance far from Adyar (Madras), i.e. Ahmednagar (Maharashtra), while he was a political detenue as a German citizen. The *Pauṣkara Saṃhitā* was published in 1934 at Melkote (Karnataka) and edited by H. H. Yatiraj Muni. The first classical *Pāñcarātra Saṃhitā* to receive competent editing thus happens to be the *Jayākhya Saṃhitā*.

In fine, it cannot be termed to be an over-estimate that the Baroda edition of the *Jayākhya Saṃhitā* by Bhattacharyya has benefited multi-disciplinary scholarship of present and future.

NOTES

1. Baroda, 1967.
2. Adyar, 1916.
3. Pune, 19[illegible]6.
4. Madras, 1974, published by Pāñcarātra Parishodhan Parishad, Ed. Seetha Padmanabhan.
5. Cf. Appendix 2.
6. *Pauṣkara Saṃhitā*, Ed. 1991, R.S. Vidyapeetha, Tirupati.
7. Cf. Appendix 3.

2

The *Maṇḍa* and the *-la* of the Term *Maṇḍala*

ALEX WAYMAN

The topic of *maṇḍala* is of great importance for Buddhist Tantra. Due to the wide dispersal of concrete *maṇḍalas*, and their depiction in books, the usual form of these designs is rather well understood, but usually identified only by brief captions. The attendant symbolism is not well understood, even though some authoritative papers have been written, by Tucci and others.[1]

My paper is not on the intricate symbolism of these designs, but on the two-part division of the term *maṇḍala* as indicated by the Tibetan translation *dkyil 'khor*, and by the varied explanations of these two parts, in effect, interpreting the term *maṇḍala* as made up of two semantic parts, *maṇḍa* and *la*. It is frequent in Tantra to attribute a well-determined semantic to what in usual Sanskrit grammar is a suffix having rather vague meaning, if any.

Hitherto I have been working on various explanations for the two parts of this term, but my recent work on the *Vairocanābhisaṃbodhi-tantra* has uncovered a different explanation that was sufficiently intriguing for me to examine that whole matter again, and incidentally to decide whether the *maṇḍa* of the term *bodhimaṇḍa* (in connection with the Tree of Enlightenment) can be identified with the *maṇḍa* of *maṇḍala*.

My first reference is the footnote in *Mkhas grub rje's Fundamentals of the Buddhist Tantras*, p. 270.[2] Saraha in his commentary on the *Buddhakapālatantra* said *maṇḍa* means pith (or core) (*dkyil ni sñiṅ po'o*); *-la* means taking it (*'khor ni de len pa*). Now to be added is Tsoṅ-kha-pa's comment in his great commentary on the *Śrī-Cakrasaṃvara-laghu-tantra*, towards the end of the first chapter. He gives the same information as Saraha, but in the case of *-la* says *lāti ni len pa'o* which cites the finite form of the Sanskrit verb, 'takes, obtains' (*lāti*) for T. *len pa*; and then states:[3]

/sñiṅ po len pa'i phyi naṅ gi dkyil 'khor ni thig la sogs pas bri ba daṅ/ yid kyis bri ba ste bsgom ar bya'o/.

one should cultivate the outer and inner *maṇḍala*, i.e. 'taking (*len pa*) the core (*sñiṅ po*), by drawing with thread and so on (in the outer case), and by drawing with the mind (in the inner case).

This clarifies that the two-part division of *maṇḍala* applies as well to the mental *maṇḍala* as it does to the concrete physical *maṇḍala*.

This same footnote of Mkhas gurb rje's work cited the detailed commentary by Padmavajra on Buddhaguhya's *Tantrārthāvatāra*, which calls those two that were mentioned by Tson-kha-pa two kinds of conventional *maṇḍala*, i.e. the 'individual nature *maṇḍala*' is the mental one, and 'reflected-image *maṇḍala*' is the outer one. An example of these conventional ones is when in the middle is the Lord of the Family (i.e. the core), surrounded by the retinue (i.e. the taking of it). This is the reverse of the Buddhist meditation practice of reflecting an object into the mind, in which case the mental form is called the *ālambana*, because in the case of the *maṇḍala* it must be realized in the mind and then reflected outward, on the ground, etc. That mentioned commentary on Buddhaguhya's work states also an 'absolute' kind of *maṇḍala*, where the core is the 'mind of enlightenment' (*bodhicitta*), and the enclosing element is the *vidyā-jñāna* that comprehends it. Here the expression *vidyā-jñāna* evidently means 'the vidyā kind of *jñāna*',[4] presumably the three *vidyā* (clear visions) which legend attributes to the Buddha during the night of enlightenment, because 'taking' or realizing the 'mind of enlightenment'.

My article 'Reflections on Barabudur as a *Maṇḍala* published in a work on that monument, described the theory of *maṇḍala* in Vajravarman's commentary on the *Sarvadurgatipariśodhana-tantra*.[5] A later work on this Tantra by Skorupski identifies Vajravarman as a native of Sri Lanka (ancient Ceylon),[6] which agrees with the theory given in that article that his tantrism reflects the school of the 'Golden Isles' (presently Indonesia). I there gave my solution of *maṇḍa* and *-la* in terms of Vajravarman's categories of *maṇḍalas*. However, I have returned to the original text to rethink my solutions and now have an improvement to offer.

We should note that Vajravarman usually gives both the *maṇḍala* of inhabitants (adheya) and the *maṇḍala* of habitation (ādhāra), i.e. where the inhabitants are. Vajravarman describes five kinds of *maṇḍala*, (1) the receptacle *maṇḍala*, (2) the causal *maṇḍala*, (3) the means *maṇḍala*, (4) the *maṇḍala* of path, (5) the *maṇḍala* of fruit. Before treating them individually, I should mention that this commentator's categories use the first two for the ancient Buddhist division of the world into the receptacle world (*bhājana-loka*) and the sentient world (*sattva-loka*), while the third amounts to a classification of the habitation (*ādhāra*) *maṇḍalas*. His fourth and fifth also go together as the Buddhist path and its fruit. To take them individually:

1. The receptacle *maṇḍala* consists of Mt. Meru, the continents, etc. The five Buddhas are identified with Mt. Meru in its centre. So when the sixteen male diamond beings are the seven rocky mountains, their seven separating oceans, and two other features,[7] and the sixteen goddesses are the four main continents, eight lesser continents, and four great trees, these male diamond beings and the goddesses should be counted as the retinue. Hence, Mt. Meru, identified with the five Buddhas, is the *maṇḍa*; and the mountains, etc., identified with the sixteen male diamond beings and the sixteen goddesses, are the *-la*. Then the outer black mountain, plus the four elements and space which are the palace, constitute the *ādhāra-maṇḍala*.
2. The causal *maṇḍala* is generation. The five personal aggregates (skandha) are the five Buddhas, constituting the *maṇḍa*. The four elements are the four consort goddesses. The tripartition of the world into sense field, object field, and perception field is done for eye, ear, nose, and tongue, to make twelve, plus corporeal field and tangibles, then manodhātu and dharmadhātu, in all sixteen, identified with the sixteen male diamond beings. Then the six subjective and six objective sense bases (*āyatana*) are the twelve goddesses. Thus the elements (*dhātu*) and the sense bases (*āyatana*) identified with the male diamond beings and the goddesses, are the *-la*. Then the eight parts of hands and feet, called the eight posts, the four orifices called the four gates, and other bodily parts identified with parts of the *maṇḍala*—palace—amount to the habitation *maṇḍala*.
3. The means *maṇḍala*. As mentioned earlier, this is simply a classification of the various habitation (*ādhāra*) *maṇḍalas*.[8]
4. The *maṇḍala* of path. While this is feasibly explained in terms

of the first five perfections (pāramitā), the text here treats the path by way of the thirty-seven *bodhi-pakṣya-dharma* (nature's accessory to enlightenment). The five powers (*bala*) are the five Buddhas, hence the *maṇḍa*. Here, the power of faith (*śraddhā-bala*) is the Tathāgata Vairocana; the Power of mindfulness (smṛti), Durgatipariśodhana (= Akṣobhya); the power of *samādhi*, Ratnaketu (= Ratnasambhava); the power of insight (*prajñā*), Śākyamuni (later, Amitābha); the power of striving (*vīrya*), Saṃkusumita (= Amoghasiddhi). Then, for the retinue, the *-la*, there are the four *smṛtyupasthānas*, identified with four goddesses, Buddhalocanā, etc.; the five faculties (*indriya*), the seven members of enlightenment (*bodhyaṅga*), and the four feet of magical power (*ṛddhipāda*), identified with the sixteen diamond beings; the eightfold Noble Path, identified with a set of eight goddesses; the four right efforts (*samyakprahāṇa*), with the four goddesses, carrying the diamond hook, etc. For the place where they are, the *ādhāra*, i.e. *maitrī* ,and the remaining four immeasurables, are the four gates; the four samādhis are the four toraṇas (archways); the eight liberations are the eight posts; the four Noble Truths are the four corners; the four Dhyānas are the four jewelled borders (*pha khu*); the nine *samāpattis* are the nets and half-nets (*dra ba dra phyed*).

5. *Maṇḍala* of fruit (*phala*). This is of two kinds—the manner of the Dharmakāya and the manner of the Sambhogakāya. For the manner of the Dharmakāya I accept the information of Padmavajra's commentary, above alluded to, about the absolute *maṇḍala*, namely that here the manner of the Dharmakāya, the nature of Dharmadhātu-jñāna—which is the basis for all supramundane knowledge and is intrinsically pure, and is the nature of Vairocana—should be taken as the core (*maṇḍa*). Then for the near-retinue, as the *-la*, there is the mirror-like wisdom, as the culmination of insight (*prajñā*), the nature of Durgatipariśodhana; the sameness wisdom, having a non-appreceiving nature and which cannot be elsewhere, the Buddha Ratnaketu; the discriminate wisdom, with unmistaken reflection on all the knowable, the nature of Śākyamuni; the procedure-of-duty wisdom, performing the aim of sentient beings, the nature of Saṃkusumita. The outer retinue is also the *-la*, namely, the four gates of liberation

identified with the four consort goddesses; the sixteenth voidnesses identified with the sixteen diamond beings, beginning with Vajrasattva; eight perferctions (*pāramitā*) (*dāna, śīla, kṣānti, vīrya, prajñā, dhyāna, praṇidhāna,* and *upāya* in that order), identified with eight offering goddesses in the standard order; finally, the four sublime abodes (*brahma-vihāra*), identified with the four gatekeeper goddesses. Presumably because the Dharmakāya represents the Nirvāṇa without fixed abode (*apratiṣṭhita-nirvāṇa*), no 'habitation *maṇḍala*' is mentioned.

For the *maṇḍala* in the manner of the Sambhogakāya, the text states: Where (*gaṅ du*) the Bhagavat Vairocana, with best of all (aspects), superior to gods and men; because arisen from the Dharmakāya, has the method of the five wisdoms (jñāna); by means of the Nirmāṇakāya, for the sake of living beings, is engaged with the five senses; (where) for the sake of the trainees, has the perfection of the five sense objects in the bejewelled palace; and is the sole Buddha experiencing by way of this Tantra (the *Sarvadurgatipariśodhana-tantra*).

In the article on Barabudur as a *maṇḍala* I also speculated that these two kinds of '*maṇḍalas* of the fruit' in the respective manners of the Dharmakāya and the Sambhogakāya might be the proto-types of the two *maṇḍalas* of the Shingon sect of Japan, known as the Diamond *Maṇḍala* and Womb (or Compassion) *Maṇḍala*.[9] A point in favour of the theory is that Vairocana is the Central Buddha in the two *maṇḍalas* of the fruit, as well as in the two *maṇḍalas* of the Shingon. Now that I have made a study of the *Vairocanābhisambodhi-tantra,* the second chapter of which yields the *Karuṇāgarbha-maṇḍala* that is elaborated into one of the two Shingon *maṇḍalas,* I have a more solid basis for such judgments. Given that the '*Diamond Maṇḍala*' of the Shingon sect is drawn from the first part of the *Tattvasaṃgraha-tantra,* but is more elaborated in the temple banner of the Shingon than is found in the scripture; and given that it is also the case with the temple banner of the Karuṇāgarbha-*maṇḍala* as compared with the scripture; we can conclude that to make a judgment about relation to the two foregoing '*maṇḍalas* of the fruit', it would be necessary to stay close to the scriptures. If we do so, I still feel there is a relation between the two pairs of *maṇḍalas.*

Let us now consider what the *Vairocanābhisambodhi-tantra* has to say about the topic of this paper. In Ch. II the prose immediately following verse 44 runs as follows (as I translate):

Thereupon Vajrapāṇi asked the Bhagavat: "Bhagavat, what is the name of this *maṇḍala*? What is a '*maṇḍala*'?" The Bhagavat responded, "Master of the Secret Ones, as to '*maṇḍala*' the *maṇḍa* of the *maṇḍala* is the arising of a Buddha; the *-la* is the Complete, its higher; what is a *maṇḍa* is not otherwise: hence the term '*maṇḍala*'. Master of the Secret Ones, however, this enlarged *maṇḍala* is called 'Mahākaruṇāgarbhodbhava' (arising in the womb of great compassion), because it rescues the uncertainty of the sentient realm. It is the empowerment by the Tathāgatas for uncountable eons of the right procedure for the incomparable right perfected enlightenment (bodhi)."

This explanation of the term *maṇḍala* should be taken as a special explanation of this particular scripture. What is meant can be stated this way: By the term *maṇḍa* this scripture means the deities on the central lotus, who are Vairocana in the middle and the other four Buddhas on four of the eight petals (the other four being vacant). So far this agrees with the usage already observed. Also, by *-la* this explanation intends the expansion of the *maṇḍala* to include all the retinue deities, and this too agrees with the explanations given above. What is special to this explanation is the claim that completing the *maṇḍala* by way of the retinue is the 'Complete, its higher'; in short that the *maṇḍa* can account for the arising of a Buddha, but not a Complete Buddha. In the terminology of this scripture, one becomes Buddha through 'omniscient knowledge' (*sarvajñajñāna*), and then a Complete Buddha through 'the empowerment materialized' (*vikur-vitādhiṣṭhāna*). Thus, what this scripture calls the 'enlarged *maṇḍala*' can be expressed as 'the empowerment materialized'. The scripture's remark, 'what is a *maṇḍa* is not otherwise' points to a sense of the Buddha's title 'Tathāgata'. The meaning of the title is that the Buddhas have 'gone' (*gata*) the same way (*tathā*). So the *maṇḍa* is not otherwise. This implies that the *-la* is otherwise. This is the other meaning of the title Tathāgata, namely, that the Buddha preaches or performs in the world as (*tathā*) he learned (*āgata*); this is 'the empowerment materialized' through the retinue. Hence '*khor* of *dkyil' khor* implicates the retinue.

This brings me to the final topic: the *maṇḍa* of the term *bodhimaṇḍa*, which is used for the terrace or seat of enlightenment, namely the spot under the Tree of Enlightenment upon which Gautama sat. This term *bodhimaṇḍa* therefore is a kind of 'habitation-*maṇḍala*' which was noticed earlier, as the place where the events occur. It follows that the term *maṇḍa*, being employed in the expression *bodhi maṇḍa,* is indeed the *maṇḍa* of a *maṇḍala* but not the *maṇḍala* of the inhabitants, the Budda or his retinue. Still the term *bodhimaṇḍa* indicates a privileged habitation, mystically the navel of earth. It is also where the future Buddha touches the earth. So the poet Aśvaghosa in the *Buddhacarita,* Canto XIII, 67-8:[10]

For whatever were those deeds committed by him for enlightenment, today is their ordained time. Thus is he seated in this seat in the exact manner as were the former *munis.*

For this is the navel of the earth goddess's surface endowed with a *dhāman* (power) by the supreme totality. There is no other spot of earth which can withstand his thrust of intense concentration (*samādhi*).

We may conclude that the 'habitation-*maṇḍala*' must accord with the 'inhabitant-*maṇḍala*'. Hence, great care is taken to prepare the *maṇḍala* of habitation, preparatory to inviting the deities to take their seats.

NOTES

Extra note I: The work on the *Vairocanābhisambodhi-tantra* mentioned above was published as The *Enlightenment of Vairocana,* by Alex Wayman, Book One, and by R. Tajima, Book Two, Delhi: Motilal Banarsidass, 1992. Included is the entire second chapter, generously annotated.

Extra note II: Since the topic is the *maṇḍala,* one should notice that Benoytosh Bhattacharyya, who contributed so mightily to basic research texts for Buddhist Tantra, put out the *Niṣpannayogāvalī* of Mahāpaṇḍita Abhayākaragupta (Baroda: Oriental Institute, 1949), containing the main contents of 26 important *maṇḍalas.*

1. For example, Giuseppe Tucci, *The Theory and Practice of the Maṇḍala* (English translation, London, 1961): Alex Wayman, *The Buddhist Tantras: Light on Indo-Tibetan Esotericism* (New York, 1973), Ch. 9, 'Symbolism of the Maṇḍala-Palace'.
2. This is the work translated from the Tibetan by F.D. Lessing and Alex Wayman (The Hague, 1968).
3. Photo. edn. of the Peking canon (PTT), vol. 157, p. 20-5-2.
4. Cf. Alex Wayman, *Calming the Mind and Discerning the Real: Buddhist Meditation and the Middle View,* from the *Lam rim chen mo* of Tsoṅ-kha-pa (New York, 1978), pp. 42-3.
5. Cf. *Barabudur,* Berkeley Buddhist Studies Series 2 (Berkeley, 1981), pp. 146-9.

6. Tadeusz Skorupski, *The Sarvadurgatipariśodhana Tantra* (Delhi, 1983), p. xxv.
7. The two are, according to the Tibetan (Peking edn.) *lcags sbabs* (read: *sbubs*) apparently the 'steel-tipped arrow' (that whisses when shot) and the '*khor lo can*', apparently the discus, PTT Vol. 76. p. 133-1-4.
8. For these *maṇḍalas*, PTT Vol. 76, pp. 133-2-8ff., I here give the main details from my article (n. 5, above). They are of two kinds, (A) comprised by inner nature and (B) comprised by outer nature. (A) is of two kinds: (1) comprised of sensory support (*ālambana*), namely, the five outer senses and the mind; and (2) comprised by the dominant power (*adhipati-bala*), either sensory aim outward or sensory aim inward. (B) is also of four kinds: (metal) casting (*lugs su blugs pa*); in relief ('*bur*): coloured (*tshon*) with wet colours or with powdered (dry) colours: figured (*byug pa*) i.e. with fine wood or with mud).
9. Cf. Barabudur (n. 5, above), pp. 161-2.
10. Cf. Alex Wayman, 'Śākyamuni, Founder of Buddhism', *Studia Missionalia*, Vol. 33 (1984), p. 79.

3

Representations of *Aṣṭa-mahābodhisattvas* from Nalanda An Iconographic Study

DEBALA MITRA

In an interesting article[1] Pratapaditya Pal has brought to our notice an early representation of the *Aṣṭa-mahābodhisattva-maṇḍala* on an almost circular terracotta plaque (Fig. 1),[2] now housed in the Metropolitan Museum of Art, New York. As per his caption below the photograph, the plaque is 4.75 in. high, belongs to Uttar Pradesh, and dates to the sixth century AD. Considering the somewhat effaced condition of the plaque which I could not examine personally, I quote the observations of Pal:

> In the center of the plaque and within a shrine is seated a Tathāgata displaying the gesture of turning the wheel of the Law (*dharma-cakrapravartanamudrā*). He is surrounded by eight figures who are certainly bodhisattvas, although, because of the rather effaced condition of the plaque, it is somewhat difficult to identify each individually. The figure to the right of the Tathāgata holds a full-blown lotus and is clearly Avalokiteśvara. The figure on the left is provided with a water pot and must therefore be identified with Maitreya.
>
> What is of great significance is that the Metropolitan plaque cannot be dated any later than AD 600 and more likely is a work of the fifth century, as is indicated by paleographical features and the stylistic traits of the figures. Note particularly the hair style of some of the bodhisattvas, while the physiognomy of the figure immediately above the Tathāgata seems straight out of Ahicchatrā. This rather unostentatious plaque, which has remained unnoticed in the storage of the Metropolitan Museum since its acquisition in 1933, is therefore the earliest plastic representation of the *Ashta-mahābodhisattva-maṇḍala* known from India.[3]

The Metropolitan plaque certainly establishes the antiquity of the cult in India proper. It is also apparent that often there is great divergence between an actual representation and the textual material. Apart from the fact that the artists in the different areas very likely employed diverse textual traditions, which often resulted in variant interpretations, such plaques as that in the Metropolitan must also have frequently served as visual aids to the artists. Such small plaques must have been carried by pilgrims both as souvenirs and as prophylactic emblems from one country to another, just as the Tibetan traveller carried his *gau*. And then if they were used as models, because of their diminutive size, there could occur significant inconsistencies in the ultimate copy.[4]

The plaque (The Metropolitan Museum of Art, no. 33.50.11) with its composition and minute letters within short spaces of compartments bears the stamp of a master artist who was responsible for the aesthetically-carved matrix or mould meant for producing numerous plaques with the *maṇḍala* of the Tathāgata encircled by eight Bodhisattvas. This theme, no doubt, enjoyed great popularity in Buddhist countries. Evidently, such inexpensive plaques were in great demand among devotees and pilgrims of meagre and moderate means, desirous of earning merit by their gifts at Buddhist centres and also carrying these portable objects to their countries.

The plaque is divided into nine compartments by borders decorated either with a row of diamond-shaped motifs or with a triangular or wavy line. The central compartment having a superstructure, with an enormous *āmalaka* (possibly crowned by a tiny finial) above a *tri-ratha khurā*-shaped *chajjā*-like member supported by two visible ornate oblong pillars, represents the facade of a shrine housing the image of a Tathāgata (Vairocana or more probably Śākyamuni Buddha), seated in *vajra-paryāṅkāsana* on the pericarp of a lotus with a single row or petals, in *dharma-cakrapravatana-mudrā*; below the lotus is the moulded *tri-ratha* base of the shrine. The eight compartments (four squarish at cardinal directions and four triangular in intermediate directions) contain each the figure of a Bodhisattva. From the photograph it appears that most of the Bodhisattvas, seated each on a lotus (petals are indistinct), are sparsely bejewelled and have a halo behind their heads and shoulders. Unfortunately, the attributes in the hands of most of the Bodhisattvas are effaced beyond precise recognition. The two figures flanking the Tathāgata have already been identified by Pal as Avalokiteśvara holding the long stalk of a full-blown lotus in his left palm and Maitreya with a water-pot (spouted ?) supported by a flower(?) having its stalk rising perhaps from the left palm resting on the left knee. With an identical coiffure in the form of the *jaṭā-bhāra* gathered on the top of the head, both are seated in the *mahārājalīlā* posture. The ornaments are not clear in the case of Avalokiteśvara who might have displayed *vara-mudrā* with his right palm placed on his right leg. The right hand of Maitreya is raised, perhaps in *abhaya-mudrā* or *vandanā-mudrā*. The third Bodhisattva, who is within the triangular compartment below the squarish compartment of Maitreya, appears to be Mañjuśrī, distinguished by his *śikhaṇḍaka-kākapakṣa* coiffure and a short *hāra* possibly strung with the ring of a cylindrical amulet. His left forearm is seen horizontally in front of his waist; the palm might have held the stalk of an *utpala* supporting a book(?) which is somewhat curved. As in the case of the other three Bodhisattvas in triangular compartments, Mañjuśrī is seated with one knee slightly raised and the other leg extended to some extent on the lotus-seat, squeezed in *mahārājalīlā* posture into the narrow space. The Bodhisattva below the squarish compartment of Avalokiteśvara may stand for Vajrapāṇi, as there is a semblance of *vajra* (thunderbolt) on a stalked flower held in his left palm but he lacks the crown. The Bodhisattva above the compartment of Avalokiteśvara and within a triangular compartment presents, like Vajrapāṇi(?) and the corresponding figure on the right, tresses of hair on two sides of his face, reminiscent of the wig-like coiffure, a legacy of the Gupta period. Whether he holds any object with right palm (possibly having the tips of his thumb and index-finger touching) held near the chest could not be determined; he carries with his left hand the stalk of a flower appearing like a lotus. The Bodhisattva, within the squarish compartment above the shrine of the Tathāgata, is seated in *vajra-paryaṅkāsana*. Near his left palm (inner side visible) is the stalk of a flower or bud. If it supports a *maṇi* (which is not unlikely), he may represent Ākāśagarbha. His right palm is placed on his right knee. The right palm of the Bodhisattva (within the next compartment, triangular) is either in *abhaya-mudrā* or *vandanābhinayī*. The Bodhisattva inside the squarish compartment below the shrine is seated in *lalitāsana* with his hanging right foot perched on a lotus and shows *vara-mudrā* with his right palm. The attribute in his left hand is uncertain. It is tempting to identify the figure with Kṣitigarbha. The attributes of Samantabhadra and Sarvanivaraṇa-Viṣkambhin could not be ascertained.

The space, left by the figures of the Tathāgata and eight Bodhisattvas, inside the shrine and eight compartments is replete with tiny but well-formed letters (some, of course, effaced). These letters, as far as I could read, record the Buddhist creed in all the compartments and the shrine. On palaeographic grounds, the writing is assignable to about the seventh century AD.

Fortunately, I located photographs (Figs. 2, 3 and 5)[5] of three major fragments of three identical or analogous plaques with minute letters, apart from two small pieces belonging to two of these fragments from the Archaeological Site Museum of Nalanda (District Nalanda, Bihar) in the photo-archives of the Museums Branch of the Archaeological Survey of India. The Acc. nos. of the three fragments are 00951, 12910 and 12902 as seen in the records of the Museums Branch. The diameter of the terracotta or clay fragment bearing Acc. no. 00951 (Fig. 2) is recorded as 4.75 in. This particular fragment has preserved the figures of the Tathāgata and five Bodhisattvas (including Avalokiteśvara) and the lower part of the sixth. These figures are practically identical with the corresponding ones of the plaque of the Metropolitan Museum of Art except perhaps in one feature in the case of Mañjuśrī whose right forearm appears to be raised almost vertically instead of turning towards his right chest (as seen in the photograph of the Metropolitan Museum of Art). This minor deviation (if it is so, as this part of the Metropolitan plaque is somewhat defaced and damaged) would indicate that this piece of Nalanda is from another mould prepared by the same artist. The second piece (in two fragments joined together, stated to be clay), Acc. no. 12910 (Fig. 3), shows, apart from the preaching Tathāgata (head broken off), five Bodhisattvas (major part of the head of Maitreya broken off), including Avalokiteśvara and Mañjuśrī. This one plaque and the Metropolitan plaque appear to be from the same mould. To these fragments (joined together) may belong the piece bearing Acc. no. 11986 bearing the head of Maitreya, above which is the seated Bodhisattva in a triangular compartment (Fig. 4). The third fragment, Acc. no. 12902 (Fig. 5), stated to be of clay, has preserved the preaching Tathāgata and four of the Bodhisattvas—one below the shrine of Tathāgata and three Bodhisattvas (including Avalokiteśvara) on our left side. The available part of this fragment matches with the corresponding part of the Metropolitan plaque. The small piece bearing Acc. no. 03212 formed part of the right side (viewer's) of Acc. no. 12902 as shown in Fig. 5. All the available compartments in these fragments and smaller pieces teem with tiny letters recording the Buddhist creed.

As the shape, size and material of the plaques, mode of depiction of the figures of the Tathāgata and Bodhisattvas, the icono-compositional scheme, the vacant spaces of the compartments teeming with tiny letters of the Buddhist creed and plastic style of the figures of the fragmentary plaques are so akin to those of the Metropolitan plaque that it is not unreasonable to assume that the Metropolitan plaque originated in Nalanda.

II

That the theme of the array of eight great Bodhisattvas enjoyed considerable popularity at the important Buddhist centre of Nalanda for a considerable time is testified by a number of antiquities not only in terracotta (or clay) but in metal and stone. Pal has already referred to a bronze *stūpa.*[6]

The bronze *stūpa,* found at Nalanda, is now in the National Museum (Acc. no. 49. 129), New Delhi, and is about 40 cm. high. It is datable to about the ninth century AD.

The *stūpa* (Figs. 6, 7, 8 and 9)[7] consists of (i) a four-legged squarish platform with a flight of four steps in central part of all the four sides, (ii) an octagonal drum with eight niches showing the eight great incidents of the life of Buddha at different places, (iii) a hemispherical dome with a *viśva-padma* (with rising stamens) at the base, (iv) a squarish *harmikā* with a projected moulding (inverted *khurā*) at the top, and (v) *chatrāvalī* with a *yaṣṭi* having a moulded base and gradually-diminishing disc-shaped *chatras* (eight discs are available). The steps leading to Buddha in *bhūmisparśa-mudrā* (against the central niche of one side of the drum) are inscribed with the Buddhist creed, now practically effaced.

There are eight seated Bodhisattvas, each within a shallow squarish niche flanking the flight of steps on the four sides of the platform. By virtue of their placements, they would remind one of the guardians of directions (*dikpālas*) in Brahmanical temples. They are seated in a plain facet-like seat in a somewhat relaxed posture with both legs folded, but the foot of one leg slightly projects from the seat downwards. Each of them wears an *antarīya* and an *upavīta* (except perhaps one). The two-armed figures have suffered from abrasion and corrosion.

Starting on the side (Fig. 6) with Buddha in *bhūmisparśa-mudrā* (against the drum above the flight of steps) we find on the sinister of the platform the sparsely-bejewelled Bodhisattva Sarvanivaraṇa-Viṣkambhin (Fig. 6), devoid of ear-ornaments. With his right palm in *vyākhyāna-mudrā*, he holds with his left palm (resting on his left knee) the stalk of an *utpala*(?) supporting the pole of a banner.

To the dexter of the flight of steps of this very side is the sparsely-bejewelled Avalokiteśvara (Fig. 6) with the *jaṭā-mukuṭa* bereft of ear-ornaments. With his damaged right palm on the knee, he carries with his left palm (placed on the plain seat) the stalk of an abraded lotus.

Moving clockwise, the figure of the next Bodhisattva (Fig. 7) is badly damaged. It possibly represents Maitreya (perhaps with *jaṭā-mukuṭa*), sparsely bejewelled and devoid of ear-ornaments. On his forehead is a raised circular mark. With his damaged right palm against the chest he holds with his left palm perhaps a *nāgakesara* branch, mostly defaced.

The Bodhisattva Samantabhadra (Fig. 7) is adorned with *valayas*, armlets, a beaded string for a *hāra*, a circular ear-stud in his left ear (the ear-ornament in his right ear damaged) and a short crown. He carries with his slightly-raised right palm the hilt of a partly-broken sword, the left palm resting on the plain seat.

The fifth Bodhisattva on the next side is the bejewelled Kṣitigarbha (Fig. 8) with his right palm touching the chest. Resting on his left knee, the left palm holds a stalk ending in three oval or heart-shaped objects (abraded) which may represent a *kalpadruma*.

The sixth (Fig. 8) is the bejewelled Vajrapāṇi bearing a thunderbolt with his right palm against his chest, the left palm resting on his left knee.

The seventh Bodhisattva (Fig. 9) on the next side of the *stūpa* is the bejewelled Mañjuśrī with his characteristic *śikhaṇḍaka-kākapakṣa* coiffure. His ornaments include ear-studs and the distinctive neck-string with a central medallion. With his right palm (thumb and index-finger touching) in *vitarka-mudrā*, he bears with his left palm (resting on the plain seat) the stalk of an *utpala*.

With a mark on his forehead, the bejewelled eighth Bodhisattva (Fig. 9), Khagarbha or Ākāśagarbha, wears a folded *uttarīya* in the *upavītī* fashion. He holds a jewel with his right palm (wrist supported on the knee) and with the left palm (resting on the plain seat) a stalk supporting a defaced object (somewhat tulip-shaped; a bowl with jewels?).

III

The bronzes housed in the Archaeological Site Museum at Nalanda include the individual images of eight great Bodhisattvas. From the photographs available in the albums of the Museum Branch of the Archaeological Survey of India it is possible to identify the bejewelled images of (i) Avalokiteśvara, (ii) Maitreya, (iii) Mañjuśrī, (iv) Kṣitigarbha, (v) Sarvanivaraṇa-Viṣkambhin and perhaps (vi) Ākāśagarbha (bearing a conspicuous jewel on a flower in his right hand), all seated in *lalitāsana* on the pericarp of a lotus, and forming a cognate group. The attributes of some Bodhisattvas who may fall in this group are either indistinct in the photographs or broken off. There are at least two bronze images of Kṣitigarbha, Maitreya, Mañjuśrī and Ākāśagarbha(?) and a number of images of Avalokiteśvara. Some bronze images from Nalanda have been distributed to several museums like the Indian Museum and Patna Museum.

IV

The Archaeological Site Museum at Nalanda has at least two stone architectural slabs with a Tathāgata in the company of Bodhisattvas, as could be ascertained from the photographs in the albums of the Archaeological Survey of India.[8] Unlike the already-noted plaques and also some *maṇḍala*-reliefs of Ellora in Maharashtra, the Bodhisattvas in these two long slabs are not arrayed round the central Tathāgata in the form of a *maṇḍala.* Both the slabs present a horizontal panel with a row having Śākyamuni Buddha or a transcendent Tathāgata (popularly known as Dhyānī Buddha) in the centre and Bodhisattvas on his either side. These two carved slabs do not appear to be earlier than the tenth century.

One (Acc. no. 10721 of the Nalanda Museum) of the slabs is 30 in. (76 cm.) long and 8.5 in. (21.5 cm.) high according to the records of the Museums Branch of the Archaeological Survey of India. It is *tri-ratha* on the front side and has two gradually-increasing bands and a *khurā*-shaped moulding (relieved with a triangular half-flower in the central part of the body of the *khurā*) at the base of the panel and a band and a projected *khurā*-shaped moulding (also with a triangular half-flower in the central part of its body) at the top (Fig. 10). Most probably this slab was part of a structure, say the platform of a *stūpa.* All the nine figures are seated in *vajra-paryaṅkāsana* on a lotus within their individual niches, separated from one another by pilasters having a *khurā*-shaped base (on a squarish block), a baluster-shaped shaft enclosed by a double string, a capital with mouldings and a splayed-out bracket having a triangular half-flower in its central part; the brackets support a running narrow band-like beam.

Draped in an *antarīya* and an *uttarīya* in some cases, worn in the fashion of an *upavīta*, all the two-armed Bodhisattvas, with a benign face (smiling in some cases), are adorned with ornaments like *valayas*, armlets with a central ornate piece (usually flower-shaped), a necklace, ear-ornaments in most cases and a short crown.

Starting at the extreme dexter, the first niche (with its dexter-pilaster damaged) contains Sarvanivaraṇa-Viṣkambhin showing *vara-mudrā* with his right palm and holding with his slightly-raised left hand the long pole of a banner.

Within the second niche is Samantabhadra grasping the hilt of a vertical sword with his right palm, his left palm resting on his left thigh.

The next five niches are provided on the central projection. The third accommodates Mañjughoṣa or Mañjuvara showing *dharmackara-mudrā* with two palms placed near the chest. Passing over his left arm is the stalk of an *utpala* supporting the *Prajñāpāramitā* manuscript. Adorned with large ear-studs among other ornaments, he wears a coiffure resembling the *śikhaṇḍaka-kākapakṣa* above his bejewelled crown.

Inside the fourth niche is Avalokiteśvara with neatly-arrayed *jaṭā-bhāra* above the bejewelled crown. With his right palm (having a raised mark) in *vara-mudrā*, he holds with his slightly-raised left palm the stalk of a finely-executed lotus. His folded *uttarīya* and *antarīya* are decorated with floral patterns.

The fifth niche contains the Śākyamuni Buddha, robed in an *aṅtarvāsa* and an *uttarāsaṅga* which leaves his right chest, shoulder and arm bare. With his left palm resting on the lap, he shows *bhūmisparśa-mudrā* with his right palm. His head and *uṣṇīṣa* are covered by rows of stylized curls.

Within the next niche is Maitreya with a smiling face and the *jaṭā-mukuṭa* above the crown. With his right palm (with a circular mark) in *vara-mudrā*, he carries with his raised left palm a branch of the flowering *nāgakesara* plant. His folded *uttarīya* (worn in the fashion of an *upavīta*) and also *antarīya* are decorated.

Inside the next niche is the sixth Bodhisattva with *jaṭā-mukuṭa* above the crown. He shows *vyākhyāna-mudrā* with his right palm near the chest, the left hand resting on the lap. Near his left shoulder rises the branch of a tree: if the branch is intended for the *kalpadruma*, the Bodhisattva is Kṣitigarbha.

Within the next niche is Vajrapāṇi with a thunderbolt (indistinct in the photograph) in his right palm below the chest; he holds with his left palm the stalk of an *utpala*.

The eighth Bodhisattva in the last niche is perhaps Ākāśagarbha with his right palm possibly in *abhaya-mudrā*. By the side of his left arm is a stalk of either a lotus or a flower bearing a splayed-out object.

Bearing Acc. no. 10512 of the Nalanda Museum, the available part of the frieze (Fig. 11), possibly of an architectural piece, is reported to be 23.75 in. (nearly 60 cm.) long. It is in two fragments as seen in the photograph of the Archaeological Survey of India. The available part (in two fragments) presents the figures of seven Bodhisattvas and Vairocana. As Vairocana is in the fourth niche instead of the fifth, it is inevitable to conclude that the missing figure of the Bodhisattva had been carved on a separate stone slab which was joined with the dexter-end of the available portion (broken into two fragments). This conclusion is confirmed by the existence of nearly half of a cramp-chase on the top (Fig. 12) of the dexter-end of the available part (in two fragments) which was clamped by an iron cramp with the missing slab.

All the available seven figures of Bodhisattvas and Vairocana are seen seated on *viśva-padmas* within a row of niches with *ghaṭa*-shaped bases (*ghaṭas* are decorated with lotus-petals), round (or octagonal) shafts with vertical lines and capitals with three mouldings; over the topmost splayed-out moulding is the plain squarish abacus, from which the trefoil arch springs up. Between the arches is a prominent diamond-shaped floral motif, while above the topmost moulding of the arches are two coiled stalks of foliated leaves with a heart-shaped motif in between. Running below the *viśva-padma* seats (of the figures) and the *ghaṭa*-shaped bases of the pilasters is a horizontal band, below which is a recess, the projected bottom band appearing like a moulding.

Attired in an *antarīya* fastened by a belt with an ornate clasp, the Bodhisattvas are adorned with *valayas*, armlets with a central piece resembling a triangular half-flower, a *hāra* having a row of closely-arrayed bead-shaped pendants, ear-ornaments in most cases, and crowns (appearing like the *karaṇḍa-mukuṭa* in some cases). All of them wear an *upavīta* and have a mark on the forehead.

Starting from the left (on the dexter) niche of the available part, the first figure wearing ear-studs and a folded *uttarīya* is seated in *sattva-paryaṅkāsana*. In his right palm (held near the chest) is a damaged thunderbolt. The attribute in his left palm (resting against his left thigh) appears to be a bell. If this is correct, the figure represents Vajrasattva instead of Vajrapāṇi who is not depicted in this architectural piece. Vajrasattva is conceived here as a Bodhisattva. He is noted as one of the sixteen Bodhisattvas, all with Vajra in the first part of their names. All these sixteen (Vajra-)Bodhisattvas are described in the *Vajradhātu-maṇḍala* (*Maṇḍala* no. 19)[9] of the published *Niṣpannayogāvalī*. The bejewelled Vajrasattva who tops the list of the sixteen Bodhisattvas is noted in the *Maṇḍala* as holding a thunderbolt with his right palm and seated in *sattva-paryaṅkāsana*. That Vajrasattva (and fifteen others) is considered a Bodhisattva is specifically noted in this *Maṇḍala*: *Vajrasattvādayo hi ṣoḍaśabodhisattvāḥ svasvādhipati-tathāgatābhimukhāḥ*.[10]

The Bodhisattva within the next niche is Samantabhadra, clasping with his slightly-raised right palm the hilt of a sword (held almost straight); his left palm (hanging from his raised left knee) holds the stalk of an *utpala* bearing an object which could not be identified from the available photograph. Wearing large ear-studs and other ornaments, he is seated in the *mahārājalīlā* posture with his left knee raised.

With his right palm possibly in *vyākhyāna-mudrā*, Avalokiteśvara, the Bodhisattva in the next niche, carries the long stalk of a full-blown lotus with his left palm resting against the lower part of his left leg near the knee. Wearing a *jaṭā-mukuṭa* bearing a figure of Amitābha(?), he is seated in a posture somewhat like the *mahārājalīlā*, but the foot of his folded left leg passes behind his slanting right leg with the raised knee.

Within the next niche is the two-armed Vairocana, seated in *vajra-paryaṅkāsana* on a *viśva-padma*. Robed in an *antarvāsa* fastened by an ornate girdle, he is bedecked with *valayas*, armlets with a triangular floral motif, a necklace, ear-ornaments and a *mukuṭa* at the base of the conically-arrayed coiffure. He displays *dharmacakra-mudrā* (?).

The next niche houses Maitreya with the high *jaṭā-mukuṭa* bearing a *caitya*. Possibly he does not wear ear-ornaments. With his right palm in *vara-mudrā*, he holds with his left palm (near the chest) a branch with *nāgakesara* flowers. His sitting posture is like that of Avalokiteśvara, but his left knee is raised.

Within the next niche is Mañjuśrī wearing ear-studs. Seated in the *mahārājalīlā* posture, he carried with his left palm (hanging from his raised left knee) the stalk of an *utpala* supporting a manuscript.

The Bodhisattva inside the next niche shows perhaps the *vitarka-mudrā* and holds with his left palm (hanging from his raised left knee) possibly a long narrow pennon-like flag with a pole curved like a stalk. If the identification of the flag is correct, the figure represents Sarvanivaraṇa-Viṣkambhin. He is seated also in the *mahārājalīlā* posture.

The sinister-edge of the last niche along with the pilaster is broken off. With his right arm damaged, the Bodhisattva is seated in *mahārājalīlā*. The attribute held in his left hand is also damaged. He may represent either Ksitigarbha or Ākāśagarbha, one of whom is missing in the photograph and was evidently represented on the missing stone slab which was originally clamped with the extreme dexter of the present slab (in two fragments).

Taking a turn (at right angles) from the last niche towards our right, we find a standing figure of Buddha with his right palm in *vyākhyāna-mudrā* (Fig. 12).

V

Before closing my paper on the figures of Aṣṭa-mahābodhisattvas from Nalanda. I would like to refer to a spectacular sculpture at Jagdishpur near Nalanda. This sculpture,[11] more than life-size and datable to about the tenth century AD, depicts *aṣṭa-mahāprātihāryas* (eight great miracles or life-events) of Śākyamuni Buddha. It presents in its lowest part eight two-armed Bodhisattvas, four each in two flanks at the extremities beyond the pedestal of Buddha (in *bhūmisparśa-mudrā*) carved with the figures of Māra and his daughters, apart from the figures of the earth-goddess and Aparājitā (two witnesses).[12] Seated on either fully-blossomed double-petalled lotuses or *viśva-padmas*, all the Bodhisattvas are robed in *antarīyas* held by belts or girdless and richly adorned with anklets, *valayas*, armlets with an ornate piece, *ratnopavītas*, necklaces, ear-ornaments and *mukuṭas*. The coiffure or *mukuṭa* varies in some cases. Behind all of them are haloes (with a semicircular top), edged by tongues of flames, except perhaps at the top having a floral motif as seen in two cases in one of the photographs reproduced here.

In each flank there are four Bodhisattvas, the upper pair immediately above the lower pair. Of the lower pair on the dexter-side (Fig. 13),[13] the one on the viewer's left is seated with his right foot (leg partially bent and knee raised) on the pericarp of a double-petalled lotus and the foot of the pendant left leg resting on a small lotus. He clutches with his right fist the hilt of a long sword (placed vertically), the left palm resting on the lotus-seat. This figure, possibly with a *karaṇḍa-mukuṭa,* represents Samantabhadra.

The Bodhisattva with a conical *karaṇḍa-mukuṭa*(?) by the left side of Samantabhadra and seated like him (but his left foot is on the double-petalled lotus and hanging right foot on a small lotus) is most probably Kṣitigarbha. He shows with his right hand *vyākhyāna-mudrā*(?) and carries in his left palm a twig with two (or three) bifurcating stalks ending in indistinct diamond-shaped objects, representing presumably the *kalpadruma.* The stalks of the two double-petalled lotuses (on which these two Bodhisattvas are seated) have issued from a common floriated stem.

The left one of the upper pair of this flank is Avalokiteśvara with the well-knit *jaṭā-mukuṭa* (having perhaps a figure of Amitābha on its front), seated in the *vajra-paryaṅkāsana* on a *viśva-padma.* With his right palm bearing a mark, in *vara-mudrā,* he holds with his slightly-raised left hand the stalk of a full-blown lotus. He wears a folded *uttarīya* in the fashion of an *upavīta.*

The Bodhisattva by the left of Avalokiteśvara is Maitreya, also in the *vajra-paryaṅkāsana* on a *viśva-padma.* Wearing the slightly-loose *jaṭā-mukuṭa,* he shows with his right palm (having a circular mark) *vyākhyāna-mudrā* (or *vitarka-mudrā*) and carries with his left palm (resting on his left knee) a branch of the *nāgakesara* flowers.

The left one of the pair of Bodhisattvas in the upper row of the sinister-flank (Fig. 14) seated in the *vajra-paryaṅkāsana* (or *sattva-paryaṅkāsana*) on a *viśva-padma* and with a decorated *antarīya* is Vajrapāṇi. Wearing a short crown with hair in gradually-decreasing rolls like *karaṇḍa-mukuṭa* and having a smiling face, he supports with his right palm (placed near the chest) a thunderbolt (balanced vertically) and holds with his left palm (resting on his left thigh) a sinuous stalk of an *utpala.*

The Bodhisattva by the left side of Vajrapāṇi is Mañjuśrī, possibly in his form of Mañjuvara. Wearing a short crown capped by the rolls of hair resembling *karaṇḍa-mukuṭa,* large ear-studs and a *hāra* strung with the ring of a central conspicuous medallion and rings of smaller pendants, he is seated in the *vajra-paryaṅkāsana* on a *viśva-padma.* He displays *dharmacakra-mudrā* with his two palms held near the chest. Passing over the arms above the elbows are two curved stalks of *utpalas*, each supporting the *Prajñāpāramitā* manuscript.

Of the two figures in the lower row, the one on the left represents Sarvanivaraṇa-Viṣkambhin, draped in a decorated *antarīya.* With a short crown capped by *karaṇḍa*-like coiffure and circular mark on the forehead, he is seated in *lalitāsana* on a double-petalled lotus, with his left foot perched on a small lotus. Possibly showing *vyākhyāna-mudrā* with his slightly-raised right palm, he carried with his left palm the stalk of a flower supporting the pole of a flag.

The Bodhisattva by his left side, clad in a decorated *antarīya* and a folded decorated *uttarīya* worn in the fashion of an *upavīta,* is also in *lalitāsana* on a double-petalled lotus (the stalk of which has issued from the floriated stem with its lowest part in the shape of a *viśva-padma* from which has emerged the stalk of the double-petalled lotus of Sarvanivaraṇa-Viṣkambhin), his hanging right foot on a small lotus. With a circular mark on the forehead and having a triple-stringed crown capped by a lotus in the centre and an ornate piece at the sides, he holds in his left palm the stalk of a double-petalled lotus supporting a carved oblong object. If the object represents a string of jewels, the Bodhisattva may stand for Ākāśagarbha. From the photograph it appears that the Bodhisattva holds with the thumb and ring-finger (?) a small longish object with a conical lower part.

NOTES

1. 'A Note on The Mandala of The Eight Bodhisattvas', *Archives of Asian Art*, Vol. XXVI, 1972-73, pp. 71-3 and Fig. 1.
2. I am beholden to Pratapaditya Pal (then Senior Curator, Indian and Southeast Asian Art, Los Angeles County Museum of Art, U.S.A.) who wrote, on my behalf, to Martin Lerner (Curator, Indian Art, The Metropolitan Museum of Art, New York) for the supply of detailed photographs that would make the inscriptions legible. Martin Lerner sent an enlarged photograph of the plaque to Pal who forwarded it to me. I record here my grateful thanks to Martin Lerner and Pratapaditya Pal for the excellent photograph.
3. Pratapaditya Pal, op. cit., p. 71.
4. Ibid., p. 73.
5. Two (Acc. nos. 12902 and 12910) of these fragmentary plaques were photographed along with fifteen other plaques and discs in a single

negative, while the third (Acc. no. 00951) was photographed along with a fragment of a larger (oblong) plaque. The illustrated photographs (copyright of the Archaeological Survey of India) are singled out from two negatives of multiple objects as a result of which these (Figs. 2, 3, 3A and 4) are not up to the mark. The details are not distinct on account of partial effacement. It could not be ascertained if the fragments are of terracotta or ill-fired clay, nor could it be found out if there are fragments of other plaques in the collection of the Nalanda Museum.

6. Pratapaditya Pal, op. cit., p. 71, Fig. 2 on pp. 72 and 73, note 3. The *stūpa*, now in the National Museum, New Delhi, is from Nalanda and is not stolen. I am not aware of the other bronze *stūpa* with figures of eight Bodhisattvas mentioned by him.
7. I am grateful to R.C. Sharma, the then Director General of the National Museum, New Delhi, for the photographs showing the four sides of the *stūpa*. The copyright of these photographs rests with the National Museum.
8. The copyright of the illustrated photographs of these two slabs belongs to the Archaeological Survey of India.
9. *Niṣpannayogāvalī of Mahāpaṇḍita Abhayākaragupta*, edited by Benoytosh Bhattacharyya (Baroda, 1949), pp. 44-7.
10. Ibid., p. 46.
11. Susan L. Huntington has illustrated this sculpture in *The "Pāla-Sena" Schools of Sculpture*, Studies in South Asian Culture, Vol. X (Leiden, 1984), Fig. 131. She suggests the date of the sculpture as the late tenth or early eleventh century AD. She has not touched upon the figures of the Bodhisattvas represented on this sculpture.

    The sculpture has been described and copiously illustrated by John C. Huntington in 'Pilgrimage as Image: the Cult of the *Aṣṭamahāprātihārya*, Part II', *Orientations*, Vol. 18, No. 8, August 1987, pp. 56ff. He dates this sculpture to the ninth century (ibid., p. 57). On page 63 he has illustrated in Fig. 16 the dexter part (i.e. at the viewer's left) with four of the Bodhisattvas, but has not furnished the description of the Bodhisattvas. He, however, notes: 'These are not part of any narrative of the life of the Buddha but are part of the Buddha's nature as the progenitor *(ārya)* of the *Aṣṭamahābodhisattva-maṇḍala* (the *maṇḍala* of the Eight Great Bodhisattvas), one of the fundamental practices of Tantric Buddhism'. Along with her article entitled 'The Case of the Two Witnesses to the Buddha's Enlightenment', Janice Leoshko has furnished an excellent illustration of this over life-size sculpture, *Marg*, Vol. XXXIX, No. 4, 1988, Fig. 14 (p. 49).
12. Janice Leoshko, op. cit., p. 50.
13. The copyright of this and the following photographs belongs to the Archaeological Survey of India.

Fig. 1: Terracotta plaque with a Tathāgata encircled by eight Bodhisattvas. The Metropolitan Museum of Art, Rogers Fund, 1933 (33.50.11).

Fig. 2: Fragment of a plaque in the Archaeological Site Museum at Nalanda.

Fig. 3: Fragment of a plaque in the Archaeological Site Museum at Nalanda.

Fig. 4: Piece of plaque forming part of Fig. 3.

Fig. 5: Two fragments (Accession nos. 12902 and 03212) of a plaque in the Site Museum at Nalanda.

Fig. 6: Bronze *stūpa* from Nalanda, now in the National Museum (New Delhi).

Fig. 7: Bronze *stūpa* from Nalanda, now in the National Museum (New Delhi).

Fig. 8: Bronze *stūpa* from Nalanda, now in the National Museum (New Delhi).

Fig. 9: Bronze *stūpa* from Nalanda, now in the National Museum (New Delhi).

Fig. 10: Architectural slab with the figures of Buddha and eight Bodhisattvas, in the Archaeological Site Museum at Nalanda.

Fig. 11: Frieze with figures of Bodhisattvas and Vairochana in the Archaeological Site Museum at Nalanda.

Fig. 12: A side view of the frieze (shown on Fig. 11) showing a cramp-chase (on the extreme left of the top) and standing figure of Buddha.

Fig. 13: Figures of the four Bodhisattvas on an image of Buddha at Jagdishpur, near Nalanda.

Fig. 14: Figures of the four Bodhisattvas on an image of Buddha at Jagdishpur, near Nalanda.

4

From the Goddesses of Plaosan to the Dhāraṇī-Maṇḍala at Alchi

LOKESH CHANDRA
SUDARSHANA DEVI SINGHAL

The goddess of eternity incarnated in the grace of images in Buddhist *maṇḍalas* has remained hidden in the folds of time. Their visions have eluded modern research in the wordless beyond. The words of the *Sarva-tathāgata-tattva-saṁgraha* have not been understood in full measure, though it is the Root Tantra of 24 *Vajradhātu-maṇḍalas.* The goddesses at Chandi Plaosan Lor have led us to explore the complex at Alchi nestling in the Himalayas.

The ninth century complex of Chandi Plaosan Lor in Indonesia has only male figures in the northern temple and only female figures in the southern temple (Casparis 1958: 32 n 179). The male figures may represent the *Vajradhātu-mahamaṇḍala* (I.1) and the female figures can be the *Dhāraṇī-Maṇḍala.* (I.2)

The identification can be made when the reliefs in both temples are available in photographs. For the present we shall see how the goddesses are configured at Alchi.

Alongwith Ajanta, Angkor, Borodudur, Gyantse Kumbum, Tunhuang and other gems of Buddhist art are the staggering luminant murals of the Alchi monastery, about 70 km. west of Leh in Ladakh. Built in the eleventh century, it is situated in fertile alluvial terraces of the Indus. It is the glory of Kashmiri style Buddhist art. Its three-storeyed Sumtsek building has *maṇḍalas* of the *Sarva-tathāgata-tattva-saṁgraha* (*STTS*), which was translated into Tibetan under the guidance of Rin chen bzan po in the tenth century. Its commentary *Tattvālokakarī* has influenced the iconography of the Alchi *maṇḍalas*, as shown by S. Toganoo. The Sino-Japanese *Kongōkai maṇḍala* has conditioned the understanding of the *Vajradhātu-maṇḍalas* (plural) and that has been a hindrance in the correct identification of the Alchi *maṇḍalas.* The nine squares in the Genzu are a Chinese configuration to accord with the geomantic consideration of the T'ang capital, and they are specific to the politico-ritual requirements of China at the time. This *maṇḍala* was copied for Kobo Daishi by the Court painter Li chên and hence has nine squares. The Tendai Vajradhātū *maṇḍala* originates in the monastic tradition and thus has only the central *maṇḍala* which as the prakṛti or prototype is the prime *maṇḍala*. The Genzu has the second *samaya-maṇḍala* (I.2) where the goddesses are replaced by symbols. Hence this *maṇḍala* I.2 on the right hand of the upper floor of Sumtsek, with goddesses as required by the fundamental text *STTS*, could not be identified correctly.

The Sarva-tathāgata-tattva-saṁgraha has six *maṇḍalas* in the first samaya:

I.1 *Vajradhātu-mahām, mahām, (Amoghavajra, Genzu, Mkhas-grub. rje, Buddhaguhya), mahābhūta-m.* (*Tajima* p. 245).
I.2 *Vajraguhya-m, dhāraṇī-m. (Amonghavajra, Mkhas. grub rje), samaya-m. (Genzu, Buddhaguhya).*
I.3 *Vajrajñānadharma-m. Vajra-sūkṣma-jñāna-m. sūkṣma-vajra-m. (Amoghavajra, Genzu), sūkṣma-m. (Genzu), dharma-m. (Tajima, Mkhas. grub. rje), dharma-cakra-m. (Buddhaguhya).*
I.4 *Vajrakāryakarma-m., pūjā-karma-m. (Amoghavajra, Genzu) pūjā-m. (Genzu), Karma-m. (Tajima, Mkhas. gurb. rje, Buddhaguhya).*
I.5 *Caturmudrā-m.*
I.6 *Ekamudrā-m.*

The *maṇḍala* I.2 contains 37 goddesses: they are in the form of *pāramitā* (*Tajima* 1959: 146). In the *Genzu maṇḍala* prevalent in Japan, the goddesses have been replaced by their symbols (*samaya*) and this is known as the *samaya-m.* in the Genzu. The *Genzu maṇḍala* was drawn for Kobo Daishi by the court painter of China, and he did not depict the goddesses, as the Emperor could not worship them. This had led to distortions in understanding the *Dhāraṇī-m.* at Alchi. The goddess *Ratnavajriṇī*, the consort of *Ratnasambhava*, had been wrongly interpreted as '*Buddha Ratnasambhava* in Female Form' (Goepper/Poncar 1984: 96 pl. 25). Goepper says: 'The figures in the Central Group are all female, perhaps because the cult image refers to a so-called "mother tantra".' He identifies 'Bodhisattva Vajrayaksa in Female Form' on p. 100 pl. 27, but she is the goddess

Tejaḥpratyāhāriṇī (*STTS* pl. 103, Gobu p. 168), and she holds two fangs (*daṁṣṭrā*). The second chapter of the *STTS* describes this *maṇḍala* of goddesses at length. The *STTS* has to be read in conjuction with its 24 *maṇḍalas*. The *Genzu maṇḍala* has pre-empted the possibility of *maṇḍalas* of goddesses, as they are not represented therein, but are substituted by symbols.

In the sumptuous Japanese work on the monastic art of Ladakh entitled *Mandara: Nishi Chibetto-no Bukkyo-no Bijutsu* (*NCBB*), it has not been realised that the *Dhāraṇī-maṇḍala* (no. 6) represents goddesses. Hence *Vajriṇī* has been identified as *Vairocana* (p. 32, pl. I.19), *Dharmavajriṇī* as *Amitābha* (p. 34, pl. I.21), *Karmavajriṇī* as *Amoghasiddhi* (p. 37, pl. I.25). Snellgrove-Skorupski (1977: 1.32 pl. v) identified it as 'a *maṇḍala* of *Vairocana*' (no. 6).

I.2.1 *Vajriṇī* is the consort of *Vairocana*. Like him she has four faces, two hands, is white in complexion, and sits on two lions. Her mantra is: *Oṁ Vajradhātvīśvarī hūṁ vajriṇī* (*STTS* p. 34). Illustrated in *NCBB* 1, 23, 25, 32 (full-page plate).

I.2.2 *Vajravajriṇī* is the *vidyā* (consort) of *Akṣobhya*, and like him she is blue is colour and sits on two elephants. Illustrated in *NCBB* 1.21.

I.2.3 *Ratnavajriṇī* is the *vidyā* (consort) of *Ratnasambhava* and shares his yellow colour and like him sits on two horses. Illustrated in *NCBB* 1.20, 22, 24.

I.2.4 *Dharmavajriṇī* is the *vidyā* (consort) of *Amitābha* and like him sits on two peacocks. Illustrated in *NCBB*.1.19, 23, 34.

I.2.5 *Karmavajriṇī* is the *vidyā* (consort) of *Amoghasiddhi* and like him her mounts are two *garuḍas*. Illustrated in *NCBB* 1.19, 21, 23, 37.

FOUR VAJRADHĀRAṆĪ

Now follow the four acolytes of *Vajravajriṇī* the consort of *Akṣobhya*. *Akṣobhya* is characterised by a *vajra* and hence their collective appellation is *vajradhāraṇyaḥ* in the *STTS* p. 34.

I.2.6 *Samantabhadrā* is the consort of *Vajrasattva*. Her *mantra* is *Oṁ vajrasatva-guhyasamaye hūṁ* (*STTS* 34). Illustrated in *NCBB* 1.21.

I.2.7 *Tathāgatāṅkuśī* is the consort of *Vajrarāja*. Her mantra is *Oṁ guhyavajrāṅkuśī hūṁ* (*STTS* 34). Illustrated in *NCBB* 1.21. Here *rāja* in *Vajarāja* is from the root *rañj* 'to please, charm delight' and does not refer to a king (rājan). It means *rañjana*. Hence she is the *aṅkuśī* or seductress.

I.2.8 *Ratirāgā* is the consort of *Vajrarāga*. Her *mantra* is *Om vajraguhyarāge rāgaya hūṁ* (*STTS* 34). She holds the bow and arrow of Cupid. Illustrated in *NCBB* 1.21.

I.2.9 *Sādhūmatī* is the consort of *Vajrasādhu*. Her *mantra* is *Om guhyavajra sādhviśvari hūṁ* (*STTS* 34).

FOUR RATNADHĀRAṆĪ

The four acolytes of *Ratnavajriṇī*, the consort of *Ratnasambhava* follow (I.2.10, 11, 12, 13). They are collectively termed *Ratnadhāraṇyaḥ* in *STTS* 34.

I.2.10 *Ratnottamā* is the consort of *Vajraratna*. Her *mantra* is *Om vajraguhyaratnasamaye hūṁ* (*STTS* 34). She holds a garland. Illustrated in *NCBB* 1.18, 20.

I.2.11 *Ratnolkā* is the consort of *Vajratejas*. Her *mantra* is *om vajraguhyaprabhe hūṁ* (*STTS* 34). She holds a shining object, being *Ratna-ulkā* and the consort of *Vajra-tejas*. Compare her drawing in the *Gobu* 49. Ilustrated in *NCBB* 1.18, 20.

1.2.12 *Dhvajāgrakeyūrā* is the consort of *Vajraketu*. Her *mantra* is *om vajradhvajāgraguhye hūṃ* (*STTS* 34). She holds a banner in her right hand. Illustrated in *NCBB* 1.18.

I.2.13 *Hāsavati* is the consort of *Vajrahāsa*. Her *mantra* is *om guhyahāsavajri hūṁ* (*STTS* 34).

FOUR DHARMADHĀRAṆĪ

The four acolytes of *Dhamavajriṇī* the consort of *Amitābha* are called *dharmadhāranyaḥ* in *STTS* 35.

I.2.14 *Vajrāmbujā* is the consort of *Vajradharma* and her *mantra* is *om Vajradharmaguhyasamaye hūṁ* (*STTS* 34). Illustrated in *NCBB* 1.18.

I.2.15 *Ādhāraṇī* is the consort of *Vajratīkṣna* and her *mantra* is *om vajrakoṣaguhye hūṁ* (*STTS* 34). The word Ādhāraṇī refers to the edge of a razor, *kṣurasaya dhārā*, like *Vajra-tīkṣṇa*. The word *koṣa* in the *mantra* is the sheath of a sword. Illustrated in *NCBB* 1.18.

I.2.16 *Sarvacakra* is the consort of *Vajrahetu*. Her *mantra* is *om vajraguhyamaṇḍale hūṁ* (*STTS* 35). Illustrated in *NCBB* 1.19. Reason (*hetu*) was an expedient to confuse adversaries, to put them in a whirlpool (*cakra*).

I.2.17 *Sahasrāvartā* is the consort of *Vajrabhāṣa*. Her *mantra* is *om vajraguhyajāpasamaye hūṁ* (*STTS* 35). Illustrated in *NCBB* 1.19.

FOUR SARVADHĀRAṆĪ

The four acolytes of *Karmavajriṇī* the consort of *Amoghasiddhi* are collectively called *sarvadhāraṇyaḥ* (*STTS* 35).

I.2.18 *Siddhottarā* is the consort of *Vajrakarma*. Her *mantra* is *om vajraguhyakarmasamaye hūṁ* (*STTS* 35). Illustrated in *NCBB* 1.19.

I.2.19 *Sarvarakṣā* is the consort of *Vajrarakṣā*. Her *mantra* is *om vajraguhyakavace hūṁ* (*STTS* 35). She holds a protective amulet (*kavaca*) of leaves with handles of peacock feathers. Illustrated in *NCBB* 1.19.

I.2.20 *Tejaḥpratyāhāriṇī* is the consort of *Vajrayakṣa*. Her *mantra* is *om guhyavajradaṁṣṭrādhāriṇī hūṁ* (*STTS* 35). As said in the *mantra*, she holds two pointed fangs (*daṁṣṭrā*).

Illustrated in *NCBB* 1.19.37, Geopper/Poncar 1984: 100 pl. 27 (very clear).

I.2.21 *Dhāraṇīmudrā* is the consort of *Vajrasandhi*. Her *mantra* is *om vajraguhya muṣṭī hūṃ* (*STTS* 35). Illustrated in *NCBB* 1.19.

FOUR KARMAVAJREŚVARI

The four acolytes of *Vajriṇī* the consort of *Vairocana* are collectively termed *karmavajreśvaryāḥ* (Gobu 63 on p. 178).

I.2.22 *Sattvavajrī* is the counterpart of *Vajra-pāramitā* in *maṇḍala* I.1. Her *mantra* is *om guhya-sattvavajrī hūṁ* (*STTS* 35). Illustrated in *NCBB* 1.21.

I.2.23 *Ratnavajrī* is the counterpart of *Ratna-pāramitā* in *maṇḍala* I.1. Her *mantra* is *om guhya-ratnavajrī hūṁ* (*STTS* 35). Illustrated in *NCBB* 1.19,20.

I.2.24 *Dharmavajrī* is the counterpart of *Dharmapāramitā* in *maṇḍala* I.1. Her *mantra* is *om guhya-dharmavajrī hūṁ* (*STTS*.35). Illustrated in *NCBB* 1.19.34.

I.2.25 *Karmavajrī* is the counterpart of *Karma-pāramitā* in *maṇḍala* I.1. Her *mantra* is *om guhya-karmavajrī hūṁ* (*STTS* 35). Illustrated in *NCBB* 1.19.37.

FOUR LĀSYĀ AND OTHERS

The four goddesses beginning with *Vajralāsyā* are shown in the outer corners. They are distinguished by their tightfitting blouses and also by their concupiscent bearing.

I.2.26 Counterpart of Vajralāsyā in *maṇḍala* I.1. She is in the lower right corner. Her *mantra* is : *om vajraguhya-ratipūjāsamaye sarvapūjāṁ pravartaya hūṁ* (*STTS* 35). Illustrated in *NCBB* 1.20.

I.2.27 Counterpart of *Vajamālā* in *maṇḍala* I.1. She is in the lower left corner. Her *mantra* is: *om vajraguhyābhiṣeka-pūjāsamaye sarvapūjāṁ pravartaya hūṁ* (*STTS* 35). Illustrated in *NCBB* 1.18.

I.2.28 Counterpart of *Vajragītā* in *maṇḍala* I. She is in the upper left corner. Her *mantra* is: *om vajraguhyagītapūjā-samaye sarvapūjām pravartaya hūṁ* (*STTS* 35). Illustrated in *NCBB* 1.19.

I.2.29 Counterpart of *Vajranṛtya* in *maṇḍala* I.1. She is in the upper right corner. Her *mantra* is: *om vajraguhyanṛtyapūjāsamaye sarvapujaṁ pravartaya hūṁ* (*STTS* 35). Illustrated in *NCBB*. 1.21.

FOUR OFFERING GODDESSES

The next four goddesses of offering are in the corners of the inner sanctum and they are surrounded by a lotiform design. This design is not found with any other goddess of the *maṇḍala*. All the four wear tight-fitting blouses. They are shown in the frontal pose, while the faces of earlier four goddesses were in profile.

I.2.30 *Guhyadhūpeśvarī* is the counterpart of *Vajradhūpā* in *maṇḍala* I.1. She is the lower right corner. Illustrated in *NCBB* I.21, 23.

I.2.31 *Guhyapuṣpā* is the counterpart of *Vajrapuṣpā* in *maṇḍala* I.I. She is in the lower left corner. Illustrated in *NCBB* 1.21, 23.

I.2.32 *Guhyadipā* is the counterpart of *Vajrālokā* in *maṇḍala* I.1. She is in the upper left corner. Illustrated in *NCBB* I.18.22.

I.2.33 *Guhyagandhā* is the counterpart of *Vajragandhā* in *maṇḍala* I.1. She is in the upper right corner. Illustrated in *NCBB* 1.19.23.

FOUR GATEKEEPERS

The four gates of the inner sanctum are guarded by four goddesses:

I.2.34 *Guhyāṅkuśī*, the consort of *Vajrāṅkuśa*, guards the eastern gate. Her *mantra* is *om guhyāṅkuśī hūṁ jaḥ jaḥ jaḥ jaḥ* (*Gobu* 68). Illustrated in *NCBB* 1.25.

I.2.35 *Ghuyapāśā*, the consort of Vajrapāśa, guards the southern gate. Her *mantra* is *om guhyapāśe hūṁ hūṁ hūṁ hūṁ* (*Gobu* 69) Illustrated in *NCBB* 1.22, 24.

I.2.36 *Guhyasphoṭā*, the consort of *Vajrasphoṭa*, guards the western gate. Her *mantra* is *om guhyasphoṭe vaṁ vaṁ vaṁ vaṁ* (*Gobu* 70). Illustrated in *NCBB* 1.23, 34.

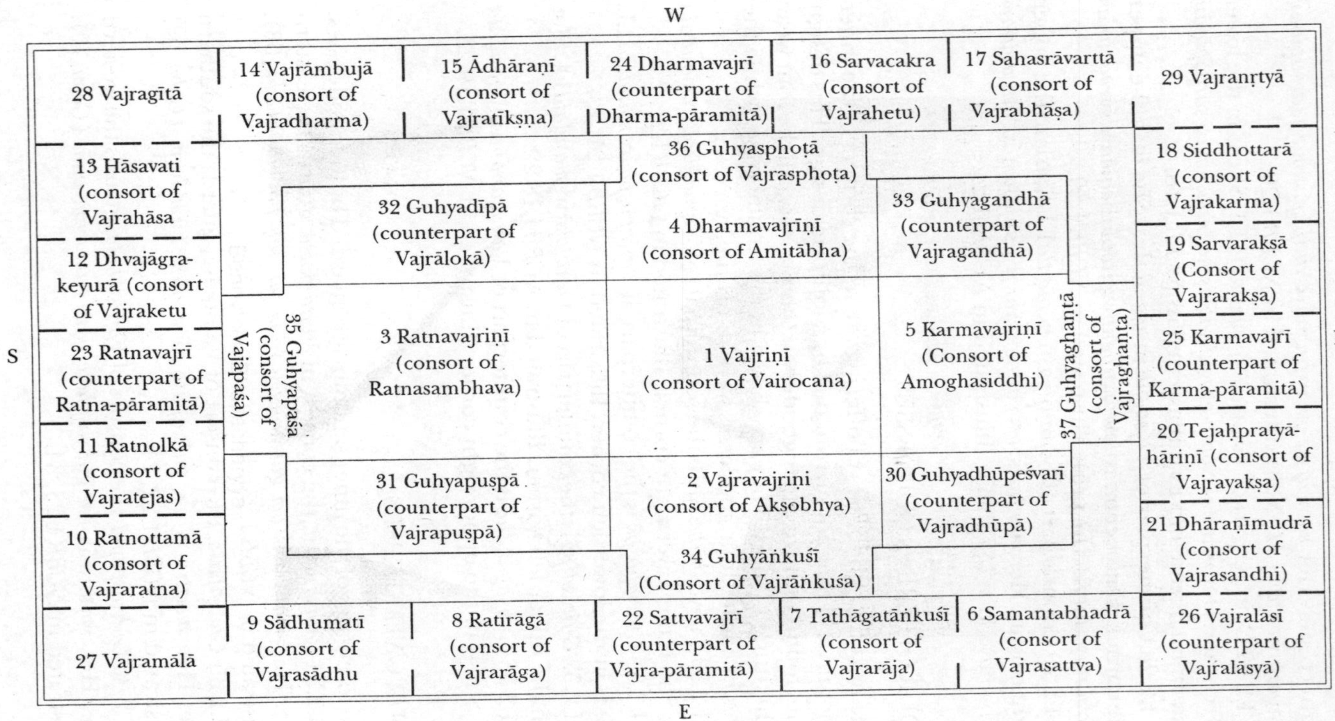

Layout of the dhāraṇī-*maṇḍala* at Alchi

Goddess	Consort	Characteristic of the Consort
1. Vajriṇī	Vairocaṇa	Four-faced, white, on lions
2. Vajravajrīṇī	Akṣobhya	blue, on elephants
3. Ratnavajrīṇī	Ratnasambhava	Yellow, on horse
4. Dharmavajriṇi	Amitābha	red, on peacocks
5. Karmavajrīṇī	Amoghasiddhi	green, on garuda
6. Samantabhadrā	Vajrasattva	vajra and bell
7. Tathāgatāṅkuśī	Vajrarāja	hook
8. Ratirāga	Vajrarāga	bow and arrow
9. Sādhūṁati	Vajrasādhu	five-pointed vajra
10. Ratnottamā	vajraratna	gem and bell
11. Ratnolkā	Vajratejas	solar disk
12. Dhvajāgrakeyūrā	Vajraketu	banner of vicitory
13. Hāsavatī	Vajrahāsa	rosary of ivory
14. Vajrāmbūjā	Vajradharma	lotus-flower
15. Ādhāraṇi	Vajratīkṣṇā	sword and book
16. Sarvacakra	Vajrahetu	eight-spoke wheel
17. Sahasrāvartā	Vajrabhāṣa	tonguetip in form of vajra
18. Siddhottarā	Vajrakarma	crossed vajra and bell
19. Sarvarakṣā	Vajrarakṣā	vaja talisman
20. Tejaḥpratyāhāriṇī	Vajrayakṣa	with large belly and protruding fangs
21. Dhāraṇīmudrā	Vajrasandhi	viśvavajra
22. Sattvavajrī	Vajrapāramitā	
23. Ratnavajrī	Ratnapāramitā	
24. Dharmavajrī	Dharmapāramitā	
25. Karmavajrī	Karmapāramitā	
26. Vajralāsī	Vajralāsya	gesture of love
27. Vajramālā	Vajramālā	garland
28. Vajragītā	Vajragīti	song
29. Vajanṛtya	Vajranṛtya	dance
30. Guhyadhūpeśvarī	Vajradhūpā	incense
31. Guhyapuṣpā	Vajrapuṣpā	flower
32. Guhyadīpā	Vajrālokā	lamp
33. Guhyagandhā	Vajragandhā	scent
34. Guhyāṅkuśī	Vajrāṅkuśa	hook
35. Guhyapāśā	Vajrapāśa	noose
36. Guhyasphoṭā	Vajrasphoṭa	chain
37. Guhyaghaṇṭā	Vajraghaṇṭa	bell

These characteristics are from Snellgrove/Skorupsha (1977: 34-5).

Plate 1: Dhāraṇī-*maṇḍala* at Alchi.

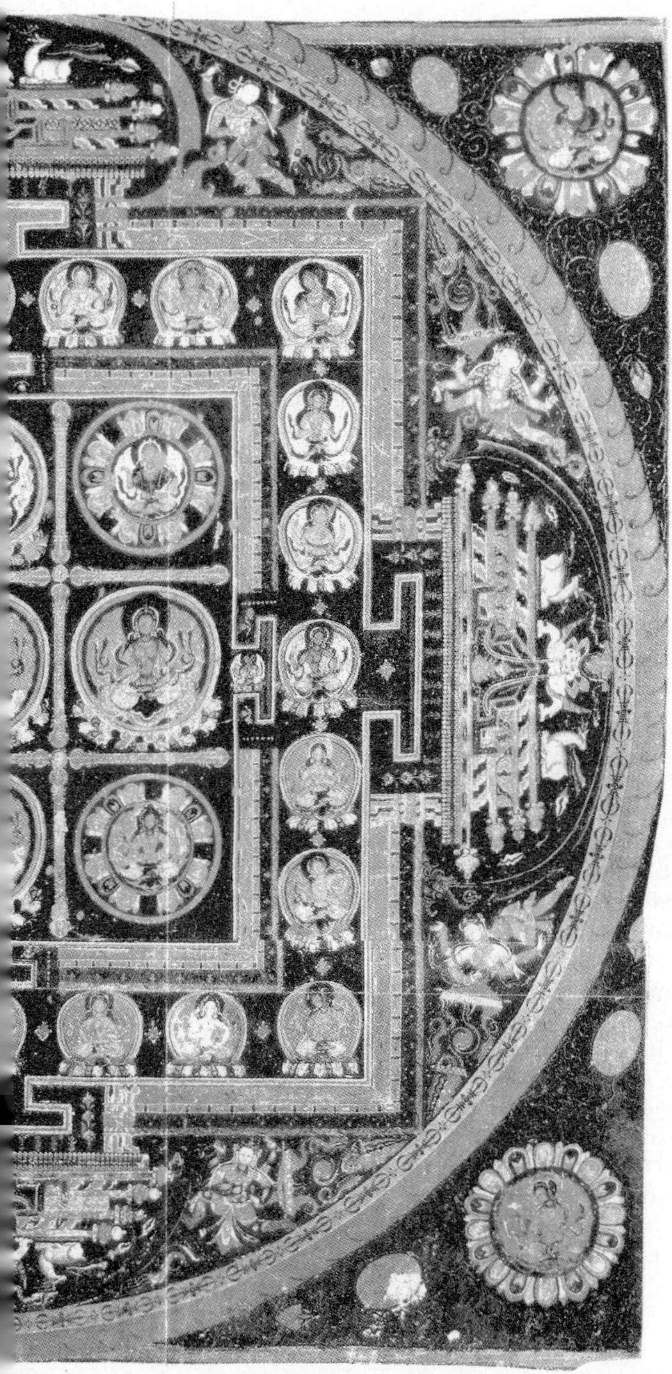

I.2.37 *Guhyaghaṇṭā*, the consort of *Vajrāveśa*, guards the northern gate. Her *mantra* is *om guhyaghaṇṭe aḥ aḥ aḥ aḥ* (*Gobu* 71). Illustrated in *NCBB* 1.19, 21, 37.

The *maṇḍala* ends here. All the goddesses have specialized *mudrās* which distinguish one from the other. A detailed study of their *mudrās* can throw light on identificatory elements. Like their god-consorts in *maṇḍala* I.1, they do not bear emblems (like hook/*aṅkuśa*, lasso/*pāśa*, etc). The specification of the goddesses by their hand-gestures is inherent in the word *mudrā* which means 'symbol, gesture sign' as well as 'feminine partner' (=*prajñā*) in *Hevajra-tantra* 1.5 4-7, 10.7, 2.2.16, 17, 20, 23, 3.16, 18, 63, 6.4, 11. For instance *Hevajra* 1.5.4 says : 'In order that one may gain release, these *Mudrā* are identified with the Five Families. She is called *Mudrā* or Sign, because she is signed with the *vajra*.'

Illustrations of the goddesses are reproduced from the vast collection of Jaroslav Poncar of the Fachhochschule, Kõln. We are grateful to him for sending these clear and detailed photographs from his photo-archives of Alchi, and also permitting us to print them. He has spent over fifteen years to document the artistic riches of this distinctive monastery.

REFERENCES

Tajima, Ryujum, Les Deux Grands Maṇḍalas et la Doctrine de l'Esoterisme Shingon, Tokyo: Bulletin de la Maison Franco—Japanaise, 1959. Tokyo and Presses Universitaires de France, Paris.

Snelgrove, David L. and Skorupski, Tadeusz, The Cultural Heritage of Ladakh, Volume I, Central Ladakh, Boulder: Prajna Press, 1977.

Casparis 1950, J.G. de Casparis, Prasasti Indonesia I, Inscripties uit de, Cailendratijd, Bandung (A.C. Nix & Co.).

Casparis, John G. de.

———Selected Inscriptions from the 7th to the 9th Century A.D. Prasasti Indonesia diterbikan oleh Dinas Purbakala Republik Indonesia, Vol. 2. Bandung: Masa Baru, 1956.

———Short Inscriptions from Tiaṇḍi Plaosan Lord. Berita Dinas Purbakala, Bulletin of the Archaeological Service of the Republic of Indonesia, no. 4. Jakarta: Archaeological Service of the Republic of Indonesia, 1958.

5

Sanskritic Buddhism in South-East Asia

INDIRA Y. JUNGHARE

I. INTRODUCTION[1]

It has been assumed that the Buddhism in South-East Asian countries, though differing somewhat in regional practices, is basically of the Theravāda or Hīnayāna school. It is true that Buddhism of Thailand, Sri Lanka and Burma is basically orthodox Theravāda: it is not so in Indonesia, Malaysia, Cambodia and Laos. This is not to say that it is basically a form of Mahāyāna Buddhism, but rather that there are elements involved in or alongside the Theravāda Buddhism of these regions which, to the trained observer obviously mirror certain characteristics of Sanskritic or Brahmanic Hinduism.

A discrepancy exists between the philosophy of Theravāda Buddhism and the practices of the Buddhist populations of Cambodia and Laos. Theoretically, Theravāda Buddhism does not allow for a pantheon of gods and goddesses; nor does it permit the use of ritualistic practices. Yet, the ordinary people of these countries worship various deities, some of which are of Hindu origin. Similarly, ancestral and spirit worship is quite common. On the logical level, the Theravāda belief in the no-soul (*anattā*) theory seems contradictory to merit-making ceremonies for the benefit of the souls of the deceased. The seeming contradictions between the highest ideals and goals of Theravāda Buddhism and the living tradition in South-East Asia has been the subject of considerable confusion and amazement to scholars.[2]

In reality, contraries do exist side by side, and explanations that seek to differentiate teaching and practice, the ideal and the actual, the great tradition and the folk or popular tradition, run the risk of sacrificing the interwoven fabric of religion. Buddhism in the South-East Asian countries allows for the co-existence of sophisticated metaphysics along with its differing commonly held beliefs and practices. In fact, the popular religions of these countries include not only the local, but also Brahmanic beliefs and practices.

The purpose of this paper is to examine the nature of Buddhism of Cambodia and Laos and show that Buddhism of those countries is Sanskritic as well as syncretic, based upon the fact that each contains an underlying pattern which to a great extent also underlies Brahmanic Hinduism. It is commonly asserted by scholars that Buddhism is 'Hinduism for export'. On the philosophical level, such a statement would be difficult to defend, based upon Gotama's teachings, e.g. 'Anattā', or non-self, and his attitudes towards ritualism. However, it will be shown that on the practical level, such a statement can find strong support. This will be accomplished as follows. First, we will attempt to present clear and concise definitions of the terms 'Sanskritic' and 'Sanskritization', in order to clarify the scope and focus of our subject material, as these terms could be misleading if not understood in this context. Second, a historical survey of the syncretic process leading to the Sanskritization of Sout-East Asia will be presented, paying special attention to our areas of interest, which will conclude with the presentation of the characteristics of modern Laotian and Cambodian Buddhist practice, with particular regard to Hinduism and Mahāyāna Buddhism on one hand, and Theravāda Buddhism and native folk-religion on the other. Third, the pattern which we find characteristic of both Sanskritic Hinduism and Sanskritic Buddhism will be presented, paying special attention to the role of the Sanskrit language in the preservation and perpetuation of this model. Finally, the implications of this theoretical model for the study of both language and religion will be presented. In particular, the claim that the nature of Buddhism in South-East Asian countries, excluding Burma, Sri Lanka and Thailand, is similar to that of Hinduism with various levels or layers, Sanskritic or Classical ideas being at the centre, serving as the base for the complex whole of faith and its practice, will be presented.

II. DEFINITION OF TERMS

Sanskritic

The term Sanskritic pertains to Sanskrit, the language of classical Hinduism and of the original texts of Mahāyāna Buddhism. The language of the canonical texts of the Theravāda Buddhism, on the other hand, is Pali, a Middle Indo-Aryan dialect, derived from Old Indo-Aryan. It is assumed that Māgadhī, the Middle Indo-Aryan language, the native tongue of Buddha, provided the basis for the formalization of Pali.[3] The term 'Sanskritic Buddhism' is not limited to the Buddhism of the Sanskrit texts. In this paper it simply means the Buddhism in which Sanskritic elements are found. We see various levels, regional, folk, popular and classical, operative in the whole composite picture of Hinduism. Similarly, various levels seem to have contributed to the making of the synthetic Buddhism of Indochina, and the Sanskritic level is one of them.

Sanskritization

M.N. Srinivas, who is generally assumed to have introduced the term 'Sanskritization' in 1952, states the following:

> Sanskritization may be briefly defined as the process by which a 'low' caste or tribe or other group takes over the customs, ritual, beliefs, ideology and style of life of a high and, in particular, a 'twice born' (dvija) caste. The Sanskritization of a group has usually the effect of improving its position in the local caste hierarchy. It normally presupposes either an improvement in the economic or political position of the group concerned or a higher group self-consciousness resulting from its contact with a source of the 'Great Tradition' of Hinduism such as a pilgrim centre or monastery or a proselytizing sect. . . . Its influence is not confined to Hindus, but is visible even in sects and religious groups outside Hinduism.[4]

This provides us with a very general notion of the concept of Sanskritization within the subcontinent of India with a hint at its applicability to outside cultures. For our purposes, the reference to caste relations will not be applicable in its literal sense, but rather should be viewed as dealing with what is a less formal, though still existent group hierarchy. Our focus is on the process 'very much akin to what anthropologists call acculturation' whereby aspects of the culture of the upper strata 'reached the lowest of the groups by a process of percolation from top to bottom through intermediaries'.[5]

In India, this process has also been called 'Brahminization', as Sanskrit culture was reserved in its fullness to the upper caste. As we will show, this process cannot be confined to South Asia alone; rather, this process goes far beyond the borders of India, and in our area of focus, Buddhism, we find such a process very apparent. The study of Cambodian and Laotian will be presented diachronically, for, in order to see the nature of Buddhism and consequently the process of Sanskritization and amalgamation of Sanskritic elements with the indigenous and of Pali origin, we must examine the cultural history of Cambodia and Laos, which has been tied with that of India. Although the early history of Indian culture is quite obscure, archaeologists and historians assume that India came in contact with Cambodia as well as other parts of Indo-China including Laos around third century BC.[6]

III. HISTORICAL ANTECEDENTS

The history of South-East Asia has been shaped by processes of syncretism which began during the first millennium AD.[7] Syncretism in that period was of two primary types: (1) the Syncretism within Hinduism, mainly of the two sects: Śaivism and Vaiṣṇavism, and (2) the Syncretism of Hinduism and Buddhism, particularly of Śaivism and Mahāyāna Buddhism, i.e. of the Śaivaite Maheśvara and the Mahāyānist Lokeśvara. Both kinds of syncretism seem to have begun in Indo-China as early as the Funan period about the middle of the first to the middle of the sixth century and reached peak in the twelfth century.[8]

The process of syncretism was a key element in the formation of Hinduism and its branches. Both Śaivism and Vaiṣṇavism received their forms during the fourth to ninth centuries. It is generally accepted that the Śiva of Hinduism developed from the merger of a form of the fierce Vedic god Rudra, and 'Śiva', meaning 'auspicious', a popular Dravidian deity, and the Vedic Viṣṇu, a solar deity, was developed from its connection with the Dravidian deity Kṛṣṇa. In order to meet the challenges of Buddhism, Hinduism attempted to combine the monotheisms of Śiva and Viṣṇu with a vast polytheism, and these two great personal deities took the place of the pantheon of the Vedas. Furthermore, in order to satisfy the monotheists, Viṣṇu and Śiva were combined into one–Harihara. The Trimūrti, or Hindu trinity, was completed by the addition of Brahmā drawn from *Brahman.* To the Vaiṣṇavites the Trimūrti consisted of Viṣṇu, Śiva as Viṣṇu and Brahmā as Viṣṇu, while to the Śaivaites, Śiva became the pivot of the Trimūrti.[9] Brahmā, other than being a cult figure, has been scarcely more than the third member of the Trimūrti.

Both Śaivism and Vaiṣṇavism existed side by side in Cambodia as early as the beginning of the seventh century. The first manifestation of Ḥarihara, a combination of Viṣṇu and Śiva in a single body, Viṣṇu (= Hari) on the right and Śiva (= Hara) on the left, is represented in many statues found in Chenla during the seventh and eighth centuries.[10] Also, two inscriptions of the reign of Iśānavarman I—Vat Chakret and Ang Pou[11]—record the erection of images of Harihara. Some of the stone and bronze figures of that deity are the most noteworthy specimens of early Khmer statuary. The cult of Harihara, even though it did not have a wide acceptance in India, was confined almost exclusively to Cambodia among all of the Hinduized states of South-East Asia.[12]

There is evidence that some of the legends of Viṣṇu, in his manifestations other than Harihara, were known in the early inscriptions of the Chenla period. An inscription of Bhavavarman I, first king of Chenla, shows that a sister of that king married an Indian brāhmaṇa and that they made gifts to the temple of Viṣṇu, on the Mekong near the present border of Laos.

At the beginning of the Khmer empire, i.e. in the reign of Jayavarman II, first king of the Kambuja, or Angkor, Śaivism became firmly established as the state cult in the form of *devarāja*. In 802, when the monarch founded his capital on Mahendraparvata (PhnomnKulen), a brāhmaṇa named Hiraṇyadama performed a tantric ritual and invested the king with divine power in order for the Kambujadeśa to have a sovereign king. The central divinity of this new state-cult was the king himself–conceived as a form of Śiva—combined with the notion of the god-king, or *devarāja*. The visible symbol of this cult was a *liṅga* set up on the central altar of a pyramid temple, the symbolic centre of the Empire, in imitation of Mount Meru, centre of the universe in Hindu cosmology.[13] The cult of *devarāja* was more of a state cult than a religious sect, and did not interfere with other forms of worship or prevent a king of another faith from ascending the throne and building a chief temple of his own faith, as long as he loyally maintained the state cult.

Although the worship of the *devarāja* was established as a state cult, Viṣṇu-worship was very popular during the reign of Jayavarman II and his son and successor, Jayavarman III. Many monuments were dedicated to Viṣṇu on Mahendraparvata, the early capital of Jayavarman II. According to the inscriptional record, the wife of Jayavarman II and his son Jayavarman III were Vaiṣṇavites.

In judging the relative strength of Vaiṣṇavism during these reigns, by names and foundations, it must be borne is mind that Śaivism and

Vaiṣṇavism are related cults of Hinduism, differing from each other chiefly in the relative rank assigned to the two deities. Śaivites sometimes bore Vaiṣṇavite names and the most ardent Śaivite monarch could, with perfect propriety, make a foundation to Viṣṇu and *vice versa*. Regardless, the existence of Vaiṣṇavite names and foundations is in the some sense a measure of the strength of Vaiṣṇavism during the period.

The tenth and eleventh centuries were marked by the development of Śaivism and Mahāyāna Buddhism, with Vaiṣṇavism being quiescent during the period. However, Vaiṣṇavism's eventual triumph in Cambodia seems to have begun at the end of the eleventh century with the coming of the dynasty of Mahīdharapura. A king from this dynasty, namely Jayavarman VI, adored Campeśvara (Viṣṇu) and made a rich donation to this temple of Kok Po according to the inscription of Preah Vihear.

The reign of Sūryavarman II (1112-50) was the golden age of Vaiṣṇavism in Cambodia. Buddhism, which had flourished under Sūryavarman I and was to blossom forth in great splendour under Jayavarman VII, was temporally at rest. The Śaivism of this period—in the form of the *devarāja* cult—was official and perfunctory. Inscriptions show that foundations were still made at the old Śaivaite shrines of Preah Vihear, Vat Phu, and Phnom Sandak.[14]

The process of apotheosis or deification was so prevalent that Sūryavarman II identified himself with the worship of *devarāja* and he combined his own image with that of Śiva, setting up his temple as a *Suryeśvara*. The idea of *devarāja*, under the support of Divākarapaṇḍita, who had crowned three kings and received the honour of apotheosis, began to be replaced by the idea of Visnurāja. Vaiṣṇavism became strangely interwoven with the old state Śaivism and began to raise itself to a position of equality under the guise of Śaivism. Finally, the Central Temple, the ultimate architectural symbol of Śaivism, with its *prasats*, terraces, and galleries, and even a central deity, was taken over by Vaiṣṇavism, and Angkor Wat—the *summum bonum* of Śaivic architectural aspiration—became the abode of a Viṣṇurāja. Thus, the syncretism of Śaivism and Vaiṣṇavism seems from this time to have been complete—in a larger Hinduism.[15] It seems incorrect to say that Śaivism triumphed over Vaiṣṇavism in Cambodia. The last great Śaivic temple of Cambodia was the Baphuon. Angkor Wat was the last great Hindu temple in Cambodia and was dedicated to Viṣṇu and its decorations were Vaiṣṇavic; only its forms were Saivic.

Perhaps even more intriguing is the syncretism of Śaivism and Mahāyāna Buddhism between Maheśvara, a manifestation of Śiva, and the Bodhisattva Avalokiteśvara or Lokeśvara as he was generally called in Indo-China. This syncretism seems to have its roots in the birth of Mahāyānism in India. When, in about the second century of our era, the bodhisattvas were added to Mahāyānism, some of them derived their names and characteristics from the Brahmānic gods. Thus, Vajrapāṇi took his name from the thunderbolt (*vajra*) of Indra along with some of the characteristics of that deity. Avalokiteśvara was compounded of two words, *avalokita* 'looking on' and Īśvara 'lord', an epithet of Śiva. As Avalokiteśvara became prominent in Cambodia in the latter part of the reign of Jayavarman VII, his representations contained many of the characteristics of Śiva.

Indications of the close relationship between Maheśvara and the bodhisattva Lokeśvara appeared in Indo-China as early as the fifth century, during the Funan period. About 484, King Kaundinya Jayavarman sent the Buddhist monk Nāgasena on an embassy to the emperor of China. Nāgasena, in his letter to the emperor, first praised Maheśvara and then Lokeśvara, and finally characterized each in his characteristic role of god of mercy. The Buddhism of South-East Asia of this period was Mahāyānist.

During the period, Buddhism had been undergoing change in India. In 643, at a council called by King Harṣa—at which the Chinese Buddhist pilgrim Hsuan-tsang was present—Mahāyāna Buddhism was approved and Hīnayāna was rejected.[16] Those of the latter sects who were not absorbed by other sects withdrew to Ceylon, and Hīnayāna all but disappeared from the land of its birth. It is not believed that Hīnayāṇa was driven out of India by persecution. It lost in fair competition, because of its extremity: strict monasticism and inexorable doctrines of transmigration and retribution. It could not meet the desires and needs of the Indian people as well as the reforms of the Mahāyānists. Whereas the Hināyānist hope of deliverence lay only in attainment of Nirvāṇa, the Māhāyanists offered the more attractive prospect of universal attainment of Buddhahood through Bodhisattvaship.

After the death of Harṣa (AD 647), the kingdom of Kanauj declined and the hegemony of the Ganges valley fell to the kingdom of Bengal. Here, under the protection of the Pāla dynasty (730-1060), Mahāyāna, with a whole hierarchy of Bodhisattvas and other supernatural beings, became indoctrinated with mysticism, magic practices, shamanism, Tantrism and what not, that which the popular

Śaivaite sect was beginning to take on. As the Mahāyāna lost ground to the new Hindu sects, Mahāyānist monks spread to Burma and South-East Asia. The Śailendra dynasty which ruled over much of Java, Sumatra and the Malay peninsula during the eighth and ninth centuries became a great centre from which Mahāyāna was relayed to all parts of Indo-China and to western Indonesia, allowing it to become the chief form of Buddhism in those regions. It is known that this dynasty was in close contact with northern India at this time. The outburst of Buddhist architecture and art in central Java of which Borobudur is the chief specimen bears witness to this Buddhist movement, mixed, however, as in India, with Hindu elements. Relations between Campā and Java seem to have been close at this time, which may account for the upsurge of Mahāyāna in Campā.[17] Cambodia, recently at war with the Mahārāja (Śailendra), seems to have been little affected by the Mahāyānist movement at this time.

With the establishment of the Khmer Empire and the state cult of *devarāja* in 802, Buddhism fell into the background and played a very minor role until the reign of Rājendravarman II, near the middle of the tenth century. Rājendravarman sought the assistance of every faction, including that of Mahāyānists, in regaining the throne which his uncle Jayavarman IV and, after his death, his son had forcibly occupied. An inscription tells us that Rājendravarman made a study of Buddhist doctrine. His chief minister, Kavindrārimathana—apparently the first Buddhist minister of the Kambuja period—erected a sanctuary at Bat Chum, the first Buddhist sanctuary of the Angkor period, dedicated to Buddha and the Bodhisattvas Lokeśvara, Vajrapāṇi and Prajñāpāramitā, and built Buddhist foundations at other sanctuaries.[18]

Jayavarman V (968-1001), son and successor of Rājendravarman II, also had a Buddhist minister, Kīrtipaṇḍita, who, with the acquiescence of the king, laboured to establish Mahāyāna by bringing from foreign lands treaties and commentaries on Mahāyānist philosophy. Buddhist inscriptions of the reign of Jayavarman V show the development of Buddhism under these two kings. The inscription of Phum Banteay Neang, in the province of Battambang, whose last date is 986, celebrates the erection of images of Prajñāpāramitā, 'Mother of the Buddhas', and of Lokeśvara.[19]

Buddhism in the reign of the monarchs Rājendravarman II and Jayavarman V was raised to a level with Śaivism by dressing it in Śaivic form. The inscription of Srei Santhor provided that a *purohita* should be versed in Buddhist doctrine and on festival days should bathe the image of the Buddha and recite Buddhist prayers. Thus Buddhism was raised in status by having its rites performed in the same forms as Śaivism and through Śaivite agencies.

Although both the kings, Rājendravarman II and Jayavarman V helped to establish Buddhism in Cambodia and were also friendly to Vaiṣṇavism, they were loyal Śaivites, devoted to the cult of *devarāja* and ancestor-worship.

Sūryavarman I was the first Buddhist king of the Angkor period who seems to have established a new capital with a Buddhist central temple on the site of the later Bayon. Briggs is of the opinion that the new central idol of the temple was a sort of Buddharāja and the new central temple became Sūryavarman I's mausoleum after his death.

Buddhism was somewhat dormant during the period of Udayadityavarman II (1050-66) and Harṣavarman III (1066-90) as these kings were mildly Śaivite. It was in 1067, the first year of Harṣavarman III's reign, that an unusual *caturmūrti* was erected, composed of Brahmā, Viṣṇu and the Buddha—the latter substituted for Śiva—and as a whole consecrated to Śiva.

With the advent of the Mahīdharapura dynasty, at the beginning of the twelfth century, Vaiṣṇavism became the dominant religion and reached its zenith under Sūryavarman II. Buddhism, however, continued to occupy a subordinate position. The reign of Sūryavarman II, representative of the best Ankorean art, was followed by a period of dissension during which Prince Jayavarman, who had the best claim to the throne, went on a long pilgrimage to Campā. After his return, he restored order and was crowned Jayavarman VII.

Jayavarman VII was a Mahāyānist of the Yogācāra (idealist) school. Like the monuments, most of the sculptured figures of ancient Cambodia belong to the reign of Jayavarman VII. The temple Preah Khan of Angkor was dedicated to Lokeśvara, Ta Prohm to Prajñāpāramitā, and Bayon to the Buddha, which formed the Buddhic Trinity, according to Coedes. The inscription of Ta Prohm states that 260 small statues were deposited in that temple, while those of Preah Khan numbered 515.[20] These idols were almost, it not all, funerary images, i.e. statues of princes, princesses, or dignitaries, raised to apotheosis and represented under the traits of a Buddhic divinity, principally Lokeśvara for the men and Tārā or Prajñāpāramitā for the women.[21]

Lokeśvara was the leading deity of the period and many images of him appeared, some of which are unique to that time, and have never since appeared in Cambodia or elsewhere, including a new type of Lokeśvara which shows the amalgamation with Maheśvara. This syncretization had been slowly taking place in Cambodia, as shown by the bodhisattvas of the preceding period. But its progress was undoubtedly enhanced at this period by an influx of Mahāyānist monks from north India. Mahāyāna was already being absorbed there by Śaivism—both impregnated with Tantrism, mysticism and magic practices—or, one can say, Mahāyāna was becoming amalgamated with Śaivism. After the Muslim invasion, Hinduism based on caste and family survived, but Mahāyāna, centered in its monasteries, could not outlive their destruction.

The syncretism of Lokeśvara and Śiva in Cambodia was possibly due to the fact that Śaivism had its counterpart to the doctrine of the compassionate Lokeśvara in the cult of Maheśvara, which was associated with the *liṅga* in Indo-China. These two cults became so similar that they flourished side by side without friction, almost without distinction in some cases. The similarity even extended to the personality and attributes of the two deities. Lokeśvara was pictured at Angkor with the four arms, four faces, the frontal eye, and sometimes even with the trident and twining serpents of Śiva.[22]

This syncretism had other implications at this time. It is mentioned earlier that in the reign of Jayavarman V Buddhism had been brought to a level with Śaivism by adopting Śaivic forms. This syncretism of Mahāyāna with state Śaivism, in Brigg's opinion, must have resulted in the development of a Buddharāja and his substitution for the *devarāja.* This phenomenon is parallel to the substitution of Viṣṇurāja for the *devarāja* during the reign of Sūryavarman II, which had resulted from the syncretism of Vaiṣṇavism and Śaivism.

The substitution of Buddharāja and the transformation of the Bayon into a pyramid-temple occurred in the reign of Jayavarman VII. Bayon was originally dedicated to Lokeśvara. The figure found in the front and in other places in the figure of Lokeśvara, and the four faces of the towers of the Bayon and its walls are the faces of Lokeśvara in the image of Jayavarman VII, with whom he is conceived to have been united

It is certain that the Bayon was finally dedicated to the Buddharāja—the Buddha with the characteristic features of Jayavarman VII. As the idea that he was the living Buddha began to grow on

Jayavarman VII, he conceived the idea of a Buddharāja—himself apotheosized as the Buddha—in place of the temple on the flat plan which he was building. The result was the Bayon and the enormous statue of the Buddha found there. These changes are attributed to the third period of the Bayon style.

Theravāda Buddhism was imposed on the region at the end of the thirteenth century, through the political power of the Thais. It is very interesting to note that at this time, in South-East Asia as a whole, the Mahāyāna Buddhist and Hindu elements became inter-twined and identified with one another, and Tantrism reached its peak both in the regions of Cambodia and Laos and India. From this point up to the present. Theravāda was to become the dominant religion of the area.[23] What is extremely interesting, however, is the fact that though for the past seven hundred years Theravāda has been the dominant religion of the areas of both Cambodia and Laos, the effect of the Brahmānical tradition continues to play a key role in the religious practices of these areas. In Laos, Brahmānical rites are of common occurrence in relation to marriage, birth, and death, and few Laotians are strangers to the names of Indian gods, as they are invoked in association with Buddha in prayer and ritual.[24]

This tradition has been dominant to the extreme of being carried overseas to the United States. The Cambodian and Laotian monasteries in the Minneapolis area of Minnesota both contain huge statues of Buddha which are placed on large platforms surrounded by a multitude of images of the Buddha, of differing sizes and many materials, such as wood, stone, bronze, copper, alabaster and plaster, plain and gilded. These images are worshipped through washing, lighting of candles, offerings of flowers and fruits, incense sticks, and resounding gongs. The entire picture reminds one of Hindu temple worship, differing only in the images which are present. Just as the Hindus worship at a home shrine as in temple worship, Buddhists have a similar practice. Many restaurants in Minneapolis contain small shrines of Buddhist deities, with offerings of various fruits and other objects, and many Cambodian and Laotian Buddhists have shrines in their home at which they make ceremonial offerings to the Buddha and other figures.

Some Buddhist pagodas and temples have various images of attendant beings and miscellaneous worshipping animals. Some walls of the monasteries in Minnesota contained pictures from the

Jātaka tales 'Stories of Buddha's Birth', which depicted Buddha in association with particular Hindu gods such as Kṛṣṇa, Rāma, and Hanumān, in previous incarnations.

IV. ANALYSIS

The purpose behind presenting a historical survey as well as an account of current practice in the United States is to give the reader an understanding of the great impact which Sanskritization had upon South-East Asia through both Brahmānical Hinduism and Mahāyāna Buddhism. From the first through the seventh century the acculturation of Brahmānical elements was the process by which popular and political status was both attested and concretized. From the seventh to the thirteenth centuries, Mahāyāna Buddhism was the dominant religion of the state, which slightly modified the objects of worship, but did not significantly change the underlying process of the inculcation of Sanskrit names and rituals, in this case Mahāyāna Buddhist. The continuity between these two traditions is apparent in the breakdown of the barriers between them which occurred near the end of the thirteenth century. Just prior to the institution of Theravāda Buddhism through the Thai political power, Buddha became identified with Śiva and Viṣṇu, and the greater part of the Hindu pantheon was absorbed into Mahāyāna Buddhism.[25]

The deep seated influence which these Sanskrit traditions had and continue to have upon the religion of this area is the central point which we want to understand. The character of modern Buddhist practice in this area testifies just to this fact, with the continuance of Brahmānical ritual practice within the framework of Theravāda Buddhism in both the Cambodian and Laotian religious practice. Under a 'Buddhist veneer' these cultures continue to preserve the traditions which sprang from the process whereby 'a native chief adopted the civilization of the foreigners and increased his status and power thereby'.[26] Therevāda Buddhism thus has had to modify itself to this state of affairs, and though attempting to preserve its pure Pali core within the bounds of its rigid monasticism, has allowed lay practice to extend itself into practices which run completely counter to its principles: ancestor worship, shamanism, and the association of a Hindu pantheon of deities around a central figure, Buddha.

In *A Thousand Lives Away*, Winston L. King presents a theoretical framework as to the different levels of operation within Buddhist practice.

> But it is equally true, it seems, that it is the relation of the total mass of ideas and practices to the central ideal that holds the structure together in what is something of a truly organic unity, articulating its relationship, and making genuine intercommunication (or at least understanding) possible between the various levels.[27]

What King articulates is the idea that Buddhism is comprised of a dynamic interrelationship between several different levels of philosophy and ritual, from the completely orthodox centre of Nirvāṇa and the Buddha to the level of folk religion. At the centre are the ideals of Theravāda Buddhism, such as the philosophical concepts of *dukkha* and *anattā,* as well as the notion of meditation as being one if not the essential, practice which leads to release from cyclic existence. On the level of the layperson, there is a greater range, from the relatively small number who have some knowledge of meditation, to the level of folk devotee, which places Buddha at the head of a pantheon of deities.

In Cambodia and Laos, this structure hinges upon the Sanskritization which has occurred over the course of the past centuries. In the Theravāda Buddhism of this area, the dynamics between the orthodox and unorthodox practice is the underlying substratum of Hindu ideas and beliefs which have been subsumed into the cultures. Theravāda Buddhism, instead of making a great impact upon the beliefs and rituals upon these areas, has rather been forced to adapt itself to a heterogeneity owing much to the Hindu tradition.[28] This is ironic in a certain sense, because as many scholars would agree, Buddhism arose in India as a religion aimed at obviating superstitious belies and practices and such, intently asserting that gods, as well as mortals, were trapped within *saṃsāra* or cyclic existence, a state which cannot ever lead to permanent peace. The notion of a pantheon of gods with the Buddha at its head, for example, is reminiscent of the henotheism which is so characteristic of any sort of sectarian Hinduism. Beyond its possession of particular practices and of the Pali language, which are essentially Buddhist, Theravāda Buddhism has not ever been able to completely overshadow the worship of Hindu deities, nor change the underlying cultural structures which propagates the process of Sanskritizaton within society.

There are several reasons why Sanskrit operates in such a way that it allows for this process to occur with such success and veracity. First of all, as meaning 'refined' or 'the language of the God', it is a rich, sophisticated religious language which, in the great emphasis on its followers, provides a level of complexity which is not accessible to all of society. As such, Sanskrit has a tendency to be mystifying, in that at the 'higher' level on which it operates, it is esoteric and unintelligible to those who are at 'lower' levels of sophistication. Furthermore, Sanskrit, as being representative of India, is representative of a spiritual tradition which is often referred to as the 'Motherland' or 'Holy Land' of religious beliefs and practices, which provides the notion of the association with a more truly religious source.

The relationship of these two elements are the key to our understanding of these cultures; on the one hand we have an attempt to use the syncretic Sanskrit language for the purpose of instantiating political authority, i.e. the *devarāja*, and on the other hand, a tracing back of the pre-Aryan metaphysical roots in shamanism, fertility worship, and ancestor worship which is found in these areas. The central concept is that Sanskrit functions as a vehicle for the organization of seemingly discordant practices into a harmonic, yet hierarchical relationship, establishing authority through its organization, yet at the same time being able in a unique way to be culturally fluid.

V. CONCLUSION

Following the understanding of the great impact that the process of Sanskritization has upon the development and the propagation of culture in these areas, one is led to the conclusion that South-East Asia as a whole can be considered to be characterized by elements which have their roots in Sanskrit tradition. We have called the Buddhism of Cambodia and Laos 'Sanskritic' due to the underlying substratum of Brahmanic ritualism and Sanskrit terminology which began in the first century and continues to play a defining role in the religious practices of these countries. The applicability of the paradigm of the orthodox *v.* folk traditions, as well as the application of the process of Sanskritizaton to other areas and languages is a definite possibility. Also, the relationship between Westernization and Sanskritization is an interesting issue which has a definite relation to our thesis, if we question what has resulted from the interactions of Sanskritic religion with western culture. One might as well question to what extent the Pali language, though less sophisticated, has inherited the Sanskritic quality of setting up a dynamic relationship between the orthodox and the folk tradition, and whether it has a power of unification and mystification similar to Sanskritization which it has inherited from its precursor. We have chosen to concentrate on one specific area and one particular linguistic strain, and as such, these other implications are beyond the scope of the present paper, yet show promise in terms of further folklore, linguistic, and religious study.

NOTES

1. I would like to acknowledge the work of my Research Assistant Stuart Sarbacker, for his contribution towards the organization and completion of this paper, and to express my appreciation to the scholars at the IX World Sanskrit Conference for their comments. An earlier version of this paper was presented at the IX World Sanskrit Conference held in Melbourne, Australia, from 9 to 15 January 1994
2. Lawrence Palmer Briggs, 'The Syncretism of Religions in Southeast Asia, especially in the Khmer Empire', *Journal of the American Oriental Society,* 71 (1951), pp. 230-49.
3. Kogen Mizuno, *Buddhist Sūtras: Origin, Development Transmission* (Tokyo, 1980), p. 29.
4. M.N. Srinivas, *The Cohesive Role of Sanskritization and other Essays* (Delhi, 1989), pp. 56-7.
5. K.K. Gangadharan, *Sociology of Revivalism* (New Delhi, 1970), pp. 59-60.
6. Manamohan Ghosh, *A History of Cambodia* (Saigon, 1960), p. 30.
7. Briggs, ibid., p. 230.
8. Ibid.
9. Briggs, ibid., p. 231.
10. Ibid.; Larry Briggs gives illustrations in his book *A Pilgrimage to Angkor* (Oakland, 1943), pp. 77-9.
11. Briggs, ibid., p. 232; see also Aususte Berth, 'Inscriptions sanscrites du Cambodge' (ISC), Academie des Inscriptions et Belles Letters: Notices et Extraits ds Manuscripts (Paris, 1885).
12. Briggs, ibid., p. 232.
13. Heine-Geldern, 'Conceptions of State and Kingship in Southeast Asia', South-East Asia program, Data Paper No. 18, Ithaca: Cornell University, 1958, pp. 87-8.
14. Briggs, ibid., p. 237.

15. Ibid.
16. Ramesh Chandra Mujumdar, *Hindu Colonies in the Far East* (Calcutta, 1963), pp. 175-206.
17. Briggs, op. cit., p. 240.
18. Coedes, 'Les Inscriptions de Bat Chum', *Journal of Asian Studies* ser. 10, 8(1912). 12A, St. 21.
19. Bergaigne, ISC, No. 52, Phum Bantei Neang, p. 178 (see Briggs, p. 241).
20. George Coedes, 'La Stelle de ta Prohm', *Bulletin de l'Ecole Francaise d'Extreme Orient* (BEFEO), 1906, p. 37 (see Briggs, p. 245).
21. Coedes, 'Nouvelles decouvertes a Angkor', BEFEO, Nos. 20-1 (1939): 19.
22. L. Finot, 'Outlines of the History of Buddhism in Indo-China', *Indian Historical Quarterly*, Vol. II, No. 4 (Dec. 1926), pp. 675-84.
23. Majumdar, 'Buddhism in South-East Asia', *Indian Historical Quarterly*, Vol. XXXII, Nos. 2 and 3 (June and Sept. 1956), pp. 297-303.
24. Dawee Daweewarn, *Brahmanism in South-East Asia* (New Delhi, 1982), pp. 255-60.
25. Majumdar, op. cit., p. 303.
26. D.G.E. Hall, *A History of South-East Asia* (New York, 1955), p. 19.
27. King, Winston L., *A Thousand Lives Away* (Cambridge, 1964), p. 68 (see also pp. 41-84).
28. Hall, ibid., p. 19.

6

Kula in the Indo-Tibetan Tantra Literature

SUNITI KUMAR PATHAK

KULA

According to the ancient Indian diction *kula* is a socio-ethnic term. It generally refers to a family or genealogical tree with progenitors and successive descents such as, Ikṣvāku Kula in respect of Daśratha and his son Rāma. Kṛṣṇa belonged to the Yadu-Kula. The Upaniṣad texts like *Chāndyogya* (3/12.6) and *Bṛhadāraṇyaka* (1.5.21) used *kula* in the sense of successive family (*anvaya*). It is not *gotra* which may be equivalent to a clan. Also in words like Kulācāra (family custom), and in Kulācārya a family priest or geneologist were indicated.

In course of time *kula* denoted a high noble family or a House in the English diction maintaining the purity of blood and prestige of the tradition of a particular family, e.g. Kulāṅganā opposite to varāṅganā. In the latter case *akula* suggested that of a mixed origin or middling in character. In the ancient astronomy of India *akula-vāra* referred to the Wednesday, i.e. the day after *bhaumavāra*, Tuesday which was praised as the principal or the first day of a week.

K.C. Pandeya in his *Abhinavagupta* elaborately mentioned the uses of *kula* and *kaula* in the context of Śaiva practice in Kashmir. A Śaiva practitioner according to Mādhavācārya (*Sarvadarśana-saṁgraha*, p. 190) endeavours to achieve the monistic spiritual self-response (*pratyabhijñā*) in unification of the phenomenon and nomenon as the sublime, or Paraśiva. In due course *pratyabhijñā* response tended to different monistic views (*mata*) like Krama (in gradation) and Kula successive respondent in practice developed among the Śaiva practitioners. A Śaiva practitioner analyses the psycho-physical experiences in three broad factors, namely, *anubhava* or *pratyakṣa*: direct knowledge or perception of a phenomenon; *smṛti*: memory inclined to the previous impression caused by direct knowledge of a phenomenon; *pratyabhijñā* the union of previous impression; and direct knowledge, an experience in apperception of reality.

Pratyabhijñā becomes a psychic experience of knowledge in a practitioner's mind in effulgence of the Self or nomenon against the opposite direction of a phenomenon (*pratipamātmā-bhimukhyena jñānaṃ prakāśaḥ*), as described in the *Īśvara pratyabhijñā-vimarśinī* (Pt I, 19-20). The Śaiva practitioners claim that the *pratyabhijñā* experience is of non-Vedic origin as propounded in their Āgamas like *Siddhāgama, Mālinī-āgama* and *Vāmakāgama.*

In the Tantra traditions of India divergence and convergence had been occasional as and when required by an individual practitioner or by a group. *Pratyabhijñā* thereby becomes a kind of vibratum in spiritual experience when the phenomenon is submerged with the nomenon. It was therefore named *spanda* in the context of the monentary visualization or that in experience of unification of one's individual egoistic self with the All-pervading Self, Īśvara or Śiva (*ahamīśvara eva nānya ityevaṃ yaḥ sākṣāt-kāla sā pratyahbhijñā,* (*Sarvadarśanasaṅgraha*), *Om, Sivo'haṃ, Sivo'haṃ, Sivo'ham.* That means, the sublime (*anuttara*) would merge with the individual will (*icchā*) and its response (*unmeṣa*). With reference to the potential power (*śakti*) latent in an individual the Universal psychic power (*citśakti*) becomes amalgamated with will-power (*icchāśakti*) and the Knowing or responsive power (*jñānaśakti*). The *Tantrāloka* reads:

anuttara parecchā ca parāparatayā sthita/
unmeṣa śaktirjñānānakhaya tvapareti nigadyati//

Tantrāloka 3.249

As the threefold power have been delineated in this thought process, it is popularly known as *Trika* among the Śaivaites. *Kula* and thereby *kaula,* thus enter in the Tantra with a specific import as the *Trika* procedure in Śaiva practice. Abhinavagupta in his *Parāriṃśikā* describes *kula* in the following lines:

(i) *Kula* is the effulgent rays of the cosmic luminaries (*jyotirliṅga* of Śiva).
(ii) *Kula* is the sublime (*anuttara*) experience.
(iii) *Kula* is the gross experience of the assimilation of the phenomenon and the nomenon, i.e. that of the expression of the unification of the individual self with the all-pervading

Self (*śivātmā*) in which potential-power (*śakti*) prevails. The Eternal-self (*sadāśiva*) and five primaries become one.

(iv) The all-inclusive phenomenon in which the gross and the subtle manifests, is *kula.*

The above unified experience of *kula* fails to go beyond the phenomonal orbit whether gross or subtle. He who also goes above such experience is *akula,* i.e. Śiva who holds no manifestation (*avabhāsa*).

Kula has many other references also:

(a) *Kula* is the *yāmala* or union of the sublime principles like Śiva (*anuttara*) and Śakti (*anuttarā*).

(b) *Kula* is therefore Śiva and Śakti unified.

(c) That is, *kula* is the manifestation of the Self.

(d) Thus, *kula* becomes the body of an individual.

(e) *Kula,* being a manifestation of the self in the human body is fit to experience the Supreme Bliss (*paramānanda*).

(f) *Kula* is also the transitory phenomenal world (*jagat*) which originates out of the potential creative power (*prasavinī-śakti*).

(g) Thus, *kula* is the independent cause appearing in emergence (*udaya*) and dissolution (*laya*). In that respect, *kula* is beyond the transitory phenomenal world; despite the constituted world is within the above independent cause (*kāraṇaṃ kāraṇānām,. patiḥ patinam*).

The derivative explanation of cohesive conjoining of *ku* and *la* may tend to project unification of Śiva and Śakti in *yāmala* manifestation (*kuṃ lāteti kula*).

K.C. Pandeya opined that the viewpoint of *kula* among the Śaiva practitioners probably appeared earlier than the *Pratyabhijñā* or *Trika.* Here, *kula* and *kaula* may not also be one and the same and that requires separate elaboration. Matsyendra, otherwise known as Macchanda, probably conjoined form of *mat* (mine or I) and *chanda* (independent Will) of the fifth century was the innovator of *Kula-mata,* as Pandeya presumes. However, *Kula-mata* had spread in India and abroad on account of its wide Tantra potential, i.e. unification of the phenomenal world with the nomenon, the global earth with the cosmic universe, and the internal with the external, in quest of the blissful self-nature within the solar universe.

INDO-TIBETAN LITERATURE

Indo-Tibetan literature suggests broadly the Indian texts which had been carried to Tibet since the seventh century and translated into Tibetan. Traditionally a systematic procedure was observed by the joint endeavours of an Indian Paṇḍita, expert on the subject matter of a particular text, in collaboration with a Tibetan well-versed *lo tsa ba* translator. Those translated texts were subsequently codified and collected under two heads the Kanjur (*bka' 'gyur*) Buddhavacana and the Tanjur (*bstan 'gyur*) śāstra works of mostly Indian origin. Again, the Tantra texts belonging to the *Rñin rgyud* (Old Tantra) and the *Rgyud gsar ma* (New Tantra) are diverse.

Here Indo-Tibetan does not refer to an ethnic identity as that is applied by Fr. Hermann in respect to the Bhotia or Bhutia, of the Indian Himalayas. They had been ethnic Tibetans of Mongoloid stock. It cannot be denied that the majority of Bhotias in India profess Buddhism and hold faith in Indo-Tibetan literature, especially the two cannonical collections. They speak either Tibetan or its offshoot dialects in the Indian Himalayas.

KULA IN THE BUDDHIST TEXTS

In the Buddhist literature in Sanskrit, Pali and Apabhraṃśa, *kula* generally suggests a family which corresponds to '*rigs*' in Tibetan. Gautama, the Buddha was born in the Śākyakula or Śākya-family. The Buddhist texts occasionally refer to *kula -putra* (Pali *kalaputra*) and *kuladuhitā* in the context of those who fervently adhered to the Bodhi mind (*bodhicitta*) exclusively.

Among the Tantra practitioners of the Buddhists, the term *kula* holds distinct significance, though the Tibetan equivalent '*rigs*' does not vary.

Tantra in general is divided into four broad sections,

(i) *kriyā-tantra* onritualistic performances in respect of a practitioner
(ii) *ācāra-tantra* for observance of the prescribed way of life
(iii) *yoga-tantra* referring to esoteric practices and
(iv) *jñāna-tantra* leading to spiritual awakening by knowing the true nature of the phenomenal world and beyond.

The Buddhist name of *ācāra* is *caryā* and that of *jñāna* is *anuttara-yoga,* sublime esoteric practice. Accordingly the Tantra texts, as available in Sanskrit, Apabhraṃśa and their translation in Tibetan have been distributed in the above four divisions. As a result of that the conceptual descriptions of terms like *kula* are different. The *Caryāgītikośavyākhyā,* which belongs to the Yoga-tantra division, describes *kula* as the *avadhutikā naḍī* the central nerve among the three principal nerves of a human body. *Kumārga-candrādikaṃ yasyāmādhyūtyā layam gacchati, sā prakṛti-pariśuddhāvadhūtikā kula śabdena boddhavya* (p. 126). On the other hand *Guhyasamājatantra* and its *pradīpadyotana* commentary derive *Kum latiti kulam* by referring to jewel-like elite beings on the earth. *Kuḥ pṛthivī, tān tadvyavasthitān sattvān ratnadānena lāli svikaratīti kulaḥ,* i.e. *ratnaketuḥ.* This text belongs to the Yogatantra class.

Kula thus becomes multiple with reference to the efficacy of excelling in jewel-like effulgence. *Hevajratantra,* which is of Yoga tantra class enumerates *kula* as given below:

1. *Tathāgata-kula*: Adherent to the knowing of the intrinsic nature of the phenomena in the same way as it is and becoming in the same way as the former Buddhas came in the past.
2. *Padmakula*: The family governed by Ārya Avalokiteśvara who sees all beings of the worlds with an eye of compassion uninterruptedly.
3. *Vajrakula*: Bodhisattva Samantabhadra with his adamantine vajra knowledge, protects the *Buddha vacana* or saying of the Buddha, by overcoming inimical evil in the mind.
4. *Karmakula*: In the Yogatantra, the actions (*karma*) with the purified mind generate a specified power in rising towards the Buddhahood.
5. *Ratnakula*: Leading to mundane prosperity together with spiritual progress by generating potential efficiency.

These five represent the five aggregates with reference to five primary elements of the world.

Kalanaṃ pañca-bhūtānāṃ pañca-skandha-svarūpinam/
klyate gaṇyate'anena kulamitya-bhidhīyate//

(*Hevajratantra* I.9-10)

These five *kulas* are enumerated in accordance with five Buddhas of the Anuttarayoga (esoteric achievement)

(a) Akṣobhya : *dveṣa kula* (remover of persons' hatred)
(b) Ratnasambhava : *krodhakula* (remover of persons' avarice)
(c) Amitābha : *mohakula* (remover of persons' delusion)
(d) Amoghasiddhi : *lobhakula* (remover of persons' greed)
(e) Vairocana : *rāgakula* (remover of persons' allurement)

In addition, *Vajradhara-kula* is the sixth one.
Thus the *Hevajratantra* reads:

kulāni ṣaḍvidhanyahect saṃkṣepeṇa tu pañcadhā/
pañcācca traividhyaṃ yānti kāya vākcitta bhedena//

The sixfold *kula* which may be briefly five will be threefold according to the body, the speech and the mind of the Buddha. These three are:

(i) Tathāgatakula
(ii) Padmakula
(iii) Vajrakula as explained earlier.

These are regarded as *lokottara* or supramundane in relation to the *kriyā-tantra* and the *caryā-tantra*. The three are the order of high, middle and low depending on a practitioner's capacity for practice from the rudimentary stage.

Again, the *laukika kula* or mundane family of *kriyā-tantra* are:

(i) *Pañcaka (pauṣṭika) kula* refer to five *kuñcuka* or mental filth like allurement, stupidity, etc.
(ii) *Maṇikula*: Dispels the poverty of the material requirement and that of the mind.
(iii) *Laukikakula*: Consists of the six worlds in the wheel of existence (*bhavacakra*).

In elucidation of the *kula* as stated above the *Ārya-subāhu-paripṛcchā-tantra-piṇḍārtha-vṛtti* of an anonymous author (Toh 2673) becomes a source in Tibetan.

The *Mañjuśrīmūlakapa-tantra* (1912 : 37. V.13-14) which is regarded as the *Kriyā-tantra* with an emphasis on *mantra* practice mentions seven *kulas* broadly.

kule saptamake proktā mudrā gandharvamāśritā/
tathāṣṭamake mudrā kulebhyo parikirtitā //
sarve mudrā samakhyatā aparaśca sugatāhvaya/
pṛthak pṛthak mantreṣu laukikeśa sa-saugate//

Again, the *mudrā* with reference to the *kula* may be three-fold. In respect of Bodhisattva the Tathāgato-hṛdaya-mudrā is *mahāmudrā*. For the Maṇikula deities like Jambhala and Jālendra *mudrā* is separate. Similarly Pañeka-kula holds *yakula mudrā*. Also for the Pratyeka-buddha and the Śrāvaka the *mudrās* differ. For instance, *cintāmaṇi-kula mudrā, saṅghāṭī-mudrā, buddhalocana-mudrā, māmakimudrā, bhogavatīmudrā* require separate discussion elsewhere. The mode of application of a *mudrā* in connection with the initiation in a particular kula of deities determines the plurality in ritualistic procedure of the *Kriyātantra* primarily.

An institutional order in conducting a *kula* is also set up in the Buddhist Tantra literature. For instance, in respect of the Tathāgata-kula, Bhagavan Śākyamuni is the Kuleśa or Pradhāna (Tibetan *gso bo*) the progenitor of the Tathāgata kula; while Mañjuśrī becomes the Kulādhipati, conductor of the family. Again, the five protecting mother (Tibetan *yum*) deities pañca-Vidyārajñī such as (1) Sahasrapramardanī, (2) Mahāmāyūrī, (3) Pratisarā, (4) Sītavatī, and (5) Mantranusariṇī (dhāriṇī) together with (Māyā) mārīcī become the Mother (*Kulapālāka*) of the family.

In glorification of the deities of Tathāgata Kula, the *uṣṇīṣa* or crowns of the family are (i) Uṣṇīṣa-vijaya, (ii) Vimala-uṣṇīṣa, and (iii) Sitātapatrā-uṣṇīṣa. No other *kula* holds *uṣṇīṣa*.

Besides the five protecting mother-deities (pancaraṣksa-mātṛkā) several male and female fierce deities belong to the Tathāgata Kula. In this regard, several Dhāraṇī texts have come down to safeguard a practitioner initiated in the Tathāgata Kula.

Moreover, many messenger beings (*dūta dūtī*) are enumerated to maintain the order in the family such as Sumukha-nāma-dhāraṇī (Toh. 614). Bahu-putra-pratisaraṇa-nāma-dhāraṇī (Toh. 615), may be cited here.

Lastly, the heavenly beings (*deva, devaputra*), the *nāgas* (serpentile beings), *yakṣa* (treasure-keeper) and others are regarded as inmates of the Tathāgata family.

Similarly, the Padmakula is also headed by Bhagavan Śākyạmuni. Avalokiteśvara is the Kulādhipati with Tārā the protecting deity (*mātṛkā*). Hayagrīva and Parṇa-śabarī are the deities who safeguard the family. Pratyaṅgirā and Mahālakṣmi are deities belonging to the Padma Kula.

In case of the Vajra Kula, the Kuleśa or *pradhāna* progenitor expels all veils of ignorance which tend to evil conduct as the *Sarvakarmāvaraṇa-viśodhanī dhārṇi* (Toh 743) refers. Obviously, Vajrapāṇi Bodhisattva leads the *kula* as the *adhipati*. Vajravidāraṇī-Tārā becomes the mother of the family. Alike the above *kulas*, there are many fierce (a) deities and (b) messengers of *Vajrakula* as the following texts mention, e.g.

(a) *Kuṇḍālyāmṛta dhāraṇi* (Toh 755).
(b) *Mahabala (mahāyāna-sūtra)-dhāraṇī* (Toh 757)
Vajraśṛṅikhala-Tantra (Toh 758)
Vajratuṇḍa (Toh 759)
Vajralohatuṇḍa (Toh 760)

However, in the (i) *Maṇikula*, (ii) *Pañcaka kula* and (iii) *Laukika-kula*, no such orderliness is found. Despite that, several texts preserved in the Kanjur (*bka' 'gyur*) refer to the above. Thus

(i) *Maṇibhadra-dhāraṇī* (Toh 764)
Maṇibhadra-kalpa (Toh 765)
Maṇibhadra-yakṣasena-kalpa
Jambhala-jalendra (yathālabdha)-kalpa (Toh 770),
Nartakapara-kalpa (Toh 766-767), etc.
(ii) *Mekhala-(Vidyarājñi)-dhāraṇī* (Toh 772)
(iii) (*Maheśvāra Vidyāmantrarājñī*), Rig snags *kyi* rgyal mo chen mo (Toh 773) (Alternative reading-suggests Vidyā (*mantra-dhara-rāja-maheśvara-nāma*).

PLURALITY IN KULA

Plurality in *kula* among the Buddhist practitioners, as preserved in Tibetan translation, show the diversity in the Tantra literature. The distribution of *kula* as practised by the Buddhists was based on ritualistic divergence which appeared institutionally. In course of time, the significance of *kula* was modified from a genealogical continuity to a traditional heritage in successive order in academic learning, in social rituals, or in spiritual practices. The connotation of kula changed culturally among the Tantra practitioners, Buddhist and non-Buddhist. The variations in connotation of kula may be noticed when *kula* had been equivalent to śakti the potent power. Obviously, Śiva becomes *akula* or *kuleśa,* progenitor. Thereby the total unification (*sāmarasya*) of Kulākula is described as Kaula or Kaulika.

> *akulaṃ Śiva ityuktaṃ kulaṃ śakti prakīrtitā/*
> *kulākulanusandhan-nipuṇaḥ kaulikaḥ priye//*
>
> (*Kulārṇava-tantra* 17.27)

Genealogical descent at the individual level of Upaniṣadic times underwent a new social structure (Kuladharma) among the Tantra practitioners. And that has been continuing up to the present day practitioners, Ramprasad Sen, Kamalākānta, Āgamavāgīśa, etc. The socio-cultural environment of the Tantra practitioners thus holds different lineages of practices (*ācāra*). Thereby, Tantra treatises (*śāstra*) have been multi-dimensional and innumerable.

As a result a vast Tantra literature referring to the aforesaid *kula* of family could grow among the Buddhists in India up to the twelfth century from the pre-Christian period. A sizeable number of those Tantra texts were carried to Tibet and have been preserved in Tibetan translation. Some texts related to the aforesaid *kula* division among the Buddhist practitioners are mentioned in the Appendix. It may be noted that the Sūtra and the Tantra in Buddhist literature are so close because many *sūtra* texts have been included in the Tantra section and *vice versa.*

In spite of multiple number of the *kula* in the Tantra, according to divergence in practices, the common objective of a Tantra practitioner is how to render the service (*lokakalyāṇa*), whether material or spiritual, that an individual can do for the persons around the Kalyāṇamitra, avowed altruistic practitioner.

APPENDIX

Translated Buddhist Texts in the Kangyur

1. *Tathāgatakula*

(a) *Kuleśa: (rigs Kyi gtso bo)*
Text: Ārya-pratītya-samutpāda-nāma-mahāyāna sūtra (Toh. 520)
Anantamukhasādhaka-nama-dhāraṇī (Toh. 525)
Ārya pratītyasamutpāda dhāraṇī (Toh. 521)
Trisamaya-vyūharāja-nāma-tantra (Toh. 502)
Sarva-tathāgatādhiṣṭhāna-hṛdaya-guhya-dhatukaraṇḍa-nāma-dhāraṇī mahāyāna-sūtra (Toh. 507)
Raśmi-vimala-viruddha-prabhā-dhāraṇī (Toh. 510)

(b) *Kulādhipati: (rigs Kyi bdag bo)*
Āryamañjuśrīmūlakalpa-(tantra) Toh. 343.
Mañjuśrī-siddhaikavīra-tantra (Toh. 544)

(c) *Kulamātṛkā: (rigs kyi yum).*
Mārīcī- nāma-dhāraṇī (Toh. 564)
Mārīcīkalpa (Toh. 565)
Māyāmārīcī-saptaśata-nāma (Toh. 566)

(d) *Kulōṣṇīṣa (rigs Kyi gtsag tor/gtsag tor Kyi rigs)*
Sarva-tathāgatoṣṇīṣa-sitātapatra-nāma-aparājitā-pratyaṅgirā-nāma-vidyarājñī (Toh. 590), also 591, 592, 593 be referred).
Uṣṇīṣavijaya-dhāraṇī (Toh. 596)
Sarva-durgati-pariśodhani-uṣṇīṣavijayaa-nāma-dhāraṇī (Toh. 597)
Uṣṇīṣavijaya-dhāraṇī-Kalpa (Toh. 598)
Vimalōṣṇīṣa-dhāraṇī (Toh. 599)
Uṣṇīṣajvala-nāma-dhāraṇī (gtsug for 'bar ba toh. 600 resembles to the first chapter of the Kulādhipati/text, Mañjuśrīmūlakalpa-tantra (Toh. 343)

Note: No *kula* other than the Tathāgatakula holds Kulōṣṇīṣa texts.

(e) *Kulakrodhaka (rigs kyi khro bo)*
Krodhavijayakalpaguhya-tantra (Toh. 604)
Ārya-Vaja-bhairava-dhāraṇī (Toh. 605)
Dhvajāgrakeyurā dhāraṇī (Toh. 612)
Cundi/(ṇḍi)-devī-dhāraṇī (Toh. 613)

(f) *Kula-dūtādūti (rigs kyi pho ña dan pho na mo)*
Sumukha-nāma-dhāraṇī (Toh. 614)
Bahuputra-pratisaraṇa-nāma-dhāraṇī (Toh. 615)
Tohuku catalogue Nos. 616-33 be referred
including Coravidhvaṃsana-nāma-dhāraṇī (Toh. 629) and
Acalakalpa-tantra (Toh. 631).

(g) *Kula-Bodhisattva and suddhavasika deva (byaṅ chub sems dpa' rigs daṅ gnas jsaṅ Iha.*
Lastly, many Tantra and Dhāraṇī texts of the Tathāgata-Kula are preserved in the Kanjur dealing with the

(i) Bodhisattvas and (ii) Sudhāvasika-deva who associated with the Tathāgatas. Such as,

(i) Maitreya, Mañjuśrī Bodhisattvas are included.
(ii) Mahāmega sūtra (Toh. 658)
Vasudhārā-nāma-dhāraṇī (Toh. 660)
Amṛtabhava-nāma-dhāraṇī (Toh. 645)
Jvālāmukhī-dhāraṇī (kha 'bar maii gzuṅs) Toh. 647
Gaṇapati-dhāraṇī (Toh. 665)
Gaṇapati-Tantra (Toh. 666)
Śrī-Mahākāla-tantra (Toh. 667

2. *Padmakula*:

(a) Ārya-aparimitāyurijñāna-nāma-māhāyāna-sūtra (Toh. 674 and 675)
Ārya-aparimitāyurjñānahṛdaya-nāma-dhāraṇī (Toh. 676)
(b) Ārya-avalokiteśvara-padmajāla-kula-tantra-rāja-nāma (Toh. 681)
Avalokiteśvara-siṃhanāda-dhāraṇī (Toh. 703 and 704)
Ārya-amoghapāśahṛdaya-nāma mahāyāna-sūtra (Toh. 682)
Ārya-amoghapāśa-hṛdaya-nāma-dhāraṇī (Toh. 683)

Amoghapāśa-kalparāja-tantra (Toh.686) and
its dhāraṇī (Toh. 687) with Kalparājavidhi (Toh. 689).

(c) Sarva-tathāgata-mātṛ-tārā-viśvakarma-bhava-tantra (Toh. 726)
Namastare ekaviṃśaṭi-stotra-guṇa-sahita (Toh. 438).
Āryatārā (bhaṭṭārikā) nāmāṣṭaśataka (Toh. 727 and 728).

(d) not applicable.

(e) Hayagrīva-dhāraṇī (Toh. 733)
Parṇaśabari-sūtra (Toh. 735)
Parṇaśabari-nāma dhāraṇī (Toh. 736)

(f) Balavatī-nāma-pratyaṅgirā (Toh. 737)
Mahālakṣmi-sūtra (Toh. 740)

3. *Vajrakula*

(a) Sarva-karmavarṇana-visadhani-dhāraṇī (Toh. 743)

(b) Ārya-Vajra paṭala-nāma-mahātantra (Toh. 744)
Bhutaḍāmara-tantra (Toh. 747)
Vajracaṇḍa-tantra texts (Toh. 458-460)
Vajravidāraṇa-nāma-dhāraṇī (Toh. 750)
Vajrameraśikhara-kuṭāgāra-dhāraṇī (Toh. 751)

Also, Acintya-sūtra (Toh. 47), and Tathāgata-cintya-guhyanirrdeśa-Sūtra (Toh. 48) ?
be also referred here.

(c) Anala pramahani dhāraṇī (Toh. 752)

(d) not applicable.

(e) and (f) Texts have already been mentioned.

7

The Bodhisattva Ideal A Chronological Survey

MEENA V. TALIM

The present study investigates the origin and growth of the Bodhisattva ideal from the chronological point of view, mainly on the basis of literary sources. In the days of Buddha the ideal of the Arhant was well established and had taken a formidable shape, approved by Buddha himself. However after the demise of Buddha, there was much religious fervour and the Bodhisattva ideal began to emerge. This process of rising up on the horizon is reflected in the Buddhist literature.

The Vinaya text forms an earlier portion of Ti-piṭaka. It advocates Arhant ideal along with the earliest principles of Hīnayāna dogma. Here we come across an interesting episode about Buddha and an Ājīvaka monk. Buddha decided to preach to the world at the injunction of Lord Brahmā and went to meet the Pañcavaggiya monks (five monks). On his way, at Gayā, he met an Ājīvaka ascetic named Upaka who asked him 'Who is your master? And whose religion do you follow?'[1] To him Buddha answered 'I am an Arhant in this world and I am the master, the incomparable one'.[2] One can notice here that stress is given on the word *arhant*, denoting the *arhant* ideal. This is the first and the earliest example. Again, when Buddha met the five monks they addressed him as 'brother' (*āvusovādena*), and he admonished them saying, 'Do not address Tathāgata as brother, for oh monks, he is an Arhant and Tathāgata, the enlightened one.'[3] He then taught them the doctrine of *dukkha*, *anattā* and *anicattā*. At Vārāṇasi he met Yasa,[4] the son of a rich merchant who was the first householder to convert to the Buddhist faith. To him the Buddha taught Dharma consisting of the four noble truths and the eightfold noble path. This points out that Dharma to monks and householders was one and the same, even adoption of the methods. In all these earlier episodes we hardly hear about pāramitās or Bodhisattvas which means that the Bodhisattva ideal had not emerged as yet.

The Cullavagga mentions the first and second Buddhist councils which were obviously summoned for establishing Buddha's norms and rectifying the disorder in the monasteries. Neither council discussed anything regarding the Bodhisattva ideal. In the first all the attention was on stabilization of the Buddhist religion. In the second council, held a century after the demise of Buddha, all controversial points were taken for discussion but they were more of disciplinary nature than dogmatic. On the whole the Cullavagga and Mahāvagga preach about the four noble truths, eightfold noble path, impermanence, *karma*, etc., coherent to the ideal of *arhant*.

The third Buddhist council held in the third century BC produced a valuable book named *Kathāvatthu*. This book discusses a few points regarding the Bodhisattva. This means that by Aśokan period Buddhist community knew about the Bodhisattva ideal and was widely aware of it. It would be interesting to glance at the questions raised in this book:

Bodhisatto issariyakāmakārikāhetu vinipātaṃ gacchati iti?

(Does Bodhisattva accept evil state for the sake of a godly act?)[5]

Bodhisatto issariyakāmakārikāhetu gabbhaseyyaṃ okkamati ti?

(Does Buddhisattva take birth in the womb for the sake of a godly act?)[6]

Bodhisatto issariyakāmakārikāhetu dukkarakārikaṃ akāso ti?

(Does Bodhisattva perform a hard task for the sake of a godly act?)[7]

Bodhisatto issariyakāmakārikāhetu apastapaṃ akāsī ti?

(Does Bodhisattva perform severe penances for the sake of a godly act?)[8]

Bodhisatto issariyakāmakārikāhetu ajjaṃ satthāraṃ uddiso ti?

[Does Bodhisattva follow other (heretic) masters for the sake of a godly act?][9]

All these questions are superficial and casual; they do not discuss the ideal thoroughly. Besides all the propositions are rejected under the pretext that there is no evidence of a *sutta* (in the Tipiṭaka) which would give consent to such proposals. Whatever may be the attitude of the Kathāvatthu writers, whether to ridicule or discourage the Bodhisattva ideals, one can not find any definite shape in the book which would indicate the progress of the ideal in the third century BC.

The Jātakas are collection of Bodhisattva stories forming a separate section of the Pali literature. In all these stories the hero is Bodhisattva performing one of the acts of the ten *paramitas* (perfections). Some of them are very old and go back to the second century BC. The archaeological evidence at Sāñci and Bhārhut speak about these Jātakas. The gateways (*toraṇas*) of the *stūpas* reveal many popular Jātaka stories. However, the actual text does not show any demarcation line between Arhant and Bodhisattva. In the Jātakas the Bodhisattva appears as a mere future Buddha working along with the line of arhant. Paramitas explained in the Jātaka are garbed as vows of purification. Bodhisattvahood is not looked upon as a special principle or dogmatic theory in this text.

Hīnayānis believe in ten perfections (*dasa-pāramita*) and Mahāyānis in six. In the Jātakas and early Pali books ten *pāramitas* appear as a natural development of Hīnayāna philosophy. No separate entity was attached to Bodhisattva and *pāramitas* nor was any attempt made to bifurcate from Hīnayāna philosophy. It was very popular amongst the householders perhaps on psychological grounds. R. Kimura feels 'Jātaka stories existed already in the third century BC and Jātaka cult was prevalent among common people of the time.'[10] However people then seem to have been ignorant about the future development of the Bodhisattva and *pāramitā* concepts which were to form an important tenet of Buddhism. Rhys Davids remarks, 'It is important to notice that in not one of these instances of earliest composition that were called Jātakas is the Buddha identified in his previous birth with an animal. He is identified only with famous sages and teachers of old time. This was the first idea to be attached to the word Jātaka.'[11]

A similar attitude can be noticed in the *Nidāna Kathā*', written between the first century BC and the first century AD. However, in this period more thinking is done on this topic, Bodhisattva is given more scope and the theory begins to take shape. *'Dure'-nidāna'* which occupies a special portion of this book is indicative of the growth of the Bodhisattva ideal. *Buddhavaṁśa*, and *Cariyā Piṭaka* are the two books of Tipiṭaka which reveal the deification of Buddha not evident in the earlier books of the Tipiṭaka. Winternitz has pointed out that the '*Durenidāna*' of *Nidānakathā* is directly connected with the *Buddhavaṃśa* and *Cariya Pitaka*, and is a mere commentary on an extract from these two texts.[12] The twenty-four Buddhas mentioned in all these books were Bodhisattvas in their former lives, who strove for Buddhahood. Thus knowingly or unknowingly the Bodhisattva ideal was finding firm ground. Probably in this period three types of Bodhis were recognized namely Śrāvaka, Pratyeka and Samyaka. Corresponding to these three kinds of Bodhi, three Yānas developed, Śrāvaka (Savakayāna), Pratyeka (Pacceka Yāna) and Samyaka (Sammaka Yāna). The last was subsequently known as Bodhiasttva Yāna and later on imbibed in Mahāyāna. The first two were known as Hīnayāna.

The Arhant ideal, as we have stated, was heading towards the rise of the Bodhisattva. In the process, Pratyeka Buddha and Samyaka Buddha were introduced. It seems that many monks in the Saṅgha recognized unrest in the order and the self-centredness of monks. Introduction of Pratyeka Buddha and Samyaka Buddha was an act of compromise. Pratyeka Buddha was Buddha for himself and Samyaka was not only for himself but also for mankind. Psychologically speaking this was the right step, for those who were introvert could adapt to Pratyekà and extroverts could opt for Samyaka. However, this adjustment could last only for a century or two. The Samyaka ideal grew fast and ultimately culminated in the Bodhisattva ideal and arhantavādins did not accept the Pratyeka Buddha theory totally. This resulted in the decline of Pratyeka Buddha in Theravāda.

In the beginning an attempt was made to stick to the original traditions. The introduction of Pacceka Buddha and Sammaka Buddha show that it was not totally successful. The later *Tipiṭaka* books began to speak about Pacceka Buddhas. *Therigāthā* very reverentially refers to Pacceka Buddhas. Theris like Citta,[13] Dantikā,[14] Bhaddākapilāni,[15] and Mahāpajāpati Gotamī[16] give all the credit for their present successful renunciated life to the Pacceka Buddha, to whom they had offered flowers in their previous lives.

A non-canonical book written in about first century AD named the *Milinda Pañha* refers to these theories very casually. In the chapter on dilemna, Pacceka-bhumi is compared with Savaka-bhumi, where the latter is considered superior to the former. The reason given is that the Arhant's mind is more receptive (as regards all that disciples can do or aspire), it quickly grasps and acts with ease. Pacceka Buddha, on the other hand performs it with difficulty and acts slowly.[17] It further enlightens us, 'Pacceka Buddhas are dependent on themselves alone, waiting on no teacher, lonely dwellers like solitary born of rhinoceros, who as far as their own higher life is concerned, have pure hearts, free from stain'—this thinking process, so far as their own province is concerned are brought quickly. But as regards all that is especially within a perfect Buddha, they are brought with difficulty into and more slowly.[18] These few references of *Milinda Pañha* are important for they reveal strong adherence to the arhant ideal and feeble recognition of Pacceka Buddha.

Earlier Mahāyāna texts, more or less of the same period are also very informative. Let us take Mahāvastu which is undoubtedly old and has much in common with the Pāli canon. The nucleus of this book orginated as far back as the second century BC even though it was enlarged in the fourth century AD.[19] This work stands on the threshold of Hīnayāna and enters into the realm of Mahāyāna. Hence there is much assimilation. 'A very favourite theme in these is the glorification of the exceeding self denial and generosity of the Bodhisattva.'[20] The *Khaḍgaviṣāṇa Sutra* praises Pratyeka Buddha as does the Suttanipāta of the Pāli canon.

Another early Mahāyāna text is the *Lalita Vistāra* which was translated into Chinese as early as the first century AD[21] Here one can notice the definite growth of Bodhisattva. In this book the Master is always described as surrounded by 12,000 monks and 32,000 Bodhisattvas or more, all rejoicing in the knowledge of a Bodhisattva. This tendency started growing strongly and rapidly. *Jātaka mālā* of Āryasura or the entire Avadāna literature praise the Bodhisattva ideal. The arhant ideal lagged far behind and Mahāyāna literature of the later period completely engulfed it with the Bodhisattva ideal. The Bodhisattva ideal which established its identity by the beginning of the first century began to grow speedily.

Why was the Bodhisattva ideal not given much scope in early Buddhism? This question perplexes the mind, especially when one takes into account the life of the Buddha and his attitude towards humanity. He was the first Indian philosopher who was involved with social uplift. Every moment of his life was dedicated to the peace of mankind. He was a man closer to the Bodhisattva ideal than the Arhant ideal, and yet the Arhant ideal was first put forth. Why?

One has to find out the answer in ancient Indian traditions and history. The Aryans as nomadic people came down to India and were enamoured by the beauty of Indian flora and fauna. They composed many hymns in early *Ṛgveda*, in praise of nature and found divinity in nature. They started worshipping nature very objectively. In due course sages began to seek spiritual power from them, by invoking powers through performances of sacrifices. At the time of Upaniṣads metaphysics and mysticism were also included in Indian philosophy. 'Upaniṣads appear to have been added to the Vedas with the object of investigating more definitely such abstruse problems as the origin of soul, and the reciprocal connection of spirit and matter.'[22] Vedas and Upaniṣads laid the foundations of Indian philosophy. Monastic attitudes attached to philosophy were confirmed. A period came when philosophers and seekers of new theories began to remain aloof from the society, somewhat like a modern scientist. They kept on making new experiments and inventing new theories but had no time to look into the needs of common people. The earlier Vedic sages at least gave 'Varṇa' and Āśrama systems to society, but later the tendency was to remain aloof. This became a philosophical pattern. The period of this however reveals the material gains more than spiritual ones. Society had a say over philosophers and sages were involved in social affairs. Barring this period the pattern remained the same before the rise of Buddha. Śramaṇa cults widened this gap and in course of time, by the sixth century BC there were sixty-two heresies in India.[23]

After making a survey of these different heresies one feels that the revolts were against philosophical patterns laid down traditionally. Sages as pointed out in *Digha Nikāya* began to say that you may make a heap of human skeletons on the bank of the Ganga or you perform sacrifices on its banks—there is no demerit (*akusala*) or merit (*kusala*). Such type of teachers were uprooting the very core of philosophical traditions. They were not fools to propagate evil as no evil, good as bad, but they had chosen an extreme way to denounce the traditional pattern. Along with this nihilistic attitude one can observe a sort of social awareness in this philosophical group. Mahāvīra and Buddha belonged to one such group and their ways were more constructive as they channelised philosophical fervour to social needs. Buddha was aware of this trend and calls his way the *majjhimapaṭipadā* the middle path. This middle path demanded compromises with existing traditions and one of them was the Arhant ideal. This was one that contained highest philosophical sense, parallel to the early Indian philosophical tradition, but its approach, methods and manifestation were within the reach of ordinary people. Unlike the Vedas or Upaniṣads Buddhism did not demand intellectuals but could be understood by a man of average intelligence. Besides this, the average man was elevated to intellectual level. Some of his earlier doctrinal tenets were similar to those of the Upaniṣads: *anattā, dukkha, aniccatā karma,* etc., even as the approach was absolutely novel.

Buddha was a revolutionary in many respects. In a class bound society he proclaimed equality; in a *yajña*-centered society he showed the futility of *yajña* and in a ritual stricken society he propagated rationality. He was a great man, struggling on the forefront, carrying with him social problems and tenets of philosophy at the same time. In such a situation it would have been dangerous to promote the Bodhisattva philosophy. The Bodhisattva ideal can only be successful and progressive if it can wade through the vigorous and disciplined philosophy of arhantship. A certain period of training was essential for the growth of the Bodhisattva ideal.

The doctrines of *karma* and *pāramitā* evolved to give rise to the Bodhisattva ideal. Thus through *arhantship* ideal emerged the ideal of the Bodhisattva.

Besides the earlier disciples of Buddha who made a constructive contribution to the growth of Buddhism, were mostly from the Brāhmaṇa class. The three Jaṭila brothers, Sāriputta, Maggallana, Kassapa and many others were already trained and well versed in Brāhmaṇical theologies. Due to this background they found no difficulty in understanding *arhantship* and Nibbāṇa. Psychologically this group of monks was prepared for this ideal. At the same time one should remember that they were the earliest disciples of the Buddha to propagate the doctrine. Hence the question of the Bodhisattva ideal did not arise in the early days of Buddhism. One may say that the arhant ideal was essential for the proper growth of the Bodhisattva ideal, for it could control and check the emotional natural tendencies that lie in the Bodhisattva ideal.

Thus we observe that nearly four to five centuries were required for the firm fixation of the Bodhisattva ideal, i.e. from the fifth century BC to the first century AD. Then this ideal took a steady but rapid growth and by the fourth century was gloriously marching ahead. In this period it blossomed with philosophies of great scholars like Aśvaghoṣa, Nāgārajuṇa, Vasu-Bandhu, Dignāga, Dharmakirti,

Candrakīrti, and many others. One must note that this progress and growth of the Bodhisattva ideal in India was growth and progress of Buddhism as a whole.

We further observe that in the later Mahāyāna schools, Bodhisattva offered his merit over to mankind and all people were blessed with his merit, which they had not earned themselves by exertion or performing pāramitās. The transference of merit of Bodhisattva made it easy way for devotees to attain salvation. Bodhisattvas like Amitābha and Avalokiteśvara became saviours of mankind. These two Bodhisattvas were later considered equal to Buddha and sometimes even a little superior to him. The Bodhisattvas of earlier Theravāda and Mahāyāna schools were meant to set an example before mankind, as how to achieve emancipation by practising *pāramitās,* numbering ten or six respectively. However later on this attitude changed completely.

Yogācāra, Vijñānavāda, Sukhavativuha, Tantric and many later schools (fourth to seventh centuries) totally changed the original Bodhisattva ideal and thereby its position in Budhist philosophy. By the seventh century the Vajrayāna school's propagation of mantras, dhariṇis and diagrams began to assume increasing importance and popularity. By the eleventh century Vajrayāna established esoteric Buddhism through Tantric teachings. All these new inovations reduced the importance of the original Bodhisattva ideal.

NOTES

1. *Mahāvgga,* Nalanda Mahāvihara Pub. 1956, p. 11.
2. Ibid.
3. Ibid., p. 12.
4. Ibid., p. 19.
5. *Kathāvatthu,* ed. Jagidish Kassapo, Nalanda Pub.; 1961, p. 535.
6. Ibid., p. 536.
7. Ibid., p. 537.
8. Ibid., p. 537.
9. Ibid., p. 537.
10. R. Kimura, *Historical Study of Terms Hīnayāna and Mahāyāna* (Calcutta, 1927), p. 131.
11. T.W. Rhys Davids, *Buddhist India* (London, 1911), p. 196.
12. M. Winternitz, *A History of Indian Literature,* Vol. II. (Calcutta, 1933).
13. E. Muller, *Paramattha Dipani,* Vol. P.T.S. edn. (London, 1893), p. 33.
14. Ibid., p. 51.

15. Ibid., p. 68.
16. Ibid., p. 140.
17. R.D. Vadekar, *Milinda Panha* (Bombay, 1940), p. 107.
18. Max Muller, *Questions of King Milinda*, S.B.E., Vol. XXXV (Oxford, 1890), p. 158.
19. M. Winternitz, ibid., p. 247.
20. Ibid., p. 244.
21. Ibid., p. 253.
22. M. Monier Williams, *Indian Wisdom*.
23. N.K. Bhagwat, *Digha Nikaya*, Vol. I (Bombay).

8

Goddess Vajravārāhī An Iconographic Study

MALLAR MITRA

The Buddhist goddess Vajravārāhī derives her name from the excrescence near her ear which resembles the face of a sow. Alice Getty in *The Gods of Northern Buddhism*[1] has recorded an interesting legend about Vajravārāhī. In Tibet the abbess of a monastery had an excrescence behind her head which resembled a sow's head. Yun-gar, a Mongol warrior, while attacking the monastery, challenged the abbess to come forth and show her sow-head. When the army invaded the place, they found that the place was inhabited by pigs and sows led by a sow bigger than the others. Yun-gar was surprised and stopped the pillage. Immediately the pigs and sows were transformed into monks and the largest sow into the abbess herself. Yun-gar became a convert and enriched the monastery.

The popularity of the goddess is evident from the fact that as many as eleven *sādhanas* of the *Sādhanamālā*[2] are devoted to her. A Tantra known as *Vajravārāhī Tantra* is centred on her. The *Niṣpannayogāvalī* of Abhayākaragupta[3] has also described her, not as an independent goddess but as the reflection (*svābha*) of Saṃbara and Hevajra.

She has been described as a goddess (*bhagavatī*) in *Sādhanas* 217, 218, 219, 221, 226 and 227 and as a *ḍākinī* in *Sādhana* 221. The excrescence is mentioned only in one *Sādhana* (224) which describes her as *vajraghoṇā*. The *Yamāri-maṇḍala* of the *Niṣpannayogāvalī* calls her *ghoṇamukhī*.[4]

Exactly when the goddess came into existence is not known. There is no doubt that she is a late introduction to the Buddhist pantheon. Of the *sādhanas* describing her, only one (217) has the name of its author. He is Mahāpaṇḍita Avadhūta Śrīmad Advayavajra who is believed to have flourished in around AD 978-1030.[5] The *Sādhana* (255) of two armed Sambara written by Ratnākaragupta also mentions her. Ratnākaragupta has been dated to about 1100.[6]

No image of the deity so far found in India (noticed by me) can be ascribed earlier than the tenth century and it is likely that the concept emerged some time in the ninth-tenth century.

The popularity of this Vajrayāna Buddhist goddess was due to the fact that she could fulfil the desires of devotees (*sarvvasiddhipradāyikā*). Her *mantra* is supposed to be very powerful. How powerful is her *mantra* is known from *Sādhana* 218.[7] By uttering her *mantra* seven or eight lakh times, the worshipper becomes expert in all *śāstras* and arts; he acquires good memory, bravery, versatility and becomes a good debator. He will never be troubled with fever, poison and *ḍākinīs.* Whatever he would eat would turn into nectar. If a person after the attainment of *siddhi* (perfection) gives a piece of chalk on which the *mantra* is uttered in the hands of an illiterate, the illiterate person would become a poet. Interestingly, the unknown author of this *sādhana* claims that by uttering her *mantra* two lakh times he would write the *sādhana* effortlessly.

Vajravārāhī who is the emanation of Tathāgata Vairocana[8] is known in many forms: two-armed, four-armed, and in the embrace of her consorts.

I

TWO-ARMED FORMS

Under this head six varieties of Vajravārāhī are noticed. The first variety is described in *Sādhana* 217[9] written by Advayavajra. According to this *sādhana,* the goddess is red like a promegranate flower (*dāḍimakusuma*). She is two-armed, her right palm showing the *tarjanī,* and wields a thunderbolt. With her left hand she bears a *karoṭaka* (skull-cup) and a *khaṭvāṅga.* Single-faced and three-eyed, she has dishevelled hair. She is marked with six auspicious symbols (*ṣanmudrā-mudritā*)[10] and is nude (*digambarā*). She is the essence of five kinds of knowledge and is the embodiment of *sahaja* pleasure. She stands in the *pratyālīḍha* posture trampling Bhairava and Kālarātri. She is bejewelled with a garland of heads still wet with the blood she drinks.

In the four cardinal directions there are four goddesses on the four petals of the lotus (on which Vajravārāhī stands). Beginning in the east, there are Ḍākinī, Lāmā, Khaṇḍarohā and Rūpiṇī. They are respectively of black/blue (*kṛṣṇa*), green (*śyāma*), red (*rakta*) and white (*gaura*) complexion. All the four are single-faced, three-eyed and four-armed, holding in their right hands a *ḍamaru* and a *kartri* and in the left a *kapāla* and *khaṭvāṅga*. They are bejewelled with five *mudrās*, nude, and have dishevelled hair, and stand in the *ālīḍha* posture. On the intermediate petals there are four *kapālas* filled with the four thoughts of knowledge (*bodhicittādi pūrṇāni kapālāni*). Her *mantra* is: *oṃ vajravairocanīye huṃ huṃ phaṭ svāhā*.

The description of the second variety is found in *Sādhana* 218, entitled *Prajñālokasādhana*. According to this *Sādhana* she is a young girl of sixteen years, as white as the autumn moon (*śaradindudhavalā*) and three-eyed, the eyes being round and red. Her face appears somewhat terrible with bare fangs. Her dishevelled hair is decorated with different kinds of flowers: half the hair is tied and attached with a *vajra* and a *kapāla*. She is decorated with *cakrī* (crown), *kuṇḍala* (ear-rings), *kaṇṭhi* (necklace), *rūcaka* (bracelets), and *mekhalā* (girdle). She is wearing a long garland of fifty severed heads. She is nude and stands in the *ālīḍha* posture on the *ajñānapuruṣa*[12] placed on the orb of the sun above a lotus. With her right palm brandishing a thunderbolt adorned with three banners, she threatens the *ajñānapuruṣa* and holds in the left hand *padmabhājana* (skull-cup) filled with the blood of four Māras. Against her shoulder (*bāhadaṇḍāsaṃsakta*) is a *khaṭvāṅga*.

In the third variety, described in *Sādhana* 219,[13] she is red in complexion. She holds in her left palm a noose of the syllable *hriḥ* and with the right a *vajrāṅkuśa* (elephant-goad surmounted by a *vajra*) which resembles the bud of a red *utpala*.

The fourth form is invoked in rituals performed with the purpose of bewitching men and women. *Sādhana* 220 entitled *Vajravārāhyā vaśyavidhiḥ* describes this form.[14] She is nude, has dishevelled hair and is dancing holding a *kartri* and a *kapāla* near her navel.

In the fifth form also the two-armed goddess is dancing. This form is described in *Sādhanas* 226 and 227 entitled *Saṃkṣipta Vajravārāhī sādhanam*.[15] Vajravārāhī who is single-faced and two-armed is of terrible appearance (*pralayānala-sannibhāṃ*). She holds a *vajrikā* with her right palm showing the *tarjanī*. In the left hand she has a *kapāla* and attached to her hand (*bāhudaṇḍāsakta*) is a *khaṭvāṅga* decorated with a banner (*viśvapatākā*). She dances the *tāṇḍava* dance in the *pratyālīḍha* posture, trampling under her feet Bhairava and Kālarātri. She is three-eyed, clad with space (*digvāsā*, i.e. nude), has dishevelled hair, wears a girdle of pieces of bones (*khaṇḍa-maṇḍitamekhalā*), is decorated with all kinds of ornaments and a garland of heads. Her face is distorted (*vikṛtānanā*) and terrible, with bare fangs (*daṃsṭrākarālavadanā*). On her head is a *viśva-vajra*, a garland of *vajras* and *kapālas*.

The sixth variety of two-armed Vajravārāhī is known as *Ūrdhavapādavajravārāhī*. Her iconographical features are described in *Sādhana* 226.[16] This *sādhana* originated in *Oḍiyānavajrapīṭha*. According to the *sādhana*, she is red, three-eyed and nude. With dishevelled hairs, she wears a girdle of pieces of bones (*khaṇḍa-maṇḍitamekhalā*) and a garland of fifty (*śatārdha*) human heads, still wet. In her left hand she holds a *kapāla* full of the blood of wicked Māras (*duṣṭamārādya-sṛgdharam*). With the right palm showing the *tarjanī*, she holds a *vajra*.

tarjayantīṃ diśaḥ sarvaduṣṭatarjanavajṛkām/
kalpavahṇimahātejāṃ sravantīṃ rūdhirapriyām//

Her legs are raised up. On the four petals of the lotus are (from the east) Ḍākinī, Lāmā, Khaṇḍarohā and Rūpiṇī. In the intermediate corners are four skull-cups (*karoṭāścatvāraḥ*). The *mantra* of Vajravārāhī is *oṃ sarvvabuddhaḍākinīye vajravarṇanīye huṃ huṃ phaṭ phaṭ svāhā.*

II

FOUR-ARMED FORM

The four-armed form of Vajravārāhī is described in *Sādhana* 224.[17] According to this *Sādhana* she is red in complexion and nude, had a crown of *kapālas* and her hair bristles upwards. She is decorated with five *mudrās* (*pañcamudropetāṃ*). She is four-armed, holding in her right hands a *vajra* and a *vajrāṅkuśa* (a goad surmounted by a *vajra*) and in the two left, *kapāla-khaṭvāṅga* and *tarjanīpāśa* (a noose in the palm showing *tarjanī*).

She is single-faced and three-eyed. With frowning eyebrows her face is awful (*karālavadanā*). She has an adamantine excrescence (*vajraghoṇā*). She is terrible-looking (*subhīṣanā*). Her belly is protruding (*vṛhadudarā*) and her tongue is also protruding (*lalajihvā*). She stands in the *ālīḍha* posture on a corpse.

III

VAJRAVĀRĀHĪ AS THE SVĀBHA PRAJÑĀ OF GODS

Vajravārāhī as the *svābha* of the three-faced, six-armed Saptākṣara is described in *Sādhana* 250,[18] written by Durjayacandra whose date is not known. Her legs are around the knee of Saptākṣara. Regarding her attributes, the *Sādhana* says: *yathā nāthasya tathā Vajravārāhyāpi bhujādikam.* The attributes in the hands of her *nātha* Saptāksāra who tramples on Bhairava and Kālarātri are: a *vajra* and a *ghaṇṭā* in the first pair of hands: the wet human skin (*naracarmmādra*) in the second pair of hands: and a *triśūla* (in the right hand) and a *kapāla-khaṭvāṅga* (in the left hand) in the third pair of hands.

Her form as the *svābha* of Saptākṣara described in *Sādhana* 251[19] (written by Advayavajra) is slightly different. Her attributes have been described as almost similar to those in Saptākṣara's hands. The three-faced and six-armed Saptākṣara embraces Vajravārāhī with the main pair of hands holding a *vajra* and a *ghaṇṭā*: with the upper hands he holds human skin (*naracarmma*), the remaining two hands bearing *triśūla* and *khaṭvāṅgakapāla.* Regarding Vajravārāhī's attributes, the *Sādhana* says: *yathā nāthasya tathā Vajravārāhyā varṇabhujādikaṃ kintu naracarmma tyaktva tatkarābhyāṃ dhanur-bāṇadhāriṇī devī bhagavajjā nudvayaṃ samāveṣṭya.* It is, therefore, clear that Vajravārāhī, whose legs are around the knees of Saptākṣara, holds the same attributes as her *nātha* but not the *naracarmma.* She holds a bow and an arrow instead.

The description of Vajravārāhī in the embrance of two-armed Sambara is found in the *Sādhana* 255[20] entitled *dvibhuja-Sambaropadeśaḥ.* She holds a *vajra* and a *kapāla* full of blood. The *khaṭvāṅga* is her girdle (*khaṭvāṅgamekhalā*). She is of red complexion, three-eyed and wears a garland of several heads. With dishevelled hair, she is endowed with five *mudrās,* and is without garment (*digvastrā*). She has the figure of Buddha on her crown (*Buddha-śekharā*). Tathāgata is not explicity named.

The iconographic features of Vajravārāhī embraced by the main hands of twelve-armed Sambara are found in the *Sambaramaṇḍala* of the *Niṣpannayogāvalī.*[21] She is red, nude, single-faced, three-eyed, has dishevelled hair, and wears a girdle made of broken *kapālas.* She holds a *vajra* with the raised hand showing *tarjanī* and with the hand embracing (her partner) she bears a *kapāla*, from which blood tickles down. She wears a garland of dry human heads, has the aureole of the rays of the sun, and is decorated with five *mudrās*.

Vajravārāhī is the *svābha* of four-armed Hevajra, according to the *Saptadaśātmaka-Hevajra-maṇḍala* of the *Niṣpannayogāvalī*.[22] The single-faced and four-armed Hevajra holds with one right hand a *vajra* and with the left a skull-cup, full of blood and marked with a *vajra*. With the other two hands he embraces his *śakti* Vajravārāhī, his own reflection. Vajravārāhī's iconographical features are, however, not described.

In the *Navātmaka-Heruka-maṇḍala* of the *Niṣpannayogāvalī*.[23] She is in the embrace of the four-armed Heruka. In *Sādhana* 221[24] she has been described as the principal queen of Heruka (*Herukadevasya agramahiṣī*). Both these texts are silent about her features.

IV

HER PLACE IN THE *MAṆḌALA*

She is one of the divinities in the *maṇḍala* of Yamāri. The *Yamāri-maṇḍala*[25] of the *Niṣpannayogāvalī* places her in the *nairṛita* corner. She has been described as *ghoṇamukhī* (sow-faced) and *dveṣakālārisadṛśī*.

IMAGES

A. India

Images of Vajravārāhī are rare in India. Of the two images illustrated here one hails from Chauduar (Orissa) and the other from Sringirikhi (Bihar).

(i)

An image of Vajravārāhī (Pl. 1) was found by Ramaprasad Chanda in a modern Vaiṣṇava temple in Chauduar, District Cuttack, Orissa.[26] The image cannot be located at present but from the photograph[27] it appears that it was an excellent one. The image is of stone and can be dated to the tenth-eleventh century.

Vajravārāhī is bejewelled in anklets, an ornate girdle of two strings with bell-shaped pendants and hanging wavy garlands (spaced by pendants), *valayas*, beaded armlets, a beaded *hāra*, a necklace and ear-rings and a tiara. From the photograph it appear that she is not wearing any cloth.

The single-headed goddess with dishevelled hair is two-armed. Her eyes are round and her expression angry. Her right hand hangs downwards and the palm exhibits the *tarjanī-mudrā* and holds a *vajra* (thunderbolt). Her left hand, stretched upwards, holds a *kapāla* (skull-cup). From her left shoulder hangs a *khaṭvāṅga* (with a *vajra* at the top and bottom) which touches the ground.

Vajravārāhī stands in a posture akin to the *ālīḍha* stance. She tramples with her right foot the emaciated figure of Kālarātri and near her left foot is a male figure, presumably Bhairava. Both Bhairava and Kālarātri are lying on their backs on the ground.

Near the left leg of Vajravārāhī is a female figure, seated with legs folded, hands joined in the *añjali-mudrā*. She represents a devotee or a donor. Slightly above the head of the female is a male standing on a *viśva-padma*. Draped in an *antarīya* and an *uttarīya*, he is holding an indistinct object detween joined palms. The identity of this figure cannot be ascertained. The possibility of his being one of the four companions of Vajravārāhī is ruled out, as his figure does not conform with that of any of them, described in the *sādhanas*.

Behind the right leg of Vajravārāhī is a male figure, seated in the *Vajraparyaṅkāsana* on a *viśva-padma* holding a *vajra* in his right palm placed near the chest. His left hand [holding a *ghaṇṭā* (?)] is placed on the left thigh. He appears to be Vajrasattva.

The back-slab shows flames. At the top corners of the back-slab are seen two flying *vidyādharas*. At the top, in the centre, there is a full-blown lotus.

The image tallies with the description of Vajravārāhī given in *Sādhana* 217, but she stands in the *ālīḍha* posture, not in the *pratyālīḍha* attitude as enjoined by the *Sādhana*.

(ii)

The image of Vajravārāhī (Pl. 2)[28] found at Sringirikhi, Rajgir, Bihar, is preserved in the Patna Museum (no. 10540). The black stone image, is datable to the eleventh century and is in a fine state of preservation.

Vajravārāhī is bejewelled with beaded anklets, an ornate girdle with a beaded string (from which hang down wavy garlands, spaced by pendants), bangles, armlets with a central triangular shaped projection, a necklace, a beaded *hāra*, an *upavīta* of two strings (one beaded, and the other plain), a long garland (crossing her knees), ear-ornaments and a tiara.

She is three-eyed; the normal eyes are round and angry and her open mouth shows her teeth. The hair is let loose. There appears to be an excrescence resembling a sow-face by the left side of her natural face.

The two-armed Vajravārāhī holds with her right hand, hanging down, a *kartri.* Her raised left hand holds a *kapāla.* She holds a *khaṭvāṅga* with her left elbow.

The goddess stands in the *ālīḍha* posture, trampling under her right foot the emaciated Kālarātri and under her left foot Bhairava. Both Kālarātri and Bhairava are lying on the pericarp of a *viśva-padma.* The back-slab around her is incised with the marks of flames.

At the top of the conical upper part of the back-slab above the head of Vajravārāhī is the figure of the Tathāgata Vairocana seated in the *vajraparyaṅkāsana* on a lotus, displaying the *dharmachakra-mudrā* with his hands.

The attributes *kartri* and *kapāla* are prescribed for her in *Sādhana* 220 where, however, she is required to be in the dancing pose.

B. Nepal

Of the many images of Vajravārāhī found in Nepal, two bronze images and a sketch drawn by a modern Nepalese artist are described in the following pages.

(i)

An image of Vajravārāhī (Pl. 3) made of bronze is preserved in the collection of H.K. Swali.[29] Datable to about 1400, it hails from Nepal.

The fierce-looking one-faced, three-eyed goddess with contracted eye-brows and visible teeth and fang is bejewelled with *nūpuras,* a highly ornate girdle with chains ending in bell-shaped and bud-shaped pendants, bracelets, armlets, a beaded *hāra,* a necklace, a long garland with human heads, *kuṇḍalas* and a *mukuṭa.* From the right side of her head projects the head of a *vārāhī.*

The two-armed goddess holds in her raised right hand a *vajra* and in the left, near her heart, a *kapāla.* She is dancing in the *ardhaparyaṅka* attitude with right leg folded, and the left resting on a disc placed over the figure of a man, lying on the pericarp of a *viśva-padma* with hands kept behind his head.

The image is in accordance with *Sādhana* 218. In the image, however, she is dancing on the *ajñānapuruṣa.* According to the *sādhana* she is standing in the *ālīḍha* posture on the *ajñānapuruṣa.*

(ii)

A bronze image of Vajravārāhī (Pl. 4) from Nepal is preserved in the Baroda Museum (No. Af. 5.90).[30] The image is 8.5 inches high and 6 inches wide and can be ascribed to the fifteenth century.

Vajravārāhī does not wear any garment. She is fierce looking with three round eyes, open mouth and dishevelled hair. She has an excrescence near her right ear which resembles the face of a sow.

She is adorned with headed *nūpuras,* an ornate girdle with three chains ending in pendants, beaded *valayas,* armlets (plain below, beaded above), a necklace with a pendant, a *hāra* of *channavīra* type with a circular floral design from which issue three long chains ending in pendants, a long garland made of beads reaching up to the knees, *kuṇḍalas,* a *mukuṭa* on the head having five crests, each set with a human skull and arranged in the shape of a flame of fire. Above and below the five skulls are green jewels.

The raised right hand of the two-armed goddess holds a *kartri* surmounted by a *vajra* and the left hand near the chest carries a *kapāla* full of flesh.

The goddess dances with her right leg folded and the left slightly bent. Below the left leg is a corpse, lying face down on the oblong seat over the pedestal. His head and face are covered with hair. On the fringe of the pedestal (4.5 inches X 2.5 inches) nineteen lotuses are engraved, nine in front and five on each side. The semi-circular aureole behind the goddess is decorated with flames.

(iii)

A sketch of Vajravārāhī with the label *Vajravārāhī* drawn by a Nepalese artist (Pl. 5) has been reproduced by Benoytosh Bhattacharyya.[31]

Bejewelled with anklets, bangles, *hāras,* a long garland of human heads, armlets, ear-rings, a short crown, the three-eyed Vajravārāhī with an excrescence near the right ear in the form of the head of a sow holds a *kartri* with her raised right arm and a *kapāla* in the left resting against the chest. A trident decorated with human heads passes through her bent left forearm.

She dances in the *ardhaparyaṅka* with right leg folded and the left resting on a man lying on his chest on the pericarp of a single-petalled lotus.

C. Tibet

Images of Vajravārāhī are profuse in number in Tibet.

(i)

An image of Vajravārāhī is preserved in the William B. Whitney Tibetan Lamaist Collection (Pl. 6) at the American Museum of Natural History, New York.[32] This bronze image is 8 inches high.

The three-eyed goddess with visible teeth is bejewelled with anklets of beaded strings, a girdle, bangles, a necklace of beaded strings, a *hāra,* a long garland with skulls, *kuṇḍalas* and a *mukuṭa.* Near her right ear is the head of a *vārāhī.*

The two-armed goddess holds in the raised right hand a *kartri* and in the left, placed near the chest, a *kapāla.* Resting against her left shoulder is a long *khaṭvāṅga.* She dances in the *ardhaparyaṅka* posture.

This image follows *Sādhana* 220. However, the sow-face and *khaṭvāṅga* are not mentioned in this *sādhana.*

(ii)

An image of Vajravārāhī (Pl. 7) is in the collection of the Newark Museum, Newark.[33] The image (32.6 cm. high) made of silver (gilt with gold) hails from Central Regions, Tibet. It is datable to the sixteenth century.

The single-faced goddess with three eyes, open mouth showing teeth looks somewhat angry. She is adorned with anklets, an ornamented girdle with loops, bangles, armlets, a necklace, a *hāra* of the *channavīra* type with hanging pendants, ear-ornaments and a *mukuṭa* decorated with skulls. Most of her ornaments are inset with semi-precious stones. She is dancing in the *ardha-paryaṅka.* Both the emblems in the hands of the two-armed goddess are now missing.

Above her right ear on the right side of her head is the projecting sow-head which proves her identity as Vajravārāhī.

D. Central Asia

A tangka from Khara Khoto, Central Asia, dated before AD 1227 has a representation of Vajravārāhī (Pl. 8). The *tangka* (110.5 cm. X 68.5 cm.) is now in the Museum Hermitage, Leningrad.[34]

Vajravārāhī is of red complexion, single-faced and three-eyed. With bulging eyed, mouth slightly open showing teeth including the canine ones, the goddess looks fierce.

She is draped in a long folded, white *uttarīya* decorated with floral motifs, which hangs on her both sides. She is profusely adorned with anklets, an ornate girdle, bracelets, armlets, a *hāra*, a highly elaborated necklace, and *kuṇḍalas*. She wears a long garland strung with the hair of human heads of different colours and a crown decorated with five skulls; on the central skull is a crescent on which is placed a wheel capped by a half-*vajra*. Her dishevelled black hair falls on her back. On either side of her head is a floating ribbon. To the right of her head is the sow-head, now defaced.

The two-armed goddess holds a *vajra-kartri* in her raised right hand; the left, held near the chest, carries a *kapāla*. In the crook of her left arm she bears a white *khaṭvāṅga* crowned by three successive skulls capped by a half-*vajra*. The upper part of the *khaṭvāṅga* is tied by a blue banner.

She is dancing in the *ardhaparyaṅka* with right leg folded and the left resting on a red disc placed on the chest of a male figure, possibly Bhairava, lying on his back on the pericarp of a *viśva-padma*. He is draped in a short cloth, and wearing bangles, a *hāra*, a short *mukuṭa* at the base of her loose black hair rising upwards in the form of an elongated triangle.

The figure of Vajravārāhī is surrounded by an aureole with tongues of flames. Against the background of the aureole are six females who are her companions. The three on her right are red, green and blue, and the three on her left yellow, white and dark blue. All six are single-headed, three-eyed, bejewelled, and have a row of five skulls on the head against the base of the loose hair falling on her back. Each of them is standing in the *pratyālīḍha* posture trampling a two-armed male lying on his back on the pericarp of a single-petalled lotus. The male figure resembles the one under Vajravārāhī's foot. Five of the six figures are four-armed holding the same attributes in their hands; a *kartri* and a *ḍamaru* in the right palm and a *khaṭvāṅga* and a *kapāla* in the left. The sixth figure, the red one, is three-faced and six-armed; she holds in her three right hands a *vajra-kartri*, an *ankuśa*, a *ḍamaru* and in her three left a *khaṭvāṅga*, a *pāśa* and *kapāla*.

The oblong surrounding the aureole has human figures with palms joined, animals eating corpses, severed limbs, trees, bones, skulls and eight *stūpas* which have been identified as cemeteries.[35]

On the four borders of the *tangka* are four rows of figures. The top row has five figures, the central one being twelve-armed Sambara of blue complexion embracing Vajravārāhī with his main pair of hands. Two-armed Vajravārāhī is wearing a *mukuṭa* decorated with skulls at the base of dishevelled hair. In her raised right palms she holds a *kartri* and the left hand is at the back of her consort. The couple is flanked by two figures on either side: the ones on the dexter are red and green and the sinister ones are yellow and blue. All the four are bejewelled, wear long garlands of skulls and a *mukuṭa* of five skulls on their heads. They stand in the *pratyālīḍha*, are single-faced, three-eyed and four armed.

All the four hold in the upper right palm a *ḍamaru*, in the upper left a *khaṭvāṅga*, and in the lower left kept against the chest a *kapāla*. The attribute in the lower right palm of the red figure is a *kartri*: it is defaced on the palms of the other figures.

On the two vertical sides are five figures seated within compartments; the five on the dexter, from the bottom are: a bearded saint; two figures seated on a tiger; a monk seated on a cushion; a male seated with his consort; and a standing monk, holding with his two hands a *khakhara* and a begging bowl. The figures on the sinister from bottom to top are a seated bearded saint; a bejewelled male on a elephant with a man standing behind; a man seated on a red cushion holding two fish in a bowl; a bearded man seated on a red cushion raising his right hand with two fingers pointing towards the direction of the sun; and a monk standing on a cushion.

On the bottom panel are six bejewelled dancing women holding offerings in their hands.

E. China

A figure of Vajravārāhī (Pl. 9) executed in silk embroidery (22.8 cm. X 16.8 cm.) belongs to the collection of Carolyn and Wesley Halpert.[36]

It is of Chinese or Tibeto-Chinese origin and datable to the thirteenth or fourteenth century.

The three-eyed goddess is draped in along *uttarīya* which coming from her back hangs down her knees. She is decked in anklets, a girdle, bangles, armlets, a necklace, ear-studs, a long garland strung with the hair of human heads and a *mukuṭa* decorated with human skulls.

She is two-armed, holding in her raised right hand a *vajra-kartri* and in her left palm resting against her chest a *kapāla*. A *khaṭvāṅga*, the top part of which is tied with a banner and surmounted by three successive skulls capped by a half-*vajra*, passes through the crook of her left arm and hangs down.

She is dancing in the *ardhaparyaṅka* with right leg folded and left bent, resting on the chest of a man who is lying on his back on the pericarp of a lotus. His feet are crossed, his hair is dishevelled, his right hand rests over his head and left rests along his body. Around the figure are rings of flames.

The mildness of the figure, the delicate ring of loose flames, the pastel colouring, and the silk-embroidery technique itself all point to a Chinese origin. In fact, this is a choice example reflective of the interrelationships between Tibet and China during the 13th and 14th centuries.[37]

F. Vajravārāhī in the Embrace of Sambara

(i)

An image of Vajravārāhī (Pl. 10) in the embrace of the two-armed Sambara belongs to the Zimmerman Family Collection.[38] The image, made of brass with silver inlay and remains of gold foil and pigment is 33 cm. high. Originally belonging to the Central Regions, Tibet or Western Tibet, it is datable to the twelfth or thirteenth century.

In this image Sambara who is single-faced, three-eyed, moustached and bearded bears an angry facial expression with visible teeth and fangs. He is draped in an *uttarīya* and bejewelled with anklets, leg-ornaments, bangles, armlets and *kuṇḍalas*. He is wearing a *mukuṭa* of skulls: over the central skull is a *viśvavajra*. On the top of the head within a shrine is the figure of Tathāgata Vairocana showing the *dharmacakra-mudrā* with his two hands.

The two arms of Sambara holding a *vajra* and a *ghaṇṭā* are crossed against the back of Vajravārāhī.

Vajravārāhī is bejewelled with anklets, leg ornaments, a highly ornate girdle with loops and pendants, a *hāra*, a necklace, a garland with human skulls and a short *mukuṭa* with with human skulls at the base of her hair dishevelled and resting on her back. The two-armed goddess holds with her raised right hand a *vajra* and her left encircles the neck of Sambara and holds a *kapāla*. Her left leg is stretched parallel to the leg of her consort and the feet of the couple trample a human figure, presumably Kālarātri. Her right leg is around Sambara's waist. The human figure under Sambara's left leg is probably Bhairava. Both Kālarātri and Bhairava are lying on their back on a pedestal. This image conforms with the description of the goddess and her consort as given in *Sādhana* 255.

(ii)

Vajravārāhī in the embrace of Sambara is depicted in a *thangka* (gouache on cotton) (Pl. 11) from Tibet, probably Tsang. This tangka (61 cm. X 45.8 cm.) datable to the fifteenth to sixteenth century is in the Robert Hatfield Ellsworth Private Collection.[39]

In this very beautiful *thangka* four-faced, twelve-armed Sambara of dark blue complexion embraces Vajravārāhī with his main pair of hands holding a *vajra* an a *ghaṇṭā*. Vajravārāhī who is of red complexion is bejewelled with anklets, a beautiful girdle, bracelets, armlets, *kuṇḍalas* and *mukuṭa*, decorated with skulls. Her black hair falls on her back. She holds with her raised right hand a *vajra-kartri* and her left hand is at the back of Sambara. Her right leg is around Sambara's waist and her left leg and also the parallel right leg of Sambara trample a human figure. Under the foot of the bent left leg of Sambara is another figure. These two figures lying on the pericarp of a *viśva-padma* probably represent Bhairava and Kālarātri. The aureole is bordered with flames.

Above the aureole and on the four corners are human figures, each sitting within a trefoil-arched shrine. Among the figures some represent saints and monks.

G. Vajravārāhī in the Maṇḍala

Raghu Vīra and Lokesh Chandra have illustrated the *maṇḍala* of Yamāri. Yamāri is represented not in anthropomorphic form but in his theriomorphic form.[40] The surrounding gods and goddesses are depicted by their *āvudhas.* Vajravārāhī (Rdo rje phag mo) occupies the *nairrita* corner in the *maṇḍala* surrounding the principal god Yamāri. Her presence is indicated by a *vajra.*

NOTES

1. Alice Getty, *The Gods of Northern Buddhism* (Oxford, 1914), p. 117. Getty, however, has classified Vajravārāhī as a form of Mārīcī. But these two—Mārīcī and Vajravārāhī—are independent goddesses having individual characteristics.
2. *Sādhanamālā*, Part II (Baroda, 1968), edited by Benoytosh Bhattacharyya, pp. 424-3.
3. *Niṣpannayogāvali* (Baroda, 1949), edited by Benoytosh Bhattacharyya.
4. The word *ghoṇa* means nose. M. Monier Williams. *A Sanskrit English Dictionary* (Oxford, 1960), p. 37; The word *ghoṇi* means a pig. Raja Radha Kanta Deva, *Śabdakalpadrumaḥ*, Part Two (Calcutta, 1808), p. 406.
5. *Sādhanamālā* (Baroda, 1968), edited by Benoytosh Bhattacharyya, p. XCI.
6. Ibid., p. CXIII.
7. Ibid., p. 431.
8. This is known from *Sādhanas* 226 and 227 which describe her as *Vairocanakulodhbhavā.* The *Sambaramaṇḍala* of the *Niṣpannayogāvalī* mentions Vajrocana as the *Kuleśa* of Vajravārāhī.
9. *Sādhanamālā,* Vol. II, edited by Benoytosh Bhattacharyya (Baroda, 1968), pp. 424-6.
10. The six auspicious symbols are described in *Sādhana* 250 as

    kaṇṭhikā rūcakaṃ ratnamekhalāṃ bhasmasūt rakam /
    ṣhat vai pāramitā eta mudrārūpena yojitāḥ //

    'The Torque, the (two) Bracelets, a bejewelled girdle, ashes and sacred thread represent the six Pāramitās and are applied in the form of Mudrās', p. CXXXVII.
11. Ibid., pp. 426-31.
12. *Ajñānauruṣa* means ignorance personified. The position of *ajñānauruṣa* under Vajravārāhī's feet implies that she destroys all types of ignorance. This is also suggested by the emblem *kartri* in her palm. The *kartri* is used by her to cut off the ignorance.
13. *Sādhanamālā,* Part II, edited by Benoytosh Bhattacharyya (Baroda, 1968), pp. 432-3.
14. Ibid., p. 433.
15. Ibid., pp. 440-3.

16. Ibid., pp. 438-9
17. Ibid., pp. 437-8.
18. Ibid., p. 488
19. Ibid., pp. 491-2.
20. Ibid., p. 504.
21. *Niṣpannayogāvalī,* edited by Benoytosh Bhattacharyya (Baroda, 1949), p. 26.
22. Ibid., p. 14
23. Ibid., p. 21
24. *Sādhanamālā,* (Baroda, 1968), p. 435.
25. *Niṣpannayogāvalī,* (Baroda, 1949), p. 36.
26. Ramaprasad Chanda, *Exploration in Orissa,* Memoirs of the Archaeological Survey of India, No. 44 (Calcutta, 1930), 22. Chanda has described the image as a 'two-armed goddess (14.75 inches X 8 inches) standing in archer's attitude with *vajra* in her right hand and a cup (upper half of a human skull) held by her left hand'.
27. Ibid., Plate VIII, Fig. 1; R.D. Banerjee, *History of Orissa,* Vol. II (Calcutta, 1931), Illustrations, 63; N.K. Sahu, *Buddhism in Orissa* (Cuttack, 1958), pp. 206 and 207, Fig. 59.
28. The image is the black stone one (No. 10540), noticed in the *Patna Museum Catalogue of Antiquities,* ed., Parmeswari Lal Gupta (Patna, 1965), p. 66, No. 69. There it is described simply as 'Goddess'. According to the Catalogue the height of the image is 1 feet 6.5 inches; S.K. Saraswati, *Tantrayāna Art—An Album* (Calcutta, 1977), pp. LXI-LXIII, Illustration 174. Saraswati has suggested the identification of the image as that of Vajrayoginī.
29. Pratapadiya Pal, *The Arts of Nepal,* Part I (Leiden, 1974), p. 180, Fig. 287.
30. B. Bhattacharyya, 'Three Buddhist Metal Images in the Baroda Museum', *Bulletin of the Baroda State Museum Picture Gallery,* Vol. II, Pt. I (1946), p. 43.
31. Benoytosh Bhattacharyya, *The Indian Buddhist Iconography* (Calcutta, 1924), p. 105, Pl. XXXII (a).
32. Antoinette K. Gordon, *The Iconography of Tibetan Lamaism* (Tokyo, 1959), Illustration, facing p. 80.
33. Marylin M. Rhie and Robert A.F. Thurman, *Wisdom and Compassion The Sacred Art of Tibet* (New York, 1991), p. 298, Illustration 113.
34. Ibid., pp. 258-60, Illustration 93.
35. Ibid., p. 259. In fact *Sādhanas* 226 and 227 say that Vajravārāhī is placed within eight *śmaśānas* (cemeteries). *Sādhanamālā,* Vol. II (Baroda, 1968), pp. 440 and 442.
36. Marylin M. Rhie and Robert A.F. Thurman, op. cit., p. 408, Illustration 170.

37. Ibid.
38. Ibid., p. 215, Illustration 68.
39. Ibid., p. 220, Illustration 70.
40. Raghu Vira and Lokesh Chandra. *A New Tibeto-Mongol Pantheon* (New Delhi, 1967), p. 33, Illustration 15.

Plate 1: A Buddhist Goddess from Chauduar. Ramaprasad Chanda, *Memoir of the Archaeological Survey of India*, No. 44, Pl. VIII, Fig. 1.

Plate 2: S.K. Saraswati, *Tantrayāna Art—An Album* (Calcutta, 1977), Illustration 174.

Plate 3: Pratapaditya Pal, *The Arts of Nepal* (Leiden, 1974), Fig. 287.

Plate 4: Vajravārāhī. B. Bhattacharyya, *Bulletin of the Baroda State Museum and Picture Gallery*, Vol. II, Part I (Baroda, 1946).

Plate 5: Vajravārāhī. Benoytosh Bhattacharyya, *Indian Buddhist Iconography* (Calcutta, 1924), Pl. XXXII(a).

Plate 6: Vajravārāhī. A.K. Gordon, *The Iconography of Tibetan Lamaism* (Vermont and Tokyo, 1959), Illustration, p. 80.

Plate 7: Vajravārāhī. Central Regions, Tibet. Marylin M. Rhie and Robert A.F. Thurman, *Wisdom and Compassion* (New York, 1991), Pl. 113.

Plate 8: Vajravārāhī. Khara Khote, Central Asia, Tangka, gouache on cotton. Marylin M. Rhie and Robert A.F. Thurman, *Wisdom and Compassion* (New York, 1991), Pl. 93.

Plate 9: Vajravārāhī. China, Tibet, Chinese silk embroidery. Marylin M. Rhie and Robert A.F. Thurman, *Wisdom and Compassion* (New York, 1991), Pl. 170.

Plate 10: Paramsukha Chakrasamvara, Central or Western Tibet, twelfth/thirteenth century. Marylin M. Rhie and Robert A.F. Thurman, *Wisdom and Compassion* (New York, 1991), Pl. 68.

Plate 11: Paramasukha Chakrasamvara, Khara Khote, Central Asia, Tangka gouache on cotton. Marylin M. Rhie and Robert A.F. Thurman, *Wisdom and Compassion* (New York, 1991), Pl. 70.

9

History of Tantric Buddhism in Tamilnadu

G.V. SAROJA

The monks of the various sects of Buddhism of Vajrāladinne must have reached Kanchipuram by sea or land routes for spreading Buddhism in Tamilnadu. The patronage of the rulers of this Andhara region of Kanchi and of tradesmen and chieftains was the main cause of Kanchipuram becoming a great stronghold of Buddhism from where the various shades of Buddhism reached every nook and corner of Tamilnadu, Sri Lanka, South-East Asia, and Japan and China too. The monks of Banaras and Amaravati had left for the outskirts of Kanchi and Kaveripumpattinam respectively and built *vihāras*. Tantric Buddhism also reached Kanchi in the same manner.[1]

Dr. Benoytosh Bhattacharyya, while tracing the rise of Tanric Buddhism in his introduction to *Two Vajrayāna Works* declares that the seeds of Tantric Buddhism are found in original Buddhism in the form of *mudrā, mantra, maṇḍala, dhāraṇis, yoga* and *samādhi.* Buddha had to cater to the needs of his followers who craved for happiness and prosperity in this world. This is the first stage of Tantric Buddhism as found in Śāntarakṣita's and Kamalaśīla's works. *Āryamañjuśrīmūlakalpa,* a *Vaipulya Sūtra* belonging to a very early period—the fourth or fifth century—describes *mudrā, maṇḍala, mantra* and deities and presupposes earlier literature on this subject.[2]

Guhyasamājatantra mentions the term Vajrayāna, the five Dhyānī Buddhas and their families. Anaṅgavajra's *Prajñopāyavi-niścayasiddhi* of the seventh-eighth century defines *śūnyatā* as *prajñā* and *karuṇā* as the *upāya.* The merging of these two, *prajñopāya* is the *mahāsukha,* the creative principle of the universe from which innumerable Buddhas, Sambuddhas and the Śrāvakas originate. As stated by Indrabhūti in his *Jñānasiddhi,* a monk can take any food, enjoy any woman and indulge in all kinds of enjoyments which do not obstruct the way of spiritual attainment. As Bhattacharyya states, the introduction of *mahāsukha* is the first and primary cause of degenerating Buddhism.[3]

According to Wayman, the human authors of early Tantras ascribed their authorship to a celestical Buddha such as Vajradhara. He further states that the Buddhist Tantras were standardized in the Tibetan *Kanjur* as the three lower *kriyā, caryā* and *yoga* Tantras and as the higher *anuttarayoga* Tantras. The lower Tantra, the *Mahāvairocanasūtra,* has influenced the Suvarṇadvīpa (Indonesia). The famous Borobudur shrine in Java must have been constructed around the eighth-ninth century AD. The higher *Guhyasamājatantra* was popular in north India from the ninth to the twelfth century.[4]

Ramprasad Mishra points out that Mahāyāna furnished ample scope to its adherents of later days to schematize it into Mantrāyāna(naya) and Paramitāyāna(naya), from which Buddhist Tantra originated and evolved.[5]

HISTORICAL AND ARCHAEOLOGICAL EVIDENCE

Vajrabodhi, a great monk of the Vajrayāna sect, was born in the Malaya kingdom in south India according to Chinese chronicles. At the age of ten, he took his first vow, graduated from both the Nalanda and the Valabhi Universities, received the title 'Tripiṭakācārya' and studied the doctrines of Tantric Buddhism from the south Indian monk Nagābodhi.

When Kanchipuram faced a severe famine Vajrabodhi was requested to pray for rain by king Narasiṃha Pallava II. The prayer was answered. The monk then went to Ceylon from Kanchi and returned. He then left for China to spread Vajrayāna. In AD 720 with his disciple Amoghavajra he reached Ch'ang-an where another Vajrayāna monk Śubhakara lived. Vajrabodhi translated into Chinese 24 Vajrayāna texts and died in AD 741 at the age of 71.

Amoghavajra also translated Vajrayāna texts into Chinese. After his master's death he returned to India via Java and Ceylon for collecting Vajrayāna texts. The disciple was more popular than his master as he attracted high officials with his *siddhis.* In AD 772 he installed many Mañjuśrī images and popularized the Mañjuśrī cult.[6]

Siddha Nāgārjuna also belonged to Kanchi in the seventh century AD. This Tantric monk, according the Tibetan tradition, was born at Kahora which was a part of Kanchi. He became a Buddhist monk at the age of seven in order to avert an impending calamity in his life. He was regarded as one of the 84 *siddhas.*

Identifying Oḍḍiyāna with Kancipuram, Lokesh Chandra asserts that Vajrapāṇi of 'Mangostha in Oḍḍiyāna' mentioned in a Nepalese manuscript refers to the Ekambareśvara temple of Kanchi. Tārā is the presiding deity of Oḍḍiyāna. The *Vajrasekhara Tantra* of the *Yoga Tantra* division alone must have prevailed in Kanchi according to Lokesh Chandra. Vajrabodhi visited Śrī-Vijaya on his way to China and as a result Buddhists from Śrī-Vijaya came to Tamilnadu and stayed in Nagapattinam. Under the patronage of the Cola kings they built two Buddhist shrines in the early years of the eleventh century AD.

Maṇi Cintana, a Tantric master from Kashmir, embarked for China from Mamallapuram port of Kanchi and following the route of Dharmapāla reached Loyang in AD 693. He worked there until 706, constructed a monastery and passed away in AD 712.

Kanchi, Lokesh Chandra asserts, was a centre of Tantric Buddhism where the monks studied *Guhya-Piṭaka* and practised strange rites. Prajñā of Kapiśa learnt the speech of south India, studied *Yoga-Tantra, maṇḍala* and *mudrā* of the five families in more than 3,000 *gāthās.* He studied the Chinese language and embarked for China from a south Indian port.

Pointing out that the Buddhist name of Kanchi is Oḍḍiyāna, the birth place of Tantric Buddhism, Chandra writes that it was a major port of embarkation to China. Pao-ssu-wei (Maṇi Chintana) must have studied for some time in Kanchi to become an adept in the Tantric disciplines. 'He cultivated the wonder of astrology and of the art of *Dhāraṇi* in particular.'[8]

According to Conze, the Vāmācāra-Vajrayāna was founded by a succession of teachers of whom Nāgārjuna II (600-50) was 'one of the first'. It originated in north Bengal and Assam and in the West Oḍḍiyāna (perhaps the region around Peshawar). Conze does not identify Oḍḍiyāna with Kanchi. The Dakṣiṇācārya-Tantra practised by Amogha Vajra and presented in China is also stated to have originated by Nāgārjuna II.[9]

In Kanchi and in Pallur, a village near Kanchi, Dhyānī Buddha images have been located. The Kurkihar bronze images donated by the monks of Kanchi during the ninth to eleventh centuries AD contain inscriptions from which it is possible to know their names.

The names Mañjuśrī, Śukhasukha and Avalokita Siṃha are those of the Vajrayāna deities.

In 753 the Jaina monk Akalaṅka had caused the exodus of Buddhists from Kanchi particularly to Ceylon. The Sravaṇa Belgolā inscription reveals how a Jain monk overcame the Buddhas. It is stated that the Buddhist deity Tārā was overcome together with the Buddhas.[10]

The Kalyani inscriptions describe Nagapattinam as a place of pilgrimage. A Buddhist temple was constructed here during the reign of Pallava Narasiṃhavarman II as requested by the Chinese king for the sake of the Chinese Buddhist tradesmen who came to Nagapattinam. It was known as China Pagoda. Sir Walter Eliot who has seen this tower in AD 1846 has described this China tower before it was demolished by the Jesuit fathers in 1847.[11]

More than 300 bronze images of Avalokiteśvara, Siṃhanāda, Jambhala, Tārā, Vasudhārā, Maitreya and other Vajrayāna deities were found in Nagapattinam belonging to the ninth to seventeenth centuries AD according to Śrīnivasa Desikan. Some of them are displayed in the Madras Museum.[12]

The Pallavanesvaram excavation reveals the connection between Kaveripumpattinam of Tamilnadu and Amaravati and Nagarjunikonda of Andhra. Buddhist monks from Andhra must have left for Kaveripumpattinam in the fourth-fifth century. The bronze Buddha images and the terracotta figurines also reveal the Vihāra's connection with Nagapattinam during the seventh or eighth century.[13]

Potiamalai according to the Buddhist works Gaṇḍavyūha, *Tārāsukkam* and *Maṇimekalai,* is the abode of the Bodhisattva Avalokiteśvara and his consort Tārā. Avalokitesvara and Tārā cult must have been very popular in Tamilnadu. The Terur village of Kanyākumārī district contains a temple called Ilayanāyanār-koil in which a stone image of Avalokiteśvara with Tārā is found. Even in 1919, a group of Buddhist monks from Ceylon is stated to have visited this temple and worshipped the deity.[14]

TANTRIC BUDDHISM IN TAMIL LITERATURE

In the *Tiruvādavūrār Purāṇam,* Vādavūrar (Māṇikka-vācakar) is stated to have refuted the Buddhist concept of the Bodhisattva. In verse 468, it is pointed out that if the form got by the aggregation of the five *skandhas* ceases to exist, it is impossible for the Bodhisattva to take births in different *yonis* in order to be affectionate to other beings.[15] In the Jaina *Nīlakeśi* also this concept has been criticised.

In the Buddhist Tamil work *Maṇimekalai*, the concept of the *Bodhisattva* has been defined as '*poti mūlattu nātanāyōn*' (one who will become a Buddha).[16] The other terms *ṛddhi* (*alavaṟṟa irutti* or innumerable *ṛddhis*) *pāramitā* (innumerable *pāramitās*), *mantras* of the Tantric school are found. Cāttanār must have written *Maṇimekalai* during Conze's third period of Tantric Buddhism that ends in AD 1000. Conze describes the features of the third period in terms of cosmic adjustment as the clue to enlightenment.[17] This period gives importance to age old magic practices. The *cāraṇas* of *Maṇimekalai* are comparable to the *siddhas* of Tantrayāna who are stated to be in harmony with the cosmos, and move around as free agents manipulating the cosmic forces. Cāttanār's Buddhist deities teach the *mantras* for attaining supernatural powers. The *cakkaravāḷakkoṭṭam* is the model of Vajrayāna cosmology with the various *maṇḍalas* of the cosmos. In one place Cāttanār has defined liberation as '*pērinpam*' or *mahāsukha* of the Vajrayāna.

Conze has divided the emergence of Tantrayāna into three periods. The first Mantrayāna began in the fourth century AD, gained momentum after the fifth, introducing many *mantras, mudrās, maṇḍalas* and deities unsystematically. After AD 750 these were systematized in Vajrayāna and Sahajayāna which insisted on meditational practices in order to avoid scholasticism. In the tenth century, Kālacakrayāna with its emphasis on astrology appeared. Absorbing the ideas from the tribes of India, Tantrayāna assigned honoured but subordinate roles to spirits, fairies, fiends, demons, ogres and ghosts. It favoured magical practices of the agricultural population. These trends can be seen in the *Maṇimekalai,* which describes the various roles of the Catukka bhūtam (pūtam), Kantir pāvai, the Buddhist deities Maṇimekala, Cintātevī, Tīvatilakai and Campāpati. Cāttanār would have written *Maṇimekalai* during or after the third phase, around the tenth century. The influence of *Nyāya-praveśa* and Vasubandhu on Cāttanār reinforces this hypothesis.[18]

The goal of Tantra is Buddhahood attainable at the very instant with the help of the Pañcamakāras in the Vāmācara sect. Cāttanār's Buddha or a Bodhisattva is a great pure person devoid of sin. No woman can attain *nirvāṇa* as she has to take male birth and become a chief disciple of Buddha for attaining *nirvāṇa.*[19]

In *Nīlakeśi,* the tenth century work, the Jaina nun pictures how a Buddhist preceptor teaches his disciples the mode of approaching and getting wealth, etc., from a householder, the method of receiving *kañci* (gruel), etc., and condemns the practice of eating meat. Vāmācāra Tantric practices must have been practised by some of the Buddhist monks of Tamilnadu. *Nīlakeśi* condemns the obscene practices of the monks. From the manner in which the lusty monks behave licentiously as described in this Jaina work, we have to conclude that many wicked men being attracted by royal patronage shown to Buddhist monks would have joined the Saṅgha. Even drinking and *maithuna* were common among these Vāmācārins. The Verse 249 mentions the dumb, the helpless lady *upāsaka* (*upācaka pen*), prostitutes, even nuns as some of the victims.

CONCLUSION

During the period from AD 250 to 550 marked as the Kāḷabhra period and known as the 'dark age of Tamil Literature', Buddhism attained its peak in Tamilnadu, particularly in Toṇḍaimaṇḍalam. Great monks of Theravāda and Mahāyāna Buddhism crowded the Vihāras of Kanchi and other parts of Tamilnadu. Between the sixth and eleventh centuries Vajrayāna became popular, and the Pallava and Cola rulers also patronized Buddhism in the seventh and the eleventh centuries respectively. The merchant class which came from Andhra, north India, Ceylon, China and Śrī-Vijaya and settled in Tamilnadu, constructed many shrines for the Mahāyāna and Vajrayāna deities. During the same period, the Buddhists had to face three-pronged opposition of the Śaivites, Vaiṣṇavites and Jains, resulting in an exodus to other countries, or mass conversion to other faiths.

NOTES

1. G.V. Saroja, 'History of Buddhism in Tamil Nadu', mss, pp. 69-72.
2. *Two Vajrayāna Works,* edited by Benoytosh Bhattacharyya (Baroda, 1929), p. x.
3. Ibid., pp. XI-XIX
4. A.K. Narain, ed., *Studies in History of Buddhism* (Delhi, 1980), pp. 359-60.
5. Ramprasad Mishra, *Sahajayāna* (Calcutta, 1991), p. 16.
6. *History of Buddhism in Tamil Nadu,* op. cit., pp. 35-6.

7. Lokesh Chandra, *The Borobudur as a Monument of Esoteric Buddhism* (New Delhi, 1979), pp. 3-4, 73-6.
8. The Tripiṭaka—Translator Pao-ssu-wei, in *The Journal of the Institute of Asian Studies*, Vol. V, No. 2.
9. Edward Conze, *Buddhism* (New York, 1959), pp. 178-9.
10. *Epigraphia Indica*, Vol. III (1894-5, 1979), p. 186. Also in Taylor's *Catalogue*, Vol. III. 424.
11. *Indian Antiquary*, Vol. VII (1878), p. 224.
12. Desikan, *The Bronze Gallery—a Guide*, Govt. Museum, Madras, 1972, p. IX.
13. K.V. Soundararajan, in *Indian Archaeology—A Review* 1973-4, p. 25.
14. Shu Hikosaka, *Buddhism in Tamil Nadu, a New Perspective* (Madras, 1989), pp. 192-4.
15. Kaṭavul Māmuniver, *Tiruvātavurar Purāṇam*, Tiruvavatuturai Atinam, 1877.
16. U. Ve, Swaminatha Iyer, *Maṇimekalai* (Madras, 1951), 29.24-5.
17. Edward Conze, *A Short History of Buddhism* (London), p. 13. *History of Buddhism in Tamil Nadu*, op. cit., mss.
18. Ibid.
19. Ibid.

10

The Tantras
An Excursus into Origins

PRANABANANDA JASH

The emergence of Tantricism in Indian religious history effected a radical change in the outlook and character of not only Buddhism but Hinduism also. The Tantras, whether of the Buddhists or the Śaiva or the Vaiṣṇava or Śākta schools, mainly pertain to the Sādhana, i.e. religious exercises or practices, as contrasted with any abstract philosophy. The Tantrikas have not much to do with systematic metaphysical speculations, since their leading object is to expound practical methods for the realization of the ultimate truth.

The significance of the subject and the time of emergence of this particular method of worship can hardly be exaggerated. It was the age when Tantricism washed off distinctive traits of Buddhism and swept all religious sects of the country into the stream of devotional mysticism; when Buddhism began to recede into the background while Brahmanism reshaped itself into 'Hinduism'. Henceforth, Indian religious thought flowed with a new colouring. There is no denying the fact that Brahmanical sects and subsects became popular and well circulated because of the introduction of the Tantrika method of worship with its ritualistic procedures of semi-magical character that appealed to the common mass.

In fact, it was the beginning of a new age in the field of Indian religious thought which had so long been dominated by the 'bhakti-cult' or *yajñas* of Vedic character. In the opinion of the Tantrika teachers, on the other hand, the four main classes of scriptures, e.g. Veda, Smṛti, Purāṇa and Āgama are designed respectively for the four ages (*yugas*), i.e. *satya, tretā, dvāpara* and *kali*. The special type of scripture that is applicable to the era of *kali* is Āgama or Tantra. It is to be admitted that from the religious point of view the most significant and essential thing about a cult is its mode of worship. The purpose of worship is to elevate man from the level of sensibility to that of divinity by making proper use of his very senses. The salient features of this cult consists in the worship of deities in *yantra* or diagrams symbolically representing them; *mantra* or chanting of some sacred sounds; *mudrā* or various gestures made with fingers and movement of hands in different posture; *nyāsa* or the control of the breath that brings the deity in the body of the worshipper; and *bīja* or the syllables of mystic significance peculiar to each deity. These are the means by which the Sādhaka invokes, and identifies himself with his chosen deity (*iṣṭadevatā*). Tantra, in fact, enunciates a new form of *sādhana* or technique in which we find the *karma* of the Vedas, the *jñana* of the Upaniṣads and the *bhakti* of the Purāṇas and the Great Epic.[2]

In the present age the term 'Tantra' has, of course, been very loosely taken by some scholars to denote the literature of the mystical worship of female deities (Śakti) alone ignoring the fact that the Tantra enunciates particular form of worship and it is not centred on a particular cult. In the Tantrika method we can worship any God of our choice. To many scholars, however, Tantricism is identical with Śaktism—a theory which cannot be accepted. H.P. Sastri points out that Tantra 'really means the worship of Śakti or female energy'.[3] G.N. Kaviraj also holds the same view. According to him 'Tantrika worship is the worship of Śakti'.[4] It is becoming increasingly manifest that the cult of Śakti is related to the cult of the Mother Goddess on the one hand, and to the Śaiva cult, on the other.[5]

Archaeological remains in the sites of the Indus culture have disclosed that the seeds of Śaktism go back to the days of Harappa and Mohenjodaro, about the third millennium BC.[6] Again, the famous steatite seal from Mohenjodaro described by J. Marshall as a 'male god' and 'the prototype of historic Śiva' may equally be regarded as the prototype of the Tantrika Siddhas.[7] The same scholar also suggests that the well known bronze 'dancing girl' from Mahenjodaro might be taken as the prototype of Tantrika Yoginī.[8]

In this connection we may also note that the tradition of the Harappan ring stones associated with the Mother Goddess cult, found continuation in almost similar, but much more decorated, flat stone discs belonging to the early historical periods unearthed from such sites as Taxila, Kosam, Rajghat and Patliputra. One such object of the Maurya-Śuṅga period was discovered by J. Marshall at Hathial near Taxila. Marshall observed that it is three and one-fourth inches in diameter and has a perforated centre. There are four nude female figures alternating with honey-suckle designs engraved in relief around the central hole. The nude figures are the representation of the Mother Goddess.[9]

Before we come to any definite conclusion we should always bear in mind that Tantricism has so much in common with Śaivism and Śaktism that it might eventually be taken as the most ancient living faith in the world except for the elements incorporated in its body in the course of centuries. In this connection we may mention here that the earliest available Tantrika manuscript now preserved in the Asiatic Society, Calcutta, the *Kubjikāmata Tantra,* is written in about the later Gupta characters, showing that it belongs to sixth-seventh century. Another Tantrika text of the eighth century, the *Niśvāsa Saṃhitā,* is included within the catalogue of H.P. Sastri. It is stated in these texts that the Tantras preach a new doctrine of *sādhanā* that was accepted by some of the sects. On the basis of the inscription of Sdok-kak Thom (discovered in the province of Sisophon, Cambodia), P.C. Bagchi suggested the prevalence of Tantrika doctrine in South East Asia in the eighth century. The record 'mentions the introduction of the mystic cult of Devarāja along with some Tantric texts in Kambuja during the reign of king Jayavarman II who came to the throne in the Śaka year 728 (= AD 802)'. The inscription further mentions the four Tantrika texts—*Śiraścheda, Vināśika, Sammoha* and *Nayottara.* This shows that these four Tantrika texts were written in the eighth-ninth centuries and according to P.C. Bagchi 'the four Tantras were of North Indian origin'.[10] The worship of the Mother Goddess and reference to Tantras and to Dakinis may be traced to the Gangadhar inscription of the fifth century.[11] This 'shows how the Śākta cult was gradually tending towards Tantricism in the age of the Guptas'.[12]

As regards the origin of the Tantras scholars have expressed divergent opinions. H.P. Sastri opines that it was of foreign origin. While maintaining that 'Śakti worship' is the *raison d'être* of Tantra, Sastri held that 'Tantra came with the Magi priests of the Scythians'. As an argument he pointed out that wonder is expressed in the *Niśvāsatattva Saṃhitā* at the novel mode of Tantrika initiation.[13] Likewise Bhattacharyya also says that 'The introduction of Śakti worship in religion is so un-Indian that we are constrained to admit it as an external or foreign influence.'[14] Bagchi has aptly pointed out some possible foreign elements in the Tantras, but they are quite late importations and belong to a period when Tantricism had become popular in India and when India's cultural contacts with northern neighbours had become well established.[15] It is true that Tantras contain many un-Indian elements and in some Brahmanical texts (e.g. Śaṅkara's *Brahma-sūtra*, II, 2, 7-8) they are condemned. Yet it is far from the truth to regard the Tantras as a whole or Śakti worship in particular as 'un-Indian' or of foreign origin. The association of the Goddess with Ḍākinīs (mentioned in the Gangadhar inscription) and Śākinīs clearly shows how Central Asiatic influences were gradually creeping into the cult. Bagchi is of the opinion that the Śākinīs refer to the Śakas and the Ḍākinīs to the Ḍāga of Dagistan in Central Asia.[16] S.B. Dasgupta partly endorsed this view. He traced its root in the word *Ḍāka* used in Tibet in the sense of 'a wise man', the particular term being its femine form.[17] As regards foreign influence we may also note that the *Kadimata*, to which many of the Tantras belong, refers to magic, sorcery, etc., of the Himalayan and Trans-Himalayan regions.[18] Sudhakar Chattopadhyaya is also of the opinion that 'there are again practices which are specifically described as coming from Mahācīna'.[19] But J.N. Banerjea is not inclined to accept this view of alien import of the term Ḍākinī on account of this early epigraphic evidence.

> The inscription particularly emphasises the shouting propensity of the Mothers and their attendants, and the word Ḍāka and Ḍākinī may be of purely Indian origin. The suggestion may be supported by the interesting word *ghoṣiṇī* (*ghoṣa* and *ḍāka* mean the same thing) occurring in the *Atharvaveda* to denote the female attendants of the terrific god Rudra.[20]

It is interesting to note that the Tantras make no claim to historicity; instead they claim to be revelations. All the Tantras, Buddhist as well as Brahmanical, ascribe their doctrines and practices to the highest personalities in their religious hierarchy.[21] The Tantras are regarded as scriptural authority par excellence,[22] and are also often classed with the Vedas.[23] The Purāṇas recognize the Tantras as authorities on religious affairs.[24] In spite of all this, the developed Tantrika religion as it was prevalent during the early mediaeval period is not a very old religious system even if its seeds may be traced back to the remotest period of Indian civilization.

The Tantras as we have already mentioned deal with the worship of not only female deities but also with various male deities. Besides the Buddhists, we have, in fact, the Tantras of various Hindu cults, the Śaivas, the Vaiṣṇavas, the Sauras, the Gāṇapatyas, etc.[25] Of course, the Śaivas and the Śāktas were more affected by Tantrika ideas than the others. The Śakti cult, as we have mentioned earlier, almost became a synonym for Tantrika rites, often of a degrading character. Debiprasad Chattopadhyaya wrongly treats the Tantras under the impression that they are concerned only with Śākta doctrines. According to him the triangles in the *yantras* represent the *yoni* (female organ) and the *sādhaka* should always think that he has been transformed into a woman while performing his *pūjā*, and the *yoni* symbol in the diagram help him in his meditation.[26] But there is nothing of the fertility-cult or sex worship in the *yantra* as suggested by Chattopadhyay. To strengthen our contention we may quote the opinion of N.K. Brahma in the following:

> The Tantrika worshipper identifies himself in meditation with the Deity he worships and places before himself the fully blossomed condition represented by the Deity as the ideal to be realised. The Paurāṇika worshipper, on the other hand, can never think of the identity between himself and his Deity, and always bears in mind the immense difference between the infinitude of God and the finiteness of man. Here we observe that the Tantra accepts the Absolute Monism of the Upaniṣads and regards the identity between the Jiva and Śiva, the individual and the Absolute, as the Supreme ideal, although this ideal is to be realised through *upāsanā*. . . . The synthesis between the Upaniṣads and the Purāṇas, which the Tantra sought to bring about by accepting the philosophy of the former and the practical method of the latter, eminently suited the requirements of the people for whom it was intended. While recognising the difference between the individual and the Absolute, the worshipper and the worshipped, the difference which common people could in no way forget and which was emphasized by the Bhakti cult, the Tantras maintained that the attainment of the *summum bonum* consisted in overcoming that difference by unfolding the latent absoluteness of man.[27]

While dealing with the relationship between the Śaivas and the Tantras, it may be noted that the two sub-sects of the Śaivas, the Kāpālikas and the Kālāmukhas, followed the most repulsive and obnoxious practices associated with wine and women. Their practices probably show the influence of the Tantrika practices of Śaivism. Parts of *pañca-makāra* (i.e. *madya, māṃsa, matsya, mudrā,* and *maithuna*) forms of worship had been accepted by the Kāpālikas. Their practices often resembled the system known as *Vāmācāra* and *Vīrācāra.*[28] Eliot, while making a distinction between Tantricism and Śaktism opined that 'the Tantras are a simplification of religion, but on metaphysical rather than emotional lines'.[29]

The term 'Tantra' means 'that by which knowledge is spread'. According to H.P. Sastri, 'The word *tantra* means algebraic forms *mantras* or formula that would otherwise run to scores of syllables.'[30] The word 'Tantra' has been sought to be derived in the *Kāśika-vṛtti* from the root 'tan', to spread with the suffix '*ṣtran*' added. Some philosophical commentators have traced it to the root '*tatri*', or '*tantri*', i.e. to explain. The grammarians derive the word from the root 'tan', meaning 'to extend' or 'propagation'.[31] But S.N. Dasgupta thinks that 'tan' is the original form of '*tantri*' and the meaning 'explaining' is derived by narrowing the sense of spreading.[32] The original connotation of the term is any scientific or systematic discussion on any particular subject. Mention may also be made in this connection that the term is sometimes used for a book, namely, the *Pañca-tantra*, a collection of stories. The *Amarakośa* refers to this term meaning various treatises as 'a class of work teaching magical and mystical formularies'.[33] The *Kāmika Āgama* says that the Tantra is so called because it elucidates the meaning of *tattva* and *mantra*, and liberates man from bondage. The two words *tattva* and *mantra* have a special sense—*tattva* means science of the cosmic principles, and *mantra* the science of the cosmic sound. Tantra, therefore, combines the application of those two sciences (*tattva* and *mantra*) with a view of the attainment of spiritual ascendance. *Tattava* denotes different grades of the universe or universes (*bhuvanas*). *Citta* makes according to these principles of *tattvas*, and it is finally transcended experience goes to the spiritual level. Of the thirty-six *tattvas* the last two, *Śakti-tattva* and *Śiva-tattva*, are beyond the metaphysical region in the context of the universe of universes. As mentioned earlier, *mantra* is the science of the cosmic sound, it is consciousness as power. The science of cosmic sound (*śabda-brahma*) is based on the Brahman as letters of the alphabet forming the *bindu*, *bīja* and *nāda* of the garland of letters (*varṇa-mālā*). In this sense Tantra would mean a manual giving the principles of truth and mystic sounds:

Tena vipulān arthān tantra-mantra-samanvitan/
Trāṇam ca kurute yasmāt tantramityabidhayate/ /[34]

It is interpreted by Īsanaśivagurudeva Miśra as the *Śāstra* that expounds the six categories of Śaivism, e.g. *Paśu, Pāśa, Pati, Śakti, Vicāra* and *Kriyācārya.* He drives the word from the root '*tatri*' to understand:

Sauvaṣvathaurṣaṃ tu padārthakānām/
Vyūt-yadakam yat bhavatiha śāstram/
Tantritidhantiriha dhāraṇārthat //[35]

Thus, Tantra is also understood to mean a religious system or science (*Śāstra*) dealing with the means (*sādhanā*) of attaining success (*siddhi*) in secular or religious efforts. In Tibetan, the term *'royud'* (Tantra) stands for a Tantrika text, 'a ritual book for coercing deities and for other magical ceremonies'.[36] One of the large sections of the *Lahgyur* (Kanjur) which contains numerous Tantrika texts, is known as '*rayud*'. It would seem from the above discussion that the word 'Tantra' connotes several meanings but its technical meaning is a religious system now commonly called 'Tantricism', and the scriptures belonging to this system. N.N. Bhattacharyya thus mentions that 'Tantra came to mean the essentials of any religious system and, subsequently, special doctrines and rituals found only in certain forms of various religious systems. This change in the meaning, significance, and character of the word "Tantra" is quite striking and is likely to reveal many hitherto unnoticed elements that have characterised the social fabric of India through the ages.'[37]

It is thus worth noting that the Tantrika tradition is not the work of a day, it has a long history behind it. Creation, maintenance and dissolution, propitiation of gods and goddesses, religious and spiritual practices, *puraścaraṇa, ṣaṭ-karma, dhyāna, yoga* and similar other practices have been discussed in Tantrika texts like the *Vārāhī Tantra.*

In this connection we may also analyse the account of the *Piṅgalāmata Tantra,* a palm-leaf manuscript of the Nepal Darbar Library, dated Nepal Samvat-294 (= AD 1174). According to this Tantrika text it is called *Āgama* because spiritual knowledge proceeds from it to every direction. It is called *Śāstra* because everything is controlled and protected by it. It is *Jñana* because everything can be known with its help and it is Tantra because everything is always preserved and perpetuated by it.[38]

The term *Āgama* is also explained as that class of Tantra which is addressed to Pārvatī by Śiva, whereas *Nigama* refers to words spoken by Pārvatī to Śiva. The words are supposed to be formed by the initial letters of *āgata, gata* and *mata,* on the one hand, and *nirgata, giriśa* and *mata,* on the other:

Āgatam Śivavaktrebhyo gataśc girijānane/
Mataśca Vāsudevasya tasmādāgamamucyate//

Nirgatam girijāvaktad gataśca giriśaśrutau /
Mataśca Vāsudevasya tasmānnigamamucyate //

In this form of *Sādhanā*, the guru who opens the eyes of the disciple to the true meaning of texts played an important role. He guides him through dark, devious and dangerous practices to the realm of light and anoints him (*abhiṣeka*) as a peer of the spiritual kingdom.[39] Moreover, the language used in the Tantrika texts is sometimes enigmatic and has both an exoteric and esoteric meaning, and without the help of a *guru* there is every possibility of misunderstanding the proper sense of the texts. So, for a novice practitioner *dikṣa* or initiation by a *guru* is indispensable for access to the esoteric or real meaning of a particular word or sentence. An exhaustive information regarding the proper selection of *Guru* is to be noted that while the Vaiṣṇavas, Sauras and Gāṇapatyas can initiate one belonging to their respective sects, the Śāktas and the Śaivas are privileged to initiate all the sects, including their own. The *Dakṣina-ācāra-tantra-rāja* states that Gauḍa, Kerala and Kāśmīra with Kālikā, Tripurā and Tārā as goddesses, respectively, are the homes of the purer (*Dakṣiṇācāra*) sects. The *Bṛhat Gautamīya Tantra* claims that gurus from the west are the best, from the south middling, those from the Gauḍa and Kāmarūpa are inferior, and from Kaliṅga the worst.

The rudimentary idea of the Tantrika philosophy is the doctrine of *Prakṛti* and *Puruṣa* as propounded the Sāṅkhya school of thought.[40] To this school *Puruṣa* is inactive while *Prakṛti* is active, and hence *Prakṛti* is more important than *Puruṣa*. To the Śāktas, Śakti is the eternal dynamic source of all beings. It is perceived that all beings proceed from the womb of a woman who is regarded as the ultimate creative principle in terms of the 'mother', and not the 'father'.

NOTES

1. Charles Eliot, *Hinduism and Buddhism*, Vol. II, p. 281
2. N.K. Brahma, *Philosophy of Hindu Sadhana*, pp. 274ff.
3. H.P. Sastri, *Modern Buddhism*, pp. 10-11.
4. G.N. Kaviraj, *Bhāratīya Saṃskṛti aur Sādhanā*, Part I.
5. W. Durant, *Our Oriental Heritage*, Chs. VII-IX, XXIII
6. J. Marshall, *Mohenjodaro and the Indus Civilization*, Vol. I, pp. 48-58.
7. Ibid., p. 52, plate XII. 17
8. Ibid., pp. 44-5, plate XCIV. 6, 8.
9. *Archaeological Survey of India, Annual Report*, 1927-38, p. 66.

10. P.C. Bagchi, *Studies in the Tantras*, Calcutta University, p. 15.
11. *Corpus Inscriptionum Indicarum*, Vol. III., p. 44.
12. Sudhakar Chattopadhyaya, *Evolution of Theistic Section in Ancient India*, p. 160
13. B. Bhattacharyya, *An Introduction to Buddhist Esoterism*, p. 43.
14. *Indian Historical Quarterly*, 'Foreign Elements in the Tantra', Vol. VII.
15. P.C. Bagchi, op. cit., p. 51.
16. S.B. Dasgupta, *Bhātater Śakti Sādhanā O Śākta Sāhitya*, ...
17. J.N. Banerjea, *Purāṇic and Tantric Religion*, p. 128.
18. Agehanada Bharati, *The Tantric Tradition*, pp. 70-1.
19. Sudhakar Chattopadhyaya, *Reflections on the Tantras*, p. 9.
20. J.N. Banerjea, op. cit., p. 128.
21. *Guhyasamāja Tantra*, GOS, No. 53, Ch. I.
22. B. Bhattacharyya, op. cit., p. 70.
23. Kulluka Bhatta on *Manu* -II. 1.
24. R.C. Hazra, *Purānic Records on Hindu Rites and Customs*, Part II, Ch. V. pp. 260ff.
25. Woodroffe, *Shakti and Shakta*, p. 55.
26. Debiprasad Chattopadhyaya, *Lokāyata*, pp. 300ff.
27. N.K. Brahma, op. cit., pp. 278-9.
28. Pranabananda Jash, *History of Śaivism*, p. 64.
29. Sir Charles Eliot, op. cit., Vol. II, p. 121.
30. H.P. Sastri, *Notices of Sanskrit Manuscripts*, I, Preface iv.
31. V.S. Apte, *Sanskrit English Dictionary*, p. 229.
32. S.N. Dasgupta, *Philosophical Essays*, pp. 151ff.
33. Monier Williams, *Sanskrit English Dictionary*, p. 436.
34. *Cultural Heritage of India*, Vol. IV, p. 221: Woodroffe, op. cit., pp. 18-19.
35. *Īśānaśivagurudeva Paddhati*, Trivandrum Sanskrit Series, Part III, p. 28.
36. S.C. Das, *Tibetan English Dictionary*, p. 318.
37. N. N. Bhattacharyya, *History of the Tantric Religion* (Delhi, 1982), p. 2.
38. P.C. Bagchi, op. cit., p. 106.
39. The *Tantrasāra* (I. 49-52) which tries to bring the Tantrika tradition and doctrine into the orthodox line informs us with some interesting details regarding *dīkṣā* or initiation and also about the merits and demerits of the śiṣya (I. 26-33).
40. Latika Chattopadhyaya, *Self in Sāṃkhya Philosophy* (Calcutta, 1982), pp. 98ff.

11

A New Dimension to the Study of the Buddhist Tantras

VRAJ VALLABH DVIVEDI

The writing of history, especially in regard to determining the chronology of religious texts, depends on the foundation of solid proof; with the appearance of new evidence older formulations become invalid. Therefore, in order to settle the sequence of time in relation to the Buddhist and allied Tantras and to revaluate the established conclusions, simultaneously we have to pursue the same course as is ordained by the divine maxim *parikṣya bhikṣavao grāhyam.*

Here I shall assess the interpretations of a few of our scholars who have contributed and are contributing to this field of study. The approach to this case should be what the great poet Kālidāsa in his *Raghuvaṃśā* had laid down—*maṇau vajrasamutkīrṇe sūtrasyevāsti me gatiḥ.* Here, while evaluating the contents, we would like to follow the directives as given by the most revered Padmavibhuṣana Mahāmahopādhyāya Gopinath Kaviraj and in determining chronology, the method of the renowned Chintaharan Chakravarti. Long ago the way was paved by the Tibetan historical Lāmā Tāranātha whose viewpoint was considered to be fundamental by Chakravarti.

Before coming to the subject matter of this article we like to remember with respect the services rendered by three great savants. They are Haraprasad Sastri, Benoytosh Bhattacharyya and Prabodh Chandra Bagchi who have made remarkable contributions respectively to the study on the Buddhist Siddhas and their Apabhraṃśa language, Buddhist Tantras, and the interrelation of the Kaulatantras and the Tantras mentioned in the Kambuja inscriptions.

Today not only in the West, but in India as well, separate and distinctive studies on Āgama Tantraśāstra are being carried out. Scholars writing on Tantra here are mostly interested in attempting to assemble those branches (of Tantric literature) in which the practice of *pañcamakāra* (ritual-elements containing *madya* or wine, *māṃsa* or meat, *matsya* or the fish, *mudrā* or cereals and *maithuna* or sexual intercourse, collectively known as the five Ms) have been clearly enunciated. Taking this terminology (equating Tantra with *pañcamakāra*) for granted, they could not resist the temptation to introduce in their own works only those branches of this literature pertaining to such elements, ascribing them even to texts in which such elements are not present. Attempts have also been made to establish this Śāstra as of late origin and to insert a question mark on the difference between Āgama and Nigama. This line of approach is not desirable as argued in *Āgam āur Tantraśāstra ko Kavirāj jī ki Den.* There is no need to repeat the arguments here. It is a matter of satisfaction that some recent works or yantra have left out much of the said approach.[1]

The greatest problem, however, lies in the determination of the time of the introduction of the Buddhist Tantra. On the basis of the term *āśraya-parāvṛtti* as found in the *Mahāyānasūtralaṅkāra* (p. 44) of the great yogācara (*vijñānavāda*) teacher Asaṅga, the introduction of the *Guhyasamājatantra* has been settled around the fourth century AD and that of the *Āryamañjuśrīmūlakalpa* still earlier. It is apparent that this date had been fixed on the basis of an incorrect interpreta-tion of such terms as *maithuna-parāvṛtti. Parāvṛtti* means the same as is denoted by the word *pratyāhāra* used in the *Yogaśāstra* and not *viparītarati* (sexual intercourse in the reverse order). Likewise *Bhūtatantra* and *Garuḍatantra* are mentioned in the *Āryamañjuśrimulakalpa*. From the five faces of Śiva emerged one after another *Garuḍa, Dakṣiṇa (Bhairava), Bhūta, Vāma* and *Siddhānta* (Śaiva) Tantras. How can a text which quotes such Tantras be so old? That is why now-a-days no one is ready to accept the date of this Tantra prior to the sixth century.

It should be mentioned that some Japanese scholars have dated *Guhyasamājatantra* to the sixth century. N.N. Bhattacharyya accepts this date of *Guhyasamāja.* On the basis of some descriptions, the date of *Aryamañjuśrīmūlakalpa* had been lowered to the eighth century. It had been established on evidences that the original founder of the Kaulatantras was Matsyendranātha, and according to Kanti Chandra Pande[3] he flourished around the fifth-sixth centuries. The existence of the Kaula materials in the *Guhyasamājatantra* proves that its appearance took place after Matsyendranātha. According to the

Buddhist tradition among the 84 Siddhas the name of Matsyendra or Mīnanātha comes first and his time may be assigned to that period (fifth-sixth century). Prior to this date the introduction of any Tantra with Kaula materials cannot be accepted.

In *Kāmikāgama, Somasiddhānta, Svacchandatantra* and other works five streams of knowledge have been enunciated, which are Laukika, Vaidika, Ādhyātmika, Atimārgika and Māntrika, each of which is again subdivided into five branches. No complete account exists, but in the *Siddhāntaprakāśikā* of Sarvātmasambhū,[4] the Pāśupatas, Mahāvratas (Kālāmukhas) and Kāpālikas are included directly in the Atimārgika division, while the Kaulas and Śāktas are mentioned indirectly. The Mattamayūras of the Āmardaka Maṭha are not included. It is held that the introduction of the dualistic interpretation of the Śaivāgamas started with the Āmardaka Maṭha. It is possible that in a later period it was influenced by the Kaula doctrine.

Abhinavagupta has accepted the difference between the Pāśupata Śāstras introduced by Śrīkaṇṭha and Lakulīśa. This is not recognised by modern scholars. They do not recognise 28 Yogācāryas from Śveta to Lakulīśa. They hold that the emergence of the Pāśupata doctrine should be traced from Lakulīśa. We have dealt with this view eleswhere.[5] The very name Lakulīśa-Pāśupata clearly indicates its difference with the Pāśupata doctrine introduced by Śrīkaṇṭha.

Abhinavagupta holds that Lakulīśa and others were responsible for the introduction of the symbolic worship of the physical self (*kāyapūjā*) on the basis of the theory that the *brahmāṇḍa* (universe) is in *piṇḍa* (lump), i.e. the macrocosm inheres in the microcosm. Mausula and other disciples of Lakulīśa are not only mentioned in the *Svacchandatantra* but their views are correlated with those of Vaimala, Kāruka and others. The meditation of Viśvarūpa who is described in the *Netratantra* (XIII. 10) as an Ācārya of the Pāśupata doctrine and the father of Lakulīśa appears to be reflected in the *urdhvameḍha* posture of the statuette from Mohenjodaro. On the proposition of Lakulīśa *sarvadevaḥ kāyaḥ* (body is the manifestation of all gods, *Tantra* XV. 604) were founded the Kaula and Nātha doctrines with which the Sekayoga and Haṭhagoya of the Buddhist Tantras may be associated. But it should be made clear in this connection that there is difference of a century between the age of Matsyendra and that of Gorakṣa.

In the Nārāyaṇīya section of the *Mahābhārata* Śrīkaṇṭha has been regarded as the founder of the Pāśupata doctrine. There is a tradition of various streams in Pāśupatism. In the *Maitrāyaṇī Saṃhitā* and the *Taittirīya Āraṇyaka* five types of *mantras* have been ascribed to the five *mantra*-bodies of Śiva which are Tatpuruṣa, Aghora, Sadyojāta, Vāmadeva and Īśāna. Puṇḍarīka, author of the Vimalaprabhā[6] which is the commentary on the *Kālacakratantra*, has equated the five Buddhas with the five *mantra*-bodies of Śiva. This current or stream cannot be associated with the Atimārga of the Pāśupata doctrine. But it can be associated with what has been told above with regard to the nature of the Lakulīśa-Pāśupata system. Enumeration of the Śrauta Pāśupata doctrine is to be found in the Purāṇas, especially in the Vāyavīyasaṃhitā of the *Śiva Purāṇa* and in the Sūtasaṃhitā of the *Skanda Purāṇa*. Its philosophical background may be traced to the *Śvetāśvatara Upaniṣad*. According to the Śaṅkara school this tradition follows the Samaya doctrine. That which has been criticized in the *Brahmasūtra* and the *Kūrma Purāṇa* may be the Lakulīśa-Pāśupata system. In modern terminology we may describe this two-streamed Śāstra as Dakṣiṇa-mārga (right-handed way) and Vāma-mārga (left-handed way).

Our purpose in writing all this is to show that there is no need to imagine an *āstika-nāstika* difference in the Tantras, like the substitution of the word *kṛṣṭi* for *samskṛti* which is ordinarily done. The word *saṃskṛti* in its modern sense is applied in the *Mādhyandina Saṃhitā* (VII.14) of the *Śukla Yajurveda* in which occurs *yatra viśvam bhavatyekanīḍam* (XXXII. 8), the phrase adopted as a principle by the Viśvabhāratī. Divisions such as Atimārgika, Māntrika, etc., may pertain to all forms of Tantra.

The Buddhsit Tantra has been subjected to a threefold division, Vajrayāna, Kālacakrayāna and Sahajayāna, but we ought to recall that in the Kaulatantra and also in the Kashmir Śaiva Tantra which is influenced by the former, this threefold category may be discerned. In different *āhnikas* of Abhinavagupta's *Tantrāloka*, there are descriptions of different systems such as Kālodaya, Cakrodaya and Kaulatantra, in which materials of the above-mentioned division of the Buddhsit Tantra are found in great detail. The *āntaravarivasyā* (spiritual worship) of all Tantras reveals an easy (*sahaja*) condition leading to two kinds of judgements, that there is no need of external worship and that whether you perform external rituals or not, it depends on your own will; but in *sahaja* form what is done by you, you are to think whether it has made your mind pure or not. Worship by uttering of name or oblations to fire, etc., may be possible from external sources and their mental conceptions are also possible.

Buddhsit Tantras are divided into *kriyā, caryā, yoga* and *anuttara.* The Śaiva and Vaiṣṇava Āgamas are likewise divided into *vidyā, kriyā, yoga* and *caryā.* The specific contents of every division have been clearly demonstrated. Their characteristics are to be found in Sāyana-Mādhava's *Sarvadarśanasaṃgraha,* Sarvātmasambhū's *Siddhānta-prakāśikā* and other texts. However, we do not come across such clear terminologies in the Buddhist Tantras. We have dealt with the issue in our *vihagāvalokana* (preface) to the '*Sampādan ke Siddānt our Upādān*' (*Dhīḥ,* 11th *aṅka,* p. 159). In other different *aṅkas* of *Dhīḥ,* in the five articles associated with Buddhsit Tantra published in *Bhāratīya Tantraśāstra* and in the critical deliberations, the extent of this fourfold division has been discussed.

From all these it appears that no universally accepted terminologies of this fourfold Tantra have been prepared. In the Pañcaratra Vaiṣṇava Āgamas various derivative interpretations of the term Pāñcarātra have been found, but they do not make it clear in which sense the term was originally introduced. Here also is the same case. In one place *hāsya, darśana, panyāpti* and such other acts are added to the fourfold Tantra, which should, however, be basically related only to the Anuttara Tantra. Since there was a long time-gap between the introduction of the original *śāstra* and its subsequent development, various derivative interpretations of the term Pāñcarātra came into existence in course of time. In the same way at a later period, it appears that the original significance of the terms *caryā, kriyā,* etc., sank into oblivion in Tibet. This problem can be solved only when the collected Tantras of a particular division are critically analysed for determining their extent and well-articulated interpretations of their terminologies are supplied. Now it appears that like Śaiva and Vaiṣṇava Tantras, here also all the aspects of kriyā, caryā, yoga and Anuttara Tantras have been apprehended.

In the Anuttara Tantra three sub-divisions have been made which are known as *pitṛ* (father), *mātṛ* (mother) and *advaya* (non-dual). From the Yoginī Kaula and Siddha Kaula divisions located in the *Mṛgendrāgama* (*Caryā* I. 37-9) and Kashmir Pratyabhijñā philosophy we can equate them. It seems to us that the nature of Buddhist Anuttara Tantra and that of the Kaula Tantra are same. We may compare the Kriyā, Caryā and Yoga Tantras with the Vaiṣṇava, Śaiva and Śākta Tantras following the *samaya* doctrine. We can also associate internal and external worship with the Kuṇḍalinī and Caṇḍālī Yoga, but not with Seka and Haṭhayoga.

A fourth type of worship has been described in the Kaula Tantra and Buddhist Anuttara Tantra. It pertains to *Kāya* worship. We have already given a short account of it. According to this approach, when we may invoke and worship the deity in image, *maṇḍala, paṭa* and *cakra* (*yantra*), etc., why should we not worship the self as god which is in the conscious human body? This worship of the Kāpālikas is accomplished by the materials ejected from the nine doors of the human body, while in the Kaula and Anuttara Tantra it is done by twleve-*ratnas,* five-*ratnas,* five-*pradīpas,* five-*makāras* and other materials. The whole universe is in the human body; all gods reside here; liberation may be attained in a single span of life; the aspirant should follow *unmatta-vrata*—such views are found among the followers of the Lakulīśa-Pāśupata doctrine, the Nātha sect, the Avadhuta Siddhas as also by the Śaivācāryas. In this connection, it should be stated that *Kālottara* and *Nisvāsasaṃhitā* of the Śaivāgama find mention in the *Guhyasiddhi* (VIII.12).

The methods of the Kuṇḍalinī and Caṇḍālī Yoga are described in all Tantras. Notwithstanding differences in number and name in the fourfold or sixfold *cakras,*[8] the ninefold, twelvefold or sixteenfold containers and the like, the methods remain the same. You can easily compare the methods described in the *Vasantatilaka* (X. 30-7) with those found in the *Nityaṣadaśikārṇava* (IV. 12-16). Notwithstanding terminological differences in regard to the materialization of the methods, even differences in the designations of the ultimate objectives to be achieved through such methods, we do not find any difference insofar as the methods themselves are concerned. Besides, in relation to the number and names of nerves[9] and winds,[10] and other allied features, a kind of uniformity may be observed.

The solution of the *vajradeha*[11] by means of Caṇḍālīyoga may be deemed a special characteristic of the Buddhist Tantra. Among other general characteristics of Buddhist Tantra we may refer to the thrirty-seven *bodhipakṣīya dharma,* fivefold knowledge like *ānanda,* etc., fourfold moments, fourfold bliss, fourfold *yoga,* fourforld *mudrās,* fourfold body, etc. These are found in our Mahāyāna texts. The philosopical interpretation regarding the nature of one's personal deity (*iṣṭadevatā*) is found in the tradition of each Tantra. In view of all these we are inclined to say that the development of Tantric ritual and philosophy worked out simultaneously in all forms of religion, doctrine and sect reflecting a praiseworthy attempt to bring uniformity and harmony in relation to each other, the differences and conflicts being mitigated and compromise settled. In this connection, we may refer to the conception of *caturbrahmavihāra*. Besides Pali texts its exposition is to be found in the Pātañjala *Yoga-sūtra* (I.33) and Jain *Tattvārthasūtra* (VII.11). This process is active in the field of thought, though its justification in the field of Indian philosophy, especially in that of Tantric philosophy, has not as yet been sought through this viewpoint.

The performance of sixfold yoga[12] is a basic characteristic of Buddhist Tantra. With it the Siddhis[13] have been distributed into the Buddhist and non-Buddhist divisions. By fancying of Āstika-Nāstika[14] division, studies are made of the foreign influence of the Nāstika Tantra. We have written much on the insubstantiality of this approach. The ascertainment of *saḍaṅga-yoga* has been made in the Śaiva, Vaiṣṇava and Śākta Tantras as well as in the Upaniṣads, Purāṇas, Gītābhāṣya, etc. The *yama* (abstinence) and *niyama* (observances) of Pātañjala yoga reveal the separate states of *samaya* of *saṃvara* of the Tantra which the disciple receives from his teacher after initiation, and *āsana* (bodily posture) is the basic ingredient of Tantric worship. By correlating *anusmṛti* of the Buddhist Tantra, the same of the Śaiva Tantra, the *japa* of the Vaiṣṇava and Pāśupata doctrine and *tarka* of Kashmir Śaivism with the remaining five *yogāṅgas* the six forms of *yoga* may be settled. Variations may be observed in regard to certain features, but the basic structure is everywhere the same. Elsewhere[15] we have reviewed P.V. Kane's approach to the sixfold *yoga*.

Eight kinds of *siddhis* (attainments) such as *khadga, añjana* and *pādalepa*, have been described in the Buddhist Tantras. These are also contained in the *Vasantatilaka* (IV.9.10-38). The commentator (p. 74) has clearly defined all these. These may be regarded as the Buddhist *siddhis*. In the list of non-Buddhist *siddhis, animā*, etc., have been incorprorated. But we find that these are described in ancient Śākta Tantras like *Nityaṣodaśikārṇava* and comparatively late Tantras such as the *Śaktisaṅgama*. Siddhis such as *animā* are also described in the Buddhist Tantras. The commentator on the *Vasantatilaka* (p. 74) has divided *siddhis* into *laukika* (mundane) and *lokottara* (supramundane). Accordingly, we may place such attainments as *khaḍga, añjana*, etc., in the supramental group. At least we may say that in all branches of the Tantraśāstra the mundane attainments have received prominence while in all the branches of the *yoga* śāstra the supramundane *siddhis* have been emphasized.

In this connection the influence of the Buddhist on the non-Buddhist Tantra has been much emphasized. In the Sanskrit *upodghāta* (pp. 20-1) of the fourth part of the *Śaktisaṅgamatantra* we have dealt with the early and late divisions of the Tantra. Tantras existing prior to Abhinavagupta will be collated in the ancient division while those which appeared after him will be in the younger division. The influence of the Buddhist Tantra may be discerned on those of the younger group but not those which belong to the older group. Instead here we find the reverse phenomenon. We have already had the occasion to refer to *Kālottara* and *Niśvāsasaṃhitā* mentioned in the *Guhyasiddhi* (VIII.12). It is also to be remembered that like the *Prajñā-pāramitā*, in the store of verses at least 13 recensions of *Kālottarāgama* may be found. We are strongly of the opinion that the study of Hīnayāna should be made in terms of the Vedic literature and *Mahābhārata*, that of Mahāyāna in terms of the Āgamas and Puraṇic literature and that of Vajrayāna in terms of Kaulatantra.

We have dealt with the five divisions comprising Laukika, Vaidika, etc., of the Tantraśāstra, especially as found in the texts of the Śaivāgama. It is better to avail ourselves of the opportunity to divide on the basis of the text rather than insisting on artificial and imaginary divisions like Āstika-Nāstika and so forth. Accordingly, we can include the Tantras of Kaula nature into the Atimārgika division.[16] Working on the nature of the Atimārgika Tantras we have found that there is no need to imagine external influence. The 14 and 15 canonical *vidyāsthānas* are respectively dealt with in the commentary on the *Vasantatilaka*[17] under the categories *parayūthya* and *svayūthya*. In the introduction of the *Siddhānta-prakāśikā* we have made a comparative survey of all these.

Special account of the *mātṛkā, mālinī* and *bhūtalipi* as well as *mantra* and *mudrā* may be found in the *upodghāta* of the *Nityaṣodaśikārṇava* (pp. 62-78). The alphabetical (vowels and consonants) division of the *mātṛkās* are made in the Buddhist Tantras in the forms of Āli and Kāli. In other places these are called *bīja* and *yoni*. The division of *mantra* into *hṛdaya, upahṛdaya*, etc., is a characteristic of the Buddhist Tantras. In other Tantras which are of later origin these have also been incorporated. The term *'mudrā'* has been used in the Tantra-śāstra and Yogaśāstra in numerous senses.[18] The determination of fourfold *mudrā* is a unique characteristic of the Buddhist Tantra. The

Caturmudrā incorporated in the *Advayavajrasaṃgraha* really belongs not to Advayavajra but to Nāgārjuna. In this text details of the four *mudrās* are to be found.

A short account of the Pīṭhas, Upapīṭhas, etc., are to be found in the *Upodghāta* (pp. 78-83) of the *Nityaṣodaśikārṇava.* Detailed account of the Buddhist Pīṭhas, Upapīṭhas, etc., is provided in the articles under the title *Bauddha Tantroṅ meṅ Pīṭhapīṭhādi ka Vivecan* published in *Dhih,* vols. 1, 3, 10-11 and 21. The correlation of the external Pīṭhas with internal Pīṭhas is met with in the Kaula as well as in the Buddhist Tantras. In the Buddhist Tantras along with four Pīṭhas[19] accounts of the 24 and 32 Pīṭhas are especially found. Apart from the *Hevajratantra,* the 24 Pīṭhas[20] are found in *Cakrasaṃvara* and other Buddhist Tantras. In the Śākta Tantras[21] 51, in Rāghavabhaṭṭa's commentary on the *Śaradātilaka* 64 (I.85) and the Purāṇas[22] 108 Pīṭhas, their names and identifications, are found.

Here, evidence is put forward to supplement that the determination of the said topics has been made in all Āgama-Nigamas. In the beginning of this article, the reference of the terms 'Āgama' and 'Nigama' has some purpose. Detailed discussion of the derivative significance of these two terms on the basis of Abhinavagupta's interpretation is to be found in my Sanskrit article *Purāṇānāṃ Nūnamāgamānuvartitvam* (pp. 107-8) published in the second series of the collection of my Sanskrit articles entitled *Nigamāgamīyaṃ Saṃskrtidarśanam.* Abhinavagupta says that even in the statements of Bhagavān Buddha and Kapila Muni there should be a distinction in the Āgamas. According to this interpretation the Nigamas of the literature dealing with *traivarṇika* (pertaining to three *varṇas*) subjects and the Āgamas of the entire Indian literature dealing with subjects pertaining to all the *varṇas* may be mutually correlated.

In two verses of the *Vārāhītantra* it is said that the *śāstra* taught by Śiva is Āgama and that taught by Devī is Nigama. I have reviewed this statement also in the said article (p. 108). Bhagavatī or Devī is regarded as the propounder of the *śāstra* of the Kashmir Śākta Krama philosophy, but such *śāstras* are placed in the Āgama division. In the *Kulacuḍāmaṇi* published at Calcutta the term Nigama has been suffixed, but we should remember what Kṣemarāja, the pupil of Abhinavagupta, has quoted from the *Kulacuḍāmaṇi* in his own *Śivasūtravimarsiṇī,* is not found in this edition. Therefore we admit that this new term has not been referred to in texts prior to Abhinavagupta.

We are all acquainted with the burning of Kāma by Śiva and the victory over Māra by Buddha. Kālidāsa in his *Kumārasambhava* and Aśvaghoṣa in his *Buddhacarita* have narrated these legends in an impressive manner with the superb touch of the poetic *adbhutarasa.* The question arises how this Kāma-burning and Māra-defeating society eventually became victim to the same Kāma (the force of sensualism). From the legends found in the *Rāmāyaṇa, Mahābhārata* and Purāṇas we find that due to a momentary lack of self-control many great ascetics deviated from their paths of acquiring spiritual merit. The excess of the faculty of attachment may be its cause. Instead of forcibly repressing this indomitable instinct if means were suggested for its alleviation it would be more beneficial to mankind, is a belief at the root of this change. In the Śruti is it is said:

What Manu has said is medicine.

And Manu says:

Na māṃsabhakṣaṇe doṣo na madya na ca maithune/
Pravṛttireṣā bhūtānāṃ nivṛttistu mahāphalā//

What is the medicine in the statement of Manu? Its secret lies in *nivṛttistu mahāphalā.* We admit this statement of Rāmacandra *yadannaḥ puruṣo bhavati tadannāstasya devatāḥ* as found in the *Rāmāyaṇa* is the beginning of a new outlook meant for the salvation of men indulged in wine, meat, etc. Its purpose is the alleviation of attachment, not indulgence. Today this statement of Nilapata[23] as found in the *Yaśastilaka-campū* finds currency everywhere.

Strīmudrāṃ jhyaṣaketanasya mahatīṃ sarvārthasampatkarīm
Ye mohādavadhīrayanti kudhiyo mithyāphalānveṣiṇaḥ/
Te tenaiva nihatya nirdayataraṃ muṇḍīkṛtā luñcitāḥ
Kecit pañcaśikhakṛtāśca jaṭinaḥ kāpālikāscāpre//

NOTES

1. In the Tarkapāda of the *Brahmasūtra,* Sāṅkhya-Yoga, Nyāya-Vaiśeṣika, Pāśupata-Pañcarātra and other systems along with Buddhism and Jainism have been declared as non-Vedic. On the other hand, in the Nārāyaṇīya section of the Śānti-parvan of the *Mahābhārata,* Sāṅkhya, Yoga, Pāñcarātra, Pāśupata and Vedāraṇyaka have been equally acknowledged as authoritative. After Ācārya Śaṅkara, the Vaiṣṇavas and Śaivas attempted to base their views on the Vedas and the process

of bringing them in line with the Veda was complete during the time of Bhāskara Rāya. According to these exponents there is no difference between the Nigamas and Āgamas. Its evil effect was that the liberal outlook of the Tantras was blurred before the old Vedic perspective. There was a seminar (6-12. Feb. 1992) at Sarnath on Indian Tantrism. In the proceedings of the deliberations of the fifth and sixth days this twofold approach is to be found.

2. 'The Contribution of Kavirāj jī to Āgama and Tantraśāstra' in *Āgam āur Tantraśāstra,* (Delhi, 1984), pp. 1-26. Regarding recent works N.N. Bhattacharyya's *History of the Tantric Religion,* New Delhi, 1982, and S.C. Bannerji's *A Brief History of the Tantric Literature* (Calcutta 1988), may be mentioned.
3. *Abhinavagupta: An Historical and Philosophical Study,* Chowkhamba Sanskrit Series, 2nd edn (Varanasi, 1963), pp. 545-8.
4. Along with Madhusudana Sarasvatī's *Prasthānabheda* this book has been published from Śaivabhāratī Saudha Pratiṣṭhāna, Jangambāḍi Maṭha, Vārāṇasī in 1963. One of its editions has been published in the *Sodhapatrikā* (Research Series) of the Sarasvati Mahal Pustakalaya of Tanjore, part 23, 1984.
5. See 'Pāśupata, Kāpālika and Kālāmukha doctrine' in the Tantrāgama section in the *History of Sanskrit Literature* published by the Uttar Pradesh Sanskrit Academy, Lucknow.
6. *Pañcavaktrāṇi pañcabrahmalakṣaṇāni jaṭāmukuṭadharāṇī/*
Atra Sadyo vairocanaḥ vāmadevomitābhaḥ, aghorao ratnasambhavaḥ, tatpuruṣo'moghasiddhiḥ īṣāṇo'kṣobhya (Part 2, p. 186).
7. The references to *Kālottara* and *Niśvāsasaṃhitā* in the *Guhyasiddhi* (VIII.12) are meant to support the foregoing formulations. These two texts belong to the Siddhānta Śaivagama. 28 Āgamas from *Kāmika* to *Vātula* are know as Siddhāntaśāstra. Have all these Śāstras, 32 or 64 Bhairavāgamas, 64 Tantras, 18 Purāṇas, Upapurāṇas and Smṛtis appeared at the same time ? Chintaharan Chakravarti and Lāma Tāranātha have referred to the founder-teacher of various Tantrāgamas. Matsyendranātha is famous as the founder of Kaulaśāstra. Whether individual texts of all these Śāstras were composed separately, or were compiled at various assemblies, as was done in the Buddhist Saṅgītis, we do not know.
8. Cakras are 4 in number in most Buddhist Tantras and also in the Vaiṣṇava *Sātvatasaṃhitā*. The number of Cakras has been determined as 6 in the *Kālacakratantra* and other Śaiva-Śākta Tantras. Puṇḍarīka, the commentator of the *Kālacakratantra* says that the Cakras are 18 in number. In the *Dīpika* commentary on the *Yoginīhṛdaya* 32 Cakras are mentioned on the evidence of the *Svacchandasaṃgraha.*
9. In all texts on Indian Tantra and Yoga the number of nerves (*nāḍis*)

are stated to be 72. Among these 10, 3 and at least 1 have been given greater importance. The nerves Iḍā, Piṅgalā and Suṣumnā are described in the Buddhist Tantras respectively as Lalanā, Rasanā and Avadhūtī. In the *Vasantatilaka* and other works in terms of the 37 *bodhipakṣīya dharma* 37 nerves have been determined in the Ḍākinī group. See 7th *nirdeśa* and the *upodghāta* (pp. 22-32) of the *Vasantatilaka.* Such account is not found elsewhere.

10. Like *nāḍi* the number of *vāyus* (vital airs) are counted as 5 or 10. In the *Yoginīhṛdayadīpikā* (p. 317) 16 *vāyus* are mentioned. 14 *vāyus* are referred to in the *Liṅga Purāṇa* (I. 86. 83-4) in which the *Vairambha-vāyu* as mentioned in the *Vasantatilaka* (VIII. 6) is also included.
11. In the workshop held at Sarnath (6-12 Feb. 1992) on Indian Tantrism this had been discussed in the paper of Pitṛtantra while in the paper entitled 'Vajadeha in the Mātṛtantra' the concept of *Vajradeha* and its allied *nāḍi, cakra, vāyu, tilaka, vindu,* etc., have been dealt with. Here a brief account of the process of the origin of the human body is also found. We may hold that in other branches of Tantra and Yoga Śāstra these have been referred to in one way or another.
12. For the Ṣaḍanga Yoga see the *Upodghāta* (pp. 117-19) of the *Nityaṣodaśikārṇava.*
13. Analysis of various *siddhis* is to be found in the Sanskrit *upodhāta* (pp. 86-7) of the Chinnamastā-khaṇḍa of the *Śaktisaṅgamatantra.*
14. For the division *āṣtika-nāstika* of the Tantra and foreign influence on them see *Āgama aur Tantraśāstra,* pp. 6-9.
15. Ibid., p. 18, n. 2.
16. The following is stated about the characteristics or *Atimārga* and *Atimārgikas* in the *Svacchandatantra* (XI. 182-3): *atītaṃ buddhibhāvanā-matimārgaṃ prakīrtitam / lokātītam tu yajñānamatimārgamiti smṛtam// lokaśca pasavaḥ proktāḥ sṛṣṭisaṃhārakarmaṇi / teṣāmatitāste jñeyā ye atimārge vyavasthitāḥ/*
17. Vasantatilakānāṃ Sādhanopāyikā, Sāvyākhya, p. 72. See *Durlabh Bauddha Grantha Saudha Yojana,* Central Institute of Higher Tibetan Studies, Sarnath 1990.
18. For the selection of the term *mudrā,* the need of *mudrā,* the use of *mudrā* in four senses in Buddhist Tantra, etc., see 'Some Mudras in the Buddhist Tantras' in *Dhīḥ,* Vol. I, pp. 113-15. In *Mahārthamañjarī-parimala* of Maheśvarānanda the following meaning is attributed to *mudrā*: *Mudrā svātmanaḥ parameśvaratvopapādanāya sārīram prati kalpamānaḥ karacaraṇādisannivesaviseṣo veśadhāraṇaviśeṣaśca/ mahatī tu mudrā paryantato rāve (vimarśo) evāntarbhavati* (p. 106). Here the characteristics of *mahāmudrā* are not different from the fourfold *mudrā* described in the Buddhist Tantras and *Veśadhāraṇa, laksaṇa-karṇika, rucaka,* etc., of the ancient Pāśupata and Buddhist sixfold

mudrās. The above characteristics indicated by Maheśvarānanda pertain also to the *mahāmudrā, mahābandha*, etc., comprising 10 *mudrās* and the twofold and threefold *khecarimudrā* mentioned in the third upadeśa of the *Haṭhayogapradīpikā*. For particulars about *mudrā* see the *upodghāta* (pp. 75-8) of the *Nityaṣodaśikārṇava*.

19. Mention of the four pīṭhas—Kāmarūpa, Pūrṇagiri, Jālandhara and Oḍiyāna—are found in all branches of Tantraśāstra. In *Sādhanamālā* (pp. 453, 485) Jālandhara has been located in Śrīhaṭṭa (Shylet). In Buddist literature a Tantric work named *Catuṣpīṭha* is mentioned. There those are named *atma, para, yoga* and *tattva*. These names have no connection with the four Pīṭhas. These are names of the four parts of the text.
20. For these 24 Pīṭhas and 32 other Pīṭhas mentioned in the *Hevajra Tantra* see *Dhiḥ*, Vol. I, pp. 137-48.
21. For the 51 Piṭhas mentioned in the Śākta Tantras, see D.C. Sircar, The *Śākta Piṭhas*, JBBRAS, 1948, pp. 1-108.
22. For the 108 Mahāpīṭhas and Upapīṭhas see Karuna S. Dvivedi's 'Purāṇagata Yoga evam Tantra' in the *History of Sanskrit Literature*, Uttar Pradesh Samskrta Samsthana, Lucknow.
23. In the Śrāddhaprakaraṇa of the *Kūrma Purāṇa* (II. 22.35) the Pākhaṇḍis and those who wear dress of blue and colour red ochre are declared to be unfit for invitation. There (II. 33.10) it is also stated that if a Brāhmaṇa wears blue or red he will have to purify himself with *pañcagavya*, etc. In the collection of *Old Articles* (pp. 109-13) of Mahāpaṇḍita Rāhula Sāṅkrityayan, the Nīlapaṭa-darśana has been discussed in connection with the origin of Vajrayāna. Somadeva has quoted a verse of Nilapaṭa. In Krishna Kanta Handiki's *Yaśastilakacampū and Indian Culture* (p. 44) another verse of Nīlapaṭa collected from the *Saduktikarṇāmṛta* has been quoted. He has also quoted a similar verse from Bhartṛhari. The purpose of all these is same. The event referred to by Mahāpaṇḍita Rāhula Sāṅkrityayan in connection with Nīlapaṭa-philosophy may be ascribed to 515-24. K.C. Pande has fixed the date of Matsyendranātha, the founder of the Kaula system, around this period.

Translated from Hindi by N.N. Bhattacharyya

12

Colour Symbolism in Tantric Buddhism

T.K. BISWAS

In Tantric Buddhism, references to five colours (*pañca-varṇa*) are frequently met with. The colours are white, yellow, red, blue and green. That these colours were often symbolic is substantiated quite clearly in a passage in the *Caṇḍamahāroṣaṇa Tantra* which runs thus:

> *Kṛṣṇahi māraṇe dveṣe*
> *Śvetaḥ śāntau mātava api*
> *Pītaḥ stambhane puṣtau*
> *Vaśyākṛṣte tu lohitaḥ*
> *Śyāmā uccātane khyātaḥ*

This means the colour black symbolises killing and anger, white denotes rest and thinking, yellow stands for restraining and nourishing, red subjugation and summoning, and green means exorcisim.[1]

The five Dhyānī Buddhas, Vairocana, Ratnasambhava, Akṣobhya, Amitābha and Amoghasiddhi are endowed with five different body colours in their *sādhanās.* White is prescribed for Vairocana, it symbolises delusion; Ratnasambha is yellow in body colour, that denotes pride; Akṣobhya is blue bodied, which stands for hatred; Amitābha's red body signifies passion; and the green colour of Amoghasiddhi symbolizes envy.[2]

The *Mahāvairocana-Sūtra* states that a *maṇḍala* should be painted in five colours. It further prescribes that one should start at the interior of the *maṇḍala* with white and to be followed by red, yellow, blue and black.[3] The *Cakrasambhāra-tantra* preseribes that the walls of a *maṇḍala* should be painted in five colours and should maintain the order of black in the interior followed by white, yellow, red and green.[4] In certain *maṇḍalas,* the four directions within the palace are indicated by colours. The east is indicated by white, west by red, north by green and the south by yellow while the centre is painted blue. The *Kālacakra-tantra,* however, prescribes a completely different colour scheme to indicate different directions: the colour black indicates east, yellow west, white north, and red stands for the south. In any case, the protecting circle of a *maṇḍala* is usually drawn in red.

The reference to the five colours has been made also in an altogether different context. In the processes of purification and empowering sense organs in the course of visualizing goddess Tārā, the *sādhanā* includes the references to five colours:

The devotee having identified himself as Tārā, visualizes a white '*oṃ tāre svāhā*' upon his eyes, a blue '*oṃ tuttāre svāhā*' upon his ears, a yellow '*oṃ ture svāhā*' on the nose, a red '*oṃ tu svāhā*' on his tongue and a green '*oṃ tārenī svāhā*' on the top of his head.[5] According to Tibetan tradition the word '*huṃ*' although blue in colour radiates five different colours. The dot (drop) on the crescent should be blue, the crescent is white, the head is yellow, the syllable 'ha' is red and the vowel ū is of green colour.[6]

The four elements, air, fire, water and earth are identified in the *Kālacakra-tantra* with four different colours: either blue or black, red, white and yellow, respectively.[7] These four elements, are depicted as semi-circular, triangular, circular, and square, respectively. The *Guhyasamājatantra* and the *Advayavajra Saṃgraha* refer to the female personifications of colours while the *Hevajra tantra* prescribes golden, dark, moonstone colour and the colour of sapphire, for the above elements.[8]

The Yoga-tantra symbolizes the 'triad' Kāya (body), Vāc (speech) and Citta (mind) in three different colours, viz., white, red, and blue, respectively. They may also be represented by the white syllable 'oṃ', the red syllable 'āḥ' and the blue syllable 'huṃ' and these syllables empower one to visualize the deity and give life and power to an image.[9] Akṣobhya, who rules over *citta-cakra* or *citta maṇḍala,* is represented by a blue *vajra*; Amitābha who presides over *vāc-cakra* or *vāc-maṇḍala* is symbolized as a red lotus flower or a red *vajra* while Vairocana who presides over Kāya is represented either by a white *vajra* or a white wheel or circle (of *Cakrasaṃvara Tantra, Niṣpannayogāvalī* and *Sādhanamālā*).[10]

The notion of the polarity of colours is found to have been entertained in Tantric Buddhism. For instance, the polarity of black and white may be taken up. The colour black denotes darkness. It is inauspicious; it symbolizes *avidyā* and represents evil. The colour white represents light; it is auspicious; it denotes *vidyā* and stands for the good.

The Tibetan Buddhists refer to two kinds of light, a set of intensive light which is endowed with brilliant and clear colour; and a dull light which appears in broken colours. The former leads to enlightenment and the state of Buddhahood, the latter results in rebirth in the misery of *saṃsāra.*

Early Tantras refer to certain deities as encircled by a red and a white aureole. *Bodhicaryāvatāra* takes these as colours of semen and menstrual blood. In Tantra, the red and white represent the polarity of female-male principles, it has underlying unity and inseparability of opposites. The white semen (*śukra*) is the symbol of light and stands both for *saṃsāra* and *nirvāṇa.* Red represents female principle and also denotes a white male.

The male-female principles are present both in men and women. The thought of enlightenment (*bodhi-citta*) represents the union of insight (*prajñā*) and means (*upāya*) of red and white colours, respectively and this union leads to a great bliss (*mahā-sukha*). Red and white drops flow in the channels of all human beings dissolving into the indestructible drop white at the top and red at the bottom. Thus Sun may be conceived as a red moon and similarly, the lunar disc as both white and red.[12] In the structural patterns of a *maṇḍala,* the union of insight (*prajñā*) and means (*upāya*) is expressed by male-female deities embracing each other (*yab-yum*) and in this process the discrimination between the two is removed and dichotomies are withdrawn. The white Vajradhara and black Vajratma dissolve into one, says *Hevajra Tanra.*[13]

Besides the five common colours, in Vajrayāna, the colour gold is found to be given adequate importance. In Tibet, it is believed that the colour of gold synthesizes all colours.[14] The Buddhas and Boddhisattvas in Tibet are painted in gold.[15] The colour gold is mentioned in relation to the time of the birth of Gautama, the period of his attainment of enlightenment, and also his demise. The Bodisattvas and their path are compared with gold. Bodhisattva Mañjuśrī and his *śakti.* Prajñāpāramitā appear as golden coloured since they personify six perfections. It is also held that those born in Sukhāvatī have the colour of molten gold. The visualization of Tārā, accompanies a verse: with devotion I invite you who have the colour of refined gold, more greatly splendid than the Sun.[16] It is further said that one's guru be visualized as golden.

The colour yellow symbolizes pride, prosperity, affluence, the south, the element of earth, the aggregate of sensations, the wisdom of equality, etc.

The colour green denotes envy, the multitude, the element of air, the aggregate of the concept of consciousness and the accomplishment of wisdom. Green is the combination of white (pacifying), yellow (affluence) and blue (destruction).[17] The goddess Tārā who covers a whole range of such functions is depicted as green. The colour blue symbolizes hatred, destruction, killing, the element of space or air, unchangeability, firmness of mind, the wisdom of *dharma-dhātu* and the aggregate of consciousness.

There is a reference in the *Ratnagotravibhāga* that residing in the inconceivable act of Thatagata, the Buddha never casts off the sky-quality (*ākāśa-svabhāvatā*) of his body.[18] According to the *Mahā-prajñāpāramitā Śāstra,* both mind and space are luminous, pure and boundless. The space is referred to as illusory and non-real blue sky. A pure mind is also conceived as an extensive sky and a flawless blue beryl.

The event of enlightenment, and the unchangeability of enlightened mind, is represented by the dhyānī Buddha Akṣobhya. He is blue in colour and he governs the blue circle of the mind within a *maṇḍala.*[19] Similarly, Cakrasambhāra appears blue since he does not change from the *dharmadhātujñāna.* Incidentally, a reference may also be made to the bodies of Buddha that evolved from the Dharma-kāya. These bodies are inconceiveable. *Samādhirāja-Sūtra* records that 'it is not easy to comprehend the body of Tathāgata even through his marks and determine whether it is blue, blue coloured, apparently blue or blue like.'[20]

The colour white symbolizes delusion, pacification, purity, the element of water, the aggregate of form perception, goodness, maleness and the wisdom of discrimination. White also stands for compassion and the perfection of *nirvāṇa.* In the yoga-tantra the five pronged *vajra* is visualized as white symbolizing non-discursive knowledge which is Vairocana's heart.[21] The colour red symbolizes passion, hatred, subjugation, empowerment, the west, the element of fire, the aggregate of sensation and perceptions. It symbolizes a female. The colour red also represents compassion (*karuṇā*). All deities in *Mahākaruṇāgarbha maṇḍala* sit on a red lotus.[22] Red is also the colour of Vajravārāhī as a sign of her devotion to the service of all sentient beings.[23] Red eyes in a deity signify a wrathful and fierce character: but such eyes may also mean kindness and compassion. Expressions like '*Kṛpayā locane rakte*' (*Hevajra Tantra*) and '*Kṛpayā dṛṣtya lohite*' (*Mahākāla Tantra*) point in that direction.[24]

When the image makers were in confusion how to make the image of Buddha, they were provided with certain *mahāpuruṣa lakaṣaṇam.* These included golden skin (*suvarṇa varṇa*) dark blue eyes (*ati nīla netra*), very white teeth (*Suśukladanta*), black hair (*asita keśa*), black eyebrows (*asitha bhrū*), lips red like vimba fruit (*Vimbavatraktoṣṭha*), copper-red feet and palms (*tāmralohitapāṇi padatala*).[25]

Before the conception of the Lord, Māyādevī dreamt of an elephant. According to *Mahāvastu* the elephant looked gleaming like snowwhite silver (*himarajatanibha*),[26] it is also described as the young sun with the hue of gold (*mahārka-cāruvarṇa*). The fasting Gautama is described as black or dark brown, like the *madgura* fish (cf. *Mahāvastu*).[27]

Thus it appears that references to colours prevailed during the period of conceptual beginning of the image of the Buddha and were mostly referred to as similies but by the time of Tantric Buddhism, the colours became evidently symbolic and artists were compelled to understand the symbolism and apply it to the visualization of deities. In painting Tantraya deities, the artist had no freedom at all.

NOTES

1. George Christopher, *The Caṇḍamahāroṣanatantra* (New Haven, 1974), p. 25. A different pattern of colour symbolism is referred to in the *Mahākālatantra,* edited by Stablein William George, Columbia University, 1976, pp. 118-25.
2. See *Guhyasamājatantra,* edited by B. Bhattacharyya (Baroda, 1931), Ch. 13.
3. Tajima Ryujun, *Etude sur le Mahāvairocanasūtra* (Paris, 1936), Ch. 2.
4. Kazi Dawa Samdup, *Śrīcakrasambhara Tantra* (London and Calcutta, 1919), p. 18.
5. Stephen Beyer, *The Cult of Tārā: Magic and Rituals in Tibet,* (Berkeley, 1978), p. 275.

6. Kazi Dawa Samdup, *Cakrasambhāratantra* (London and Calcutta, 1919), p. 4 and also see Govinda Angarika, *Foundation of Tibetan Mysticism* (York Beach, 1969), p. 188.
7. *Kālacakratantra: Exposition of Dalai Lama XIV*, edited by Jeffery Hopkins, (Dharamasala, 1985).
8. Giusppe Tucci, *Tibetan Painted Scrolls*, (Rome 1949), Vol. 2, p. 601.
9. Rolf A. Stein, *Tibetan Civilization*, (Standford, California, 1972), p. 187 and also see Roger Jackson, *Wheel of Time: The Kālacakra Context* (New York, 1991).
10. Vide *Cakrasambhāratantra*, op. cit., pp. 30-3, 47 and 51, also see *Niṣpannayogāvalī*, edited by B. Bhattacharyya (Baroda, 1949), pp. 12-13 and *Sādhanamālā*, edited by B. Bhattacharyya, p. 218.
11. Marion L. Matics, *Entering the Path of Enlightenment, The Bodhicaryāvatāra of Buddhist Poet Śāntideva* (pp. 8-11 and 158).
12. Stephen Beyer, op. cit., p. 122 and cf. *Cakrasambhāratantra*, op. cit., p. 177.
13. *Hevajratantra*, I. 8-9, edited by David L. Snellgrove (London, 1959).
14. Giusppe Tucci, *The Religion of Tibet* (Berkeley, 1980), p. 77.
15. Giusppe Tucci, op. cit., Vol. I, pp. 288f.
16. Stephen Beyer, op. cit., p. 336.
17. Lo Bue, *Buddhaguhyas' Dharmamaṇḍalasūtra* in 'Orientalia losephi, Tucci Memorial Dicata Serie Orientale', Rome, 56, 1-3, pp. 787-807.
18. Takasaki Jikido, *A Study of Ratnagotravibhāga* (Rome, 1966), p. 193.
19. de Mallamann, *Introduction al Iconographique do tantrism Buddhique* (Paris, 1975), p. 91.
20. Regamey Konstanty, *Three Chapters from the Samādhirāja Sūtra*, (Warszawa, 1938).
21. Glenn H. Mullin, *Meditations on the Lower Tantras*, etc. (Dharmasala, 1983), p. 55.
22. Tajima Ryujum, op. cit.
23. See *Cakrasambhāratantra*, op. cit., p. 27.
24. See *Hevajratantra* II. IX. II. and *Mahākāla Tantra*, op. cit., p. 122.
25. Ph. Faucaux, ed., *Lalitavistara* (Paris, 1984), pp. 95-9.
26. *Mahāvastu* I, p. 162.
27. *Mahāvastu* II, pp. 111-29.

13

Concept of Mudrā in Japanese (Shingon) Esoteric Buddhism

KALPAKAM SANKARNARAYAN
YORITOMI MOTOHIRO

INTRODUCTION

Shingon is the name of a Buddhist sect in Japan founded by Kobō Daishi in AD 807. It was known at that time in China as 'Chenyen' and it was there that Kobō Daishi, who was then called Kukai studied it and took it to Japan.

'Shingon' means 'true word', and its teaching is esoteric. The element of secrecy has always played a prominent part in the doctrine and in entirety it is taught only to initiates. It is considered to be a teaching that was first imparted by Buddha Mahāvairocana in his spiritual body and its full and perfect instruction is given only by oral transmission to qualified disciples. Shingon is spoken of as the sect of Dhāraṇīs and the secret teachings of all the Tathāgatas. Although some of the secret teaching has been divulged to the world in these modern days, much is still withheld: for, according to Shingon, certain religious truths and practices can only be taught orally and are known by a secret communication between teacher and pupil, and are never to be given out through the printed page or in a crowded assembly. In other words, they are esoteric in the fullest sense of the term. To study 'Shingon' on its esoteric side, it is necessary to have a personal teacher who initiates his pupil into the secret practices and the deeper significance of the doctrine. Nevertheless, there is in Shingon much of great interest which is communicable and many books on Shingon doctrine have been written.

One teacher has given a brief definition of Shingon—'To say the words of the Buddha is the way to walk with the Buddha.'[1] Another has said 'To realize Buddhahood in this life, in this body, that is

Shingon.'[2] My own definition is 'All is ONE; Realize That. That is the *True Word*'. '*Shin*' means 'true and genuine', '*gon*' signifies 'word' or teaching, so '*Shingon*' means 'the teaching of the *true words. Shingon* is the translation of the Sanskrit '*mantra*' and hence the sect is often called 'Mantrayāna'.

This Mantrayāna or Shingon sect of Japanese (Kukai's) Esoteric Buddhism lay stress on *mantra, mudrā* and *maṇḍala* (rather, 'speech', 'body' and 'mind').

We have discussed the concept of *mantra* in detail elsewhere.[3] Here we are taking the concept of '*mudrā*' in Shingon Buddhism.

The term allows for a variety of related but distinct meanings, indicated in the first and second parts of this section. In Tantric terminology, *mudrā* is the means whereby the candidate affiliates his body with that of the Buddha.[4] As for the general use of *mudrās*, the Tantras both mirror and transcend the non-tantric precedents. Accordingly, this topic will be discussed under three headings: (1) *mudrā* in non-Tantric Buddhism, (2) The Tantric use of *mudrās* in general and (3) The special fourfold classification of mudrā as found in the scripture.

NON-TANTRIC USAGE

The root meaning of *mudrā* is the signet ring whereby a prince or king marked a letter or goods as his own; a primitive derived meaning is the effect produced by the impression of the ring, namely, a seal.[5] Quite early in Buddhist tradition *mudrā* acquired the metaphorical meaning of a hand-gesture distinctive to a specific action in the life of Buddha.[6] The Hīnayāna monks employ hand gestures in their initiation ceremonies: by these symbols the initiate is helped to realize in himself the attitudes of the Buddha.[7]

THE TANTRAYĀNA USAGE

The Tantrayāna incorporates into itself the non-Tantric meanings of *mudrā* and also creates several more metaphorical usages of the term. Thus, in the Tantras, *mudrā* connotes the following:

(i) hand-gesture,
(ii) physical adornment,
(iii) mark to indicate Tathāgata lineage,

(iv) a person so marked, whether as a deity or a female officient at initiations,
(v) the meditational level of Tantric perfection,
(vi) insight as one of the two major Tantric Virtues.

In Shingon Buddhism the *mudrā* is used as a vehicle to experience the phenomenal world as it is. Unlike a *mantra* and *maṇḍala*—which aid the mind-aspect to focus, become sedimented and finally enter into first order body-mind-awareness—a *mudrā* is a vehicle which focuses upon the body aspect. A *mudrā*, the hand-posture, like the *mantra* and *maṇḍala* at once symbolizes the all pervasive character of the Dharmakāya while being a concrete representative of the *dharma.* Once the practice of *mudrā* gestures has been sedimented, it too can aid the practitioner to enter into first order body-mind-awareness. *Mudrās* correspond to the mystery of body and the reality of 'Sound, word, and reality'. The *mudrā* provides the focus for the body - aspect that symbolizes 'the meaning of these words'. A *mudrā* is the 'Body of the Dharmakaya Symbolized'.[8]

As hand gesture, *mudrā* generates the presence of the *maṇḍala* deity.[9] In this instance, the hand gesture is shaped according to the form of the hand symbol (*ciñha*).[10] The *mudrā* indicated specific adornments which symbolize both the Tathāgata Buddha and a special knowledge. The adornments associated with the Buddhas are: circlet, Akṣobhya; earring, Amitābha; necklace, Ratnasambhava; bracelet, Vairocana; belt, Amoghasiddhi.[11]

MUDRĀ IN EARLY BUDDHISM

In early Buddhism, the *mudrā* was a 'seal or any instrument used for sealing, to seal or to confirm by a "seal", and the stamp or impression attached to some object to show that it is genuine'. The three distinguished teachings (*dharmas*) of Buddhism, that is, all *dharmas* are *anitya,* all *dharmas* are *anātmā* and *nirvāṇa* is *śānta',* were termed *tri-dharma-mudrā.*[12]

MAHĀYĀNA BUDDHISM

In Mahāyāna Buddhism, *buddha-mudrā* or *six-pāramitā-mudrā* was used. The term *mudrā* in three usages indicates, as does a seal, that it is true and not false.[13]

Concurrently, hand-gestures became known as *hasta-mudrā* (hand-symbol). The kind of *mudrā* started to appear in the Chinese Buddhist scriptures in sixth century AD.

In the *Mou-li-man-t'u-lo chou-ching* translated in the Liang Dynasty (502-56),[14] sixteen *hasta-mudrā* were mentioned as religious symbols of the actions and merits of Buddha. In the *T'o-lo-nichi-ching* translated by Atikūṭa in AD 653-4, over three hundred *hasta-mudrās* were explained, and the held-objects of Buddhas or Boddhisattvas, such as lotus flowers, sword, *vajra*-pounder, *stūpa,* etc., were called *ciñha-mudrā* (sign-symbol). These held objects (*jimotsu* in Japanese) are the religious concrete symols of the inner witness or pledge (*samaya*) of Buddha. Here, *chinha-mudrā* (sign-symbols) were identified with *Samayas,* and *mudrā* lifted its position up to *Mudrā.* The concrete *mudrā* (*hasta-mudrā* and *cinha-mudrā*) became the religious symbol (*mudrā*) of the actions, merits and inner witness or pledge (*samaya*) of Buddhas.

Therefore, the commentary of *Mahāvairocana-Sūtra* states *mudrā* is the symbol of *Dharma-dhātu* (the world of *Dharma*). By *mudrā* is the body of *Dharma-dhātu* symbolized.[15]

In *Mahāvairocana Sūtra,* the concrete religious symbols (*mudrās*) were *hasta-mudrās* and *ciñha-mudrās.* However, in the *Vajraśekhara-sūtra,*[16] *mudrā* is called *jñāna-mudrā* (wisdom symbol) and classified into four parts under the name of *mahā, samaya, karma* and *dharma.* *Mahā-jñāna mudrā* is body-postures representing all concrete religious objects, that is images, written *bīja-mantras* and *samayas. Samaya-jñāna-mudrā* is the *hasta-mudrās* of *samaya,* i.e. the hand gestures in which hand and fingers express *samayas* (*stupa, vajra, padma,* etc.). *Karma-jñāna-mudrā* is *hasta-mudrā* of the *karma* (action) of Buddha, (i.e. the hand-gestures representing Buddha's Compassion, turning wheel, enlightenment, etc.). *Dharma-jñāna-mudrā* is Shingons.

The terms *maha, samaya, karma* and *dharma* used in the *Vajraśekhara-Sūtra* are identical with the terms used in the classification of *maṇḍalas* which we have discussed in detail elsewhere.[17] *Mahā-jñāna-mudrā* including *Ciñha-mudrās* are the symbols of *manasguhya* (the secret of mind), both *samaya-jñāna*-and *Karma jñāna-mudrās* (i.e. *hasta mudrās* in the *Mahāvairocana Sūtra*) the symbols of *Kāya-guhya* (the secrets of body) and *dharma-jñāna-mudrās* are the symbols of *Vāc-guhya* (the secret of speech). Therefore, *mudrā,* the abstract verbal symbol, which was postulated from the concrete symbol *mudrā* is identical with *maṇḍalas,* i.e. the symbol of the whole manifestation of *Dharma-kāya.*

HASTA-*MUDRĀS* IN SHINGON BUDDHISM

In a broad sense, the term *mudrā* is *Mudrā* (the symbol) of the whole universe and includes Shingons as a part of it, but in the narrow sense, or in common use, it signifies *hasta-mudrā* (hand-symbol). The term 'Mudrā' is generally translated *phyag-rgya* in Tibetan. *Phyag* in the Tibetan language is the honoric word for *Lag*- the hand, and *rgya* means 'seal' or 'sign'. Therefore, the Tibetan rendeirng *phyag-rgya* meaning literally 'hand-sign' indicates the gesture or the manner in which the hand and figures are held by Buddha, by priests, etc.[18]

Hasta-mudrās in Shingon Buddhism are divided into two main types. One is the natural type of *hasta-mudrā* and the other the artificial type. The former is the hand-gesture in which hand and fingers express something in a natural way. The latter is the hand-gestures in which hand and fingers, following certain conventions,[19] indicate or symbolize some particular thing in an artificial way. *Karma-jñāna-mudrā* and *samaya-jñāna-mudrā* in the *Vajraśekhara-sūtras* correspond practically to these two types.

The origin of the natural types of hand-gestures in India can be traced back to the folk-dances in Ancient India which were performed at festivals. Basham says:

> The most striking feature of the Indian dance is undoubtedly the hand gesture (*mudrā*). By a beautiful and complicated code, the hand alone is capable of potraying not only a wide range of exotions, but gods, animals, men, natural scenery, actions and so on. Some hundreds of *mudrās* are classified in later text books, and they are used not only in the dance, but ... in religious worship and iconography.[20]

The first appearance of *hasta-mudrā* in Buddhism was in Gandhāra and to a lesser extent at Mathura as well.[21] *Mudrā* of joining the hands (*anjali-mudrā*), *mudrā* of meditation (*dhyāna-mudrā*), *mudrā* that bestows (*da*) a wish or boon (*varada-mudrā*),[22] *mudrā* which grants the absence of fear (*abhaya-mudrā*), *mudrā* of conjuring the earth to witness (*bhūmi-sparśa-mudrā*),[23] and *mudrā* of turning the wheel of *dharma* (*dharma-cakra mudrā*), all of these are *hasta-mudrās* seen in Gandhāra Buddhist art. They are respectively the symbols of devotion, meditation, compassion, awakening, pledge, and enlightenment of the Buddha, symbols of what the Buddha had done in his life.

The appearance of Buddhist images as concrete religious objects marked an epoch in the history of Buddhism. In the *Pan-cheu-san-mei ching* translated by Lokarakṣa in the second century (soon after the age of Gandhara art), Buddha's images were considered very important for *samādhi* (contemplation).[24] In the *Kuan-fo-San-mei-Lal-Cing*, translated by Buddhabhadra in the early fifth century, religious symbols like the lotus flower, *maṇi and dharmacakra* were considered the *karma* (action) of Buddha and were objects of contemplation.[24]

In the *Mon-li-man-t'u-lochou-ching* translated in the time of the Liang Dynasty (502-56), *hasta-mudrās* represented in Buddhist images became the actual hand-gestures of the *Sādhaka* (practitioner). In the *T'o-lo-ni-chi-ching* translated by Atikūṭa in (AD 653-4) the gestures increased in number to over three hundred, and in the commentary of the *Mahāvairocana Sūtra,* they were systematically organized under the source of all hand-gestures, *hasta-mudrā-mātṛkā,* which is the four types of fists and the twelve types of hand clasps.[25]

Then in the *Vajraśekhara Sūtra,* all hand-gestures are classified into *samaya-jñāna-mudrā* and *karma-jñāna-mudrā.* Before describing several concrete *hasta-mudrās* (the symbols of *Kāya-guhya*) performed with Shingon (the symbols of *Vāc-guhya*), we shall discuss *samayas* (the symbols of *manas-guhya*).

SAMAYA AND *SAMAYAS*

The Significnace of the Term 'Samaya'

Symbols other than those expressed by bodily representations (hand-gestures, body-gestures, and *Shingons*) are called *ciñha-mudrā* or *samaya.* The *ciñha-mudrā* is identical to the 'sign-symbol' of Paul Tillich who says

> Many things—like special parts of the Church building, like the Candles, like the water at the entrance of the Roman Church, like the cross in all churches, especailly Protestant Churches—were originally only signs, but in use became symbols; call them sign-symbols, signs, which have become symbols.[27]

The term *samaya* derived from 'Sam + i' (to come together) has been used with various significations, which can be arranged in the following ways:

(i) Coming together, meeting or a place of meeting; (ii) coming to a mutual understanding, agreement, conditions of agreement; (iii) convention, conventional rule, established law or practice; (iv) oppotunity, occasion, appointed or proper time, (v) sign, hint, indication, (vi) solemn address or speech.[28]

In the 'revealed' Buddhism, the three meanings of the term which are generally used are (1) an assembly, (2) an 'established rule or doctrine', and (3) a 'time against *kāla*'.[29]

Kāla (time) is the source from which arise all things, heaven and earth, good and bad; however there is no such thing as a reality apart from the successive events. Time (*samaya*) is a notion derived from the distinction perceivable within the composite whole of interrelated events. 'We perceive the course of events, give the name "time" to this universal order of succession and draw the distinction of part and future, the remembered and the anticipated, the not any more and the not yet, in contrast with that which is here now, the present.'[30]

Therefore, in the teaching of the Buddha, *samaya* is used more often, and it is only rarely that '*kāla*' for 'time' is used.

In Shingon Buddhism, the basis for interpretation of the term '*samaya*' lies in its original etymology. *Samaya* is a compound of *Sam-aya.*[31] '*Sam*' is the prefix meaning 'with', 'together', 'in association', and with intensive force 'thoroughly', 'completely' and 'universally'. *Aya* derived from i (to go) means 'going'. The term '*samaya*' is interpreted in a similar manner as the term *upāya* (*upa* - *aya* literally means 'going' or 'forward or near to'), is the ascending and descending approach and their 'means'.

According to Buddha-guhya (eighth century) a Tibetan comentator of the *Mahāvairocana-Sūtra,* the term '*samaya*' is on the one hand, going (*-aya*) thoroughly (*sam-*) to Buddha from man, i.e. the state of *Bodhi* (enlightenment) and the path to it, and on the other, coming (*-aya*) universally (*sam-*) from Buddha to man, i.e. the state of *karuṇā* (compassion) and its activities.[32]

In short the term *samaya* connotes four significations, i.e. (1) going up to *Bodhi,* (2) *Bodhi* as such, (3) *karuṇā* as such, and (4) coming down from *karuṇā.*

Samaya, is the essential symbol of *Bodhi* and *karuṇā*: *Bodhi* (enlightenment, or inner witness) and *karuṇā* (compassion or vow) are symbolized by *samaya.* 'Going up and coming down or "ascending and descending" or "Self-benefiting" (*jiri*) and benefiting other (*rita*)' approaches. This double-edged (*upāya*) is the inherent activity of *samaya,* i.e. *Bodhi* and *karuṇā.Samaya* symbolizes both *Bodhi* and *karuṇā* or in other words, *Bodhi* and *karuṇā* are two aspects of *samaya.*

In the last part of the significance of the letter *Hūm,* Kūkai explains the letter '*hūm*' from the view point of the two aspects of *samaya* in this manner: The written letter '*hūm*' is composed of three parts: '*ha*', *ṁ* and *ū*. The centre letter 'ha' signifying the sound of laughing '*ha-ha-ha*', represents the great pleasures. The upper part (.) '*m*' represents the *samaya* or enlightenment, self-benefiting, and the lower part 'ū' the *samaya* of compassion, or benefitting others. All *Tathāgatas,* envisaging equally these two aspects of *samaya* reside in great pleasure. Therefore, the significance of '*hūm*' is to envisage equally the two aspects of *samaya* and to please greatly.[33]

In the ninth volume of the commentary of the *Mahāvairocana Sūtra, samaya* is also explained as having four significations, equality, vow, awakening and disposal of hindrances.[34]

Equality is to envisage the three secrets (*tri-guhya*) of Buddha and the three actions (*tri-karma*) of man without discrimination and to equate the former with the latter, and this is, in a word, *Bodhi.* Vow is a solemn promise of Buddha to benefit others or to save all sentient beings from suffering. This is *karuṇā.* Awakening and disposal of hindrances indicate the activities of *karuṇā.*

The long and short of it is that the term *samaya* that appeared recurrently as an essential verbal symbol in Shingon Buddhism, signified 'equality' and 'vow' and *samaya* is the symbol of both *Bodhi* and *karuṇā.*[35]

Now we must take up the term *samaya* with its relationship to *samaya.*

SAMAYA AND *SAMAYA*

In Shingon Buddhism, the term used for *samaya* is '*samayegyo*', '*gyo*' (Chinese, *hsiry*) means 'figure', 'form' 'appearance': Therefore *samaya* is a concrete figure of *Samaya.* In the Tibetan Tantric scriptures, the term *'samaya'* is usually translated as '*dam-tshig*' which means literally 'a sacred or solemn vow'.

As explained earlier, *samaya* is the symbol of *Bodhi* and *karuṇā.* Every honourable one, opens the gate of his enlightenment for others. And by opening the gate, the honourable one pledges himself to save all sentient beings. Then, the honourable one, in order to make his pledge known to this followers, holds various *ciñha-*

mudrā, as the symbols of his pledge. There are *samayas.* These *samayas* are also called *gyo* (figures) of *pāramitā,* i.e. the symbols by which man can reach enlightenment.[36]

To sum up, *samaya* is the symbols of *samaya* which represents *Bodhi* and *karuṇā.* In other words, *samaya* represents the natures of the minds of the deities.[37] Here we can very clearly see that *samaya* and *Samaya-s* form a double system of symbols. *Samaya* is the essential abstract verbal symbol of *Bodhi* and *karuṇā* and *samaya* the subordinate, concrete, non-verbal symbol of *samaya.* Man can approach *Samaya* through *samaya,* and Buddha shows *samaya* to man in *Samaya.*

Samayas started to appear in the Chinese Buddhist scriptures in the time of the early T'ang Dynasty (618-907). In the Buddhist scriptures translated by Chin-t' ung and Atikūṭa in the middle of seventh century, the held-objects of Buddha or of Bodhisattvas, being separated from their holders, appear independently as *ciñha-mudrā,* and are begun to be called *samaya.*[38]

Ciñha-mudrās such as *vajra, padma,* moon circle, *caitya* or *stūpa,* etc., have their own long history of symbols.

Vajra was the thunderbolt or sceptre of Indra in the *Ṛg Veda*[39] and was also a weapon used in ancient India. The term '*Vajra*' refers to its resistance, which can smash anything.[40] In Shingon Buddhism, the *vajra* is generally used as a symbol of wisdom and power over illusions and evil spirits. There are three kinds. The single-pronged *vajra* represents the *Tathāgata,* the three pronged one the three secrets or the three families of all deities, (Buddha, Padma and Vajra), and the five pronged one the five wisdoms of Buddha.[41]

Lotus and moon symbolism are thought to have been introduced from Mesopotamia.[42] In Shingon Buddhism, the former symbolizes the merits and compassion of Buddha, and the latter the inner witness of Buddha or Enlightenment.

The symbolism of *caitya* or *stūpa* has its origin in the pupular belief of ancient India. The cult of the *caitya* was that of secret spots and it was the cult of the *caitya* that Buddhism made its own.[43] In Shingon Buddism, *caitya* or *stūpa* symbolizes the assembly of all *Tathāgatas* or the collection of the merits of *Mahāvairocana Buddha.*

We have no further intention to analyse in detail each of the *ciñha-mudrās.* We must, however, be aware of the fact that of these sign-symbols have their proto-type in the popular belief of ancient India, and in the course of time they had been incorporated and adapted into the system of Buddhism, and that at the daybreak of *Mantra-*

yāna, they, being called *Samaya,* became the symbol of *samaya.*

Truly the formation of this symbol system, the '*Samaya-Samayas*' marked a new epoch of the 'Secret of Buddhism'. All corporeal, perceptible, and concrete existences were considered to be the symbols of *Samaya,* and through these symbols (*Samayas*) man was able to approach or attain the final goal of Enlightenment.

This symbol-system of '*Samaya-Samayas*' is based on the religious experience of 'non-duality' (*advaita*) of concrete existence and abstract principle (*ji-ri funi*) and 'one-ness' of matter and mind. In Shingon Buddhism, this religious exerience is expressed in this manner: 'All concrete things or phenomena are identical with the truth' (*Soku-ji-ji-shin*)' or 'That which appears is as such the path (*tō-sō-soku-dō*).'

The truth of this symbol-system as a religion is that by which man, unifying the opposition of concrete existence and abstract principle, harmonizing the confrontation of that which has form and that which has no form, experiences *tathatā* (suchness) of *dharma.*

If man understood that truth of this symbol-system and through a single object did envisage and experience the Inner-witness of *Dharma-Kāya,* it would appear to him that many and every existence in the universe is nothing but *samaya.*

Kūkai, drawing a line of demarcation between the 'revealed' doctrine and the 'secret' doctrine by this symbol system, says, 'In the 'revealed' doctrine, are Earth, Water, Fire, Wind, etc., treated as non-sentient objects, but in the 'secret' doctrine, they are explained as *samay*-bodies of *Tathāgata.*[43]

In Shingon Buddhism, 'Earth, Water, Fire, Wind, Space and Consciousness' are termed *Roku-dai* (Skt. *Sad mahā-bhūtāni* literally meaning six-great-beings), which we shall treat as a compound symbol later. This represents not six elements but *samaya*-bodies of *tathāgata;* this is what Kūkai would like to emphasize.

Historically speaking, among three symbols, first, Shingons (*mantras, dhāraṇīs* and other words of prayer) were introduced into Buddhism; secondly *hasta-mudrās* (hand-gestures) especially the natural type of time, and *ciñha-mudrās* (sign symbols) were incorporated into the system of Buddhism; thirdly these *ciñha-mudrās,* called *samaya,* became the symbol of *samaya* and concurrently the artificial type of *hasta-mudrā* (including that of *samaya* were devised; ultimately all of these symbols were compounded as three symbols of *Sam-mitsu.*

There is no further necessity to discuss these three symbols of *Sam-mitsu*. However, without the description of several concrete examples of these symbols, it would appear as if something was omitted and therefore, as a finishing touch, selecting the five kinds of practices of *Goshin-bō* (the dharma of protecting body) from among a great number of practices, we shall describe a concrete example of the smybols of *Sam-mitsu*.

GOSHIN-BŌ

Goshin-bō (literally the *dharma* of protecting body)[45] is one of the most important practices performed by Shingon priests. The main purpose of this practice is the protection and purification of the Practitioner, and this practice is performed before any other practices or rites in Shingon Buddhism.

Goshin-bō consists of five kinds of practice and each has its own *mudrā*, *shingon* and *samādhi* (contemplation):

(i) 'Purifiying Three Karmas'

(a) *Mudrā*: *mifu-renge* (Skt. *kudmala*), the unopened lotus hand-clasp:

(The two hands are placed together, palm against palm. Between the hands a slight space is left. Ten fingers[46] join, and only the middle fingers are slightly separated to leave an opening).

This *mudrā* represents the lotus flower just beginning to bloom. It is the symbol of 'starting out for *Bodhi*'.

(b) *Shingon*: *Oṁ Svabhava—Śuddha-Sarva-dharma-svabhāva Śuddhohaṁ* (Oṁ ! All dharmas which are pure by nature: I am pure in its nature!).[47]
Chanting the *shingon*, bring the *mudrā* to the five parts of the body: forehead, right and left shoulders, breast and throat, then to contemplate.

(c) *Samādhi*: By *Kaji* (*adhiṣṭhāna*), the ten evil things (Skt. *daśakuśala*) produced by three *karmas* are removed and purified, then is bathed the body and the innermost heart is purified.

(ii) 'The *Samaya* of the Buddha family'.[48]

(a) *Mudrā: buccho-in* (Skt. *uṣṇīṣa-mudrā*) the *mudrā* representing 'the head of Buddha': (The ten fingers are brought together, but between the hands a slight space is left. Then bend the index fingers and attach the tips to the middle part of middle fingers. The two thumbs subjoin the index fingers). This *Mudrā* is called that of the head of Buddha, because the three fingers, little ring and middle, represent the head of Buddha and the space between the middle and index fingers his eyes.

(b) *Shingon: Oṁ tathāgatodbhavāya svāhā* (Oṁ! For the arising of *Tathāgata*: hail!).[49]

(c) *Samādhi*: All *Tathāgatas* in the Buddha family *adhiṣṭhāna* (empower) the *Sādhaka*, and have him purify immediately his body-*karma*, extinguish his sinful actions, and enlarge his wisdom.

(iii) 'The *Samaya* of the Lotus Family'

(a) *Mudrā: hachiyo-in*, the *mudrā* of eight petals, or *Kaifu-renge*; full-bloomed lotus:
(The two hands are placed together, palm against palm. Space is left between them. Leave the tips of the thumbs and little fingers joined and the rest of the six fingers open with their tips bent slightly). This forms the eight petals of the full-bloomed lotus.

(b) *Shingon: Oṁ Padmodbhavāya Svāhā* (Oṁ! For the arising of Lotus, hail!).

(c) *Samādhi: Avalokiteśvara—bodhisattva* and the holy ones of the lotus family *adhiṣṭhana* (empower) the *Sādhaka* and have him immediately purify his *mouth-karma*, and make his speech dignified, a pleasure to listen to, eloquent and fluent.

(iv) 'The *Samaya* of the Diamond family'

(a) *mudrā: Sanko-kongō-in*, the *mudrā* of the three pronged *vajra*:
(Lay the left hand with palm downwards and the right hand with palm upwards, and place the two hands back to back. Interlock thumbs to little fingers, and other three fingers of both hands, i.e. index, middle, and ring form the three-pronged *vajra*).

The three-pronged *vajra* of the ritght hand represents the *Sam-mitsu* of the Buddha, and that of the left hand the *Sam-mitsu* of the people, and the interlocking of the body symbolizes its unification, i.e. *Sam-mitsu-Kaji*.

(b) *Shingon*: *Oṁ Vajradbhavāya Svāhā*: (Oṁ! For the arising of *Vajra* hail!).

(c) *Samādhi*: Bodhisattvas of *vajra-dhātu* (the world of *vajra*) and the holy ones in *vajra* family *adhiṣṭhāna* (empower) the *sādhaka*, and have him purify his mind-*karma*, verify his *bodhi*-mind, actualize his *Samadhi*, and have him immediately attain *Nirvāṇa*.

(v) 'The Protection of the Body by Wearing Armour'

(a) *mudrā: naibaku-Sanko-in*, the *mudrā* of the three-pronged *vajra* made by the inner-bond first:
(Ten fingers are joined with the tips on the inside. Raise both middle fingers and join their tips. Both Index fingers hook behind the middle fingers, but not attached to them. Both thumbs are extended and pressed against the closed ring fingers).
This *mudrā* represents the three-pronged *vajra* of the armour, which is considered as a symbol that keeps the *Sādhaka* away from evil desires, just as the armour is protection to the body from the attacks of the enemy.

(b) *Shingon: Oṁ Vajrāgni - Pradīptāya Svāhā* (Oṁ! For the blazing of *Vajra*-fire, hail!).

(c) *Samādhi*: Because the *Sādhaka* wears the Armour of Great Compassion of *Tathāgata*, to every devil and intruder, the sight of the power of *Sādhaka* which is brilliant just like the bright sun, brings forth their compassionate minds, and they are unable to intrude upon him. No sinful just or action can infect him. Getting rid of all sufferings, he attains the highest enlightenment (*anuttara-samyak-saṁbodhi*).

CONCLUSION

Like *mantras* and *maṇḍalas*, the most important aspect of the various kinds of *Shingon mudrās* is their functional role as catalysts which aid the practitioner to experience the phenomenal world as it is primordially given to consciousness. The Shingon pedagogy is consistent with Indian Śaivāgamic-Śaiva tantric *mudrās* or *nyasas,* and also with indigenous Japanese cultural characteristics. *Mudrās* denote both the means and goal of the Tantric path. The development of meanings, from mark and gesture to meditative state, help one see how Tantric matters incorporated the practices of the earlier Buddhist tradition into their own method for enlightenment. This paper also sought to show that this path, largely meditational in character, is in essential continuity with its Buddhist antecedents. The *mudrā* in shingon emphasizes the Somatic aspect of practice for attainting enlightenment with this present body, which makes Japanese esoteric Buddhism unique.

NOTES

1. Beatrice Lane Suzuki, *Shingon School of Mahāyāna Buddhism,* Research Institute of Esoteric Buddhist Culture, Koyasan University, Japan, p. 89.
2. Ibid.
3. K. Sankarnarayan, 'Concept of Mantra in Buddhist Tantra', International Seminar Proceedings on *Indo-Tibetan Buddhist Tantra* held by Central Institute of Indo-Tibetan Higher Studies, Saranath, Varanasi, India.
4. *Buddhist Tantra,* pp. 31, 36.
5. A. Macdonnell, *A Practical Sanskrit Dictionary* (London, 1929), rpt Oxford Unversity Press, 1969, p. 231.
6. *Religious Structure of Tantric Buddhism,* p. 194.
7. Ibid. Padma Sudhi in her work on *Symbols of Art, Religion and Philosophy,* discusses '*Mudrā*' in Ch. III. 'The word *Mudrā* as in Nirvana Tantra in its Pātala 11 described mudrra as mu = mukti and drā = dāyinī, i.e. which brings "beatitude".'

   Pṛthukāstaṇḍulā mṛṣṭā godhūma caṇakadayah
   tasya nāma bhaveddevī mudrā muktipradāyinī// p. 47.

   Kulārṇava-tantra derives the word from *mud* meaning delight, 'dravya' causal of *dru* and says *mudrās* (ritual fingers and hand poses) should be shown in worship and are so known because they give delight to the Gods and make their minds melt (with compositions for the worshippers). But *Śāradā Tilaka* derives from *mud* and *rā* (to give) and according to it *mudrā* means that delights the gods -

   mudaṁ rāti dadātīti mudreti nirvacanam ataeva
   taddarśanena devatāharṣopattiḥ/
   Mudaṁ kurvanti devānām manāṁsi drāvayanti ca

tasmān mudrā iti khyata darśitavyah kuleśvari//- 23.106.
Buddhist concept of *Mudrā* is discussed in detail by A. Wayman *Yoga of the Guhya Samāja Tantra* (Delhi, 1973), pp. 238-9.

8. *Mikkyo Bunka* by S. Toganoo (3) p. 61.
9. S. Dasgupta, *Buddhist Tantra,* p. 50.
10. *The Tantric Tradition,* p. 194.
11. Agehanada Bharati, *Hevajra Tantra,* edited by Snellgrove, viii. 17; II. vi. 3-5.
12. Kauṭilya's *Artha Śāstra*, the term signifies 'a seal'. *Cf.* Zimmer, *Philosophies of India*, p. 126.
13. For instance, 'the seal of Buddha' appeared in one of the sixteen chapters of *Pan-Chen-San-mei-Ching* translated by Lokarakṣa.
14. *Taisho,* Vol. 19, pp. 658b-64c.
15. Ibid. Vol. 39, p. 714a
16. *Vajraśekhara Sūtra* edited by Max Müller, p. 97.
17. *Japanese (Kūkai's Shingon) Esoteric Buddhism with Indian Perspective,* (under preparation by Yoritomi Motohiro, Shuchin University, Kyoto, Japan and Kalpakam Sankarnarayan, K.J. Somajya Centre of Buddhist Studies, Bombay, India).
18. Cf. H.A. Jaschke, *A Tibetan-English Dictionary* (London, 1881), p. 347.
19. E. Saunders, *Mudrā,* op. cit., pp. 32-3.
20. A.L. Basham, *The Wonder that was India,* p. 387.
21. Dietrich Seckel, *The Art of Buddhism,* tr. Ann. E. Keep (New York, 1964), p. 167.
22. Heinrich Zimmer, *The Art of Indian Asia,* completed and edited by Joseph Campbell, Vol. I, p. 165.
23. Ibid., pp. 175-7.
24. *Taisho,* Vol. 13, p. 899c.
25. Ibid., Vol. 15. p. 688c.
26. E. Saunders, *Mudrā,* pp. 38-42.
27. Paul Tillich, *Theology of Culture,* p. 65.
28. Monier Williams, *A Sanskrit English Dictionary.* Oxford, p. 1164a.
29. *Buddhist English Dictionary,* Vol. 2, p. 1679c.
30. *Nāgārjuna's Philosophy as presented in Mahā Prajñāpāramitā Śāstra,* edited by K. Venkata Ramanan, pp. 194-200.
31. Monier Williams, p. 1164a.
32. *Mandara no Kenkyu,* Toganoo, p. 263.
33. Yoshito S. Hakeda, *Kūkai and his Major Works* (New York, 1967), p. 56.
34. *Taisho,* Vol. 39, p. 674c.
35. Ibid., Vol. 4, pp. 18, 43, 59.
36. Ibid., Vol. 1, p. 844.
37. Ferdinand D. Lessing and Alex Wayman, *Fundamentals of Buddhsit Tantra,* p. 228, n. 23.

38. Matsunaga Yukei, *Mikkyo no Rekishi or the History of Esoteric Buddhism*, pp. 45-6.
39. *Ṛg Veda* 1.83; 32.3.
40. Cf. *Rishukyo no Kenkyu or the Study of Naya-Sūtra* by Toganoo, p. 447.
41. Explanation given by the Abbot of Koyasan Monastry, Koyasan, Japan.
42. Cf. Heinrich Zimmer, *Myths and Symbols in Indian Art and Civilization*, p. 71.
43. A.L. Basham, *The Wonder that was India*, p. 262.
44. *Daishi*, Vol. 2, p. 511.
45. *The Study of Goshin-bo*, Vol. 4.
46. Five fingers of both hands represent various things, such as *pañca-skanda* (five aggregates), pañca-*indriyāṇi* (the five roots), the five elements (*pañca-mahā-bhūta*), the five *dhyānī* Buddhas, the five letter, etc. See E. Saunders, op. cit., pp. 32-4.
47. Cf. Benoytosh Bhattacharyya, *An Introduction to Buddhist Esoterism*, Varanasi, 2nd revd edn.
48. This is one of the three families (*tri-kula*). In the *Mahāvairocana Sūtra* all deities (*Tathāgata*, Bodhisattvas and Vidyā-rajas) are classified into three families (tri-kula): Buddha Family, Lotus Family and Vajra Family.
49. *Svāhā* is the sacred word signifying 'may there be success'! the origin of which can be traced back to *Ṛg Veda*. Cf. Waddell, *The Dhāraṇī Cult in Buddhism*, p. 161.

14

Social Perspective of Tantrism A Religion of the Kali Age

BHASKAR CHATTERJEE

Tantrism is the religion of the Kali age. *The Kulārṇava Tantra* says: *Kṛte śrutyakta ācārastretāyāṁ smṛti—sambhavāḥ Dvāpare tu purāṇoktaṁ kalau āgamo kevelaṁ,*[1] that is, in the Kṛta or Satya age the religious scripture is Śruti (the Veda and Upaniṣad), in the Tretā age Smṛti (the Dharmaśāstra), in the Dvāpra age the Purāṇa, and in the Kali age the Tantra (Āgama). The *Mahānirvāṇa Tantra*[2] and other Tantra works also lay down the same rule. In the Satya age men are said to have been living in a golden age, as human relations were quite cordial. Men lived in a society where the means of production and the method of distribution were under the supervision of the community as a whole. There was hardly any shortage of food or other bare necessities of life. 'Plain living and high thinking' was the motto of life. The way of life was, therefore, thoroughly religious in every sense of the term. In a class-less society or a society in which there was hardly any hard and fast rule of caste, jealousy and hatred were totally absent. It was a sort of heavenly life, a description of which is to be found in the Buddhist *Digha Nikāya* and the Śānti Parvaṇ of the *Mahābhārata.*[3] It is learnt from such textual evidence that in the Kṛta age there was no state, as people did not require rule by coercion (*Daṇḍa*). But social conditions gradually deteriorated with the origin of institutions like the family, private property and caste system (implying social-distinctions). Because it was difficult to maintain these institutions without codified law and its implementation.[4] The *Smṛtikāras* or the authors of the Dharmaśāstras codified the law (*Dharma*) and the state originated for their implementation. Law was supposed to be a body of rules (*Ācāras*) regulating every aspect of life. Thus began the dependence of men on the state for their welfare and happiness. The king who promised to give protection automatically attracted the allegiance of the people. In the eyes of the common people the king was 'a god on the earth' (*Mahatī devatā hi eṣā naraūpeṇa tiṣṭhati*—Manu, VII).[5] Power, glory, wealth, slendour and above all, capacity to do good to those who are *śiṣṭa,* i.e. law-abiding, owing allegiance to the authority, are some of the significant attributes of both the ķing and the god. To the people living far away from the capital, the king remained unseen and unknown. They could however meet occasionally the officials who represented the king. Thus the king and his *amātyas* (bureaucracy) served as the model for the hierarchical Puraṇic pantheon. With increasing dependence on the state, men became more and more infirm, lacking initiative for hard work. They were devotees of divinities presiding over the coveted things of life such as wealth beauty, power, etc. The Purāṇas catered to their needs and paved the way towards the emergence of different religious sects. The ultimate goal of life was attainment of heaven, an imaginary abode providing pleasures of all kinds. The devotee (*sādhaka*) sumbitted his prayers to his *Iṣṭadevatā* (a special divinity chosen for one's worship). In the Kali age men do not have even the capacity, longevity or moral strength necessary for the application of *Bhakti-mārga.* They have become so weak that in order to avoid physical, mental and intellectual exertion, they have shifted their allegiance from God to guru who is supposed to give directions of the easiest way to the ultimate and common end of all Śāstras. Fulfilment of desire may be held to be the common end of all religions, whatever might be the nature of desire. For the average people, desire is of a temporal nature, while for the highly advanced devotees the desire is spiritual.

The Tantras distinguish three classes of men according to their temperament, disposition and character: *paśubhāva* (animal), *vīrabhāva* (heroic) and *divyabhāva* (divine).[6] The *paśu* is the man bound by the *pāśas* (bonds) which, according to the *Kulārṇava Tantra,* are *dayā* (pity), *moha* (delusion), *bhaya* (fear), *lajjā* (shame), *ghṛṇa* (disgust), *kula* (family), *śila* (custom) and *varṇa* (caste).[7] The people of higher categories belong to *vīrabhāva* and *divyabhāva.* However, Tantrism is primarily the religion meant for those who lead a family-life (*gṛhastha*) in a caste society. The *vīras* who are distinguished from the *paśus* are anarchists and ignore the traditional sentiments and rules of family and caste. But one can hardly begin one's religious life as a *vīra* without crossing the initial stage of *paśu*, that of a 'social animal'.

Tantrik worship is free from Vedic exclusiveness, whether based on caste or sex. As the *Gautamīya Tantra* observes: 'The Tantra is for all men, of whatever caste, and for all women' (*Sarvavarṇādhikāraśca nārīṇāṁ yogya eva ca*).[8] In the *Setubandha*-commentary of the *Vāmakeśvara Tantra* it is said that tantrika sādhanā is suitable for the dvijāti, Śudra, saṁkara-caste and women.[9] The Śudras have no right to make use of the Gāyatrī but can take initiation for Tāntrik sādhanā. The *Viśvasāra Tantra* says that women and Śudras can worship as per rules of the Āgama (*Āgamokta vidhānena strī śudraścaiva pūjayet*).[10] The Kaulamārga is open to all castes, according to the *Kulārṇava Tantra*. It appears, therefore, that the Tantrik writers have not ignored the caste system, although they have ruled out caste restrictions in religious life.

The *Varṇāśrama* has been modified in Tantrism. The *Mahānirvāṇa Tantra* (Ch. VIII, verse 8) states that in the Kali age there are only two āśramas, the *gārhasthya* and the *saṁnyāsa* (*avadhūta*).[11] It has been enjoined that Tantrik sannyāsa can be adopted by all castes. But one should not enter into Avadhūtāśrama neglecting old parents, faithful wife and children. This, no doubt, implies the significant role of a gṛhastha in social life. A householder can very well prove to be a sādhaka, if he has sincerity of purpose. The *Mahānirvāṇa Tantra* advises all to remain gṛhastha with devotion to Brahma (*Brahmaniṣṭho gṛhasthaḥ syād*).[12] However, women have been granted the right to adopt the life of an avadhūtī. In the *Muṇḍamālā Tantra* it has been said that an avadhūta is like Śiva Himself, while an avadhūtī is like goddess Śiva (*Avadhūti Śiva devī*).[13]

The Tāntrik view of society is opposite to that of the Śruti and the Smṛti. From the Smārta point of view, a Śudra is unfit for sacraments, vows and religious instruction (*Manu Saṃhitā*, IV). In the Śānti Parvaṇ of the *Mahābhārata* it is clearly laid down that a Śudra is not entitled to the Vedic 'dharma'. Similar views had been expressed with regard to the religious rights of women. Again, āśrama-dharma or duties to be performed in the four stages of life have been explained in the *Dharmasūtras, Arthaśāstra* and *Dharmaśāstras*. On the other hand, the Tantras have extended recognition to the religious rights of both the Śudras and women. Again, the Tantras have recognized the greatest value of the life of a householder and have questioned the relevance of *Brahmācārya* and *Vānaprastha* in the Kali age. There is little doubt that Tantrism is unvedic in its social perspective. That seems to be the reason why the Tantras have been denounced in the Purāṇas like the *Varāha, Kūrma, Liṅga, Brahmavaivarta, Skanda, Śāmba,* etc.[14] Aparārka (thirteenth century) in his commentary on *Yājñavalkya* (I.7) has stated: 'The Tantras should not be condemned but still they have no authority or validity in all their parts.'[15] Bendall has observed in the introduction to his edition of *Śikṣa-samuccaya* that the 'Tantras developed a form of religion which was brought to the level of very thinly veiled *Kāmaśāstra*'.[16] This has an indirect reference to the *Vīrācāra.* These particular practices formed only a part of the Tantras and were meant only for the select few. In the *Kulārṇava Tantra*[17] it has been a said:

Nectar drinking is the union of Kuṇḍali Śakti with the Moon cit (*ciccandra*). Others are but wine-drinkers (VV. 107-8). The true meat-eater is he who has merged his citta in the Supremo (V.109). He who controls his senses and unites them with Ātmā is a fish-eater. The rest do but kill animals (V.110). True sexual union is the union of Parā-Śakti (Kuṇḍali) with Ātmā; others do but have carnal connection with women' (VV.111-12).

Bhaskarācārya in his *Setubandha* has pointed out that it was with a view to dissuade ordinary people from the observance of these very difficult practices that even the Tantra and the Purāṇa works are found to speak adversely against them.[18]

Distinctions between higher and lower groups has never been made in the Tantras in the ordinary social sense. The religious path, as noted above, was left open to all irrespective of caste and sex. But the guru, the spiritual guide, who has been given the most exalted position in the tantrik system, is given the liberty to analyse the spiritual aptitude of his disciples. He makes the classification called *Kula.* There are five such *Kulas,* technically called Ḍombī, Naṭī, Rajakī, Caṇḍālī and Brāhmāṇi.[19] The *Tantrasāra* (Ch. 1) says that good qualities are required in the disciple.[20] In the *Matsya-sūkta-Tantra* (Ch. XIII) and *Prāṇātoṣinī* (. 108)[21] the qualifications of a good disciple are stated to be good birth, purity of soul (*sūddhātmā*), and capacity for enjoyment, combined with desire for liberation (*puruśārtha-parāyaṇaḥ*). Those who are lewd (*kāmuka*), adulterous (*paradārātura*) constantly addicted to sin (*sadā pāpa-kriya*), ignorant, slothful and devoid of religion should be rejected , according to the

Mahārudra-Yāmala [1 khanda (Ch. XV) and 2 khanda (Ch. II)].[22] Therefore, on this parameter there is little scope for distinctions between higher and lower caste people. Raghunandana seems to have made a misreading of the actual condition in his *Tithitattva* (Durgā Pūjā section) when he states that higher caste people were not to take part in the Kaula rites of the Tantras.[23]

Although from the point of view of Tantra writers, the Ṭantras were meant for the Kali age and the Vedas for the Satya age, it has been suggested by non-Tāntrik modern scholars that Tantrism had its origin in pre-Vedic times, and that Tāntrik rites originated in primitive fertility cults.[24] Sorcery, fertility rites and secret tribal cults continued to be practised by those who avoided the official 'civilised' religion but tried to achieve special powers and material prosperty. Primitive fertility rites are said to have appeared in a sublimated form as Tantrism. That is, the higher class of people systematized those rites and found for them a philosophy of their own.

The Sāṁkhya theory of creation, as envisaged in the Tantras, upholds the predominant role of the Mother-Goddess or *Śakti*. The dual process of involution and evolution of *Śakti* is said to have formed the foundation of thc Tāntrik *yogasādhanā*. The process of evolution is presumed to be caused by *Vāmācāra* which, according to some, represents the original version of Tantrism. The said *ācāra* or practice is explained as one in which women participate. The participation of women in rites for agricultural production is suggested to be the foundation of Tāntrik belief and practice.[25] It is believed by some that the predominance of the *Śakti* cult or the cult of the Mother is to be traced in a social form that was on the threshold of agrarian economy.

If the cult of the Mother-Goddess is held to be the foundation of Tantrism, it is to the life of Mohenjodaro and Harappa that we must trace the source of Tantrism.[26] The figure of Proto-Śiva is found depicted on a Mohenjodaro-seal in yogic posture, being surrounded by a number of beasts. The Mother-Goddess is represented by a large number of terracotta figurines, portraying standing semi-nude female figures. The lower part of an Indus seal is occupied by a row of seven female spirits or deities, probably the precursors of later *saptamātṛkās*. Several artefacts represent *liṅga* and *yoni* symbols. The archaeological evidence leaves little doubt that the cult of fertility was prevalent side by side with the worship of Father-God (Proto-Siva) and a Mother-

Goddess (later Śakti).[27] It is difficult to ascertain whether the Harappan people had a matriarchal society. But there is least doubt that their society was not at the threshold of agrarian economy, as they had developed an urban society and economy on the basis of surplus agricultural production. It has been observed: 'Concrete elements of the material conditions to which Tantrism owed its origin must have somehow or other survived in the general social fabric of later India to sustain and nourish these ideological elements.'[28] The observation does not satisfactorily explain the position.

Tāntrik rites are traced by some scholars in the later Vedic texts, and in Buddhist and Jain literature.[29] But the Tantras cannot be said to have existed as a distinct system before the sixth century AD. Manuscripts of several early Tāntrik texts, such as fragments of the *Sarvajñānottara tantra, Kubjikā Tantra, Niśvāsa Saṃhitā* and *Saura Saṃhitā*, are found to be in Gupta or transitional Gupta characters.[30] The word 'Tantra' occurs in an inscription of the first quarter of the fifth century in the village of Gangdhar (Jhalwar, M.P.). In lines 22-3 of the record mention is made of the (Divine Mothers), filled full of Ḍākinīs, who stir up the very oceans with the mighty wind rising from the Tāntrik rites of their religion.[31] Again it has been suggested that persons well-versed in the *maṇḍalakrama* (mentioned in Ch. 58 of the *Bṛhatsaṃhitā*), entitled to instal the images of the Divine Mothers, might have been Tāntrik Śakti-worsippers.[32] The concept of the *Śakti-pīṭhas,* which was based on the Tāntrik concept of the intimate association of Śakti with Bhairava (the terrific aspect of Śiva), was well known in the seventh century and was observed by Hiuen Tsang.[33]

However, if the tribal-folk base of Tantrism is assumed, as it has been actually done by a group of scholars, the new phenomenon in the religious life promoted social harmony by forging uniting ties between the folk and elite cultures. It is doubtful if the folk-religion merged in the official civilized religion, for people often found the official civilized religion out of their reach and preferred to continue with their own primitive beliefs and practices. This is evident from the continuity of tribal-folk religions alongside with Tantrism.

From the available evidence it appears that Tantrism, whatever its antiquity, came to be regarded as a distinct religion from the sixth century. If that be so, the Kali age may be supposed to have begun in this century. As has been pointed out above, the Tantras were meant for the Kali age. In the Gupta/post-Gupta period liberal endowments in the form of numerous land-grants were made in favour of the Brāhmaṇical and Buddhist religious institutions. Brahmin gurus and Buddhist ācāryās found ample scope of making an investigation for developing a new system of beliefs and practices known as Tantrism. By the twelfth century their new scientific discoveries about the human body of 3.5 crores of *nāḍis,*[34] both gross and subtle, and six *cakras* with the thousand-petalled lotus at the top,[35] gave unprecedented scope for the sādhaka to search for the absolute truth within himself. 'Individualistic in character, it is the outcome of longing for intimate communion with the Divine.'[36]

Some scholars have assumed that during the post-Gupta period under feudal influence and on account of numerous land-grants made to the monasteries Buddhism degenerated into the worst forms of Tantricism.[37] But neither feudal influence nor land-endowments in large number can satisfactorily explain degeneration, if any. The erotic sculptures of Puri, Konarak and Khajuraho were not necessarily inspired by Tantrik practices of the early medieval period, as is assumed by some.[38] The tradition of eroticism was maintained by sculptors even at Sanchi, Amaravati, Mathura and Ellora in earlier periods.

In the early centuries of the Christian era, mercantile support benefitted the Buddhist *saṁgha.* This is evident from numerous donation-records listed by Lüders.[40] Again, from the *Kāmasūtra* of Vātsyāyana we have vivid descriptions of orgies in which city-bred men (Nāgaraka) could have involved themselves.[41] Lust of the basest type could be satisfied, it may be reasonably assumed, by those called *Seṭṭhis* and *Ibhyas* in the Jātakas. During the Gupta/post-Gupta period, when emphasis had shifted from the mercantile agrarian economy, the landed gentry of different cateogories began the process of exploitng the peasantry. The entire poulation was divided into two sections, the landed aristocracy on the one hand and the vast population of peasants on the other. It was but natural for the peasant population, mostly Śudras, to seek a way of escape or liberation from the miseries which were caused by exploitation by the aristocracy. Tantrism provided the common people with the easiest way of escape from mundane miseries. This explains why the people took to the mystic and individualistic Tāntrik method as the prop of life. The socio-religious trend that had its beginning in the sixth century became mature by the sixteenth century, when the Vaiṣṇava Bhakti movement, in a changed Indo-Islamic social background, questioned the authority of the Tantras in the Kali age.

NOTES

1. John Woodroffe, *Introduction to Tantra-Śāstra* (Madras, 1956), p. 40.
2. Ibid., p. 41.
3. R.S. Sharma, *Aspects of Political Ideas and Institutions in Ancient India* (New Delhi, 1959), pp. 33-9.
4. Ibid., pp. 41, 49, 54.
5. V.P. Verma, *Studies in Hindu Political Thought* (Delhi, 1959), pp. 239ff.
6. Woodroffe, op. cit., p. 58.
7. Ibid.
8. Ibid., p. 31.
9. Sukhamay Bhattacharya Sastri, *Tantra Parichay* (Visva Bharati, B.S. 1359), p. 18.
10. Ibid., p. 39.
11. Woodroffe, op. cit., pp. 32-3.
12. Sastri, op. cit., p. 66.
13. Ibid.
14. Chintaharan Chakrabarti, *Tantras: Studies on their Religion and Literature,* (Calcutta, 1963), pp. 32-3.
15. Ibid., p. 37.
16. Ibid., p. 36.
17. Taranatha Vidyaratana, *Kulārṇava Tantra* (Delhi, 1973), Introduction.
18. Chakrabarti, op. cit., p. 36 fn.
19. R.C. Majumder (ed.), *History of Bengal,* Vol. I (Dacca, 1943), p. 421.
20. Woodroffe, op. cit., p. 66 fn. 4.
21. Ibid., fn. 5.
22. Ibid., fn. 6.
23. Chakrabarti, op. cit., p. 36. fn. 18.
24. D.D. Kosambi, *The Culture and Civilization of Ancient India* (New Delhi, 1962), p. 105.
25. D.P. Chattopadhyay, *Lokāyata* (New Delhi, 1985), pp. 269ff.
26. Ibid., pp. 262-5.
27. E. Mackay, *Early Indus Civilization* (New Delhi, 1976), Pl. XVII. 9, pp. 58, 62; R.C. Majumdar (ed), *The Vedic Age* (Bombay, 1971), p. 189.
28. Chattopadhyay, op. cit., p. 323.
29. Ibid., pp. 10-16.
30. Ibid., p. 20.

31. Fleet (ed.), *Corpus Inscriptionum Indicarum*, Vol. III, p. 72.
32. J.N. Banerjea, *Development of Hindu Iconography* (Calcutta, 1956), p. 494.
33. Ibid.
34. Woodroffe, op. cit., pp. 47-8.
35. Ibid., pp. 48-57.
36. D.N. Bose and Hiralal Haldar, *Tantras: Their Philosophy and Occult Secrets* (Calcutta, 1956), p. 55.
37. R.S. Sharma, *Perspectives in Social and Economic History of Early India* (New Delhi, 1983), p. 238.
38. R.C. Majumdar (ed.), *The Struggle for Empire* (Bombay, 1979), p. 653.
39. Ibid.
40. H. Lüders, *List of Brahmi Inscriptions, Appendix to Epigrphia Indica*, Vol. X.
41. H.C. Chakladar, *Social Life in Ancient India* (*Study in Vatsyayana's Kāmasūtra*) (New Delhi, 1984), Ch. V, pp. 144-71.

15

The Cult of Tārā in Historical Perspective

N.N. BHATTACHARYYA

According to the Mahāyāna Buddhist conception, Tārā is the primordial female energy, the consort of Avalokiteśvara, who enables her devotees to surmount all sorts of dangers and calamities. Prayer to this goddess removes the eight *mahābhayas* (great dangers). She is also known as the goddess Prajñāpāramitā, as it is by the fulfilment of this *pāramitā* that a Bodhisattva reaches the goal. Sometimes she is conceived as the supreme being, 'the mother of all the Buddhas and Bodhisaattvas'. She became a very popular deity in India during the early centuries after Christ when the Mahāyāna pantheon was developing rapidly. The conception of this goddess is, however, primitive and it is quite possible that in course of her conceptual development she had absorbed within herself a number of divinities representing different aspects of the Female Principle. The epithets *tāra* and *tāriṇī*, attributed to the Devī in the *Mahābhārata* and the Purāṇas may be traced to the *Yajurveda* in which the term *tāra,* meaning 'saviour' is an appellation of Śiva. Then there is the Sanskrit *tārā* or *tārakā* meaning a star, and the word might easily represent the name of a goddess dwelling among the stars. Many such streams later culminated in the conception of Tārā whose cult was established in different parts of India by the sixth century.

The earliest reference to a Buddhist worshipper of Tārā is found in Subandhu's *Vāsavadattā.*[1] From the seventh century onwards, the influence of Buddhist Tārā began to be felt upon the religious systems of India and abroad. In India, the development of the Śākta religion received momentum from the Tārā cult of the Buddhists. The Śākta Tārā, also called Ugratārā, Ekajaṭā and Nīla-Sarasvatī, is undoubtedly an adaptation of the Mahāyāna Buddhist goddess of the same name. Tārā also has a place as a Śāsanadevatā in the Jain pantheon, her other name being Dhāriṇī.

The gods and goddesses are the symbols of the Buddhist conceptions of the four elements and five constituents of a being. Earth is represented by the goddess Locanā, water by Māmakī, fire by Pāṇḍaravāsini and air by Tārā while the five constituents of a being are represented by the five Dhyānī Buddhas, and as such adepts should realize that the female sex is the source of all. The goddess Tārā occurs in the *Mañjuśrīmūlakalpa*[2] in her various forms like Bhṛkuṭi, Locanā, Māmakī, Śvetā, Pāṇḍaravāsinī, Sutārā, etc. She is described as Vidyārājñī who is full of compassion. Tārā is elevated to the position of the highest deity in the *Mahāpratyaṅgirādhāraṇī*, a fragment of which is found in Central Asia, in which she is described as a goddess of white colour, wearing a garland of *vajras* and having the figure of Vairocana on her crown. From the seventh century onwards, we find the exuberance of Tārā-stotras (cf. the *Sarangdhārā-stotras* composed in praise of Tārā by the eighth century Kashmiri poet Sarvajñamitra) and the goddess is elevated to the position of mother of all Buddhas. A Rāṣṭrakūṭa inscription refers to the great veneration in which the goddess Tārā was held by the Pāla kings of eastern India whose standard bore the representation of Bhagavatī Tārā.[3] From the Banpur copper plates of the Somavaṃśī king Indraratha it appears that the cult of Tārā was popular in Orissa. A twelfth century Nalanda inscription refers to the construction of a Tārā temple. A thirteenth century copper plate from Mainamati records the dedication of a *vihāra* to Tārā in the town of Paṭṭikera.[4]

In Śaktism Tārā is conceptually the same as Kālī. According to the *Śaktisangamatantra* there is no difference between Tārā, Kālī, Tipurasundarī and Chinnamastā (Vajrayoginī of the Buddhist tradition). The relation between Kālī and Tārā is the same as that between Śiva and Śakti. According to the *Tārātantra*,[6] without initiation into the Tārā cult one cannot attain happiness, liberation or fame. In the *Tārārahasya*[7] it is said that because she is the saviour of all, she is known as Tārā and as such she is definitely identical with Kālī. In the *Kubjikātantra*[8] it is said that because she protects she is known as Tārā and Tārinī. Tārā is one of the ten goddesses of the Mahāvidyā category. Her *mantras* are numerous and she is invoked in three forms, Ekajaṭā, Ugratārā and Nīlasarasvatī.[9] Ekajaṭā has dishevelled hair and her matted locks represent Rudra, which accounts for her name. Ugratārā is so called because she protects mankind from grave (*ugra*) disasters. According to another tradition she appear at the middle of the night to save her devotee from all fearful (*ugra*) consequences.[10] The name of Nīlasarasvatī is due to the fact that originally she appeared in Cola lake situated on the west of Meru. Her blue colour is the reflection of her own rays in the lake. The secret *mantra* of Ugratārā is *oṃ hriṃ striṃ huṃ phaṭ*. According to the *Tantrasāra*,[11] if this *mantra* be prefixed by *śrī*, it gives all forms of prosperity, if *hriṃ* be prefixed it fulfils all forms of desire, and if *aiṃ* be prefixed it bestows all forms of attainments through speech or utterances. If *oṃ* be omitted from the *mantra* or Ugratārā the rest becomes the *mantra* or Ekajaṭā. If both *oṃ* and *phaṭ* be omitted the three other sounds turn to be the *mantra* of Nīlasarasvatī. She is also called Kullukā. Quoting *Matsyasukta*, the *Tantrasāra*[12] says that the Tārā-*mantras* fulfil all attainments. Their knowledge bring liberation within the span of life. He who utters these *mantras* is endowed with poetic imagination and mastery over all sciences. He becomes as rich as Kubera and as learned as Bṛhaspati. In the king's court he receives honour, in legal disputes he becomes the winner, and in business he becomes successful.

The *dhyānas* or conceptual meditations of Tārā are found in various Śākta Tantras. According to the *Nīlatantra*,[13] she is garlanded with human skulls, seated in *pratyālīḍha* pose (the left leg is outstretched while the right is slightly bent and placed behind). She is short, pot-bellied. Her waist is guarded by tiger skin. She is youthful and endowed with five *mudrās*, and four-armed; her tongue is outstretched, and her appearance is fearful. She is the bestower of boons. Her two right hands contain a sword and a knife and two left hands hold a skull and a lotus. She has a single mane which is brown. Her crest contains the god Akṣobhya (one of the five Dhyānī Buddhas) in the form of a snake. Her three eyes are round and resemble the roundness of the sun. With a smiling face she is decked with womanly ornaments. She sits on a white lotus issuing out of the primordial waters. According to the *Tāriṇītantra*[14] she is black, with a protruding belly. She has a reddish face and well developed breasts. Dressed in a red garment she is surrounded by a great serpent and seated on a corpse. Her eyes are fixed on the tip of her nose. Her upper right hand contains a lotus and the lower right hand is in the boon-giving pose. Her upper left hand contains a wine-pot and lower left hand is in the pose of giving protection. Her sacred thread is a snake. She is three-eyed, having a long nose, long legs, a tall body and a long togue. The sun, the moon and fire are her three eyes. A tiger's skin serves as her headdress.

Apart from Ugratārā and Nīlasarasvatī, another tradition refers to eight other forms of Tārā: Tārā, Ugrā, Mahogrā, Vajrā, Kālī, Sarasvatī, Kāmeśvarī and Bhadrakālī.[15] In the *Nīlatantra* Nīlasarasvatī is described as standing on a corpse with a smiling face, with three eyes looking like lotus and with dagger, skull, and lotus and in her four hands. She is equated with Vagīśvarī who is like a wish-fulfilling tree to her devotees and resort of all. She bestows success and poetic imagination upon all. Her short body is full of pride. She looks brighter owing to her embellishment with serpents, tiger-skin, bell and garland of skulls. She resides on her *dhyānamantras.* She has three forms—gross, subtle and that which is beyond comprehension. Even Brahmā, Viṣṇu and Śiva worship her.[16] The eight verses in which Tārā has been lauded in the *Nīlatantra* are known as the *Tārāṣṭaka.* He who reads this *Tārāṣṭaka* with purity of body and mind thrice a day attains the power of composing poetry, becomes master of all sciences and receives Lakṣmī, the goddess of wealth and prosperity, permanently, so that he can enjoy all the enjoyable things. He possesses fame, a beautiful body, sound health and popularity and is destined to have permanent salvation after his death. Apart from reading this *Tārāṣṭaka* one should also read the *kavaca* of Tārā which is recorded in the *Rudrayāmala.*[17] The seer of *Tārākavaca* is Akṣobhya, metre *triṣṭubh,* god Tārā, and *viniyoga* (application) success in all fields. In this *kavaca* Tārā is invoked for protection and success. *Hrim, strim, hum* and *phaṭ* are all suggestive of protection which is sought from Tārā in her various forms.

Tārā is foremost among Buddhist goddesses. It appears that her cult was introduced in the Mahāyāna pantheon in the sixth century. Hiuen Tsang found many Tārā images in northern India. Originally there were two basic types in her conception, *saumya* (benign) and *ugra* (terrible). Later we come across twenty-one forms of her. The Mahāyāna pantheon is headed by five Dhyānī Buddhas, their colours being white, green, yellow and blue. Accordingly Tārā is also conceived in terms of five colours, among which her white and green forms belong to the benign category while yellow, red and blue to the terrible category.[18] Tārā was introduced in Buddhism as the consort of Avalokiteśvara. As the supreme Female Principle of Tantric Buddhism she was elevated to such a position that all other Buddhist goddesses came to be regarded as her manifestation. This is why Tārā became the common name of all Buddhist goddesses. For practical purposes, however, only those deities can be called Tārās to whom the *mantra* '*Oṃ Tare Tuttāre Ture Svāhā*' is assigned. In the simplest form Tārā carries a lotus in the left hand and exhibits the *varada mudrā* in the right. Some Tārā images bear the miniature image of Amoghasiddhi on their crowns but others may not have any effigy of the Dhyānī Buddha. In Tantric works there are so many different varieties of Tārā that it is practically impossible to classify them correctly without reference to their peculiar colour.[19]

In 1874 Rasik Mohan Chatterjee brought out a series of Hindu Tantric texts from Bengali manuscripts and published them in the Bengali script. Among the works he brought out were Brahmānada's *Tārārasasya,* the *Rudrayāmala* and the *Mahācināċārakrama,* all of which refer to the Vāmācāra practices connected with the worship of Tārā as being brought by the sage Vasiṣṭha who was instructed by the Buddha himself. The rituals are of Chinese origin. The *Tārātantra*[21] opens with the following question of Devī Tārā or Mahānīlasarasvatī: 'Thou didst speak of two Kula-Bhairavas, Buddha and Vasiṣṭha. Tell me, by what *mantra* they became Siddha.' The same Tantra defines a Bhairava as one who purifies these five (Ms) and after offering the same (to the god) partakes thereof. Buddha then is said to be Kula Bhairava.[22] In 1900, Haraprasad Sastri painted out the connection of the goddess Tārā with Tibet and China and of the Vāmācāra practices with these of China.[23] The story recorded in the *Tārātantra* describes how Vasiṣṭha went to Mahācīna to get instruction from the Buddha. He brought from there the cult known as *Mahācīnakramācāra* which prescribes the worship of Mahācinatārā. Sylvan Levi also holds, on the authority of the *Tārātantra,* and other works cited by Śastri, that the worship of Tārā and the Tantric Vāmācāra practices, involving the use of Five Ms came from China.[24] Sir John Woodroffe takes a similar view.[25]

A.K. Maitra, the editor of the *Tārātantra,* gives quotations from both the *Rudrayāmala* and the *Brahmayāmala* which narrate the story of Vasiṣṭha obtaining Vāmācāra practices from China. According to the *Rudrayāmala,*[26] Vasiṣṭha practised for six thousand years severe austerities in a lonely spot, but the goddess did not appear to him. Thereupon he went to his father Brahmā and asked for a different *mantra.* Brahmā advised him to carry on his austerities. Vasiṣṭha complied, and this time when the goddess did not appear he became angry, and having sipped water uttered a terrible curse. Thereupon the goddess appeared to him and pointed out that he had not taken the right mode of *sādhanā*. She advised him to go to Mahācīna, the country of Bauddhas. Vasiṣṭha then went to China where Buddha was established (*budahapratiṣṭha*). Having repeatedly bowed to the ground he said to the Buddha:

> Protect me, O Mahādeva, the imperishable one, in the form of Buddha. I am humble Vasiṣṭha, son of Brahmā. For my perturbed mind I have come here for the *sādhanā* of the Mahādevī.... But doubts assail my mind (*bhayāni santi me hṛdi*) having seen the methods (*ācāra*). Remove them and also the weakness of my mind which is inclined to the Vedic way (*vedagāminī*). O Lord, here I find rites which are outside Veda (*vedabahiṣkṛta*). How is that wine, meat, women are drunk, eaten and enjoyed by Siddhas who are naked (*digambara*), high (*vara*) and about to drink blood (*raktapānodyata*). They drink constantly and enjoy beautiful women (*muhurmuhu prapivanti ramayanti varāṅganān*).... They are beyond the Vedas (*vedasyāgocarāḥ*) and always indulged in wine and women (*madyastrisevaniratāḥ*).... How can inclinations to such things purify mind? How can there by *siddhi* without Vedic rites?

The Buddha was not perturbed at these direct questions but delivered a lecture on the duties of the Kaulas and explained to him their mysteries and utility and acquainted him with the secret rites and practices connected therewith. Again in the *Brahmayāmala*[27] the same story is repeated, but with a slight modification. Now Vasiṣṭha is asked by the Devī to go to Mahācīna and get himself initiated into *cīnācāra*. Vasiṣṭha went there to see a land inhabited by great *sādhakas* and thousands of beautiful and youthful women, full of mirth, by the inspiration of wine and making suggestive gestures. He was surprised to see Buddha with eyes drooping with wine. He asked himself: 'What is Viṣṇu doing in his Buddha form? This way (*ācāra*) is opposed to Veda (*vedavādaviruddha*). I do not approve of it.' At once he heard a voice coming from air telling him not to think in this way. Being afraid he sought refuge with Buddha who explained to him the mysteries of the Tāriṇī (Tārā) cult which involved Five Ma-kāras, known as Cīnācāra.

The cult of Tārā passed from India to Tibet where the she came to be known as Sgrol-ma or Dol-ma in the Tibetan translation of her name. Like her husband Avalokiteśvara she was also conceptualized in numerous forms. Her cult, also went to China as the Śakti or Avalokiteśvara. But in China, as S.K. Chatterji[28] has demonstrated, Avalokiteśvara was already on the way to transformation from a god to a goddess through the influence of the pre-Buddhist (Taoist and Confucian) Mother Goddess Si-Wang-Mu, the representative of Yin or the Female Principle. This happened in the seventh and eighth centuries, when Tārā became absolutely merged with her husband who was transformed into the goddess Kuan-yin in China. This double form of Tārā became popular in China and brought about her connection with most of the existing beliefs and rituals, especially those belonging to Taoism. The Taoist rituals which thus came into the fold of the Tārā cult in China as well as Yinism or Exaltation of the Female Principle in Taoism, which developed in that system as a corollary of the aforesaid Chinese Buddhist cult of the Female Principle, were also able to exert a counter-influence upon the development of the Indian Vāmācāra rites of both the Buddhist and non-Buddhist Tantras.

P.C. Bagchi, on the basis of a *sādhanā* found in the *Sādhanamālā*[29] has tried to establish the identify of Mahācīnatārā and Ekajaṭā whose cult is said to have been recovered by Siddha Nāgārjuna from Tibet.[30] The *sādhanā* of the goddess Ekajaṭā was discovered by him in the country of Bhoṭa. The description of Ekajaṭā is found in six different *sādhanas*[31] and closely agrees with that of Mahācīnakramatārā as found in other *sādhanas.*[32] According to the *Sammohatantra,* Nīlasarasvatī or Ugratārā was born in a lake called Cola on the western side of the Meru which was included in the Cīnadeśa. Bagchi suggested that Cola is probably to be connected with the common word for lake, *kul* or *col,* which is found with the names of many lakes to the west and north of T'ien-shan, that is to say, the pure Mongolian zone.

A number of countries beyond India are enumerated and described in the *Sammohatantra* as centres of Ṭantric culture. These are Bāhlīka (Balkh), Kirāta (hill tribes in the Himalayan zone), Bhoṭa (Tibet), Cīna (China), Mahācīna (Greater China), Maide (Media), Pārśvakika (Pārasika, Persia), Airāka (Iraq), Kamboja, Huna, Yavana, Gandhāra and Nepāla. It is not impossible that some Tantric schools associated themselves with these countries either through tradition or through the community of some mystic beliefs, whose history is not clearly known. The same Tantra holds that China alone possessed a hundred primary and seven subsidiary Tantras (*śatam tantrāni cine tu upatantrāni sapa ca*). It should also be remembered that of the earlier Śākta Pīṭhas—Kāmarūpa, Pūrṇagiri, Oḍḍiyāna and Jālandhara—there were situated on the high roads leading to countries outside India. Oḍḍiyāna was situated on the high road that connected the upper valley of the Indus with Balkh, Samarkand, etc., on the one hand and the Pamirs, Khotan, Kashgarh, etc., on the other by the Gilgit valley. Jālandhara was situated on another highway that connected Tibet with India through the Shipki pass and Kāmarūpa had to a great extent been the centre of activities of foreign peoples since very ancient times.[33]

We have already had the occasion to refer to the Tārā temples seen by the Chinese pilgrims. A ninth century Tārā image has been found at Dhāraṇi Mātā temple at the foot of the Taranga hill on the west bank of the Sabarmati in Gujarat. It was the site of the ancient Tārāpura, though later it came under the influence of Jainism.[34] In Karṇāṭaka where Tārā images have been found at Balligava (Belgami) and Dambal, an inscription of the reign of Vikramāditya VI records grants to a Tārā temple by some merchants.[35] A twelfth century Nalanda inscription found at Somapura (Paharpur in North Bengal) refers to a temple erected by a monk called Vipulaśrī which was dedicated to Aṣṭamahābhaya-Tārā, the goddess who protects her devotees from eight kinds of peril—fire, robbers, fetters, shipwreck, lions, serpents, elephants and demons. Previously the task of saving mankind from these eight great perils was entrusted to Avalokiteśvara, but later it came to the exclusive domain of Tārā. The first illustrations of this occurs at cave 9 in Ellora where Tārā is depicted as the saviour from all these.[36] Dharmasvāmin during his travels at Bodhgaya came across Tārāvihāra. He saw an image of Ārya Tārā at Vaisali, the head and body of which lean to the left, the feet unevenly placed. The right hand of the image shows *varadamudrā* and the left, three jewels. At Nalanda he found painted on a wall of the Vihāra[37] an image of Tārā without ornaments. She is illustrated in an eleventh century manuscript painting with the label *Tīrabhuktau Vaiśālī Tārā* which testifies her popularity in the said region.[38] Images of a few forms of Tārā have been found as Sarnath and Sravasti.[39] From Sirpur in Raipur district in Madhya Pradesh bronze images of Tārā have been found.[40] In a relief in Karle cave 2 Tārā is found with a lotus stalk in hand by the side of *cāmara* bearing Padmapani.[41] In Kanheri cave 90 Avalokiteśvara is found with two female figures, one of them appearing to be Tārā.[42] One panel on the right in Aurangabad cave 7 shows Lokeśvara and Tārā.[43] The Nagapattinam bronzes, especially those found near Puduveli-gopuram, include images of Tārā. Salihudam in the Śrīkakulam district has yielded a two-armed stone image of Tārā.[44]

Since there are various forms of Tārā it is difficult to classify them.

To some extent it is, however, possible if one can identify their respective *kulas* or families presided over by five Dhyānī Buddhas. There are not many Red Tārās in the *Sādhanamālā*.[45] Among them Kurukullā is an emanation of Amitābha whose image she bears on her crown. She is one faced and may have two, four, six or eight hands. When she is six-armed, she bears the effigies of the five Dhyānī Buddhas on her crown. When two-armed she is called Śukla Kurukullā. Only in this form is her colour white. All of her other forms are red in colour. When she is four-armed she is called by the names of Tārodbhāva Kurukullā, Uḍḍīyāna Kurukullā, Hevajrakrama Kurukullā and Kalpokta Kurukullā.[46] Besides there are eight-armed Aṣṭabhuja-Kurukullā and six-armed Māyājālakrama Kurukullā.[47] The *mantra* of Kurukullā is *Oṃ Kurukullā Huṃ Hrīḥ Svāhā*. Śukla or White Kurukullā is two-armed with the rosary and bowl of lotus as symbols. She sits on an animal in *vajraparyaṅka*. Tārodbhava Kurukullā is four-armed, left hands showing *abhayamudrā* and arrow and right hands bow and red lotus. Uḍḍiyāna Kurukullā is red in colour and sits in *ardhaparyaṅka* on a corpse. The first pair of her hands is in the attitude of discharging an arrow from the bow while the second pair holds a goad of flowers and a red lotus. The goddess has five skulls on the head, protruding teeth and tongue, garments of tiger-skin and brown hair rising above her head in the shape of a flame. Images of Kurukullā are found in Tibet[48] and China.[49] A few have also been found in Nepal. A Cambridge University manuscript (no. Add. 1643) illustrates Kurukullā of Kurukullāśikhara along with Tārā of Tārāpura referred to above.[50] The Banpur hoard contains two bronze images of Kurukullā. One is in sitting posture, six-armed, three-faced, three-eyed, blooming with youth. The lower right hand is in *abhayamudrā*, the middle one holds a *vajra* and the upper an arrow, whereas the left hands hold from lower to upper a stalk of *utpala, pāśa* and bow respectively. She has on her crest the image of Amitābha. The second image stands for Uḍḍīyāna Kurukullā. It is fierce in form and has a garland of skulls stretching to the waist. It is four-handed, the left upper hand holds a bow, the lower a stalk of lotus, while the right upper holds an arrow of flower and the lower a goad. She is in *ardhaparyaṅka* pose dancing on a corpse. The hair of her head rises above in the shape of a flame.[51]

In the Blue Tārā group we have Ekajaṭā and Mahācīnatārā, both emanations of Akṣobhya bearing his image on their crown.[52] We have already had the occasion to deal with both of them who are also well known Hindu Tantric goddesses. Ekajaṭā has three forms. All of them are short, youthful, pot-bellied, wrathful, one-faced and three-eyed. Having tiger-skin around their loins, brown hair rising upwards on the head and garlands hanging from their necks they stand in *pratyālīḍha* attitude on corpses. When two-armed Ekajaṭā carries a knife and skull-cup; when four-handed, arrow and sword in two right hands and bow and skull in the two left; when eight-armed she carries sword, arrow, thunderbolt and knife in her four right hands and bow, lotus, axe and skull in her four left hands.[53] Images of Ekajaṭā are found in almost all Buddhist countries of the north.[54] Mahācīnatārā is also known as Ugratārā. The Vajrayoginī temple at Sanku in Nepal contains her image.[55] Mahācīnatārā stands in *pratyālīḍha* attitude, and is awe-inspiring with a garland of heads hanging from the neck. She is short and has a protruding belly. She stands on a corpse, is decked in ornaments of snakes, has red and round eyes, wears a tiger-skin around her loins, has a protruding tongue and bare canine fangs. She carries sword and knife in two right hands and lotus and skull in the two left.[56] This *Sādhanamālā* description was the composition of Śāśvatavajra. We have already presented glimpses of the *dhyāna* of Ugratārā found in the *Tārārahasya* of Brahmānanda and *Tantrasāra* of Kṛṣṇānanda Āgamavāgīśa. The *Tantrasāra* description of Tārā is almost identical to that of Mahācīnatārā of the *Sādhanamālā*. In fact Kṛṣṇānanda has copied from the composition of Śāśvatavajra only making some grammatical corrections.

Vajratārā, Jāṅguli, Parṇaśabarī and Bhṛkuti form the Yellow Tārā group. Vajratārā has four faces and eight arms and bears the image of the Dhyānī Buddha Ratnasambhava on her crown. She is accompanied by ten goddesses when worshipped in the *maṇḍala*. They are Puṣpatārā (east), Dhūpatārā (south), Dīpatārā (west), Gandhatārā (north), Vajrāṅkuśī (eastern gate), Vajrapāśi (southern gate), Vajrasphoṭi (western gate), Vajraghaṇṭā (northern gate) Uṣṇīṣavijayā (above) and Sumbhā (below).[57] She is effulgent in her blooming youth, has swaying ear-rings, sits on the double lotus in *vajraparyaṅka* attitude and carries in her right hands thunderbolt, noose, conch and arrow and in the left *vajrāṅkuśa*, lotus, bow and *tarjanimudrā*.[58]

The Chinese collection at Peiping has an image of eight-armed Vajratārā.[59] Vajratārā is popular in Nepal and also in India. Her images have been found in many places. The Indian Museum (Calcutta) bronze image of Vajratārā is in the form of a lotus, and represents the complete *maṇḍala* with all attendant deities. It is made in such a way that it can be opened and closed at will. The petals are eight in number, and each bears the image of an attendant deity. It came from Chandipur in Bhagalpur district. A similar bronze image of Vajratārā hailing from Majvadi in Faridpur district is in the Dacca Museum. It is much mutilated and only partly preserved. The figure is within an eight-petalled lotus and the figures of eight attendants are carved on inside the petals.[60] The Buddhist site of Ratnagiri in Cuttack district, Orissa, which has yielded bronze and stone images of Tārā, shows Vajratārā on a structural *stūpa.*[61] The yellow variety of Jāṅguli has three faces and six arms and bears the image of the Dhyānī Buddha Akṣobhya on her crown. She is the Buddhist counterpart of Hindu Manasā or Viṣahari.[62] Her faces to the right and left are blue and white. She carries sword, thunderbolt and arrow in three right hands and *tarjanī* with noose, blue lotus and bow in three left hands. She rests on the expanded hood of a serpent, is decked in celestial ornaments and dress, resplendent with the auspicious marks of a virgin.[63]

Parṇaśabarī as a form of Yellow Tārā is an emanation of Akṣobhya whose effigy she bears on the crown. She has three smiling faces—blue, white and red—and six-arms holding thunderbolt, axe, arrow (right) noose, leaves and bow (right), respectively, trạmpling the *vighnas* under her feet and standing in *pratyālīḍha* attitude.[64] The Indian Museum image of Parṇaśabarī corresponds to this type.[65] The Parṇaśabarī images of the Patna Museum belonging to the Kurkihar hoard follow the types of her another tradition in which she is an emanation of Amoghasiddhi. Bhṛkuṭi of the Yellow Tārā group is an emanation of Amitābha whose image she bears on her crown. She is one-faced and four-armed, shows *varada mudrā* and rosary in the two right hands and carries the *tridaṇḍī* and *kamaṇḍalu* in the two left.[66] She is often identified with Khadiravanī Tārā and Dhanda Tārā. Reliefs of Tārā and Bhṛkuṭi are found on the right flank of the antechamber of the main pillared varandah of Cave 10 at Ellora. One should not fail to recall in this connection that Hiuen Tsang had referred to the Tārā and Bhṛkuṭi-tārā images of Potalaka moutain in south India. At Salihundam a four-armed Bhṛkuṭi image has been found.[67] The Nalanda collection of the Patna Museum contains a bronze image of four-armed standing Bhṛkuṭi belonging to about the ninth century. She holds a rosary and some unknown objects in the two right hands and a branch of a tree and *Kamaṇḍalu* in the two left hands. There are two unidentified animals on either side. In front of the pedestal are two *makaras*. A female devotee is sitting to the right in *añjalimudrā*.[68]

Among the White Tārās, we have Jāṅguli, Kurukullā, Viśvamātā Ṣaḍbhūjā Sitatārā, Caturbhūjā Sitatārā, Mṛtyuvañcana Tārā and Aṣṭamabhābhaya Tārā. White Jāṅguli is one-faced and four-armed, plays on the *vinā* with the first pair of hands and shows a white serpent and *abhaya* pose in the second.[69] White Kurukullā carries a rosary and bowl of lotus in her right and left hands respectively. She is three-eyed and wears a *jaṭāmukuṭa* which is decorated with flowers and the miniature figure of Amitābha. She sits on an animal. She is decked in bracelets, armlets, ear-rings, anklets, pearl-necklace, and celestial garments. She possesses a heart that melts with compassion.[70] Viśvamātā has been described as one-faced, with white complextion, white garments and a white serpent as her vehicle. She carries a white lotus in her left hand and holds the right in *abhaya*.[71] Ṣaḍbhūjā Sitatārā is three-faced and six armed. Her three right hands show *varadamudrā*, rosary and arrow and three left carry *utpala, padma* and bow. She sits in *ardhaparyaṅka* and bears the effigy of Amoghasiddhi on her crown. Her head is embellished with five severed heads and the crescent moon. She resides in the midst of eight cremation grounds.[72] Caturbhujā Sitatārā on her part has one face and four arms. She is accompanied by two goddesses Mārīcī and Mahāmāyūrī. She bears the images of the five Dhyānī Buddhas on her crown, exhibits the *utpala mudrā* with the first pair of hands, displays the *varada mudrā* along with *cintāmaṇi* jewel in the second right, and carries the *utpala* bud in the second left hand.[73]

In the White Tārā group of goddesses the most improtant are the Aṣṭamahābhaya-Tārā and Mṛtyuvañcana-Tārā. The distinguishing feature of the Aṣṭamahabhya Tārā is that she sits in the *ardhaparyaṅka* attitude and is surrounded by ten goddesses originating in the ten syllables of the Tārā *mantra*: *Oṃ Tāre Tuttāre Ture Svāhā*. These ten deities are identical in appearance with the principal deity.[74] She saves her devotees from eight great perils—fire, robbers, fetters, shipwreck, lions, serpents, elephants and demons. We have already had the occasion to refer to a few specimens of extant representations of this goddess.[75] Stone images corresponding to this type have been found at Ratnagiri (now in the Patna Museum), at Nalanda (now in the Nalanda Museum) and Somapara in Bangaldesh (now in the

Dacca Museum). The one in Dacca has eight miniature figures of goddesses on the *prabhāvali*, four on each side, and the figure of Vajrasattva on the extreme right corner of the pedestal.[76] The distinctive feature of Mṛtyuvañcana Tārā is that she bears a wheel on her chest. She is absolutely unattended and sits in the *vajraparyaṅka* attitude.[77] This form of Tārā is rare, the extant specimen being a stone image, now in the Rajshahi Museum, and two tenth-century bronze images now in the Nalanda Museum. One of the bronze images is seated in *vajraparyaṅka* on a lotus over a pedestal. The right hand is in *varada* with a fruit or jewel on the palm while the left holds a lotus stalk (now missing). The image wears a long necklace with *cakra*-like clasp between the breasts.[78]

The Green Tārā group comprise the goddesses Jāṅguli, Parṇaśabarī, Khadiravanī Tārā, Vaśya Tārā, Ārya Tārā, Mahattarī Tārā, Varada Tārā, Durgottariṇī Tārā and Dhanada Tārā.[79] Green Jāṅguli is four-armed and carries the *triśūla*, the peacock's features and a snake in three hands and exhibits the *abhaya mudrā* in the fourth.[80] The Green Parṇaśabarī emanates from Amoghasiddhi who is usually three-faced and six-armed, but in some cases has four arms. The Kurkihar hoard, now in the Patna Museum contains seven bronze images of the four-handed type assignable to a period between the tenth and twelfth centuries. Khadiravanī Tārā is a an emanation of Amoghasiddhi who is endowed with two hands, showing the *varada-mudrā* in the right and *utpala* in the left. She can be recognised by the figures of two attendant deities, Aśokakāntā Mārīcī and Ekajaṭā.[81] A beautiful statuette in the Baroda Museum shows the goddess in the *lalita* attitude.[82] From the Banpur copper plates of the Somavaṃśī king Indraratha (first half of the eleventh century), it appears that Khadiravanī Tārā had an honoured place in the Puri and adjoining districts of Orissa.[83] A few images of Khadiravani Tārā belonging to the Pāla period have been recovered. Vaśya Tārā and Ārya Tārā are practically the same deity with the exception that while the former sits in *bhadrāsana* (European fashion of sitting) the latter sits in the *ardhaparyaṅka* attitude. Again there is no basic difference between them and Khadiravani Tārā, becaue they all display the *varada-mudrā* in right hand, carry lotus in the left and bear the image of Amoghasiddhi on their crown.[84] The National Musuem of New Delhi contains two bronze images of this deity from Nalanda, belonging respectively to the seventh and tenth centuries Both the images are, however, standing. The Lucknow State Museum, on the other hand, has two bronze images from Naḷanda belonging to the tenth-eleventh century which are seated in *ardhaparyaṅka* having *varada* pose and *utpala* in hands and Amoghasiddhi on crest. The Nalanda collection of the Patna Museum contians three bronze images of Ārya Tārā.[85]

Among other deities of the Green Tārā Group, Mahottarī Tārā may be distinguished by the *vajraparyaṅka* posture in which she sits, and also by the fact of her being represented without a companion. Varada Tārā sits in the *ardhaparyaṅka* attitude like Ārya Tārā, but can be recognized by the prsence of four goddesses, Aśokakāntā Mārīcī, Mahāmāyūrī, Ekajaṭā and Jāṅguli. Durgottarinī Tārā has lotus for her seat, garlands of white colour, four hands carrying in the first pair noose and displaying in the second lotus and *varada mudrā.*[86] A copper plate of AD 1220 found at Mainamati records a grant of land by an official in favour of a *vihāra* dedicated to Durgottārā, apparently an abbreviation of Durgottarinī Tārā.[87] A bronze image of Dhanada Tārā, belonging to the eighth century, is now in the Nalanda Museum. It is standing with slight flexion on a lotus. The image is four-handed, right hands holding rosary and exhibiting *abhayamudrā* and left hands holding a lotus stalk and a manuscript.[88] This corresponds fully to her iconographic description according to which she is of yellowish green complextion, has one face and four hands bearing respectively *akṣamālā, varada, utpala* and *pustaka.*[89] The Kurkihar hoard of the Patna Museum contains as many as eight seated bronze images of Śyama Tārā Group. The Banpur hoard of Orissa has eleven Tārā images in bronze, all in *lalitāsana* carrying *utpala* in the left hand and exhibiting *varada* with the right. With the same hand poses there are twenty standing bronze images in the Kurkihar hoad, nine standing with a slight bend and eleven standing in *samapāda-sthānaka.*[90]

The Patna Museum contains a four armed bronze image of a crowned Tārā from Nalanda in *lalitāsana* on a single lotus pedestal. The upper right hand is broken and the left holds a *kamaṇḍalu* from which emerges a *nāgakeśara* flower. The lower right is in *abhayamudrā* and the left holds *nāgakeśara*[91] Its identification with any particular form is uncertain. Since the Tārā images have a wide variety, these can be broadly classified into two groups—ordinary (of the Ārya Tārā type) and extraordinary. Tārā is also the wife of the Dhyānī Buddha

Amoghasiddhi. Here, also known as Tāriṇī, she originates in the germ syllable *tāṃ* of golden green colour. Her recognition symbol is the green night lotus (*utpala*). She is the embodiment of the element of air. She belongs to the *karma* family and is full of jealousy.[92] Mahāśrī Tārā is an emanation of Amoghasiddhi who is endowed with two hands which exhibit the *Vyākhyāna mudrā.* She is one-faced, sits on a golden throne and is decked in a variety of flowers.[93] The Indian Museum image of Mahāśrī Tārā should be mentioned in this connection. Prasanna Tārā is an emanation of Ratnasambhāva. Her colour is yellow. She has eight faces and sixteen hands.[94] Among other forms of Tārā, Alagataru Tārā of Oḍradeśa (Orissa) is illustated on a Cambridge University Libary manuscript (no. Add. 1643) of AD 1015 which also contains painted illustrations of the two-armed seated Tārā of Candradvipa and sixteen-armed seated Cundā of Paṭṭikere. A manuscript of 1071, preserved in the Asiatic Society of Bengal, adds another famous image of Samataṭa (lower Bengal), namely, Buddhaṛddhi Bhagavatī Tārā.[95]

Tārā made her start as a simple protectress as is attested by the etymology of her name. And she always carried on as a protectress, a saviour. This form was retained all through the Indian tradition. This deity made her way into the Hindu sects and in Śaktism she was indentified with the Supreme Being, the eternal Female Principle, consort of Śiva who symbolized the Male Principle of creation. In Buddhism she also made her way as a protectress deity who was originally regarded as the consort of Amoghasiddhi, but the origins of her emantaory forms were traced to various Dhyānī Buddhas. Eventually she was not confined within the traditional Mahāyāna-Vajrayāna pantheon. She absorbed many other Buddhist goddesses in her numerous forms and ultimately became the supreme Female Principle of the Mahāyāna-Vajrayāna complex, being in eternal companionship with Avalokiteśvara and came to be regarded as the principle of Śūnyatā or Prajñā which characterized the philosophical and spiritual contents of later Buddhism. While Avalokiteśvara was the embodiment of universal compassion, Karuṇā or Upāya, she stood for universal energy and wisdom. Their union, that of Prajñā and Upāya, is for the purpose of the realization of the non-dual state, the quintessence of all entities, without which perfect wisdom is never possible.

NOTES

1. Gray's translation, p. 67.
2. XVIII. 42, 50.
3. *Eigraphia India* XXXIV, 137.
4. N.N. Bhattacharyya, *Indian Mother Goddess* (New Delhi, 1977), pp. 136-7.
5. *Śaktisaṅgama*, Sundarīkhaṇḍa IV. 51, VII. 12-14.
6. *Tārātantra*, VI. 3-4.
7. *Tārārahasya*, Paṭala I. *Tārakatvāt sadā Tārā ya Kālī saiva niścitā.*
8. *Kubjikā* quoted in *Prāṇatoṣaṇī* v.6, Vasumati ed. p. 374
9. *Tārārahasya*, Paṭala I.
10. Ibid.
11. Vasumati ed., pp. 327-8.
12. Ibid.
13. *Nīlatantra*, Paṭala IV.
14. Quoted in *Puraścayarṇava*, Taraṅga IX.
15. *Māyātantra* quoted in *Tantrasāra*, p. 347.
16. *Nīlatantra* quoted in *Tantrasāra*, pp. 539-40.
17. Quoted in *Tantrasāra*, pp. 540-2.
18. A. Getty, *Gods of Northern Buddhism* (Oxford, 1928), pp. 104ff.
19. B.T. Bhattacharyya, *Indian Buddhist Iconography* (Calcutta, 1968), p. 306.
20. Veṅkaṭeśvara Press edn, Bombay, 1908, I, p. 58ff.
21. A.K. Maitrreya ed., Varendra Research Society, Rajshahi, 1913. I.2.
22. IV. 10.
23. H.P. Sastri, *Notices of the Sanskrit Mss.*, Second Series, Vol. I (Calcutta, 1900), Pref. XXXII, p. 152.
24. S. Levi, *Nepal*, Vol. I (Paris, 1905), p. 346.
25. J. Woodroffe, *Śakti and Sakta*, 8th edn (Madras, 1975), p. 123.
26. Ch. XVII.
27. Paṭala I
28. *Journal of the Asiatic Society*, Vol. I, 1959, p. 118.
29. No. 127.
30. P.C. Bagchi, *Studies in the Tantra* (Calcutta, 1939), pp. 42-4.
31. *Sādhanamālā*, Nos. 123-8.
32. Ibid., Nos. 100, 101.
33. Bagchi, op. cit., pp. 47-9.
34. *Journal of the Gujarat Research Society*, Vol. I; (1939), pp. 67ff; Vol. VIII, 1946, p. 112.
35. Debala Mitra, *Buddhist Monuments* (Calcutta, 1969), p. 193.
36. Ibid., pp. 182, 243, 'Aṣṭamahābhaya-Tārā' in *JASB*, Vol. XXIII (1957), pp. 19-22.

37. G. Roerich and A.S. Altekar, *Biography of Dharmasvāmin* (Patna, 1959), pp. 61, 65, 90.
38. A. Foucher, *Etude Sur l' Iconographie Bouddhique,* Pt. II (Paris, 1900), Pl. VII. 1.
39. Debala Mitra, op. cit., pp. 68, 76.
40. Ibid., p. 103.
41. Ibid., p. 156
42. Ibid., p. 165
43. Ibid., p. 181
44. Ibid., pp. 197, 222.
45. A. Getty, op. cit., p. 126.
46. B.T. Bhattacharyya, *Indian Buddhist Iconography* (Calcutta, 1968), pp. 147-52.
47. For their *dhyānas* see *Sādhanamālā,* ed. B.T. Bhattacharyya, (2 Vols. GOS, XXVI, XLI) (Baroda 1925), 1928, pp. 332-63.
48. A. Getty, op. cit., pp. 126-7.
49. W.E. Clark, *Two Lamaistic Pantheon* (Cambridge, Mass., 1937), II. 105, 239; A.K. Gordon, *Iconography of Tibetan Lamaism* (New York, 1939), p. 75.
50. Debala Mitra, op. cit., p. 144.
51. N.N. Bhattacharyya in *East Indian Bronzes,* ed. S.K. Mitra, Calcutta University, 1979, p. 94.
52. B.T. Bhattacharyya, op. cit., pp. 189-91, 193-4.
53. *Sādhanamālā,* p. 266.
54. Getty., op. cit., pp. 125-6; Clark, op. cit., II, p. 284; Gordon, op. cit., p. 76.
55. B.T. Bhattacharyya, op. cit., p. 189.
56. *Sādhanamālā,* p. 210.
57. B.T. Bhattacharyya, op. cit., pp. 240-3.
58. *Sādhanamālā,* p. 179; *Niṣpannayogāvali,* ed. B.T. Bhattacharyya, GOS 109, Baroda, 1949, p. 38.
59. Clark, op. cit., II, p. 210.
60. N.K. Bhattasali, *Iconography of Buddhist and Brahmanical Sculptures in the Dacca Museum,* (Dacca, 1929), pp. 45-53, Pls. XXV-XXVII.
61. Debala Mitra, op. cit., p. 228.
62. B.T. Bhattacharyya, op. cit., pp. 191-3.
63. *Sādhanamālā,* p. 248.
64. Ibid., pp. 306-7.
65. B.T. Bhattacharyya, op. cit., p. 197.
66. Ibid., pp. 152-3; *Sādhanamālā,* p. 341.
67. Debala Mitra, op. cit., pp. 184, 192, 197.
68. N.N. Bhattacharyya, op. cit., p. 94.
69. *Sādhanamālā,* p. 253; Bhattacharyya, op. cit., pp. 191-2.

70. Ibid., pp. 362-3.
71. B.T. Bhattacharyya, op. cit., p. 308.
72. *Sādhanamālā*, p. 216; B.T. Bhattacharyya, op. cit., pp. 230-1.
73. *Sādhanamālā*, p. 215.
74. B.T. Bhattacharyya, op. cit., p. 308.
75. See Debala Mitra in *Journal of the Asiatic Society of Bengal*, Vol. XXIII (1957), pp. 19-22.
76. N.K. Bhattasali, op. cit., pp. 56-7, Pl. XXI.
77. B.T. Bhattacharyya, op. cit., p. 308.
78. N.N. Bhattacharyya, op. cit., p. 99.
79. A. Getty, op. cit., p. 123.
80. B.T. Bhattacharyya, op. cit., p. 192, 307.
81. *Sādhanamālā*, p. 176.
82. B.T. Bhattacharyya, op. cit., Fig. 168.
83. Debala Mitra op. cit., p. 225.
84. B.T. Bhattacharyya, op. cit., pp. 229-30.
85. N.N. Bhattacharyya, op. cit., pp. 229-30.
86. B.T. Bhattacharyya, op. cit., p. 307
87. Debala Mitra, op. cit., p. 244.
88. N.N. Bhattacharyya, op. cit., p. 100.
89. *Sādhanamālā*, p. 219.
90. N.N. Bhattacharyya, op. cit., p. 100.
91. *Patna Museum Catalogue of Antiquities* (Patna, 1965), pp. 121-2.
92. *Advayavajrasaṃgraha*, ed. H.P. Sastri, GOS, XL (Baroda, 1927), p. 43.
93. *Sādhanamālā*, pp. 244-5.
94. Ibid., p. 241.
95. Debala Mitra, op. cit., p. 238.

16

Vajrayoginī and Mahākāla Two Most Fearful Deities in the Buddhist Tantric Pantheon

KALPIKA MUKHERJEE

In the Buddhist Tantric pantheon we come across two types of deities, benign and fierce. The *Niṣpannayogāvali* states that in the highest stage of *sādhana*, the *bodhicitta* becomes one with *śūnyatā* that is 'essencelessness' or *prajñā*. At this stage the *sādhaka* first visualizes different colours, then the letters of the alphabet as the germ-syllable or the *bīja-mantra*. Gradually the *bīja-mantras* assume the forms of deities, first indistinctly and then in a distinct manner. These deities in the vision of a 'sādhaka' may appear in two ways: (i) beautiful, sublime, decked with beautiful ornaments, having soft expressions on their faces or (ii) in a horrible manner, with fierce expressions, decorated with the ornaments of skull and holding a skull full of blood. These fierce deities uphold a 'deepened sense of the tragedy of life' and also a desire to overcome it. These images are projections of the *sādhaka's* own mind, 'a disintegration of the psychic complex, expression of the mainfold forms of ego' by the realization of which only the *sādhaka* may ultimtely overcome it. There may be many hindrances towards attaining the ultimate goal, and one has to fight with the evil forces within oneself. Sometimes the *sādhaka* may also feel that these wrathful deities are the protectors of the influx of evil forces from the outer world. These are the guardian deities who enjoy a significant status in the Buddhist Tantra. There are a number of dreadful deities of which this paper deals with only two, Vajrayoginī, perhaps the most fearful female deity in the Buddhist Tantric pantheon, and Mahākāla, conceived as a protector deity of Buddhism known as the *dharmapāla* (Tib - *chös skyoṅ*).

For Vajrayoginī, the *Sādhanamālā*' offers four *sādhanas:* one *ārādhanavidhi*, one *Vajrayogīnyupadeśa* and one *Vajrayoginvā bali-vidhi*. These four *sādhanas* depict two distinct characteristics of the deity. *Sādhana* 232 depicts her as the most dreadful deity, without head. She is described as—*bhaṭṭārikāṃ vajrayoginīṃ ... pītavarṇaṃ svayameva svakartrikarti tasvamastaka - vāmahasta - sthitāṃ dakṣiṇahastakartrisahitaṃ ūrdhavistṛta-vāmavāhuṃ vāsāḥśūnyaṃ prasārita-dakṣiṇapadaṃ saṃkucita-vāmapadaṃ bhāvayet.*[2] She carries her own head severed by her own-self in her left hand raised upwards, in the right hand stretched downwards she carries a *kartri,* she is without clothes and stands in *ālīḍha* posture. On her left side stands Vajravarṇani of black colour; on the right side stands Vajravairocanī of yellow colour. They carry a *kartri* in their left and right hands and in their right and left hand they hold *karpara,* respectively. The first one stands in *pratyālīḍha* posture, stretching her left leg while the other stands in *ālīḍha* posture stretching her right leg. In between the two yoginīs the *sādhaka* should meditate upon a dreadful cemetery. The other three *sādhana* (*Sādhanas* 233, 234 and 236) describe her with head. In 233 she is *śavārūḍhā*—standing on a corpse. Here, she is described without any attendant. There is also a marked difference regarding the colour of the main deity. In 232 and 234 she appears as *pītavarṇa* and *kaṇaka-śyāmā* respectively. Śyāmā means beautiful, *vāmā* or *manohara.*[3] *Kaṇakaśyāmā* therefore means beautiful or bright as gold, or golden colour. The other two *sādhanas* describe her as *raktavarṇa.* She is to be worshipped in *pañcamī, aṣṭamī* and in *caturdaśī tithi,* in the cemetery.

The identity of the headless form of Vajrayoginī with that of the Hindu goddess Chinnamastā cannot be overlooked. Chinnamastā is one of the goddesses of the group of *daśamahāvidyā.* The *Prāṇtoṣaṇī* Tantra gives the following account of the origin of the goddess: one day devī Pārvatī went to the river Mandākinī, along with her attendants, Ḍākinī and Varṇiṇī, to take a bath. They were very hungry and demanded food from the Mother. On their insistence, the Mother severed her own neck with her nails. Three streams of blood gushed out. Two of these she put into the mouth of the two attendants and the third into her own mouth.[4] The *Viśvasāratantra* described the sixteen-lettered *mantra* (*ṣoḍaśākṣarī vidyā*) of Chinnamastā as *srīṃ klīṃ hrīṃ aiṃ vajravairocanīya hrīṃ hrīṃ phat svāhā.* The *vidyā* described in the *Mahākāla-saṃhitā* also mentions the name of Vajravairocanī. The word *vajra* clearly shows that this Buddhist goddess was incorporated almost without modification in the Hindu Tantric pantheon. Chinnamastā stands on Rati and Kāma, engaged in *viparītarati,* i.e. *rati* on the top.

About the time of origin of the cult of Vajrayoginī B. Bhattacharyya says that in the *Vajrayoginī-ārādhana-vidhi* the name of *siddha* Śabarapāda is mentioned. His date has been ascertained as AD 657, hence the worship of Vajrayoginī dates still earlier.[5] It seems reasonable to think that the headless form is all the more primitive than the form with head. About the other form of Vajrayoginī there is not much that is distinct from the forms of any other fierce deity.

However the headless form of Vajrayoginī reveals a deeper significance—both aesthetic and philosophical. From the aesthetic point of view the iconographic representation of Vajrayoginī apparently depicts *vībhatsa rasa* which is developed from the instinct of 'repulsion'. In this icon it is effected though the drinking of blood by the two Ḍākinīs but the underlying sentiment is *karuṇā* or universal compassion which inspires her to sustain the life of her attendants even at the cost of her own life. Such inspiration originating in compassion has been designated as *dayāvīra*, a variety of the heroic sentiment (*vīra rasa*) which ultimately culminates into *śānta* or tranquillity. Abhinavagupta, the eminent aesthetician of the eleventh century, rightly maintains that *dayāvīra* is only another name for *śānta*, thereby setting a link between the serene self possession and heroic selflessness.[6] It shows the maximum extension of ego boundaries. One becomes more and more free by being bound more and more with the extension of the self. This is the culmination of the aesthetic relish which Viśvanātha (thirteenth century) calls the 'bonded liberated state'—*yuktaviyukta daśā*.[7] This is the ultimate goal to be achieved by an artist as well by a connoisseur. Philosophically also, Vajrayoginī reveals a deeper significance. Life is procured and sustained through death and it is through the process of life and death that the cosmic energy is continuously recycled. The conception of this goddess reveals 'a basic truth that is at the very heart of things, namely that life, metabolism and nourishment necessitates continuous massive killing and death'.[8] The image of Rati and Kāma under the feet of the Hindu goddess Chinnamastā suggests that passion is subdued in favour of an altruistic, all-encompassing compassionate consciousness. The *śava* or corpse under the feet of Vajrayoginī (*Sādhana* 233) suggests that death is ignored in favour of life, though these two are connected rhythmically with inseparable relation.

However, Vajrayoginī is the composite form of *ḍākinīs* in different parts of the body. These parts are known as the *pīṭhas* and the *upapīṭhas.*[9] From the *mahāsukha-cakra* originate thirty-two *nāḍis - iha mahāsukhacakrād dvātriṃśan nāḍyaḥ prādurbhavanti - himavattva iva saritaḥ.*[10] Again these are twofold as following in the right and left directions—*eṣāṃ vāmadakṣiṇabhyāṃ pravartamānānaṃ yoginīnāṃ layabhogādhikārād dvāśaptatir avagantavyaḥ.*[11] Through *bhoga prārabdah-karma* and *kṛtakarma* are consumed and annihilated and then the individual remains in full consciousness. This is the state of cessation of all Becoming. The individual remains in his own nature or *svarūpa.* This is hinted at in the following verse of the *Śvetāśvatārā Upaniṣad:*

ārabhya karmāṇi guṇāvitāni
bhāvāṅśca sarvān viniyojayet yaḥ
teṣām abhāve kṛtakarmanāśah
karmakṣaye yāti sa tattvato'nyat.[12]

However, along with the *mūla nāḍi* the number becomes 73. It implies that the Vajrayoginī is not an individual deity but a composite deity residing inside the body.

Tradition affirms that Ācaryā Padmasambhava (eighth century) subdued all the terrible beings in Tibet but prescribed the worship of eight particular terrific deities appointed by dharmapālas (Tib. *chös skyoṅ*). Mahākāla (*nag-po-chen-pa*) is one of the dharmapālas and thus, is an important deity in the Buddhist pantheon.

Mahākāla is time personified. 'Kāla' which etymologically means that which absorbs everything within itself—*kalayati iti kāla.* The *Mahānirvāṇa Tantra* says that he is called Mahākāla because he swallows all beings; he is another form of Devī:

tava rūpam mahākālo jagat-saṃhārakārakaḥ
mahāsaṃhāra-samaye kālaḥ sarvaṃ grasiṣyati.
kalanāt sarvabhūtānāṃ mahākālaḥ prakīrtitah.[13]

'Kāla' is responsible for every creation and destruction. In the Hindu pantheon Mahākāla, another name for Śiva, becomes the highest god. On the other hand in the *Harivaṃśa* Mahākāla is one in the retinue (*gaṇa*) of Śiva and thus is reduced to a subordinate position. Mahākāla as identified with Śiva is none but the Vedic Rudra (Tib - *drag po*). In the *Ṛgveda,* Rudra does not figure as an independent deity. It is the general epithet of all the gods in their wrathful and fierce mood. In the *śatarudrīya stotra* of the *Yajurveda* Rudra has a concrete form and Śiva is one of the personalities of independent status among the hundred Rudras. In the *Atharvaveda* also the Rudras enjoy independent status.

The etymology of the 'Rudra' is doubtful. Yāska's explanation may point to an individual or to a group of people. Yāska explains the term as -*rudro rauti iti śataḥ rorudyamānodravati iti vā rodayaterva tad rudrasya rudratvam.* In the *Kūrma Purāṇa* Rudra is described as :

daṅṣṭrā-karālaṃ divi nṛtyamānam
hutāśavaktraṃ jvalanārkarūpam, . . .

The description upholds the fierceness of the deity. In the *Niruttara Tantra* Mahākāla is a form of rudra. He is described as:

dhumravarṇaṃ mahākālaṃ jaṭābhārānvitaṃ priye
trinetraṃ śivarūpañca śaktiyuktaṃ nirāmayaṃ
digambaraṃ ghorarūpaṃ nīlāñjanasamprabhaṃ
nirguṇañca guṇādhāraṃ kālisthānaṃ punaḥ punaḥ.[14]

In the Vedas Rudra is sometimes *hiraṇya-varṇa* and sometimes *aruṇa-varṇa.* In the *śatarudriya stotra* of the *Yajurveda,* Rudra is described as *nīlagrīva,* having a blue neck. In the Purāṇas Śiva's darkness of the neck (Nīlakaṇṭhatva) is due to his swallowing *kālakūṭa* a deadly poison. The Vedas do not account for this darkness. Does it imply that the leader of a tribe, whether Śiva or Rudra, had absorbed all the evils of a community and tried to construct an ideal and healthy society? Is it simply an allegory? The epithet *nīlāñjanacaya-prabham* also seems to be significant. How the *hiraṇyavarṇa Rudra-Śiva* becomes dark? Or does it signify an ethnic group altogether different from the Aryans and the Mongoloid Rudras?

Whatever it may be Mahākāla has been incorporated from the Hindu pantheon to the Buddhist pantheon as a 'dharmapāla' (*chös skyoṅ*) deity. He is dreadful in form and nature. His general description such as *'kharva', piṅgalakeśa', 'śārduladehacchada'* and *'kṛttivāsa'* remind us of the Vedic Rudra. The *Sādhanamālā* records eight *sādhanas* of Mahākāla. *Sādhana* 312 describes him as having sixteen arms. In the right set of arms he holds *'kartri', 'vajra',* elephant skin, *'mudgara', 'triśūlakhaṇḍa'* and *'yamadaṇḍa'*; in the left hands, skull full of blood, elephant skin, bell, goad, white coowrie and *'ḍamaru'*. The rest two arms are engaged in the embrace of his *'prajñā'*. He has eight faces and twentyfour eyes. He is surrounded by seven goddesses. Out of them three stand in the three cardinal points—Mahāmāyā in the east, Yamadūtī in the south and Kāladūtī in the west. All of them stand in *ālīḍha* posture. The other four goddesses, viz., Kālīka, Carcikā, Caṇḍeśvarī and Kuleśvarī occupy the four corners. They also stand in *ālīḍha* posture. It may be mentioned that both *'ālīḍha'* and *'pratyālīḍha'* postures typical to the Indian classical dance Tāṇḍava are used for depicting *'vīra' 'raudra'* and *'bhayānaka' rasas.*

Two armed Mahākāla is described in four *sādhanas* in the *Sādhanamālā. Sādhana* 304 describes Mahākāla with six arms, and 305, with four arms. He is clad with the ornaments of snakes and has tiger's skin around his waist. He is of short stature *(kharva)*, and has reddish hair (*piṅgalakeśa*). Does it not remind us of Hayagrīva (Tib-*rta-mgrin*) who is decorated with the ornaments of snakes (*sarpābharaṇabhūṣitam*), having tiger-skin as the garment (*vyāghra-carma-nivasana*), with reddish beard (*kapila-śmaśru*), and short like a dwarf (*khara-vāmanākāra*), described in *Sādhana* 259 and 260? Does it not also remind us of the Vedic Rudras, who, in all probability were described as *kimpuruṣas* and later on as *kinnaras* by the Aryans out of apathy, may be due to their very different behaviour, way of life and also look? Hence it may not be altogether meaningless to surmise that Mahākāla of the Buddhist Tantric pantheon, Śiva of Hindu mythology, Hayagrīva of the Purāṇas and Buddhist Tantra and the Kinnaras of the Trans-Himalayan region are different forms of the presumably non-Aryan Rudras. Yet it may be noted that Rudra as an associate deity has also his own place in the Buddhist Tantra.

Mahākāla has innumerable forms. In Mongolia, Mahākāla is mostly with six arms. There is also the conception of Mahākāla with four arms. In the *Niṣpannayogāvalī* Mahākāla has been conceived as belonging to the *'dharmadhatu-vāgīśvara maṇḍala'* and *'Vajrahuṃkāramaṇḍala'*. In the former *maṇḍala* he is described as *'kṛṣṇas triśūla-kapālabhṛt.* The number of faces is not mentioned. In the second '*maṇḍala*' he is of blue colour, consisting of three faces having blue, yellow and green colours, holding a trident. He belongs to the '*vāyavya dik*' and hence is of ethereal colour *vāyavyaṃ mahākālo nīlo nīlapīta-haritamukhastriśūlapāṇiḥ.* Some scholars have identified Mahākāla with Kubera on the basis of I-tsing's account that at every Indian monastery there is a deity at the door sitting with one leg pendant and holding a bag of gold.[15] But clearly the Mahākāla of Buddhist Tantra cannot be identified with Kubera in his peaceful form. In Japan Mahākāla is known in two forms once fierce and the other benign. He was known in Japan even before the introduction of esoteric Buddhism in the ninth century. In his fearful form he has three faces and six arms. In his benign form he is like an ordinary man standing on a bale of rice and wearing ordinary dress. He is worshipped daily with rice with the hope of getting wealth and is one of the seven 'gods of luck'.[16] In Tantric Buddhism however, 'he is generally worshipped in the Tantric rite of *māraṇa* and for the destruction of enemies'.[17]

Apparently therefore the image of Mahākāla depicts *raudra* (anger) and *bhayānaka* (terrible) *rasas* at a time. From the point of view of aesthetics as well as religion, the underlying emotion is *śānta* or a state of tranquillity. He is the protector and he is the well-doer of all human beings. But then how to account for his *raudra* or *bhāyanka* forms? The answer is given in the *sādhanas.* Mahākāla is the destroyer of those who are hateful and harmful to the Acaryā and *triratna.* This explanation is given in all the *sādhanas* except one, with slight variation of language.

However, the worship of Mahākāla, Śiva, Hayagrīva and Rudra over the vast tract of land shows that the Rudras had the occasion to cross the trans-Himalayan region and also the geographical boundary of Bhāratavarṣa and that Rudras in different forms were worshipped extensively among the Asian people.

NOTES

1. B. Bhattacharyya, *Niṣpannayogāvali,* Introduction.
2. B. Bhattacharyya, *Sādhanamālā,* Vol. I, Baroda Oriental Research Institute, 1928.
3. Radhakanta Dev Bahadur, *Śabdakalpadruma* (Delhi, 1961).
4. Vasumati Sahityamandir, *Prānatoṣaṇi Tantra,* 1st edn., 5-6, 378-9.
5. *Sādhanamālā,* Vol. II, Introduction.
6. Krishna Chaitanya, *Sanskrit Poetics,* Asia Publishing House, p. 334.
7. Ibid., p. 416.
8. David Kinsley, *Hindu Goddesses* (California Press, 1988), pp. 149-50.
9. Śrīkrisnācārya, *Vasantatilaka* (Saranath, 1990), 6.17, 25.
10. Ibid., p. 42
11. Ibid., p. 50
12. *Śvetāśvatara Upaniṣad* - 6/4 Anandasrama Series.
13. Arthur Avalon (ed.), *Mahānirvāṇa Tantra* - 4/30, 31, 1929.
14. B. Sharma (ed.), *Niruttara Tantra* - 4/30-1, Kalyan Mandir, 1st edn.
15. Alice Getty, *The Gods of Northern Buddhism* (Tokyo, 1962).
16. D.N. Baksi, *Hindu Divinities in Japanese Buddhist Pantheon* (Benten Publishers, 1979), pp. 36-7.
17. B. Bhattacharyya, *Indian Buddhist Iconography* (Calcutta, 1958), p. 347.

17

Parṇaśabarī: A Tantric Buddhist Goddess

PARNASABARI BHATTACHARYYA

The name Parṇaśabarī, as it implies, originally belongs to the Śabara, a wild tribe classed as Dasyus together with the Andhras, Pulindas, Mutibas and Pundras.[1] The Śabara tribe may be identical with the Sauri of Pliny and Śabaras of Ptolemy. These Śabaras were probably the ancestors of Sabaralu or Sauras of the Vigagapatan hill. They are found also in the south-east portion of Raipur district, in Sambalpur and Ganjam, in western part of Cuttuck as well as in the area around Gwalior. They are also located in the Deccan together with the Vaidarbhas and Daṇḍakas.[2]

The Buddhist deity Parṇaśabarī was undoubtedly associated with the Parṇaśabaras (leaf-clad Śabaras), mentioned in the *Bṛhatsaṃhitā* (XIV. 10; XVI. 1.33; XXXII.15) along with the Nagnaśabaras or naked Śabaras. The worship of Parṇaśabarī is effective in preventing outbreaks of epidemics and in assuring safety to the terror-striken. The epithet '*Piśācī*' given in the *mantra* shows that she was regarded as one of the demi-gods, half human, half divine. The Mahāyāna Buddhists adopted this goddess in their patheon from the non-Āryan Śabaras for their multifarious ritualistic practices as is proved from her names and attributes.[3] The goddess wears tiger-skin and leaf, holds *vajrakuṇḍala* and treads diseases and epidemics. At first she was the goddess of the Śabaras; later, when she was inducted in the higher religions, she came to be known as *sarva-śabarāṇāṃ-bhagavatī*, i.e. goddess Bhagavatī of all the Śabaras.

In the *Kulārṇavatantra*, quoted in *Jayadrathayāmala* (AD 1642) it is written that the goddess Parnaśabarī is worshipped in the house of oilmen or potters who belong to the low category in the caste hierarchy. Bāṇabhaṭṭa, mentions in his *Kādambarī* the goddess cult of the wild Śabaras and cruel rites involved therein. The *Gauḍavaho*[4] of Vākpati composed about AD 725 describes a vivid picture of the atmosphere of the temple of Vindhyavāsinī, the goddess who was worshipped by the Śabaras, with human sacrifice. It also deals with the slaying of buffalo-demon, the association of the goddess with the peacock and her blood-thirsty character. In the Sanskrit texts the goddess is mentioned frequently as Śabarī and Kirātī or Kirātinī.

In eastern India, the remains of the old and extensive culture of the Śabaras exist in different aspects. That the Śabaras had a close relations with the common people is proved by the picture of their day to day life engraved in the earthen plate of the Paharpur Temple. In different parts of Bengal, the Śabaras were incorporated in the lowest level of the caste structure. In the Durgā worship of the late medieval and also of the recent times primitive elements are found, and we may refer to *Śabarotsava* in this connection. A peculiar kind of merry-making in this festival was observed by the people on the *Daśamī tithi.*[5] During this merry-making, participants had to cover their bodies with leaves, etc., and besmear themselves with mud and other things to resemble the Śabaras. They had to jump and dance at random, sing and beat drums incoherently. In the *Kālaviveka* of Jīmutavāhana it is stated that this festival included topics and songs about sex organs and also about sexual intercourse with requisite movements of the body and that the violation of this practice incurred the rage and curse of Bhagavatī.[6] The *Bṛhaddharma Purāṇa*[7] introduces certain restrictions in this merry-making, saying:

> People should not utter before others words which are expressive of the male and female organs, etc., they should utter this during the great worship (of the goddess Durgā) in the month of Āsvina. But (even on that occasion) they should never pronouce (such words) before their mothers or daughters, or those female disciples who have not been initiated to Śakti worship.

Śūlapāṇi in his *Durgotsavaviveka* quotes an account of Śabaraotsava from the *Kālikapurāṇa*[8] according to which maidens and prostitutes must accompany the image on the day of its immersion and people must exchange words in relation to sexual organs and coitus, in default of which they would be cursed by the goddess. Raghunandana in his *Aṣṭaviṃśatitattva* mentions Śābarotsava.[9] The *Brhamāṇḍa Purāṇa* introduces some modifications with regard to the words expressive of sexual organs and acts. The description of Śābarotsava has been quoted from *Śaktisaṅgamatantra* in *Puraścaryārṇava.* In this description an explanation of using the obscence words has been given.

The name Śābarotsava shows that this festival was meant for the Śabaras. Later the cults and rituals of this goddess along with the festival were incorporated in traditional religious systems. That the Śabaras had a position in the Vajrayāna Buddhism can be proved by the evidence of the *Caryā* songs. Here a song is mentioned in which the features and attributes of Parṇaśabarī has been mentiond.[11]

Unchā unchā pāvata tanhi vasahi śabarī bālī/
Moraṅgī pīcchha parahiṇa śabarī givata guñjarī mālī//
Umata śabaro pāgala sabaro mā kara gulī guhāḍa tohari/
Nitya ghariṇī nāme sahaja sundarī//
Nānā tarubara maulila ve gaaṇata lāgelī dālī/
Ekalī śabarī e vaṇa hiṇḍai karṇakuṇḍla vajradhārī//
Tia dhāu khāṭ paḍilā śabaro mahāsuhe seji chāilī/
Śabaro bhujaṅga nairāmaṇi dārī pemha rāti pohāilī//
Hi'a tañbolā mahāsuhe kapur khāi/
Suna nairāmaṇi kaṇṭhe lāi ā mahāsuhe rāti pohāi//
Gurubāk pucchi ā bindhā niāmaha bāne/
Eke sarasandhāne bindhaha bindhaha paramāṇa baṇe//
Umata śabaro garuā roṣe/
Umata-sihara sandhi paisante śabaro laḍiva kai se//

High is the mountain (i.e. the spinal column) there; on it (i.e. in the *mahā-sukha-cakra,* which is above the spinal column) sits the Śabarī girl; she is decked with the coloured feather of the peacock and with a garland of jequirity on her neck. O exhilarated Śabara! O mad Śabara (exclaims the girl on mountain), do not revel in worldly pleasure; I am thy dear consort of the name Sahaja-sundarī (i.e. beautiful Sahaja lady). Many are the trees on the mountain, whose branches touch the sky—the Śabarī girl decked with ear-rings and the thunder plays alone in the forest. The bed-stead of the three elements (viz., body, speech and mind) are placed and the Śabara spreads the bed in great bliss and the serpent-like Śabara (i.e. the *citta*) and the goddess Nairātmā (who destroyes all the afflictions) pass their night of love on that bed.[12]

In many other Caryā songs, other aspects of the life of the Śabaras can be known.[13]

That there was a branch of Tantric Śakti worship named Śabaramārga is known from a statement of *Merutantra.* In this Tantra the five branches of the Vāmamārga, viz., Kaulika, Vāma, Cīṇakrama, Siddhāntīya and Śabara have been compared to the five fingers of the hand, while the thumb being the Kaulika; others are accordingly. The *śloka* is:

Kauliko'yaṅguṣṭhataṃ prāpto vāmo syāttarjanīmsamaḥ/
Cīnakrama madhyamān syāt siddhāntiyayavaro bhavet/
Kaniṣṭhā śabaro mārgaḥ iti vāmantu pañcadhā.//

The *Śabaratantra* does not seem to be very old, but it is highly interesting for the study of Indian folklore since it contains formulae in Arabic and reference to a Mohammedan Siddha called Ismail Pir or Ismail Yogin.

In Mahāyāna Buddhism Parṇaśabarī emanated from the Dhyānī Buddhas, Amoghasiddhi and Akṣobhya. In one of her forms, her faces are lit with pleasant smiles and in another she smiles but has an irritated expression all the same. The two images that have been discovered in eastern Bengal,[14] both have effigies of Amoghasiddhi on the crown. The *dhyāna* describing Parṇaśabarī of yellow colour with the image of Akṣobhya on her crown runs as follows:

Bhagavatīṃ pītavarṇāṃ trimukhaṃ trinetraṃ ṣaḍbhujāṃ-prathamamukhaṃ pītaṃ, daksiṇaṃ sitaṃ, vāmaṃ raktaṃ, lalitahāsiṇiṃ sarvālaṅkāradharāṃ parṇapicchikāvasanāṃ navayauvanoddhataṃ pināṃ ...dakṣiṇabhujaiḥ vajraparaśuśaradhāriṇiṃ vāmbhujaiḥ satarjanikāpāśaparṇapicchikā dhanuradhāriṇiṃ puṣpabhabaddha-jaṭāmukuṭastha Akṣobhyadhāriṇiṃ sūryyaprabhāmaṇḍalīniṃ adho vighnān nipatya sitapadmacandrāsane pratyālīḍhasthānaṃ, hrdvāmamuṣṭitar janyādho vighnaganān santarjya dakṣiṇa-vajramuṣṭiprahārābhinayāṃ... bhāvayet.[15]

The worshipper should conceive himself as (Parṇaśabarī) of yellow complexion with three faces, three eyes and six arms. Her first face is blue, the right white and the left red, and she smiles in a pleasing manner. She is decked with all sorts of ornaments, bears a garment of leaves, is arrogant in her youthful bloom, is stout in appearance and carries in her right hands the *vajra*, the *paraśu* and the arrow and in her left, the *tarjani*, with the noose, the cluster of leaves and the bow. Her *jaṭāmukuṭa* is decorated with flowers and the images of Akṣobhya; she has the effulgence of the sun as her aureole, stands in the *pratyālīḍha* attitude on the moon over the white lotus, trampling under her feet the *vighnas*. She threatens the host of other *vighnas* with the clenched fist of the left-hand exhibiting the *tarjani* against the chest and shakes her right-fist at (the host of the *vighnas*).

In her other form that is as the emanation of the Dhyānī Buddha

Amoghasiddhi, the complexion of Parṇaśabarī is green. The *mantra* calls her *piśāci* and also *sarvamārīprasamanī* or 'the destroyer of all the diseases and epidemics'. She is almost identical with the form that has been described previously, except that here her colour is green and she bears the image of Amoghasiddhi on her crown instead of that of Akṣobhya. She carries the same weapon as the previous one, but the expressions on her faces are very different; there a pleasant beaming smile, here an angry laugh. For a comparison between the two Amoghasiddhi images of Parṇaśabarī, both discovered in East Bengal, the *dhyāna* is given below:

> *Parṇaśabarīṃ hāritāṃ trimukhaṃ trinetraṃ ṣaḍbhujāṃ kṛṣṇaśukladakṣiṇavāmānāṃ vajra-paraśu-śaradaksiṇa karatrajaṃ kārmuka-patracchaṭrāsapāśatarjanivāmakara trayāṃ sakrodhahasitānanāṃ navayauvanavatīṃ sapatramālāvyāghracarmanivasanāṃ īsallambodarīṃūr dhvasaṃyatkeśim' adho aśeṣarogamārīpadākrāntāṃ Amoghasiddhimukutiṃ ātmanāṃ jhaṭiti nispādya.*[16]

The worshipper should conceive himself as Parṇaśabarī, who has green complexion, three faces, three eyes and six arms. Her right and left faces are of blue and white colour respectively. She carries in her three-right hands the *vajra*, the *paraśu* and the arrow and in her three left, the bow, the cluster of leaves and the *tarjani pāśa.* Her faces show an angry laugh. She is in the prime of youth, is decked in tiger skin and a garment of leaves, has a slightly protruding belly, and hair tied up above. She tramples under her feet various diseases and pestilences and bears the image of Amoghasiddhi on the crown.

Two images of Parṇaśabarī (173 and 174 of *IBBSDM*) have been discovered by N.K. Bhattasali. The angry laugh has been correctly depicted in the three faces and the belly slightly protrudes. To the right and left are the two divinities, Hayagrīva, the Hindu god of fever, and Śītalā, Hindu goddess of small pox and they are represented in the images as flying in opposite directions to escape the wrath of Parnaśabarī. The prostrate figures under the feet are Diseases and Pestilence, in human shape. The figure under the right leg apparently is that of man attacked by small pox, as we can judge from the circular marks all over his body; the other figure under the left foot, is probably one attacked by some fatal disease. Both the images of Parṇaśabarī are decidedly fine specimens of the Bengal School of Art.[17]

A mutilated image of Parṇaśabarī is in the Indian Museum, Calcutta. With three faces and six arms, trampling upon Ganesa and with Akṣobhya on the crown, it represents her as the protrectress from calamities (*vighnas*).[18] The Patna Museum has a good collection of images of this goddess.[19] One of them shows her seated on a single lotus throne on a high rectangular pedestal. The right leg is pendant and rests on a small figure of Ganeśa. The lower right hand is in the *varada* posture and lower left is pendant on the left knee leaning against a stock of plants. Her upper right hand holds a *vajra* and the left a *paraśu*. In another the four armed goddess is seated cross legged wearing a *karaṇḍamukuṭa*. The upper right hand holds an arrow, upper left bow and lower left a lotus stalk. The lower right is in the *varada* posture. The third figure is seated in *vajraparyaṅka*, her lower right hand being is *abhyayamudrā*. All the figures of the Patna Museum have been assigned to between the tenth and twelfth centuries. Images of Parṇaśabarī are also found in Tibet[20] and China.[21]

NOTES

1. *Aitareya Brāhmaṇa*, VII. 18.
2. *Mahābhārata* XII. 207, 42; *Matsya Purāṇa*. CXIV. 46-8; *Vāyu Purāṇa*, XLV. 126.
3. *Parṇapicchika vasanāṃ parṇapicchikā dhanurdhāriṇiṃ sarpatramālā vyāghracarmanivasanāṃ, Sādhanamālā.*
4. Vol. I, pp. LXI. and LXIV.
5. *Kālaviveka* 514, also *Kālīka Purāṇa* (Venkateswara Press edn.) 61. 21-2. Regarding the date and provenance of the present *Kālīka Purāṇa*, cf. Hazra in *ABORI*, XXII, 1-23.
6. See *Kālaviveka* 514 also *Kālīka Purāṇa*: 61. 21-2. It is difficult to believe that the action hinted by the line *bhaga, liṅga, kriyobhis = cha kriḍayayar = alarm janaḥ*, was actually practised by the people on this occasion.
7. II. VI. 81-3.
8. LXI. 17-21.
9. *Tato dhulikardama vikṣepakrīdākautukamangala bhagaliṅgābhidhānaṃ bhaga liṅgapragita paraksipta para ksepa karupam śābarotsavaṃ kuryāt.*
10. *Puraścaryārṇava* 3.11, p. 1121.22.
11. *Caryāgīti Pañcāśikā*, by Sumangal Rana, *Śabara-padanam*, 50.
12. Dasgupta S.B. *Obscure Religious Cults* (Calcutta, 1969), pp. 105-6
13. *Baragirisihara uttuṅga muṇi śabare jahi kia vāsa-Drohākoṣa* of Kānhapāda, *Dohā* No. 25 (from Dohakas' of Kānhapāda).

14. N.K. Bhattasali, *Iconography of Buddhist and Brahmanical Sculpture in the Dacca Museum* (Dacca, 1929), pp. 58-61, Pl. XXIII a-b.
15. *Sādhanamālā*, pp. 306-7; B.T. Bhattacharyya, *Indian Buddhist Iconography* (Calcutta 1968), pp. 196-7.
16. *SDM*, 308; Bhattacharyya, op. cit., pp. 233-4.
17. Bhattasali, op. cit., pp. 58-61.
18. B.T. Bhattacharyya, op. cit., p. 197.
19. *Patna Museum Catalogue of Antiquities* (Patna, 1964), pp. 150-1.
20. A.K. Gordon, *Iconography of Tibetan Lamaism* (New York, 1939), p. 71; A. Getty, *Gods of Northern Buddhism* (Oxford, 1928), pp. 134-5.
21. W.E. Clark, *The Lamaistic Pantheon*, 2 Vols. in the HOS (Cambridge, Mass., 1937), p. 278.

18

Tantric Buddhism and the Liberation of Women: Questions, Problems and Possibilities

KUMKUM ROY

I am grateful for this opportunity to pay tribute to the memory and work of a distinguished scholar. Given that my position *vis-a-vis* Tantricism in general and Tantric Buddhism in particular has been one of a relatively lay interest rather than active academic involvement, I will focus on certain questions and issues which have assumed importance within the discipline of religious studies in recent years.

There has been an increasing awareness that religion forms a central vehicle for expressing a range of social relations (e.g. Rapp 1978:3), especially in early societies. As a specific extension of this, there has been a focus on the links between institutionalized religious beliefs and practices and forms of patriarchy in a variety of contexts. This has resulted in the understanding that both religion and gender need to be taken seriously (e.g. Bynum 1986: 2). Also explicitly recognized is that religious traditions themselves are complex, and that the positions ascribed to/occupied by women even within a single tradition may vary and are not necessarily consistent. For instance, women may be viewed as members of a religious community, and may have a number of roles in that capacity, while their positions as subjects of religious discourse may be developed somewhat differently (Cameron 1994: 152). Also, current issues and interests tend to determine the focus of analysis of any living religious tradition, even when these purportedly pertain to an early period (ibid., 153).

Sponberg (1992) points out that In the context of Buddhism a number of apparently contradictory perspectives on gender can be discerned. He argues that these can be understood in terms of chronological developments, as representing responses to specific socio-historical situations, including the constraints of maintaining a monastic order, as well as a tendency towards universalizing the scope of what was viewed as the ultimate objective of Buddhism in its various forms, viz., liberation or enlightenment.

Sponberg identifies four specific trends. The first is an attempt to define liberation as gender-neutral, as open to people irrespective of birth or social identities. While this introduced a perspective which was ideally all-inclusive, it was modified in practice owing to what Sponberg classifies as institutional androcentricism, i.e. the subordination envisaged for the order of nuns *vis-a-vis* that of monks. This may have been due to societal pressures, and the need to conform to norms in order to ensure the financial viability of the monastic order. Whatever the practical exigencies, the constraints which were imposed were apparently misogynistic, and placed restrictions on women who joined the order.

At another level, there is evidence for a strand of ascetic misogyny, which is manifest in the writings of monks. Here women as objects of desire are viewed as disruptive in themselves and consequently threatening *vis-a-vis* the quest for liberation. Here is a shift from the perspective of desire as problematic in itself (a position which was, in a sense, a fundamental tenet of Buddhism), to a focus on the object of desire. What is detrimental is the latter, not the former. Finally, we have the Tantric tradition, within which women seem to have been positively valorized, and viewed as essential for the attainment of the ultimate goal.

Given the focus on the female within Tantricism tradition provides an obviously fruitful and fertile area of investigation for exploring the relationship between gender and religion. Even as the context remains somewhat problematic, Tantricism evidently incorporated elements of protest, combining a claim to universality with social inclusiveness (Shaw 1994: 21). Recognized practitioners of the tradition included princes and merchants as well as cobblers, tribal people, and outcastes. This may have been a new development, but its theoretical roots can be traced to the early Hīnayāṇa tradition, where, at one level at least, the quest for enlightenment was open to all. Thus the widening of the social base was plausible within the framework of Buddhism, even though the form in which it occurred may have represented a shift in perspective.

The inclusion of low caste or even outcaste categories such as the *dombas* has been viewed as an attempt to reverse social hierarchies within the tradition. However, as Shaw (ibid., 62) argues, this was not simply a case of reversal or inclusion: those belonging to apparently marginal groups had their own skills and traditions, which evidently enriched Tantric Buddhism. What is also likely is that the social space which was carved out by ostensibly marginal groups provided a context within which women could exercise a degree of participation which appears somewhat unprecedented (ibid., 102). This space was also one which was relatively secular and unstructured, in that it was not encomppassed within the framework of monastic institutions. As such, institutional hierarchies were absent (ibid., 97). This raises interesting questions on the connections between processes of institutionalization and the consolidation of patriarchal tendencies, which can be explored on a number of levels.

The kind of participation envisaged for women is significant. Where Tantricism marked a sharper, almost revolutionary break from earlier strands within Buddhism was in redefining the modes of attaining enlightenment. In terms of sotenology, monastic exclusiveness and celibacy were viewed as irrelevant, while heterosexual relations in ritual and spiritual context were defined as liberatory. Moreover, the possibility of attaining the final goal within a single lifetime was recognized. Clearly, this ran counter to both misogynistic tendencies, and the tendency to emphasize cessation of desire through abstinence. These developments have been viewed as being influenced by Hindu Śaktism.

Tantric traditions in general, and Tantric Buddhism in particular, have been viewed as distinctive from other religious traditions in that they recognise that women can be spiritual precepters, and initiate lineages (Shaw 1994: 6) and thus a 'source of spiritual power' (ibid., 11). The contrast with religious traditions which explicitly underscores male dominance is striking. Shaw (ibid., 139) suggests that Tantric Buddhism emerged out of the joint explorations of men and women.

In fact, women were recognized as having a role in recording the tradition. Besides, they envisaged new deities and forms of meditation, constructed new rituals, and could act as spiritual mothers (ibid., 102). However, no attempt seems to have been made to preserve the memory of these spiritual mothers, and these have to be carefully excavated by historians (ibid., 130).

As is well established, this particular tradition is rich in religious symbols, evident in visual media as well as in written treatises. As in the case of any early tradition, it is difficult to determine the chronological, and spatial limits of specific components of the tradition, and define its possible audience, readers, or spectators. This is further complicated in the case of Tantric traditions which are by definition esoteric. Thus the context within which such symbols would have been seen, understood and interpreted remains uncertain.

With the possibility of contextual understanding being thus reduced there has been a tendency to focus on the content of such symbols. These are extremely rich and vivid, and deliberately gendered. It is therefore not surprising that in a recent work on the theme Shaw (1994) begins her investigation by focusing on the imagery of the *ḍākinī* in Tantric art and literature, viewed as a liberator who combines passion with freedom. She reads these, somewhat directly, as indicating the existence of women who 'inspired and helped create these evocative female images' (ibid., 3). On another level, Shaw (ibid., 37) argues that the distinctive images available within the tradition would indicate that women were responsible for ensuring the way men viewed them.

Other figures such as Vajrayoginī, with her loose hair, skull cup, dancing on corpses, are more complex. Shaw (ibid., 28) cautions us against interpreting these as literally awesome females, arguing that what we have is a representation of a female destroying feelings of negativity. Perhaps even more complicated are representations of the beheaded Vajrayoginī depicted holding her head in her hand with blood spouting from her neck. This blood is consumed by the goddess and her female attendants. While the severing of the head and the consumption of blood have been understood to indicate the destruction of vanity (ibid., 112-14), it is surely significant that there do not seem to be representations of male deities engaged in a similar exercise. One wonders why this is so, given that vanity is not necessarily a gender specific activity.

In a sense, the representations of *mithunas* of either male and female Buddhas locked in an embrace, or of male Buddhas and their *śaktis* are more symmetrical. They tend to represent the divine couple as sometimes blissful but occasionally wrathful. The visual impact of such imagery is necessarrily varied though intrinsically linked to the valorization in Tantrism of heterosexual intercourse.

Given that such images are complex, it is likely that their interpretation has to take into account the fact that they symbolize a complex interplay between notions of gender, power, and liberation.

In other words, these symbols owe their richness to the fact that they can be interpreted differently, and that a wealth of meanings, multiple rather than unitary, lies embedded in them.

These representations are powerful, indeed gripping. However, there are obvious problems of interpreting them. Are we to understand them in direct and literal terms as indices of female power, or are they, as is the very nature of symbols, complex and multivalent? It has been suggested that religious symbols do not simply reflect or shape our understanding, but may provide a means or inverting, questioning, rejecting, or transcending definitions available in other contexts (Bynum 1986: 8). As Bynum (1986: 2) points out:

> Gender-related symbols, in their full complexity, may refer to gender in ways that affirm or reverse it, support or question it; or they may, in their basic meaning, have little at all to do with male and female roles.

Besides, the same symbol may carry different meanings for different social categories. For instance, in the context of medieval Europe, the notion that all Christians were by definition the bride of Christ meant, for women, an extension of their social experience, wheras for men it meant a reversal of their 'normal' status (ibid., 13).

There are also problems in interpreting texts. Shaw (1994: 75-6) draws attention to the fact that the language of the texts, primarily Sanskrit and Tibetan, is not conducive to preserving the identity of women authors in particular. In Sanskrit, masculine markers are used to denote any group which contains a male, irrespective of the number of females who may be incorporated within it, whereas in Tibetan there is a tendency to drop the feminine gender marker in the interest of brevity. Thus female authors or participants within the Tantric tradition tend to be rendered invisible. Shaw warns against taking the relatively few women specifically mentioned within the tradition as an accurate index of the scale of female participation. Also, it may be that those who preserved the tradition did not consider it necessary to cherish the distinct presence and voices of women Tantric practitioners.

A second problem relates to the content of text. Are we to read texts which insist that reverence be shown to women as being literally true, or are they representative of a situation where attempts were being made to create and enforce a situation where women were to be ideally treated as divine? If one accepts the second possibility, one can then raise a question as to the extent to which such prescriptions were followed. Besides, there is the problem of the extent to which such possibilities were confined to the spiritual sphere. Did they also influence secular practice? Possible answers to such questions require investigation rather than assertion.

The problem of prescritive texts can be posed *vis-a-vis* narrative traditions as well. Many stories within the Tantric tradition recount how men in search of liberation were misled or failed because they ignored women preceptors, simply because they did not conform to the external criteria considered desirable for women. Such stories can, once again, be interpreted on two levels. On the one hand they can be seen as creating a space for less structured notions of women preceptors, who are perceived as being engaged in routine activities which are not explicitly spiritual. Such a space was obviously valuable, in that it valorized the ordinary existence of women, by constructing it as a facade for a less tangible but invaluable spiritual existence. At the same time, the fact that such stories are often stereotypical, with an obvious moral, insisting on reverence for the apparently ordinary woman, suggests that the acceptance of women as preceptors was not automatic, but had to be ensured through norms and narratives.

Nevertheless, there is a certain amount of negative evidence as well: the fact that women are not represented as submissive or opres-sed, and that there is no attempt to proscribe, or prevent women from attaining positions of leadership (ibid., 74) is significant, and marks the Tantric traditions as distinctive.

Besides, there are other kinds of texts whose composition can be explicitly or implicitly attributed to women. These are rich and varied, and include manuals for the practical guidance of the initiate as well as celebratory verses, marking the attainment of enhighten-ment (Shaw 1994: 84-7). The very preservation of such compositions within the tradition is indeed significant. As gender identities are foregrounded within the traditions and considered intrinsic to the process of enlightenment, it would be interesting to compare the compositions attributed to women with those of men.

There is also the question of the position of women gurus amongst disciples of either sex. It appears that the Tantric tradition focuses far more frequently on the relationship between the woman preceptor and the male initiate than on those between woman teacher and disciple, or between male preceptors and male or female students. Part of the definition of women as preceptors involved classifying them—as best, middling and lesser—and while considerations of *gotra* and *jāti* do not seem to have been important, they were replaced by the quest for the *kulikā* (ibid., 71). This has certain similarities with classificatory schemes in erotic literature (ibid., 54). However, there seems to be a greater focus on intrinsic qualities as opposed to extrinsic attributes, and insofar as a hierarchy is discernible, it seems to move from the relatively placid woman to the more violent one. To that extent, one can talk in terms of reversal of gendered roles.

Are these variations significant, given the gendered nature of the tradition, and that of the wider social context? And if so, how are we to interpret them? One also wonders what happened to women with male gurus. Shaw, for instance, argues that the paucity of references to female supplicants for knowledge may indicate that women did not need male approval to embark on the quest for enlightenment, whereas men depended much more on female support and encouragement.

Related to this is the question of the divinity ascribed to women, who were regarded as the literal embodiments of female divinities such as Vajrayoginī, whose ambivalent nature we have noted earlier. Both men and women were expected to worship women (Shaw 1994: 40-1) in order to attain enlightenment. Yet the woman was envisaged as a deity with a difference; while offerings were to be made to her and she was to be fed, somewhat identical to the treatment envisaged for the idol in the context of image worship, the kinds of offerings were distinctive. More important, deity and devotee were expected to engage in sexual intercourse as worship.

Encounters between men and women were ideally structured around certain contexts. These include feasts, where specific items of food and drink were consumed, and men and women were expected to engage in a variety of ritual/spiritual/sexual practices. Shaw points out that women could stage such feasts independently of men (ibid., 81) and in fact could admit men if they so desired. However, there do not seem to be any instances of men admitting women to their feasts. While Shaw argues that this was because women and not men were in control of such situations, this is obviously an instance of an asymmetrical gender relationship.

On another level, the female body was envisioned positively and men were expected to demonstrate respect to women through social and ritual interaction, including and culminating in intercourse. Intercourse was not simply as a physical act, but a process of establishing communion between the participants which was emblematic of universal enlightenment (Shaw 1994: 122). Participants in the act were required to possess a distinctive vision of unity. Thus relations were probably not necessarily exploitative. There are far more detailed prescriptions for men than for women, with detailed instructions on how to approach a woman in order to win her favour. At the same time, we find many more descriptions of the attributes of the ideal woman participant. Shaw suggests that this was because it was simple for women to visualize their partner as the Buddha (ibid., 153), and because of the novelty of the methods for enlightenment, more specific instructions were necessary for men.

The roles and position of women within the specific heterosexual praxis envisioned within Tantric Buddhism have been variously interpreted. On the one hand, they have been viewed as subservient and instrumental to the avowed goal of male liberation, while on the other hand, attempts have been made to argue for an independent, active role for such women within the tradition (e.g. Shaw 1994). Shaw buttresses her position by pointing out that while women are depicted as teachers, guides, companions, and bestowers of magical power and enlightenment, the position ascribed to men seems to be somewhat subordinate (ibid., 370).

As we have seen, within Tantric traditions, men were expected to worship women symbolically as well as literally; Shaw (ibid., 70) thinks this meant that women could not/would not be dominated. She links this with a specific understanding of power, specific to Tantricism; here empowering men did not necessarily mean disempowering women (ibid., 175-6). This is likely, and power relations have been defined in a variety of ways both in terms of participants and contents in the early Indian situation. Nevertheless, given that Tantric traditions developed in situations where royal patronge seems to have been important in at least some cases, one wonders how this definition of power co-existed with more hierarchical notions. Also given that Tantric ideas recognize caste relations, which are again ideally structured in terms of differential access to power the implications of reversing caste relationships within Tantric theories and praxis require exploration. What I am suggesting is that the specific construction of gendered relations of power needs to be located within other power relations to enable us to understand its meanings and complexity.

More problematic perhaps are some of the assumptions behind

the attempt to foreground and centralize the role of women within Tantric Buddhism. Amongst these is the understanding that most textual traditions (including Tantric traditions) have been preserved and perpetuated by men, and as such reflect their preoccupations. When we find references to women authors or preceptors, these assume extraordinary significance, and represent the proverbial tip of the iceberg (Shaw 1994: 13). This assumption has been effectively employed by feminist historians working with diverse matrials and in different contexts. While gender differences are certainly discernible within textual traditions, women are often compelled to and/or deliberately disguise their voices and perceptions, casting them in what are frequently perceived as culturally more prestigious masculine modes of expression, so that the existence of a distinctive feminine voice has to be established rather than assumed—which is of course not to deny the possibility of its existence within Tantrism.

On another level, as mentioned earlier, Shaw suggests that rather than viewing women as instruments to be manipulated for purposes of salvation, Tantric texts encourage the view of women as source of power (ibid., 11). The underlying assumption is that: 'The Indian world view does not mirror Western values but includes a profound respect and veneration for the magical potencies and divine powers inherent in womanhood' (ibid., 8). Here lies an attempt to construct a unitary 'Indian worldivew', and to define its contents in terms of an understanding of woman's nature. As has been pointed out in recent years, this understanding of a single 'woman's nature has essentialist connotations, and is problematic. Even a superficial examination of the complexity of Indian traditions would warrant a more nuanced understanding on a variety of levels and would indicate that the specific components of what is regarded as woman's nature tend to vary over time and space. Thus the attempt to rehabilitate women seems to ignore the possibilities of complexities and variations in their position.

Besides there is an assumption that there is a specific Indian view of selfhood, which is distinguished from a western notion of self-hood—less bounded, and resting on a not very sharp dichotomy between spirit and flesh (Shaw 1994:10). This too is questionable. Denying the existence of dualities does not further our understanding of Indian traditions.

We need to examine the liberatory dimensions of Tantric Buddhism for women more carefully. Both textual and visual representations point to the active involvement and participation of women. At the same time, there are points of ambivalence. These need to be elucidated, as indeed is the case with the socio-political contexts within which different strands of the Tantrism emerged. In other words, the richness of the traditions requires that we move away from a unitary perspective and attempt a more complex understanding of its implications and possibilities.

REFERENCES

Bynum, Caroline Walker, Stevan Harrell, and Paula Richman (eds.) 1986. *Gender and Religion: On the Complexity of Symbols.* Boston: Beacon Press.

Bynum, Caroline Walker 1986. Introduction. The Complexity of symbols in Bynum, Caroline Walker, Stevan Harrell, and Paula Richman (eds.) 1986. *Gender and Religion: On the Complexity of Symbols,* Boston: Beacon Press, pp. 1-20.

Cameron, Averil 1994. Early Christianity and the Discourse of Female Desire in Archer, Leonie J., Susan Fischler and Maria Wyke (eds.). *Women in Ancient Societies An Illusion of the Night,* Hampshire: Macmillan, pp. 152-68.

Rapp, Rayna 1978. Women, 'Religion and Archaic Civilisations: An Introduction'. *Feminist Studies,* Vol. IV, pp. 1-5.

Shaw, Miranda 1994. *Passionate Enlighenment.* Princeton: Princeton University Press.

Sponberg, Alan 1992. 'Attitudes towards Women and the Feminine in Early Buddhism in Cabezon'. Jose lgnacio (ed.). *Buddhism, Sexuality, and Gender* (Delhi, 1992), pp. 3-36.

19

The Concept of Siddhācāryas and their Images

SHYAMALKANTI CHAKRAVARTI
SIPRA CHAKRAVARTI

In ancient Indian mythology the siddhas are regarded as a class of worshipful beings belonging to the category of the gandharvas, vidyādharas, and kinnaras who live in the *antarīkṣa* region. The siddhas of the upper air are considered to be expert in singing, dancing and playing flute. Kālidasa extolled the siddhas in his *Meghadūtam* (*Pūrvamegha*, 46) saying that they devoutly love and play the lutes. In Jaina literature thery are described as '*vyantara devatās*', intermediate gods. The concept of the siddhas changed much with the passage of time. But there is one thing common between the siddhas of the classical writers and those of mediaeval Buddhist vajrayāna faith: both are worshippers of the supreme god and possess magical powers, the latter by practising the secret *mantras.*

The Buddhist Tantric texts of the first thousand years of the Christian era, viz., the *Mañjuśrīmūlakalpa* (first century AD) *Guhyasamājatantra* (third century AD) and *Tattvasaṅgraha* (eighth century AD) describe the Buddha as the originator and instructor of the tantras, *mantras* and *maṇḍalas.* It is said that he took the easier method of salvation only to satisfy the desires of the learned and common people. 'From the Pali literature it can be easily proved that Buddha believed in the doctrine of *iddhis* or supernatural powers and mentioned four *iddhipadas* : *chhando* (will), *viriyam* (effort), *cittam* (thought) and *vimamsa* (investigation) which were conducive to the production of super human powers' (*An Introduction to Buddhist Esoterism*, p. 19). The word siddhi, according to *Hevajratantra*, means 'not so much enlightenment as perfection in magical powers.'

Mystic tantric Buddhism gradually evolved into three distinctive forms, Vajrayāna or Tantrayāna, Sahajayāna, and Kālacakrayāna. But it appears that Sahajayāna and Kālacakrayāna are two different manifestations of Vajrayāna. It shows that in spite of its separate entity, the pristine concepts of Sahajayāna life in the essential ideals of Vajrayāna and the poets, philosophers and the preachers of Sahajayāna recognize the authority of the *Guhyasamājatanatra* and other Vajrayāna texts. But the ultimate aim of all the three has the same *mahāsukha* or perfect bliss.

In all tantric systems, be it Vajrayāna, Sahajayāna or Kālacakrayāna, the worshipper must be initiated by guru or preceptor to obtain the different kinds of *abhiṣekha* from him. Then he has to pass through different stages to become a true siddha. The first two stages, *kriyā* and *caryā* are known as lower tantras. The worshipper in the beginning is admitted in the lowest rank, *kriyātantra,* where he has to follow strict rules about discipline, rites, ceremonies, and celibacy until he is considered fit for the higher stage, *caryatantra.* This rank leads one to *yogatantra* where only a competent worshipper is allowed to come in contact with the śaktis. In the Yoga and *Anuttara tantra,* a further higher stage, the worsipper has to pass through a yaugic process for the realization of Ultimate Reality. *Anuttarayogins* are exempt from all laws—human or divine. Now, they are called siddhas and possess superhuman powers to make miracles and perform marvellous feats. It is now clear that through the spiritual processes of *sādhanā* the siddhas attain siddhi or 'Supreme Realistion' and are represented by a group of Buddhist and Śaivite masters, who were the authority in esoteric tantric religion. The siddhi is again defined as *lokottara* or transcendental, and *laukika* or earthly. In *lokottara siddhi* the siddha is merged with cosmic consciousness while in *laukika siddhi* the siddha is concerned with wordly desires.

The *Guhyasamājatantra,* a text of the third-fourth century, refers to two types of siddhis—*sāmānya* (ordinary) and *uttama* (excellent). The Siddhas showing miraculous feats are called *sāmānya* whereas the attainment of Buddhahood through yoga practiced with its six limbs is known as *uttama.* Besides, *Guhyasamāja* lays down some easy processes leading to salvation, and withdraws restrictions on consumption of flesh, fish, wine and companionship of women. It advocates further a disregard of all social laws, permitting followers to sacrifical killing, stealing and committing of adultery.

The introduction of *śakti* worship as well as participation of the *śakti* in yaugic practices and the *prajñābhiṣeka* ceremony for initiation of the disciple are all mentioned in the *Guhyasamājatantra.* The attainment of perfection through the satisfaction of all desires without passing through painful processes as mentioned in the *Guhyasamājatantra* was also adopted by the siddhācāryas in the later period. The *Guhyasamājatantra* forbids *mantra, maṇḍala* and worship of the Buddhist trinity which were greatly appreciated by the tantriks and the siddhācāryas. All these liberal doctrines introduced in the *Guhyasamājatantra* attracted the attention of the siddhācāryas who boldly preached these teachings in a language that was easily understood.

In the *Pātañajalayogasūtra* there are references to eight *siddhas, animā* (atomization), *laghimā* (levitation), *mahimā* (magnification), *prāpti* (extension), *prākāmya* (efficacy), *iśitva* (sovereignty), *vaśita* (mastery over elements), *kāmavasayitva* (capacity to will actual facts). The *Brahmavaivartapurāṇa* also mentions thirty-four kinds of *siddhis* including the eight ones, thus increasing the scope of the supernatural powers of the siddhācāryas to a great extent. Some of these important siddhis are *durasravana* (power to hear distant sounds), *parakāya-praveśa* (power to enter into other people's bodies), *manojavitva* (power to go at will), *sarvajñatva* (omniscience), *vahnistambha* (power to stop the progress of fire), *jalastambha* (power to stop the current of water), *cīrajīvītva* (immortalilty), *vāyustambha* (power to stop the motion of wind), *kṣutpipāsānidrāstambha* (full control over hunger, thirst and sleep), *kāyavyūhapraveśa* (entering into all kinds of physical bodies), implying the power to go anywhere at will in a moment, *pātāla praveśa* indicating the power to go to nether region. These supernatural feats the siddhas acquired by developing psychic power and uttering *mantras.*

But the tantriks were not satisfied with all these supernatural powers. They now began to perform different rites for subduing the evil forces which are known as *ṣaṭkarma* or six rites: *śānti* (propitiatory rites), *vaśīkaraṇa* (enchanting), *stambhana* (restraining) *vidveṣana* (separating) *ucāṭana* (destruction of dwelling houses), and *māraṇa* (destruction of enemies).

According to *Tantrasāra* there are also gradations of siddhas, namely *uttama* or superior, *madhyama* or middling and *adhama* or inferior. The *uttama* siddhas can fulfil all the desires arising in the mind. The *madhyama* siddhas are able to conquer death, enter unperceived into the bodies and homes of others, commune with gods, move in the air, perform miracles, obtain erudition in all branches of knowledge, obtain omniscience, practice yoga and renounce all earthly enjoyments. The *adhama* or the lowest class obtain long life, fame, ornaments, wealth, prosperity, family, children as well as familiarity with the king. The siddhas of the *uttama* and *madhyama* rank were regarded as the *mahā siddhas* and the *adhama* (inferior) *siddhas* due to the their attachment to earthly objects were not regarded as siddhapuruṣa.

Apart from the possession of the said powers *siddhi* is also regarded as the attainment of the superhuman powers of the mind, body and sense organs, generally known as *janmaja* (co-existent) with birth, *auṣadhaja* (due to a drug) *mantraja* (due to magic syllables), *tapaja* (due to austerities), *samādhija* (due to intense meditation).

In the discussion of the siddhapuruṣa it will be pertinent to say a few words regarding the Nātha cult. According to some scholars this is essentially an esoteric Buddhist cult, later transformed into a Śaiva cult. The main reason of this hypothesis lies in the fact that in all the schools of esoterism the vital element is based on the *kāya-sādhanā* or culture of the body through the process of *hathayoga*. This process of *kāya-sādhanā* is indispensible to the realization of the supreme truth and supreme bliss. A similarity and a blending of ideas were responsible for the association of the Nātha cult with the cults of tanric Buddhism, resulting in some sort of confusion in the identification of the siddhas with the Nātha yogins. For this reason Matsyendranātha is identified with Siddhācārya Luipā in Tibetan tradition. The relation between the Nāthism and the cult of the Siddhācārya is ascertained by the fact that all important Nātha yogis like Mīnanātha or Matsyendranātha, Gorakhnātha, Jālandharī and Cauranginātha were included in the list of Buddhist siddhācāryas.

From the Tibetan sources we come to know that there were as many as eighty-four siddhapuruṣas in India and this tradition is frequently mentioned in the literature of the medieval period. Tāranāth, the Tibetan historian, remarks that during the Pāla rule of Bengal there were many *mantracaryās* who claimed to possess various *siddhis* and also demonstrated them.

Three lists of the eighty-four *mahāsiddhas* are so far available. Using the Tibetan sources Rahul Sankrityayan and W. Grünwedel mention the number of the siddhācāryas as eighty-four. Similar list has also been discovered in Java and published by Van Manen the Dutch scholar and Tibetologist. Another list of the eighty-four siddhas, (though the actual number is seventy-seven) occurs in the text *Varṇa-ratnākara* of Jyotirīśvara, the court poet of Mithila in the fourteenth century.

There is another problem regarding the chronological sequence of the siddhācāryas among the different literary sources. In tantric Buddhism the succession lists of the gurus and disciples (*guru-paramparā*) are significant because through them a paticular Tantra was handed down from guru to disciple. The *Kangyur* list of O.P. Cordier mentions Padmavajra as the earliest *mahāsiddha* followed by Anaṅgavajra, Indrabhūti, Bhagavatī, Lakṣmī, Līlavajra, Dārikapāda, Sahajayoginīcintā and Ḍombi Heruka. In the second succession list of gurus and disciples through whom *Cakrasaṃvara Tantra* was handed down, were preceded by Saraha and followed by Nāgārjuna, Śabaripā, Luipā and others. But both Tārānath and Samarkheno, the author of *Pag Sam Jon Zan* and *Cakrasaṃvara* succession list were at one in the conclusion that the name Saraha, Sarahapā, Sarahapāda, and Rāhulabhadra denoted the same person and was one of the earliest promulgators of Tantric doctrine and practices. Benoytosh Bhattacharyya after analysing the chronological sequence of the Siddhācāryas came to the conclusion that there was an interval of twelve years between each succession and considered Saraha as the earliest of the *mahāsiddhas,* around AD 633.

The names of the eighty-four siddhas as known from the Tibetan sources the *Caturasīti-siddhapravṛtti* are as follows:

(1) Lupiā (Matsyendra), (2) Lilāpā, (3) Virupā, (4) Ḍombipā, (5) Sabaripa, (6) Sarahapā, (7) Kaṅkaripā, (8) Mīnapā, (9) Gorakṣa, (10) Cauraṅga, (11) Vinapā, (12) Śāntipā, (13) Tāntipā, (14) Camaripā, (15) Khaḍgapā, (16) Nāgārjuna, (17) Kānhapā, (18) Karnaripā or Āryadeva, (19) Thaganpā, (20) Naropā, (21) Salipā, (22) Tillopā, (23) Catrapā, (24) Bhadrapā, (25) Dukhandi, (26) Ajoko, (27) Kalapo, (28) Dhombipā, (29) Kaṃkana, (30) Kambalpā, (31) Dinkpa/Dhenkipā, (32) Bhandhepā, (33) Tandhepā, (34) Kukkuripā, (35) Kucipā, (36) Dhampā, (37) Mahīpā, (38) Acinta, (39) Babhahi, (40) Nalin, (41) Bhusuku, (42) Indrabhūti, (43) Mekopā, (44) Kotolipā/ Kodālipā, (45) Kamāripā, (46) Jālandhara, (47) Rahul, (48) Dharmapā, (49) Dhokari, (50) Medhini/Medinī, (51) Pankaja, (52) Ghaṇṭapā, (53) Yogīpā, (54) Celukapā, (55) Gorua, (56) Lucika, (57) Naguni, (58) Jayānanda, (59) Pacaripā, (60) Campakapā, (61) Bhikṣaṇapā, (62) Telipā, (63) Kumaripā, (64) Caparipā, (65) Maṇibhadra or Yogini bahudi, (66) Mekhali, (67) Kankhala (Mekhala and Kankhala are two sisters), (68) Kalkal or Kolahal, (69) Kantiali, (70) Dhahuli, (71) Udhili/Udhali,

(72) Kapāla, (73) Kirpāl, (74) Sakar, (75) Sarabhakṣya, (76) Nāgabohi, (77) Dārika, (78) Putalipā, (79) Panaha, (80) Kokalipā, (81) Anaṅga, (82) Lakṣmīmkarā, (83) Samud and (84) Vyalipā/Vyadipā.

Some scholars believe the number eighty-four has some mystic significance. In the Pali *Gandhavaṃsa* it is mentioned that

> he who makes a good collection of the teachings of Buddha and causes others to do it, and who scribes and causes to be scribed the sayings of Buddha in the form of manuscript, and who gives others materials for preparing such manuscript and to preserve it, will amass immense virture equal to that which is gathered by building eighty four thousand shrines and erecting eighty four thousand monasteries.

There are also references to eighty-four yogic postures (*asanas*) in the yogic and tantric texts. The most interesting information is given in the *Skandapurāṇa* which describes in detail the eighty-four *śivaliṅgas* in eighty-four chapters.

Of the eighty-four *siddhas* mentioned in the list four are women: Maṇibhadrā or Yogini Bahudi; Mekhalī and Kankhalā, two sisters; and Lakṣmīṃkarā, a princess and sister of Mahāsiddha Indrabhūti. Another notable female ascetic was Sahajáyoginī-cintā whose name is not included in the list. It may be noted that Siddhai Mekhali of Devikot is no doubt the nun Mekhalī whose name along with Acaryā Advayavajra is associated with Devikot monastery in north Bengal. All these *siddhas* represent different socio-economic groups in society, for example, the brahmin, vaiśya, śūdra, yogī, bhikṣu, monk, farmer, weaver, hunter, cobbler, fisherman, painter and so on.

It appears that these mahāsiddhas, through their preaching and writing made the Sahajayana form of tantric Buddhism popular and acceptable to the population at large. The concept of Sahajayana was systematized by two siddhas—Sarahapada and Lakṣmiṃkarā—who strongly revolted against the conventional rituals. In Vajrayāna Buddhism the assimilation of *bodhicitta* symbolizing *karuṇā* or compassion, with *śūnyatā*, the ultimate reality, leads to *advaya* or non-duality and ultimately lays the foundation of *śakti* worship.

In the Sahajiya cult of the siddhācāryas, however, more importance was laid on the body, the epitome of the universe. They introduced *kāyasādhana* or yaugic practices and *haṭhayoga* for the realization of Truth. In the *Hevajratantra* the Lord said that without the body the realization of bliss is not possible. Saraha's *dohā* is more significant and touching when he says 'here (within the body) is the Ganga and the Yamuna, here the Gangasagara, here Prayaga and Varanasi—here the sun and moon, here the *pīṭhas* and *upapīṭhas*—I have not seen such a pilgrimage and an abode of bliss like my body.'

In the Sahajayāna *bodhicitta* is produced by the union of *prajñā* and *upāya* identified wiht female and male. This bodhicitta in the *Nirmāṇa-cakra* (navel region, body of transformation) rises in the upward motion to *dharmacakra* (heart, body of ultimate reality and cosmic unity) and *sambhogacakra* (body of bliss) and ultimately becomes still in the *uṣṇīṣakamala* and produces *sahaja* or *mahāsukha.*

It appears that the concept of *mahāsukha* is the focal point around which all tantric Buddhist cults grew and developed. The siddhācāryas of Sahajayāna proclaimed that this transcendental stage of supreme or infinite bliss can be obtained by psycho-physiological processes of yoga or through the intense emotion of love. The Sahajayāna is an admixture of tantra and yoga, laying emphasis on the purification of mind—*sahaja* realization or self realization.

The Sahajayāna cult of tantrism was widely spread in Bengal and Assam. It is generally believed that the golden period of the siddha movement lay between the eighth and twelfth centuries and there is ample evidence of a two-way traffic of siddhācāryas from eastern to southern India. Luipā, Śāntipā and Līlāpā travelled to the south and Virupā had his initiation in the south. There was a prominent centre of the siddhas in Tamilnadu. They were against ritualism, denied prevalent religious practices and *bhakti,* and strongly criticized casteism. We know of a list of twenty-five prominent members of the *siddha* movement in the south. Some were farmers, animal-rearers, hunters and fishermen. There were some dacoits who took to the siddhācārya profession. Three of this list were Brahmins. Akkppei, Kankanan, Karakkar, Thirumuttar and Macchamuni are some of the names of the Tamil siddhas. It is interesting to note that six out of this list came originally from Egypt, China and Śrīlanka.

On the basis of the composition of the texts and references to kings and dynasties as well as ācāryas in Buddhist monasteries, it is possible to ascertain the chronology of the siddhācāryas who lived and preached their doctrine from the eighth to the end of the twelfth century. During this period Pāla kings ruled in Bengal with great vigour and their patronage to tantric Buddhism gave further impetus to the development of the siddha movement in eastern India.

All the eighty-four siddhācāryas were great scholars. Some of them were teachers and monks of the different monasteries. Many enriched tantric literature through their contributions on obscure tantra texts, *sādhanās, caryās* and *dohās.* Mahāsiddha Naāgārjuna was the author of the Sādhanā of Ekajaṭā and Vajravārāhī, Sarahapāda composed Trailokyavaksaṅkara and Lokeśvara Sādhanā, Indrabhūti contributed the Sādhanā for Aṣṭabhūjā Kurukullā, Ḍombi Heruka and Kukkuripāda wrote Amṛtaprabhā and Mahāmāyā Sādhanā respectively.

In this connection it will be interesting to say a few words regarding the female siddhas who played a significant role in preaching and poularization of tantric Buddhism of Sahajayāna in the early medieval period. Of these female *siddhas* Bhagavatī Lakṣmīṃkarā in the eighth century comes foremost. She boldly projected the new theory of Sahajayāna in her work entitled *Advayasiddhi Sādhanā.* She declared that for the realization of the truth, no bathing, fasting, purifiction, or rites were necessary; one did not have to bow before a deity made of stone, wood or mud. She said that truth can only be realized by the reverence of the body, which is the abode of all gods, through concentration of mind, the sahajayoga. Without self realization the ultimate reality cannot be comprehended. She further says that there is no restriction regarding eating and drinking and the worshipper can violate laws, human or divine. But what is more important, *Lakṣmīṃkarā*'s concept of woman was far in advance of her age when she declared that no hatred should be expressed towards women who were the embodiments of the goddess Prajñā. She is also the author of many texts including *Vajrayoginī Sādhana, Lokeśvara Stotra, Bhaṭṭāraka Ārya Ekādaśamukha Avalokiteśvarasya Sādhana, Sahaja Siddhi-paddhati, Cittakalpa Parihāradrṣṭi* and others.

Sahajayogini Cintā, another female ascetic and contemporary of *Lakṣmīṃkarā* eloquently described the *mahāsukha* theory of the mind for the attainment of Buddhahood in her remarkable work *Vyaktabhāvanugatatattva Siddhi.* The literary works of other female *siddhas* are also no less important. Maṇibhadrā or Yogini Bahudi composed *Vajradāka Tantrasaya Tattva/Susthiranamapañjikā* and *vajradākavivṛtinibandha*; Mekhala wrote of *Cittacaitanyasamanaupāya.* Besides Kankhala and Mekhala, two sisters, jointly wrote on *Sanātana avartatrayamukha āgama.*

Similarly siddhas like Saraha, Virupā, Indrabhūti, Naropā/ Kambalpā, Kukkuripā, Nāgārjuna Capāripā, Tillopā, Kanhapā and Ḍombipā are specially noteworthy for their contribution of large number of works on tantra, *dohākoṣa* and *caryāgīti*. The siddhas took leading part in the development of the vernacular language and its application in literary composition. They deviated from the traditional mode of writing in Sanskrit by adopting *apabhraṃśa* or the vernacular as the medium of expression. Imbued with deep mysticism these *dohās* and *caryāpadas* of the sahajasiddhas written in *sandhyā–bhāṣā* reflect an ardent spiritual longing centring round erotic mysticism in metaphoric poetic expression. This emotional appeal of the verses later finds fuller expression in the Vaisnava *padāvāli* and Śākta and Baul songs.

There is no doubt that the cult of the siddhas was transported to Tibet from India particularly from Bengal and it was Buddhism during Pāla rule which played an important role in bringing these two countries in close proximity. It must be noted that Buddhism in Tibet was inspired and sustained by tantric Buddhism of Bengal. Tibetan lamaism was also modelled on the principle of esoteric Buddhism as it has much similarity with rituals and shamanastic practices of indigenous Bon religion. The siddhācāryas enjoyed highest spiritual prestige during the Pāla rule and may of them were engaged in teaching at the celebrated monasteries of Bengal. Tibetan monks in the course of their studies in India came in contact with them. Thus Lama drogmi (992-1074) the preceptor of Marpa acquired knowledge from the yogins of India and introduced female partnership in mystical relations. Similarly Marpa (1012-96), an important personality in Tibetan Buddhism spent twelve years in India and is said to have secret initiation from eminent Indian siddhācāryas like Naropa, the pandit of Vikramsila monastery and high priest of Vajrasana (Bodh Gaya) and from Maitripa and Kukkuripada. Even Rinchen Sang po, the greatest Tibetan translator and scholar who worked with Atisa Dipankara, was well versed in all branches of tantra and philosohy by Sraddhakaravarman.

Following the ageold tradition of the mahāsiddhas in Tibet a type of mystic yogī grew up called 'Kunlek' who popularized Buddhism among rural people. Many of these mystics came to be regarded as saints but most of them were wandering poets, the singing yogis of Tibet. The most famous of these saints was Dama Sangey, an Indian mystic of the eleventh century who lived most of his life near the border of Tibet. This shows that the cult of mahāsiddha was popular in Tibet and was almost exclusively Tibetan. Many of these siddhācāryas were historical figures and all the eighty-four mahāsiddhas were greatly venerated by the Tibetan people and were also deified by them. These mahāsiddhas are mostly represented in sculpture, murals and in *thangkas* or scroll paintings. Both in sculpture and painting they are represented in meditation seated on animal skins on lotus pedestals with the right hand showing one of the five *mudrās* of Buddha or their characteristic attributes and the left hand always holding a *kapala*. The artist portrays these siddhas with wide open eyes, parted lips and matted hair raised over the head, wearing floral and tantric bone ornaments—the *sanmudrās*, meditation sash or *yogapaṭṭa* and *upavīta*. The bone ornaments and the *kapāla*, the skull cup signify that the siddhas have overcome the profane sphere of earthly existence.

Similar to the Indian tradition of eighty-four mahasiddhas, in Tibet too there was a group of twenty-five siddhas, known as the 'Twenty-five yogis of Chingsphu', as early as the days of Padmasambhava. These siddhas were Tibetan monks who after attaining mastery in Yoga attained supernatural powers to fly through the air, walk through rock, swim like a fish, divert a river's flow on the reverse side, and achieve the great wisdom. These yogis of Chingspu were a popular theme in frescoes and temple hangings or thangkas in the monasteries of the Nyingmapa sect.

We now describe some of the interesting mural paintings, metal images and thangkas of Tibetan origin which depicted the figural features of the mahasiddhas preserved in some important museums and private collections.

The bronze figure of Mahāsiddha Heruka datable to about 1400 now in the Nasli and Alice Heeramaneck collection in New York show the acarya holding a skull cup in his left hand and thunderbolt in the right thus establishing his association with the very esoteric god Heruka. He is seated on a double petalled lotus with the bent legs apart and wears ornaments and an elaborate crossbelt over his chest. His hair is coiled into a *jaṭā* of an Indian yogī. The Mahāsiddha Heruka is also known as Ḍombi Heruka or Ḍombipā (See Pl. 43, Pal, P., *Art of Tibet*).

The Mahāsiddha Virupā in the Tibet House collection, New Delhi, executed in bronze and seated cross legged on a deerskin belongs to the fourteenth century. His hands show *dharmacakra-pravartana mudrā*. He also wears the normal yaugic belt and is decorated with flowers (See Pl. 84, Pal, P., *The Art of Tibet*).

Another fifteenth century bronze image of Mahāsiddha Virupā

hailing from Central Tibet has a long dedicatory inscription. Tradition goes that Virupā was born in Tripura in eastern India and was a great devotee of Vajravārāhi. It is said that by dint of supernatural power he stopped the sun, as he was displeased with a barmaid in a tavern. According to another story he split a statue of Śiva and converted Śaivites to Buddhism (See S. 34, Pal, P., *Art of Tibet*, 1983).

Schroeder has described three inscribed brass images of this mahasiddha from Tibet belonging to the three centuries between the fourteenth and sixteenth, executed in hollow cast technique (See Pls. 131H, 135E, 146B, Schroeder, U.V., *Indo-Tibetan Bronzes*). Two of them display usual *vyakhyana mudrā* but one is seated on a lotus pedestal with raised arm in *tarjani mudrā* and raised left leg tied with a *yogapaṭṭa* around his pot belly while his right arm is touching the pedestal. (Pl. 128C, Schroeder, U.V., *Indo -Tibetan Bronzes*).

A bare-bodied image of the Mahāsiddha ascribable between AD 1250 and 1350 is seated in the normal posture holding in his right hand a bowl and the left hand placed on the left knee. He is wearing a pair of large earrings while a thin piece of decorated scarf is seen hanging from the right shoulder (Pl. 112B, Schroeder, U.V., *Indo-Tibetan Bronzes*).

From the Yongle period (1403-24 AD) of China hails a gilt brass image of Virupa decorated chased ornaments holding his left hand in *tarjanī mudrā* with while his right hand holds a skull cup raised along his chest. He sits in the usual fashion of Virupā on an animal skin spread over his lotus pedestal. The image is inscribed with six characters of Yongle mark. This image is now preserved in the Cleveland Museum of Art (See Pl. 146B, Schroeder, U.V., *Indo-Tibetan Bronzes*).

A fifteenth century Tibetan bronze image of Mahāsiddha Dampa Sangye seated on his hauches, with hands in *vitarka mudrā,* the index fingers touching the thumbs so as to resemble a ring and the palm shown outward, is interesting. The bearded Dampa Sangye is one of the masters responsible for the successive transmission of the *Guhyasamājatantra* in Tibet. This bronze statue belongs to the Nasli and Alice Heeramaneck collection. According to the inscriptions in Tibetan character arund the base of the image this is a portrait of Dampa Sangye, also called Phadampa. He is exalted in the inscription as fully accomplished in the two spheres miraculously perfected in two bodies. He was an Indian mystic who came to Tibet shortly after the death of Atīśa Dīpankara. (See Pl. 42, Pal, P., *The Art of Tibet*).

The bronze image of Mahāsiddha Tilopā preserved in Pan Asian collection is seated on lotus holding fish and skull cup in the right and left hands, respectively. The image made in a hollow cast is decorated with chased ornaments and belongs to the sixteenth century.

Another image of Mahāsiddha Tilopā as if rising from his seat holds a fish in the right hand symbolizing the power of saving sentient beings, engaged in the ocean of worldly existence, while his left hand raises a skull cup full of blood, symbolic of his ability to confer occult power pertaining to the world *(laukika siddhi* or wordly perfection). This gilt copper image is in the collection of the Linden Museum, Stuttgart and belongs to the seventeenth century.

An identical bronze image of Tilopā showing the same posture and same attributes is in the private collection at Ticino (See Pls. 122D, 136B, Schroeder, U.V., *Indo-Tibetan Bronzes,* Pl. 89, Pal, P., *The Art of Tibet*).

Two images of Mahāsiddha Abadhutipā of the fifteenth century have been described by Schroeder, one from a private collection in Brussels and the other from the Victoria and Albert Museum. This tantric teacher is seen seated cross legged touching the lotus pedestal with this right index and little fingers, while his left arm rests on the pedestal behind his left leg. His tuft of hair is tied in a matted lock (See Pls. 131G, 131I, Schroeder, U.V., *Indo-Tibetan Bronzes*).

Of the three Mahāsiddha Kṛṣṇācārya metal images described by Schroeder two belong to the seventeenth century and display *abhayamudrā* with the right hand and the skull cup in the left, one knee raised. The third is unusual, sitting on a crouching human figure who is trying to uphold the feet of the preceptor, from touching the earth. This inscribed brass figure, decorated with chased ornaments, was executed in the sixteenth century. According to legend Kṛṣṇācārya was the siddha of Odivisa (Orissa) and a Brahmin in origin. He himself was introduced to esoteric Buddhism by Siddha Jalandharipa. In Tibetan Buddhism Kṛṣṇācārya is of particular importance to the Sakyapa sect who left mystical chants, dohas and commentaries on the tantric teaching of the Yidam Hevajra (See Pls. 122D, 136B, Schroeder, U.V., *Indo-Tibetan Bronzes.*)

A delicately modelled gilt copper image of Mahāsiddha Dombipa belonging to the nineteenth century preserved in Essen, Germany depicts the guru uplifting a *damaru* in right hand and a *kapāla* in the left resting on left thigh. The graceful swaying of the body is in harmony with the vibration of the percussion instrument held by the acarya (Pls. 126ff, Schroeder, U.V., *Indo-Tibetan Bronzes*).

The mahāsiddhas appear in Himalayan painting as early as the eleventh century. The Sumtsek monastery at Alchi provided us a unique expression of a series of mahāsiddhas on the garment of Mañjuśrī. Within a checker-board pattern formed with squares or rectangles these figures are painted in white, orange or burgundy red. Some of these are mahāsiddhas or monks, others asceties putting on yaugic sashes and still others have a band tied around their head. They are either engaged in preaching or dancing in a wide variety of postures, or having their female partners seated on lap. The mahāsiddhas sit on animal skins and have a tree beside them as well as a halo. The mahāsiddhas are among the most graceful figures of Alchi murals of unmatched splendour in the Ladakh Himalaya (See Pls. S.17, S.18, Pal, P., *Marvels of Buddhist Art*).

An early fifteenth century mural in Gyantse, Kumbum, in Central Tibet depicts a beautiful mahasiddha seated crosslegged on an animal skin offering protection. This painting demonstrates the linear rhythm of the Newari idiom. The upper part of the bare body is decorated with simple ornaments while the preceptor is adorned with a garment with *kalpalatā* design. (Pl. 20, Pal, P., *Tibetan Paintings*).

From Nor monastery in Central Tibet comes a thangka ascribable to 1600 which delineates Mahāsiddha Damrupa seated in *lalitāsana* inside a trifoiled arch within a rectangular framework of a number of Buddhist gods and goddesses, *arhats* and *lamas.* This temple banner is now in a private collection in Zurich (Pl. 40, Pal, P., *Tibetan Paintings*).

In Tibet House, New Delhi, there is a set of eleven *thangkas* depiciting the eighty-four mahāsiddhas. One of these sets is significant for our study since it contains the representations of three female siddhas—Kankhala, Mekhala and Manibhadra along with six male mahāsiddhas. The two sisters Kankhala and Mekhala are seen dancing on cloud being approached by a devotee with a retinue of servants carrying offerings. These two nude female siddhas hold trumpet and magic staff as well as *kartari* and a severed head. It is said that these two sisters chopped off their own heads to repay their debt to Kanhapa who is also shown in this *thangka* seated on rock to their right. Manibhadra is represented flying through the clouds attired in red garments. This *thangka* originally belonged to a monastary of the

Kargyu-pa sect in eastern Tibet and scholars are inclined to attribute it to the early seventeenth century.

The other *thangka* of the set shows eight mahāsiddhas—Sabaripa, Sarahapa, Kamkaripa, Minapa, Goraksa, Tsorangia Binpa and Sanlipa (Pl. 16, Pal, P., *The Art of Tibet*).

In the John Gilmore Ford Collection there are a few Tibetan *thangkas* which deserve special mention. In one mahāsiddhya Virupa has been painted seated on a leopard skin. He is dressed in a loin cloth, and a long garland of flowers hangs between his legs. His hands form the gesture of turning the wheel of Law. Before him a dakini holds out a white *kapāla* as a sacrificial bowl. The painting shows evidence of Chinese stylistic elements and Tibetan conventions of composition. He is also surrounded by five dhyānī Buddhas. The painting dates from the latter half of the eighteenth century.

Another *thangka* represents Mahāsiddha Kṛṣṇācārya holding an antelope horn in his right hand and a *kapala* in his left amidst a landscape showing Chinese influence. He is also attended by a *dakini* offering a skull-cup. Like the previous one this too dates in the latter half of the eighteenth century.

A lively painting shows two mahāsiddhas, Jalandharipa, the teacher of Virupa (seated on a rectangular platform together with a tiger and two large vessels) and Siddha Ghantavajra in the upper part of the *thangka* floating in the clouds with *vajra* and *ghaṇṭā* in his hands accompanied by his *dakini.*

In spite of controversy in chronology with regard to siddhācāryas it is generally believed that as historical personages they appeared on the scene in the seventh-eighth century, as substantiated by literary information. In art form, however, this group of Buddhist preceptors made their mark from the eleventh century onwards. In the original homeland of the siddhas, India, no visual forms have so far been recovered. Neither the Indo-Nepal nor the Chinese tradition has yet yielded any mahāsiddha paintings. Tibet, on the other hand, was the only flourishing centre for experimentation in mahāsiddha paintings and icons.

SELECT BIBLIOGRAPHY

1. Bhattacharyya, Benoytosh
   (a) *The Indian Buddhist Iconography,* Calcutta, 1987.
   (b) *Sādhanamālā,* Vols. I, II, Baroda, 1968.

(c) *The Introduction to Buddhist Esoterism,* 1980.
(d) *Guhyasamāja Tantra.*
2. Dasgupta, Sashibhusan, *Obscure Religious Cults,* Calcutta, 1962.
3. Chattopadhyaya, Alaka.
(a) *Curashi Siddhar Kahini,* Calcutta, 1988.
(b) *Atīśa and Tibet,* Calcutta, 1967.
4. Majumdar, R.C.: *History of Ancient Bengal,* Calcutta, 1971.
5. Misra, Ramprasad, *Sahajayāna.*
6. Pal, Pratapadiya
(a) *The Art of Tibet,* U.S.A., 1969.
(b) *Art of Tibet,* U.S.A., 1983.
(c) *Tibetan Paintings,* Switzerland, 1984.
7. Stein, R.A., *Tibetan Civilization,* London, 1972.
8. Snellgrove, D.L., *The Hevajra Tantra,* London, 1964.
9. Schroeder, U. Von, *Indo Tibetan Bronzes,* Hongkong, 1981.
10. Verlag, Aurum: *Tibetan Thangkas,* 1976.

20

The Basic Contents of the Siddhācāryas' Sayings from the Tibetan Translation

BHAKTI DE

A group of Buddhist esoteric practitioners appeared between the eighth and twelfth centuries in India.[1] They flourished in different parts of the land. According to Tāranātha and other scholars there was Śabarīpā at Vikramsila, Ḍombīpā in Magadha, Vīnāpā in the Gauḍa, Sarahapā in Nalanda and Bhusukpā in south India, etc.[2]

They were designated as accomplished teachers (siddhācārya) because they attained accomplishment (*siddhi*). The Siddhācāryas attained accomplishment by the innate bliss of the experiencing mind.[3] It becomes a state of supreme bliss, attained after crossing *ānanda, paramānanda* and *virāmānanda.*[4]

In this connection *Hevajratantra* mentions :

prathamāndaṃ bhavaṃ proktaṃ nirvāṇañca virāgata
madhyamānanda mātrastu sahajameti bibarjitam
no rāgo na birāgaśca madhyamaṃ nopalabhyate
trayānāṃ barjanād eva sahajaṃ bodhirucyate.[5]

The siddhācāryas were born as ordinary persons. By dint of continuous practice and sustained effort they became gradually accomplished with spiritual capability. Questions arise as to what *siddhi* is and how it is achieved.

Siddhi (perfection) literally refers to an accomplishment of the words; while *sādhanā* is a method to an accomplishment. They are interrelated. Here *sādhanā* leads us to proceed spiritually without disowning material values of the wordly life. It has two sides, pragmatic and theoretical. Both are reciprocal. So their method of application (*sādhanā*) were meant for self awareness, and further movement towards perfection. Such onward to self-recognition movement becomes both physical and mental.

So, the Siddhācārya Vade pā says:

Etakāla hau acchila svamohe
ebe mai bujhlila sad guru bohe.
ebe ciarāya moku nathā
gayaṇa samude taliā paithā.
pekhami dahadiha sabbai shunna
cia vihune pāpa na puṇṇa.[6]

Here *sadguru* meant adviser and apprentice is practitioner. So Munidatta comments:

anādi saṃsāre kalyāṇamitra saṃsargāt. Mohomiti bāhya viṣaya saṃgenānlpaklpāntaṃ tābat sthito asmi. Idāniṃ budhāna bhābāt sadgurubodha prasaṃga na mayā cityasya svarūpambagatam. Idānoṃ pabipadmasamjogākṣara sukhe cittrājo mama vinasta gamamiti prakṛtiprabhāśvara pravistamiti.[7]

The word *sādhanā* indicates *sadhi* + *anat.* In respect of a tantra practitioner among the Buddhists, *sādhanā* is like a vessel or aid by which one becomes an accomplished practitioner or *vajrasattva.*

A *vajrasattva* holds no deviation under any state of experience. In this connection the commentary of the *Hevajra tantra* mentions:

Ekāraṃ bhagamityuktam
babāram kuliṣaṃ smṛtā
mayeti calana proktaṃ
vajra dharasya lakṣaṇam.[8]

Advayavajrasaṃgraha discusses this more clearly: 'By *vajra* is meant *śūnyatā* and by *sattva* is implied pure knowledge; the identity of the two follows from the nature of *vajrasattva.*'[9]

By boarding a vessel one can make a journey to reach one's destination, that is experience spiritual bliss in the world of phenomena. The word *sādhanā* thus corresponds to the means (*upāya*) what Bodhisattva aims. Here the vessel means *dhamma* as the Pali text reads, and the *dhamma* is like a vessel (*kullupam dhammam*).

In Sahaja practice the *upāya* refers to be external; while *prajñā* (wisdom) to the potential power of the practitioner; which is internal in contrast to *upāya.* In the Tantra *upāya* is male principle;[10] and *prajñā* is female principle.[11]

Again *śūnyatā* is the self nature (*svabhāva*) of the *prajñā*; which is essencelessness.[12] *Prajñā* also is a purified and unwavering movement. Metaphorically *ālayavijñāna* is a sea without wind. No wave is formed there. Regarding this idea Śabarīpāda sang in his song:

uñcā uñcā pabatata ibasai sundari bāli
morongi pichāparhina śabarī gibata guñjarimāli.
umato śabaro pāgala śabaro mākaraguli guhāra tohori
nia gharino nāma sahaja sundarī.[13]

The *Hevajratantra* also states that *upāya* is *karuṇā* (compassion):

upāyo mahākaruṇā sarvasatvesvatma samata nu bhāva.[14]

Karuṇā also unified with *śūnyatā* undergoes in altruistic action (*seva*) in the Bodhimind (*bodhicitta*). In this regard *Prajñāviniścayasiddhi* of Advayavajra mentions:

upāyopi caturvidho bodivajeṇa varṇita
sevā vidhāna prathama dvitīāmupasādhanām
sādhanāṃ tṛtīaṃ caiva mahāsādhanaṃ caturthamiti
prathamaṃ śūnyatā bodhirdvītiam vajra saṃhati.[15]

Such an alliance is called the *prajñapāya-yoga* in the retroverive process of movement, i.e. Sahaja (innate forms). *Prajñopāya Yoga* is a kind of esoteric practice at the sublime state of experience (*anuttara yoga*), which is unified experient of the essencelssness of the world (*śūnyatā*) within the Kaya of a practitioner in the *sādhanā*.

The Tantra considers that no cause of phenomenon is out of Kāya (body) of the practitioner. The natural phenomena like forests, rivers, rocks, the moon, the sun, etc., are within the body of a practitioner. Generally the siddhācāryas were *kayāsiddhas* having the equipoised experiences in the mind and the speech of the individual. They visualize the cosmic world and the phenomenal world within the body. In this regard, siddhācārya Sarahapāda sang in his *Dohā*:

Ethu se surasari jamunā ethu se gaṅgāsāaru
ethu payāga vanārasi ethu se canda divāaru.
khettu pīṭha upapīṭha ethu mai bhanai parithayo
deha śarīsaya titha mai saha aṇṇa na dithayo.[17]

Siddhi (perfection) is the result of the *sādhanā*. The *nyāsa* (placement) of *mantra* in the mind and body become relevant. *Sidh + kti = siddhi,* i.e. accomplishment. Fulfilment arrives when an urge for action is spent. Also the endeavours for leading a disciplined way of life (*caryā*) by observing the moral precepts occur no longer. But this experience becomes incomplete until *nirvāṇa* is achieved. Nirvāṇa refers to the state of unveiling the veils of mental turbidity (*kleśāvaraṇa*) and mental knowledge (*jñeyāvaraṇa*) occuring through ignorance (*avidyā*). That is called the state of the fourth bliss or *caturthānanda.* Then the practitioner becomes *siddha* or accomplished, and acquires clairvoyant vision to see the retrospective (*atīta*) and prospective (*anāgata*). A *siddha* has no scope of being reborn. The seed of *avidyā* is boiled or burnt. In this connection Bhusuku-pāda says:

Jā su nāhi appa tāsu paretā kāhi
āi anuaṇā re jāma marama bhāva nāhi[18]

Saraha-pāda also mentions:

ambhe ṇa jaṇahu acinta joi
jāma maraṇa bhāva kaisana hoi[19]

They could show the path (*mārga*) to get rid of the filth of the ignorant mind where no suffering prevails.

The siddhācāryas were also Bodhisattvas. They abided by the teaching of Buddha. They advised afflicted persons on how they could be away from the material world. Their directions and advice were expressed in spiritual songs and in different literaty works, as shown in the appendix.

NOTES

1. Bhakti De, *Bauddha Siddhācāryader Sādhanā o Paravartī Baṅgalā Sāhitya tār Prabhāb* (Ph. D. thesis), p. 331.
2. *Caurāshi Siddho kā Vṛttānta,* ed. Dorje, pp. 157-62.
3. The innate bliss or sahajānanda is neither *bhāva* nor *nirvāṇa.* It transcends both. The *Samutika tantra* mentions its nature:
   suviśuddha mahājñānaṃ sarvadevī svarūpakam.
   vajrasattva iti khyaṃ paramasukhaṃ udhārhṛtam
   svayambhū rūpaṃ etat tu dharam kāya svarūpakam
   tasyaiva sahajā prajñā sthitatādgata rūpinī.
   Sampuṭikātantra, manuscript, p. 48b.
4. Ānanda is bliss when the *bodhicitta* is in the Nirmāṇakaya, Paramānanda in the Dharmakāya and Viramānanda in the Sambhoga kāya.
   Ānanda means ordinary transient pleasure. It represents a resemblance

of the world. In the *vicitra kṣaṇa* (special moment) there is realization of Ānanda. Here the practitioner (*sādhaka*) gets only a glimse of the world.

The second, *paramānanda,* is more intense. It is a further step towards pure bliss. The *vipāka kṣaṇa* (moment of action) there is *paramānanda.* In this moment the bliss is conditioned by knowledge. The *sādhaka* gets here the provisional world.

The third, *vīramānanda,* means detachment from wordly pleasure. *Vīramānanda* is in the *vimarda kṣaṇa* (coveted moment). It is a higher moment. The realization of this bliss is attended by the consciousness of the sublimated ego as the realizer, Vīramānanda, represents the world.

Supreme bliss is *sahajānanda* which remains in neither of these three. Here knower and knowledge (material) are lost in oneness. The *vilakṣaṇa* movement holds the Sahajānanda. In this moment the realisation of the bliss is free from any emotion of attachment or detachment.

5. *Hevajratanta,* 1.10.17.
6. Vādepā, *caryā* no : 35
7. *Caryāgītikośa,* Prabodha Candra Bagchi and Santibhiksu, p. 116.
8. *Hevajratantra,* ed. Snellgrove, p. 22a.
9. *Vajreṇa śūnyatā proktā sattvene jñāna mātratā/tādātmaṃ anayoḥ siddham vajrasattva svabhāvataḥ—Advayavajrasaṃgraha,* p. 24.
10. *Upāya puruṣa smṛtā, Hevajratantra* (Vol. II), p. 28.
11. *Joṣit tābat bhāvet prajñā,* ibid.
12. *Svarva dharmānāṃ śūnyatā, Hevajratantraṭīkā,* p. 37b.
13. *Caryāgītikosā :cārya,* No. 28.
14. *Hevajratantraṭīkā,* p. 37b.
15. *Prjñāviniscayasiddhi,* p. 211.
16. *Sarahapāda, Dohā,* Nos.188-9.
17. *Caryāgītikośa* : *Carya* No. 43.
18. Do, *Carya* No. 22
19. Those works of the Siddhācaryas are appended here which were collected by Haraprasad Sastri; these were subsequent studied by Prabodh Candra Bagchi, Sashibhusan Dasgupta, Rahul Sankrityayan and Nagendranath Cowdhuri.

APPENDIX

Luhi Pāda

1. Śrī vajrasattva sādhanā nāma
2. Buddhodaya
3. Tattvasvabhāvadhokośa gītikā dṛṣti nāma
4. Buddhadaya nāma
5. Abhisamaya vibhaṅga

Saraha Pāda

1. Śrī Buddhakapāla tantrasya pañjikā jñānvati nāma.
2. Śrī Buddhakapāla sādhanā.
3. Sarva Buddha vali vidhi.
4. Śrī Buddhakapāla nāma maṇḍaḷa vidhi krama pradyotana.
5. Dohākośa gīti.
6. Dohākośa nāma caryāgīti.
7. Dohākośopadeśa gīti nāma.
8. Kakhasya Dohā nāma.
9. Kakhasya Dohā tippaṇa.
10. Kāyakośāmṛta vajra gīta.
11. Vākakośa rucira svara vajra gīta.
12. Cittakośa ajavajra gīta.
13. Kāya vākacitta manasikaranāma.
14. Dvādaśopadeśagāthā.
15. Tattvopadeśa śikharadohā gīti nāma.
16. Bhabana dṛṣṭi caryāphala dohāgītika nāma.
17. Vasantatilaka dohā kośā gītika nāma.
18. Mahāmudropadeśa vajraguhya gīti.
19. Trailokyavaśaṃkara lokeśvara sādhanā.
20. Trailokyavaśaṃkara lokeśvara sādhanā nāma.
21. Trailokyavaśaṃkarāvaloiktesvara sādhanā.
22. Trailokyavaśaṃkarāvalokiteśvara sādhanā.
23. Adhiṣṭhāna mahākāla sādhanā nāma.
24. Mahākāla stotra.

Tanti Pāda

1. Caturyoga bhāvanā nāma.

Ḍombi Pāda

1. Gṛhyavajra tantra rājāvṛtti
2. Ekavīra *sādhanā* nāma.
3. Daśa tattva.
4. Yoga yoginīnāṃ asādhāraṇarthopadeśa nāma.
5. Gaṇacakra vidhi nāma.
6. Śrī vajra sādhanā.
7. Bhikṣavṛttināma
8. Trikramopadeśa nāma
9. Nairātma yoginī sādhanā.
10. Āryatārā yoginī sādhanā.
11. Śrī sahaja siddhi nāma.
12. Akṣaradvikopadeśa nāma.
13. Nāmasaṃgītivṛtti.
14. Ekavīra sādhanā nāma.
15. Catuṣtattva.
16. Śrī gaṇapati cakra sūrya
17. Mṛtavidhi nāma.

Jayānanda

1. Tarka mudgarekārikā nāma.
2. Madhyamakāvatāra ṭīkā nāma.

Guḍari Pāda

1. Sarvadevatā niṣpanna krama mārga nāma.

Mahī Pāda (Mahinda)

1. Vāyu tattva dohāgītikā nāma.

Kukkuri Pāda

1. Vajrasattva sādhanā.
2. Mohataraṇa kalpa nāma.
3. Mahāmāyā sādhanā maṇḍala vidhi.
4. Mahāmāyā tantranusariṇi heruka sādhanopāyikā.
5. Śrī mahāmāyā maṇḍala deva stotra.

6. Tattvasukha bhāvanānusāri yoga bhāvanopadeśa nāma.
7. Sarva paricchedana (upadeśa) nāma.
8. Śrī mahāmāyā vali vidhi.

Dharma Pāda (Dhama Pāda)

1. Sugata dṛṣṭi gītikā nāma.
2. Huṃkāra citta vindu bhāvanā krama nāma sādhanā.

Vīru Pāda

1. Dohākośanāma.
2. Chinna muṇḍa sādhanā nāma.
3. Rakta yamāri sādhanā
4. Rakta yamāntaka sādhanā
5. Prabhāsodaya karma
6. Suṇiṣprapañca tattvapodeśa nāma.
7. Yamāri yantrāvali
8. Amṛtādhiṣṭhāna nāma.
9. Śrī virūpa pāda caturasīti
10. Amṛta siddhi mūla nāma.
11. Guhyābhiṣeka prakriyā nāma
12. Amara siddhi vṛtti (sanātana siddhi) nāma.

Kaṃ Kana Pāda

1. Caryādohākośa gītikā nāma.

Āryadeva

1. Śrī caturpīṭha yoga tantra sādhanopāyika.
2. Śrī caturpīṭha tantra rāja (nāma) maṇḍalopāyikā vidhi sāra-samuccaya nāma.
3. Pradīpoddyotana nāma ṭīkā
4. Caryā melāpaka pradīpa.
5. Cittavaraṇa viśodhana nāma prakaraṇa.
6. Sādhiṣṭhāna krama abheda.
7. Śrī Guhya samāja niṣpaṇṇa kramāntaka.
8. Nirvikalpa prakaraṇa.
9. Pratipattisāra śataka.

10. Krodha bhaya nāśāni sādhana nāma.
11. Bhaya śṛlinisādhana pralayābhiseka vidhi.
12. Krodha bhaya nāśani samaya Guhya sādhana.
13. Krodha bhaya nāśani homa vidhi nāma.
14. Mahādevatraya sādhana.

Dārika Pāda

1. Śrī kālacakra tantra rājasya sekaprakriyā vṛtti vajra padodghati nāma.
2. Śrī cakrasambara sādhanā tattva saṃgraha nāma.
3. Śrī cakrasaṃvara maṇḍala vidhi tattvavatāra nāma.
4. Śrī cakrasamvara stotra sarvārtha siddhi viśuddha cuḍāmaṇi nāma.
5. Yogānusāriṇī nāma vajra yoginī ṭīkā.
6. Vajra yoginī pūjā vidhi.
7. Kaṃkāla tārana sādhana
8. Śrī uḍḍīyāna vinirgata guhya mahā guhya tattvopadeśa.
9. Saptama Siddhānta nāma.
10. Tathatā dṛṣṭi nāma.
11. Prajñā pāramitā hṛdaya sādhanā nāma.

Kṛṣṇa Pā (Kanhu pāda)

1. Mahāmāyā maṇḍala vidhi krama bodhana nāma.
2. Raktaikajatyadhiṣṭhāna vidhi.
3. Kurukullā sādhanā.
4. Vināyakarāja sādhanā nāma.
5. Śrī vajraḍākini sādhanā nāma.
6. Mahāḍhuṇḍhana mūla nāma.
7. Raṭhacakra pañcadaśa yantra.
8. Caṇḍālī Yantra.
9. Bodhisattva caryāvatārā duravabodha (pada) nirnaya nāma grantha.
10. Triskandha sādhanā nāma.

Kambala Pāda (Kamlipa)

1. Asaṃbandha dṛṣṭi nāma.
2. Asaṃbandha sargadṛṣṭi nāma.

3. Ārya prajñāpāramitopadeśa nāma.
4. Maṇḍala vidhi.
5. Ārya prajñāpārāmitopadeśa nāma.
6. Bhagavatī prajñāpāramitā navaśloka piṇḍārtha.
7. Bhagavatī prajñāpāramitā navaśloka piṇḍārthaṭīkā.
8. Ārya prajñāpāramitpadeśa nāma.
9. Maṇḍala vidhi.
10. Śrī cakrasaṃbharābhisamayaṭīkā.

Śabarī Pāda

1. Vajra yoginyabhiṣeka saṃkṣepa nāma.
2. Vajra yoginī gaṇacakra vidhi nāma.
3. Vajra Vidāraṇī nāma dhāraṇi.
4. Krodha vajra vidāraṇī nāma dhāraṇi caṇḍamahāroṣaṇa sādhana nāma.
5. Krodha vajra māraṇa krama sādhanā.

Vīnā Pā

1. Guhyābhiṣeka prakaraṇa nāma.
2. Vajraḍākiṇī niṣpaṇṇa krama.

Bhusuku Pāda

1. Bodhisattvcaryāvatarodhava praṇidhāna.
2. Kevali.
3. Āryatyaya jñāna (nāma) mahāyānasūtravṛtti.
4. Śikṣāsmuccaya kārikā.
5. Tathāgatahṛday pāpḍesana sahita saṭakṣara rakṣā vidhi.
6. Tathāgata hṛdayapādadesana.
7. Śikṣā samuccaya.
8. Śikṣā samuccaya kārikā.
9. Śrī guhyasamāja mahāyogatantrā bvalividhi nāma.
10. Sahajagīti.
11. Bodhisattva caryāvatāra.

21

Emergence of Neo-Religious Thought in Proto-Medieval Bengal

RANGAN KANTI JANA

It is difficult to throw much light on the nature of Buddhism prevalent in Bengal before the Pālas. As revealed by several literary sources, it can be at least inferred that in some parts of Bengal, Mahāyāna and Hīnayāna Buddhism existed side by side, in the pre-Pāla period. But gradually Mahāyāna Buddhism was gaining popularity for its more liberal outlook and ideals, against the ethico-religious rigour of the Hīnayāna Buddhism. From the tenth century onward Bengal Buddhism had certainly entered a new phase, influenced by esoterism, and this new phase was adorned with Tantric Buddhism and its offshoots. On the basis of art and iconography it can be said that by this time Mahāyāna Buddhism started to enter a new phase, under the influence of Tantra.

The Mantrayāna school of Mahāyāna Buddhism is considered the preparatory stage of tantric Buddhism. Afterwards several offshoots developed, enriched with new thoughts and outlook, such as Vajrayāna, Kālacakrayāna and Sahajayāna. Several exponents of these new thoughts particularly of the Vajrayāna and Sahajayāna schools, must have belonged to Bengal. The leaders of these new thoughts have been known as Siddhācāryas. So far eighty-four names of these Siddhācāryas have been found. Many of them were directly or indirectly of Buddhistic origin. Instances of Sahajayāna literature came to light with the discovery of the *Caryāpadas* and the *Dohās.* It is generally held that the authors of *Caryāpadas* and the *Dohās* flourished some time between the tenth and twelfth centuries in Bengal. The subject matter of this literature is highly mystical, focusing on esoteric doctrine and yogic theories as well as practices of the Sahajayāna school of Buddhism. A comparative study of the *Dohās* as well as of the *Caryapādas* reveals the fact that in their religious attitude, in the manner of literary representation, in imagery, in phraseology and vocabulary, and in theories, they present a definite similarity. This clearly indicates that the *Dohās* and the *Caryapādas* belong to the same literary school and the same school of thought. The authors of these literatures are celebrated by the Mahāyāna Buddhists of Nepal and Tibet, and some of them are still regarded as Saivaite Yogis in the northern India. It is evident from their literature that the Siddhācāryas and the Nātha gurus proclaim a peculiar medley of doctrines, which were never separated by any clear cut line of demarcation; possibly they had flourished under the same source or under the same condition.

It is generally believed that the Sahajayāna school is an offshoot of Tantric Buddhism, possibly of the Vajrayāna school. The prime aim of the Sahajayāna school is to realize the ultimate inborn nature of the self and the *dharmas* in a very plain and easy way, not putting any strain on human nature. The major impetus is given to the cultivation of mental power of the self through a particular form of yogic practice (Haṭhayoga), only for the upliftment and ultimate deliverance of beings. As an offshoot of Tantric Buddhism, it incorporates the heterodoxy of Buddhism in general, mixed with the spirit of Tantrisim. It is revealed from the *Dohās* and songs that the Sahajayāna school had accepted the monistic standpoint of the Upaniṣads as the highest reality, either in the form of *Mahāsukha* or the *Sahaja*. Apart from the Upaniṣadas, and the Vedānta, some other lines of thought had also merged, namely, the *Nirvāṇadhātu* of canonical Buddhism, the pure consciousness of the Vijñānavādins, the *Vajradhātu* of the Vajrayānist, the Bodhicitta in the form of the unity of *Śūnyatā* and *Karuṇā* in the idea of *Sahaja*.

The main stress is laid by the Sahajayāna exponents on the practical method for realizing ultimate bliss by the sexo-yogic practice, which is certainly a psycho-physiological process. In connection with the practical aspect, the most important factor is the selection of an appropriate preceptor and several songs mention the preceptor, who is the only and ultimate guide in the path of Sādhanā. In their literature, the human body is considered a microcosm of the universe. The practices of Haṭhayoga are prescribed for making the body perfect and mature for Sādhanā. Otherwise, supreme realization becomes negative. Another important point is that the concept of the female force, variously mentioned as the Caṇḍālī, Ḍombī, Śabarī, Yoginī, Nairāmaṇi and Sahaja Sundarī. The transcendental love and union of yogin and yoginī is garbed in the metaphors of ordinary love and sex-union of man and woman in the literature.

The 'Sahaja' (or the state of intense bliss) is variously described in the songs and *Dohās*. Tillopāda states, 'I am void, the world is void, all the three worlds are void, in the pure "Sahaja" there is neither sin nor virtue' (*Dohā* No. 34). In another *Dohā*, it is stated that 'the ultimate reality is bereft of, both merit and demerit (*Dohā* No. 29). Kāṇhapāda says,

Sahaje ṇiccala jeṇa kia–samarasa niamaṇa rāa/
Siddho so puṇa takkhaṇe ṇau–jarāmaraṇaha sa bhāa//
(*Dohā* No. 19)

The word 'Samarasa' is used frequently in the sense of 'advaya' in the songs and *Dohās*.

Bhusukupāda says,

Jima jale pāṇiā taliābheda-na jāa//
tima mana raaṇa re samarase gaaṇa samāa// (Song 43).

The meaning of 'Samarasa' can be explained thus: in the 'Sahaja'-stage, there is perception of neither 'prajñā' nor 'upāya'; there is no sense of difference anywhere. In this connection Tillopāda says that 'in Samarasa both the positive and negative aspects of the mind vanish; it is pure and free from all existence as well as non-existence' (*Dohā* No. 11).

The Mahāyāna conception of the production of 'Bodhicitta' is transformed in the Sahajayāna into the production of a state of intense bliss by sexo-yogic practices. According to the Sahajayāna school the psycho-physiological yogic practice is first applied for the production of *Bodhicitta* (the word *Bodhicitta* is synonymous with the word 'semen' in the Sahajayāna. It is the ultimate substance of the nature of the five elements such as—earth, ether, water, fire and air) through the union of the *prajñā* and the *upāya*. This Bodhicitta must be made to go upwards by the Yogic process through the different *cakras* (or Kāyas) namely the *Nirmāṇa Cakra* (which is situtated near the navel), the *Dharma Cakra* (which is situated in the heart), the *Sambhoga Cakra* (which is situated in the throat) and finally it reaches in the *uṣṇīṣa kamala* (which is situated in the head), where it produces the *Mahāsukha*. In the *Mahāsukha* (or Sahajānanda, it is neither *bhāva* nor *nirvāṇa*, it goes beyond both) all kinds of duality vanish in a unique realization of supreme bliss. It is also described as

Samarasa and *Advaya* where all kinds of duality are absorbed in a principle of non-duality and this is the ultimate goal according to the Sahajayāna school. The flow of *Bodhicitta* should be carefully regulated along the middle nerve and this is the most difficult, the vital part, of the *Sādhanā.* In this connection, the songs and *Dohās* frequently warn the beginner to take practical guidance from the preceptor at this stage. All religions impose strict rules in favour of the total annihilation of the primitive and natural tendencies of the human being, one of which is the sexual impulse. According to the Sahajayāna school, strict suppression can only make a human being neurotic and morbid. So they recommend the transformation and exaltation of the natural propensities of the human being. The sahajayāna exponents prescribe that any human being can realize the ultimate truth through initiation in the *tattva* and the practice of yoga without supressing the fundamental propensities of life. Perhaps for this reason, the Sahajayāna path has always been described as the easiest and most natural way.

External rituals and formalities had no place in the Sahajayāna school. So formal rules and regulations of other religions were vigorusly criticized.The most scathing criticisms are found in the *Dohās* of Sarahapāda. He says,

airichiṃ u ddulia cchāre/
Sīsasu vāhia e jaḍabhāreṃ //
ghorahi vaisī dīvājālī/
konahiṃ vaisī ghaḍā cālī //
akkhi ṇivesī āseṇa vandhī /
kaṇṇchiṃ khusu khusāi jaṇa dhandhī//

(*Dohā* No. 4)

kajje virahia huavaha homeṃ/
akkhi uhāvia kadueṃ dhameṃ //

(*Dohā* No. 2)

He also says,

mokṣa ki lavbhi jhāṇa pavitto/
kintah kijjai kiṇtah ṇivejjṃ //
kintah kijjai mantah sevvaṃ//

(*Dohā* No. 14)

ahimāṇa doseṃṇa Lakkhintattva/
teṇa dūsai saala jāṇu sodatta //

jhānem̩ mohia saala vi loa /
nia svahāva ṇau lakkhai koa//

(*Dohā* No. 35)

In his *Dohās*, Saraha indicates that how Sahaja can be achieved.

jahi maṇapavaṇa ṇa sañcarai-ravi sasi ṇāha pavesa/
tahi vaḍa citta visāma karu - sarahem̩ kahia uesa//

(*Dohā* No. 24)

ekku karu re mā karu veṇṇi jāne-na karaha viṇṇa/
ehu tihuaṇa Saala māhārātram̩ - ekku karu veṇṇa//

(*Dohā* No. 26)

āiṇa anta ṇa majajha ṇau ṇau bhava ṇau ṇivvāna/
ehu so parama mahāsuha ṇau para ṇau appāṇa//

(*Dohā* No. 27)

india jaththu vilaa gau ṇa ṭhiu appa sahavā/
so hale sahaja taṇu phndha-pucchahi guru pāvā/

(*Dohā* No. 29)

Apart from these, severe criticism was made by Sarahapāda of the traditional fourfold division of colours and the highest position of the Brāhmaṇa in caste society. In this connection he says 'if a man becomes a Brāhmaṇa by reciting the Vedas, let the people of the lower classes also recite the Vedas and they will also become Brahmins'. It is generally considered that the Sahajayāna school flourished in Bengal between the tenth and twelfth centuries. During that time the major political power of Bengal was the Pālas. They were Buddhist, but of liberal outlook. As revealed from the Pāla epigraphic sources, it can be said that they were inclined to maintain the existing Brahmanical varṇa system in society. The process of Sanskritization had started in Bengal long before the advent of Pāla power. In the liberal atmosphere during Pāla rule this process accelerated. By the process of Sanskritization the Brahmanical varṇa system gradually accommodated many indigenous tribes in the fold of the society. But they had to settle at the lowest stage, not losing, however, their own socio-cultural as well as religious identities. The Sahajayāna exponents were not satisfied with their position in the social hierarchy. So they criticized it. They tried to attract these peoples to the Sahajayāna fold, depicting it as their only resort from the *varṇa* exploitations of the higher castes. In this connection, Saraha says 'where the mind sets in, all bondage is torn off, there is non-dual state where every thing becomes the same; there is neither the Śūdra nor the Brāhmaṇa' (*Dohā* No. 46). The *Caryāpadas* are the only contemporary source which refer to the life of those people, regarded as almost beyond the pale of the Hindu *varṇa* system: the Ḍoma, Caṇḍāla, Śabara, etc. The same literature has also mentioned some of the professions: wood cutter, carpenter, boat-builder, boat-man, dancer, distiller, wine-seller, etc.

The prime motto of the Sahaja exponents (discarding the rituals and the formalities) was to formulate a new outlook in the religious thought, by which a human being of any caste or creed could get the scope to realize the ultimate truth (or the supreme bliss) through initiaton in the *Sahaja tattva* and the practice of yoga, not giving any strain on the natural propensities and not losing their own socio-cultural identity, obviously with the help of a Sahaja preceptor.

REFERENCES

Haraprasad Sastri, *Hājār Bachharer Purāṇa Baṅglā Bhashāy Gān O Dohā* (in Bengali) (Calcutta, 1223 BS).

N.N. Bhattacharyya, *History of Tantric Religion* (New Delhi, 1982).

P.C. Bagchi, '*Dohā* Kośa', *Journal of the Department of Letters,* Vol. XXVIII (Calcutta, 1935).

———, *Studies in the Tantras* (Calcutta, 1939).

———, *Bauddha Dharma O Sāhitya* (in Bengali) (Calcutta, 1359 BS).

S.B. Dasgupta, *An Introduction to Tantric Buddhism* (Calcutta, 1974).

S.S. Dasgupta, *Obscure Religious Cults* (Calcutta, 1976).

22

The Kālacakra School The Latest Phase of Buddhism

BISWANATH BANERJEE

In the sacred texts of the Buddhists the Buddha is said to have preached a doctrine unheard before. By his own unaided effort he realized the solution to the greatest riddle of humanity and explained to the world the Path which would make an end of suffering, leading to release from the cycle of births. What we mean by Buddhism today is, however, not the essence or fundamentals of this *new* doctrine but a religio-philosophical system which assimilated and adopted new ideas and beliefs from the society in which it developed. In course of centuries after the passing away of the Founder, the words of the Buddha underwent so many far-reaching changes and included within its fold so many diverse things that the original teachings of the Master became changed beyond recognition.

The problem of the relation of Buddhism to Brahmanism is an important factor to be considered to understand the background of Buddhism. Brahmanism as developed from the religion of Aryan India and influenced by non-Aryan contacts had by the sixth century BC become an elaborate sacrificial and sacerdotal system. It was in the midst of this that Buddhism originated. Brahmanic ideals and principles have very much influenced and guided the development of Buddhism, particularly in its later phase which is more akin to Brahmanism. The elaborate ritualistic systems together with an incorporation of a number of gods and goddesses in the later phase of Buddhism have given the religion of the Buddha a totally different form and flavour.

It was perhaps a century after the *mahāparinirvāṇa* theBuddhism began to assimilate those ideas and thoughts that ultimately led to the historical division of Buddhism into the two major schools, Hinayāna and Mahāyāna. It may be said that the broadness of outlook and the liberal attitude of Mahāyāna with its emphasis on *karuṇā* saved Buddhism from the narrow scholastic dogmatism of the earlier Buddhists, but it cannot be denied either that once the portals of this religion of rigorous moral discipline were thrown open it paved the way for the incorporation of heterogeneous ideas and practices. Various forms of popular ceremonies and thoughts crept into the ethico-religious character of Buddhism and with the process continuing from the early centuries of the Christian era till about the eighth century Buddhism incorporated the elements of *mantra, mudrā, maṇḍala* and many such other known forms. Ultimately an altogether new form of Buddhism called Vajrayāna appeared with much emphasis on rituals, meditational practices, and gods and goddesses. Some groups and sects began to emerge within the Vajrayāna with different interpretations of the cardinal principles of Buddism.

This new phase of Buddhism is more or less a kind of Tantricism and the general appellation Mantrayāna or Tantrayāna is given to all the sects or branches taken together, as their ideas and principles are based on *mantras.* In its form and characteristics this Tantra-Buddhism is much the same as the form known as Hindu Tantrism. It has been claimed that the Buddhist Tantras originated out of the Hindu Tantras and 'as regards Buddhism, Tantra stands for a Hindu conquest'.[1] This claim, however, does not stand on facts. It has to be considered in this connection that the Tantra-tradition is not the work of a day, and the principles on which the Tantras, Hindu or Buddhist, are based were not evolved by either Hinduism or Buddhism out of their own materials but were the growth of the soil utilized by both. It is also an historical fact that some Tantric trends 'arose particularly on India's extreme boundaries, some even outside Indian territory'.[2] It is indeed difficult to trace an organic relationship between Buddhism and Tantricism or to ascertain how the tanric paraphernalia crept into Buddhism. It might be that the Buddhist masters with their broad-minded receptiveness strengthened by the tendency of speading to all people including the backward frontier peoples did not hesitate to accept popular ideas and even deities in their fold. These elements were, however, fully transformed, 'purged of their primitive crudeness' and endowed with secret symbols. Many of the *maṇḍalas* of Vajrayāna reveal contact of Buddhism with frontier peoples. Different sects of Vajrayāna accepted many of ideas and institutions current among the the masses and with their tolerant universalism introduced popular indigenous deities in their *maṇḍalas* as acolytes of their chief gods. In the process popular Hindu deities like Indra, Varuṇa, Maheśvara, Viṣṇu Skanda, Kuvera, and even Kāma, the brahmanic god of love, are all admitted wholesale in Buddhism and they find their positions in *maṇḍalas,* but as the quarters. With the diversion of the Buddha's religion to this direction a large number of divine and fiendish beings also found place in Vajrayanic texts; often they assumed female forms, and sometimes monstrous appearances. In almost all texts of later Buddhism we meet with such beings as Cundā, Ambā, Ḍākinī, Yoginī, Yakṣiṇī, and a host of others like them.

The incorporation of Hindu gods and goddesses reached its limit with the development of the Kālacakra system. The most important factor for the increase of the compromising attitude of the Buddhists towards different Brahmanic sects may be traced to the advent of Islamic religion and culture. It is learnt from the Kālacakra texts that the Buddhists were faced with the social problem of the overpowering infiltration of the Semitic culture and to resist the growing influence of the foreign culture they offered to join hands with the followers of the Brahmanical religion. It is said that the purpose of introducing the Kālacakra system was to prevent people from being converted to Islam.[3] With a view to stopping the inroads of alien culture the leader of the Buddhists proposed inter-marriage and inter-dining among the Buddhist and Brahmanical families, and appealed to the latter to assemble under the banner of the one Lord Kālacakra, who to all intents and purposes appears to be a non-sectarian God. It was thought possible for all the warring elements of different religious groups to unite and fight under the leadership of such a God against foreign influence. The development of this school with abundant incorporation of Brahmanic divinities in the *maṇḍala* of the Kālacakra might have been unavoidable for a cultural fusion and united resistance to the impending danger of Islamic penetration. It was thus attempted to unite all followers of Brahma, Viṣṇu, Śiva and other sages in one family the Vajrakula, with the four-fold initiation in the Kālacakra—all differences in race, class, creed and custom were sought to be removed. Besides the developing systems of Śaivism and Vaiṣṇavism the Kālacakra school also borrowed from flourishig Manichaeanism and other foreign elements. The Kālacakra system and the concept of the Kālacakra are two important examples of the long process of culture fusion in India.

Vaiṣṇava, Śaiva and Yoga elements, along with other forms of Indian and foreign ideas have contributed significantly at one time or other to the formation of the Kālacakra system, which is certainly a syncretic one, particularly in its meditational principles. In spite of all such elements this is out and out a Buddhist system in origin, spirit and character. Its essentially Buddist character cannot be missed by anybody examining its ideas, theories and propensity.

Since the Kālacakra-Buddhists consider *kāla* or time as an important factor regulating human life and the process of the world they attach great significance to astronomical conceptions of *yoga* (variable divisions of time), *karaṇa* (astrological divisions of the day), *tithi* (lunar day), and the movemens and positions of the sun, planets and constellations. Experts in astronomy, astrology and related mathematical computations, these Buddhists interpret the fundamentals of Buddhism in relation with time and its different units. The fundamental Buddhist theory of the causal genesis, the *pratītyasamutpāda*, has been viewed in the Kālacakra text as the movement of the sun through twelve Zodiacal signs in twelve months.[4] To understand life and the cause of life, to know the real nature of the phenomenal objects, one should comprehend this movement and the process. To put an end to the mass of evils is to stop it. In the same way they explain *karuṇā* and *śūnyatā* in terms of the two fortnights and the *tithis*.[5]

Both Indian and Tibetan sources agree that this phase of Buddhism was brought to the Indian soil from a country named Śambhala about sixty years before it passed on to Tibet. It is generally accepted that the Kālacakra system penetrated into Tibet through Kashmir in AD 1027, and it was in aproximately AD 966 that it first became known in India. This phase of Buddhism exercised a potent influence in the life and thought of Tibet. The Lamaist religion is fully influenced by this system and a large number of treatises have been written by Tibetan scholars in the form of commentaries and sub-commentaries to original Sanskrit works, most of the which now appear to be lost.

Kālacakra, the Ādi-Buddha, the progentitor of all Buddhas, the unitary embodiment of *prajñā* and *upāya*, is the Lord Supreme with these Buddhists. The form of Kālacakra that a *sādhaka* should meditate upon to attain *siddhi* is like this:[6]

In the variegatd maṇḍala, on the great lotus, with the Sun above, and shedding lustre, is seated with the left leg stretched (the Lord) with the *bhūtanātha* trampled under the feet, causing horror in the minds of gods, demons, and snakes, and who is *jñānasattva* and located in the *śmaśāna,* should be meditated upon for a month and (thus) the ghosts should be controlled.[6]

In his *maṇḍala* the Lord takes his position in the centre with gods like Viṣṇu, Indra and Brahmā being assigned subordinate posts as guardians of the quarters. It is observed in the texts that the *yoga* of Śrī Kālacakra has been revealed to help men of the *kaliyuga* to attain emancipation in the present birth.

NOTES

1. M. Basu, *Tantras, A General Study,* p. 24.
2. G. Tucci, *Tibetan Painted Scrolls,* I, p. 224.
3. An interesting account on this point is found in the *Vimalaprabhā I.* See introduction to the *Kālacakratantrāja,* edited by the present author.
4. Ibid.
5. Ibid.
6. See present author's article in *Our Heritage,* 150th Anniversary Volume.

23

Female Deities in a Buddhist Tamil Epic

S.N. KANDASWAMY

With the main objective of disseminating the vital principles of Buddhism in the south, Cāttaṉār created the immortal Tamil epic *Maṇimēkalāi.* Since the epic centres around the evolution of the heroine Maṇimēkalāi into a female Bodhisattva, it was named after her. Cāttaṉār was an erudite scholar in Tamil, Pali and Sanskrit. He was an efficient logician and able exponent of Buddhist philosophy. He lived from AD 450 to 550.[1] He knew the various branches of Buddhism which were current during his life-time. He was essentially a Buddhist of the Sautrāntika-Yogācāra School founded by Vasubandhu and nurtured by Dignāga and his disciples. The salient aspects of Sautrāntika of Hinayāna and cardinal tenets of Yogācāra of Mahāyāna constituted the contents of the synthetic school of Sautrāntika-Yogācāra.[2] Since Yogācāra and Tāntricism are interrelated, it is natural that some features of Tantric Buddhism can be traced in the Buddhist *Maṇimēkalāi.* In this article, the presence of female deities and their roles as saviours of human beings, especially Buddhists, will be discussed in the light of rich materials enshrined in the *Maṇimēkalāi.*

According to Alice Getty, Hinayāna never admitted female divinities in the Buddhist pantheon.[3] Only after the advent of Tantric Buddhism did female deities became the object of adoration.[4] Normally, each male divinity or bodhisattva has a consort, and devotees would extol their glory in order to evoke their blessings. But in the Tamil epic the goddesses are independent, without a spouse, working under the command of Indra, the celestial king and sincere worshipper of Ādi Buddha. Cāttaṉār has delineated the character of at least four female deities, Maṇimēkalāi teyvam, Tīvatilakai, Campāpati and Cintādevī. Let us consider briefly the position of each of them in the epic.

GODDESS MAṆIMĒKALĀ

Maṇimēkalāi teyvam is totally a Buddhist deity, already introduced in the Jātaka stories. The *Samkha Jātaka* (No. 442) and *Mahājanaka Jātaka* (No. 539) narrate her miraculous and merciful activities. One of the duties of this deity was to protect the patrons of the Buddhist monks from all difficulties. Samkha, a patron of Buddhist monks, undertook a voyage from Banaras to Sorṇabūmi (Burma) in order to amass wealth. His ship sank in the ocean and for seven days he struggled in the tossing seas. On the seventh day Maṇimēkalāi teyvam created a big ship, put all the costly things into it, along with Samkha, and steered it herself back to Banaras. Then again Mahājanaka of Mithila Deśa was a great philanthropist, who undertook a voyage to Sorṇabumi to amass wealth. His ship also sank on the high seas and he too struggled for life for seven days. On the seventh day, Maṇimēkalāi teyvam airlifted him with all kindness and dropped him in a mango grove at Mitilai.

These two stories must have attracted Cāttaṉār. Following the themes, he introduced certain new situations from his imagination and built up the character of Maṇimēkalāi teyvam in the epic. Cāttaṉār himself was a merchant. The *Maṇimēkalāi* contains a lot of references on maritime trade. Cāttaṉār mentions ship-wrecks in three contexts, but does not make Maṇimēkalāi teyvam protect all seafaring merchants. When the ship of Kamapaḷac-ceṭṭi sank near Pukār, Maṇimēkalāi teyvam did not come to his rescue.[5] There is no evidence that this deity helped Cātuvaṉ, when the latter was struggling for life in the deep sea. Cātuvaṉ, with the help of a stray float, reached the shore and later the hilly terrain inhabited by the Nagas.[6] Cātuvaṉ was originally a hedonist, who indulged in gambling, sensual pleasures and other vices. But he renounced all of these when he became a staunch Buddhist. He was praised by Cāttaṉār as 'Naṉṟaṟi ceṭṭi', i.e. the merchant who realized what is good. But Maṇimēkalāi teyvam saved the ancestor of Kōvlaṉ, who practised Dānapāramitā and Sīlapāramitā. He was saved, because he was to become Bodhisattva in future.[7]

As described in Jātaka stories, Maṇimēkalāi teyvam is the gauridan goddess of the sea. The poet delightfully describes her as *Parappunīr pauvam pallar toḻak kāppōḷ*, i.e. she who guarded the expanded sea and was adored by many. But this deity does not hesitate to protect the Buddhist even on land. When Maṇimēkalāi was besieged by

Utayakumaraṉ in a flower garden at Kāviripūmpaṭṭiṉam, Maṇimēkalāi teyvam rescued her and placed her under protection in Maṇipallavam.

Maṇimēkalāi teyvam is a subordinate of Indra and never fails to attend Indra's festival, in the disguise of a beautiful woman of Pukār. Because Indra's festival was not celebrated in a particular year, she made the sea engulf Pukār, the city of the Colas.[8] However she also takes great delight in worshipping Buddha, worshipped by Indra. It moves anyone to read how Maṇimēkalāi teyvam, on seeing the Buddha pīṭikai at Pukār, circumambulates it with folded hands and worships with ardent devotion.[9] She also habitually praises and worships the Buddha pīṭikai, established by Indra at Maṇipallavam.[10]

Maṇimēkalāi teyvam possesses mantric powers. Assuming the form of a beautiful woman, she usually mixes with the people as one of them.[11] She will look like a climber full of flowers, when she comes down form the sky, carrying flowers, to worship Buddha.[12] She was in the habit of travelling through the high heavens. She taught the heroine, Maṇimēkalāi, the Three Mantras, viz., to take any form at will, to travel through air and to appease the appetite.[13]

Maṇimēkalāi teyvam's lightning-like body shone like a rainbow, on account of her supernatural powers.[14] The history of Nagarjunai might have helped Cāttaṉār portray this quality. Nagarjunaī, the greatest Tantric Buddhist scholar, possessed supernatural powers and his body too shone like a rainbow and he also travelled through the heavens.[15] Cāttaṉār pictures Maṇimēkalāi teyvam as an abode of beauty, lustre, tenderness and power.

Because this deity had saved his ancestor, Kōvalaṉ named his daughter, Maṇimēkalāi, after her.[16] Like her father, Maṇimēkalāi was also grateful to this deity. Maṇimēkalāi was responsible for the construction of a temple for Maṇimēkalāi teyvam at Kanci by Neṭuvēṟkiḷḷi.[17]

Maṇimēkalāi teyvam possessed the knowledge of the past, present and future. When Kōvalaṉ named his child Maṇimēkalāi, this deity appeared in Mātavi's dream that night and told her that her daughter would become a nun, causing diappointment to Kāmaṉ.[18] This deity could also expose to Cutamati, Mātavi, Maṇimēkalāi and Utayakumaraṉ their previous births.[19] She knew for certain that Utayakumaran could not leave Maṇimēkalāi, who in her turn could not easily forget Utayakumaraṉ. But this goddess determines to assist Maṇimēkalāi to become free from the bondage of love and elevates her towards nunhood. Maṇimēkalāi, who was like Kantacāli, a superior variety of paddy, was not permitted to fall into moorish or boggy soil, Utayakumaraṉ. The goddess brought Maṇimēkalāi to Maṇipallavam and made her realize her previous birth by worshipping Buddha pīṭikai. Through Tīva tilakai, she made it possible for Maṇimēkalāi to acquire the miraculous alms-bowl. She made Maṇimēkalāi learn from Aṟavaṇar the story of Āputtiraṉ and the glory of the alms-bowl.

Two individuals are mainly responsible for shaping the religious life of Maṇimēkalāi. The first half of her religious life was determined by Maṇimēkalāi teyvam, and the second half by Aṟavaṇar, who perfected it.

Maṇimēkalāi teyvam respected 'justice' more than anything else. She advised the Cola Utayakumaraṉ as follows: 'If the king violates justice, the planets will go astray. If the planets, thus, become ill disposed, the rains may fail, which in turn will make life impossible. Thus the prosperity of life depends on the king's sense of justice.' So saying, Maṇimēkalāi teyvam asked Utayakaumaran to give up his lust for Maṇimēkalai who had already become a bhikkuṇi (nun). To love a bhikkuṇi, as one would do any other woman, amounts to sin and a king should not commit such a sin.[20]

The goddess knows fully Buddhist cosmology, as is evident from her description to Cutamati of the history and structure of Cakkaravāḷakōṭṭam.[21] Even Buddha Pīṭakai respected Maṇimēkalāi teyvam, who asked the heroine to know from this deity about the life story of her husband in her previous birth.[22] Tīvatilakai also was surprised at the powers of the deity. But, Maṇimēkalāi teyvam greatly respected the venerable Bodhisattva Aṟavaṇa aṭikaḷ.[23]

Sylvan Levi states that stories of Maṇimēkalāi teyvam are in vogue in Combodia, Siam and other places. There are many places in Ceylon named after this deity.[24] Like this goddess, another Buddhist goddess, by name Tārā, became popular after the sixth century. Maṇimēkalāi teyvam's rescues of people from the sea could be an allegory denoting salvation from the sea of birth.

TĪVATILAKAI

Indra assigned different guarding duties to different Buddhist female deities. The Bhūtas were in-charge of protecting the city. The guardian deity of Madurai was Madurāpati. Maṇimēkalāi teyvam was the guardian of the seas, while Campāpati was the guardian of the lands. Likewise, Tīvatilakai was a guardian deity of islands. The name of this deity is highly suggestive of its duty. At the command of Indra, Tīvatilakai was guarding the Buddha Pīṭikai, at Maṇipallavam. She has also contact with the neighbouring islands.[25]

Tīvatilakai was a staunch devotee of Buddha. She aspired to salvation by worshipping the Lotus Feet of Buddha. She circumambulated and adored his holy foot-prints atop the Camanta mountains at Ratnadvīpa.[26] She preached the greatness of Dharma to Maṇimēkalāi.[27] The deity possessed knowledge of past, present and future. She predicted that the heroine alone would get the miraculous alms-bowl from the Kōmukhi tank on the birthday of Buddha, Vaiśāka Pūrṇimā.[28] She reminded Puṇṇiyarāsan of his previous birth as Āputtiraṉ. She was able to narrate current events also. She had great respect for Aṟavaṇaṭikaḷ. The embodiment of sympathy and love, she helped Maṇimēkalāi in her spiritual growth. She explained the significance of feeding the poor, since that was a great religious service according to Buddha.[29] As a token of gratitude, Maṇimēkalāi advised the king of Kāñci to build a temple for Tīvatilakai and celebrate an annual festival in her honour.[30]

CAMPĀPATI

Of the many temples that were founded at Pukār, the temple of Camāpati was noteworthy. Her shrine was situated in the main entrance of the public hall at Pukār. Cattaṉār calls this temple the 'Kuccarak kutikai'. Scholars opined that it was built by Gunjara architects.[31] The image of the deity was made in brick and mortar. According to the prelude of the epic, Campāpati appeared on the top of a gold moutain and then shifted to southern region. As she performed her penance under a Campa (Jambu) tree, she came to be known as 'Campāpati'. Due to the effect of penance, her lustre outdid the brilliance of rising sun. Her body was beautiful and shone like gold.[32] She was both young and old at once. Before feeding the people gathered in the open yard, Maṇimēkalāi thrice worshipped Campāpati.[33] Similarly, she adored her before she undertook her aerial journey to Jāva.[34]

Campāpati was also guarding Jambu Dvīpa.[35] Water reservoirs, public places, old and strong trees, rest house and various temples too were guarded by her.[36] Using her extraordinary power of penance, she protected the country from the invasion of Aśuras. According to

Buddhist mythology, in the beginning of the world, Pukār was known as 'Campāpati'. She was also worshipped by the sage Agasthya. In order to bring prosperity to the country, Campāpati celebrated the festival of Indra, which was subsequently continued by the Cola monarchs.

Campāpati with all kindness and compassion, conversed with a Brahmin woman Gotamai, who lost her son, and tried to remove her ignorance and agony. The woman complained that some ghost or angel had taken her son's life. She requested the goddess to revive her son so that he could take care of her blind husband. She offered her own life in return for her son's life. Nevertheless, Camāpati instructed her that though thousands of people were ready to sacrifice their life for a king, the tombs of dead kings were countless. She meant that death did not make any discrimination between an ordinary man and a king. Gotamai was not satisfied and entreated her again to revive her dead son, stating that the Vedic gods had the powers of resurrection. Then Campāpati used her unusual powers, summoning all the celestials, planets and beings, to appear before Gotamai. They consoled the bereaved woman by simply repeating the advice of Campāpati that no one could revive her dead son. This episode seems to be based on the story of Sujata or Kisagotami who was pacified by Buddha on the death of her son. Campāpati, the goddess of lands, had been glorified as the great grand deity.[37]

CINTĀDEVI

The Tamil Buddhists transformed the Hindu goddess of learning, Saraswathi, into Cintādevi. 'Cintā' means thought or mind, and Cintādevi was the ruler of mind and thought. Cāttaṉar has depicted her as being favoured by all religions.[38] There was a temple for this goddess at Madurai, the centre for Tamil learning and culture. She had a lustrous marble-like body.[39] She was in the form of an enduring and everlasting beacon of light.[40] This divine light had the power to dispell both internal and external darkness. Cintādevi was queen of all arts. She rectified defects in words and bestowed wisdom. She was compassionate and relieved the suffering of the people. When Aaputraṉ approached her in the mid-night in a rainy season to help the hunger-stricken people, he was given the miraculous alms-bowl by the goddess to appease the hunger of the lot.[41] The portions in the epic that glorify the benevolence of Cintādevi constitute the best specimen of devotional poetry.[42]

KAṆṆAKI—THE DEITY OF CHASTITY

The cult of Pattiṉi was a special feature of southern Buddhism. Some scholars identified Kaṇṇaki with the deity Tārā, the consort of Avalokiteśvara, but stories about Tārā do not agree with the biographical accounts of Kaṇṇaki. The word Tārā denotes one who helps people in crossing the sea of existence. Similarly her husband Avalokiteśvara saved his devotees from shipwreck and distress.[43] Normally, this power was exercized by female deities. Thus, Tārā bears similarity with Maṇimēkalāi teyvam and not Kaṇṇaki.

Kaṇṇaki is a totally Tamil Buddhist goddess. The *Cilapatikāram* was composed mainly to reveal the growth of Kaṇṇaki into the goddess of chastity. In this epic, all kinds of people—monarchs, subjects, men, women, deities, ascetics, family men, natives and foreigners exhibited equal reverence to the goddess of chastity.

When her husband was unjustly put to death by the Pandya king, Kaṇṇaki neither died nor was frustrated enough to renounce everything. Instead, she pointed out to the king his injustice, and destroyed the evil forces in the city by the flame of her chastity, and went to heavens with her departed husband. Ceraṉ Ceṅkuṭṭuvaṉ constructed a temple for Kaṇṇaki at Vañci. On the eve of consecration of the temple, Kajabahuī of Ceylon was the chief guest. He was instrumental for the spread of Pattiṇi Cult in Ceylon. When Maṇimēkalāi appealed to the goddess of chastity at Vañci and praised her glory, her prayer was answered. Further, the goddess informed her about the rebirth, as a male at Kapilavastu and after hearing the preachings of Buddha and entering the monastic order, she would cut the knot of birth and attain salvation.[44] Cāttaṉār has extolled her unique embodiment of chastity.[45]

CONCLUSION

As a result of the delineation of female deities and their active role and involvement in shaping the budding female Bodhisattva Maṇimēkalāi (the heroine of the epic), Cāttaṉār has revealed his association with some aspects of Tantricism, perhaps reflecting its formative period. Except goddess Maṇimēkalāi, all the rest are local

and native to the Tamil country. It is to be understood that Cāttaṉār has preserved in his epic the Tamil tradition of devotional cum Tantric Buddhism as prevalent in his period. The characteristic features of these deities deserve to be compared with those of similar deities of Buddhist Tantric traditions in the Sanskrit, Tibetan, Chinese and Japanese sources.

NOTES

1. S.N. Kandaswamy, *Buddhism as Expounded in Maṇimēkalāi,* (Annamalainagar, 1978), p. 74
2. Benoytosh Bhattacharyya, *An Introductin of Buddhist Esoterism* (Delhi, 1980), p. 35.
3. Alice Getty, *The Gods of Northern Buddhism* (Delhi, 1978), p. 175.
4. Ibid., pp. 118, 122, 137.
5. *Maṇimēkalāi,* XXV, 184-91.
6. Ibid., XVI 14-16.
7. Ibid., XXIX 23-28.
8. Ibid., XXV 197-200.
9. Ibid., V 96-105.
10. Ibid., X 3-16.
11. Ibid., V 96, VI 13, VIII 25.
12. Ibid., X 3-5: V 106-8.
13. Ibid., X 79-91.
14. Ibid., VI 9-10.
15. Sylvain Levi, 'Maṇimēkalāii, A Divinity of the Sea', *The Indian Historical Quarterly,* Vol. VII, p. 371.
16. *Maṇimēkalāi,* XXIX 29-31.
17. Ibid., XXVIII 212-16.
18. Ibid., VII 34-8, XXIX 31-3.
19. Ibid., X 18-75.
20. Ibid., VII 4-14.
21. Ibid., VI 33-8, 172-205.
22. Ibid., IX 67-9.
23. *Buddhism as Expounded in Maṇimēkalāi,* p. 157.
24. *Maṇimēkalāi* (Dr. U.V.S. edn) p. 488.
25. Ibid., XXV 213, XI 27-8.
26. Ibid., XI 21-6.
27. Ibid., XI 73-5.
28. Ibid., XI 39-47.
29. Ibid., XI 75-98.
30. Ibid., XXVII 210-16.

31. *Buddhism as Expounded in Maṇimēkalāi,* pp. 65-6.
32. *Maṇimēkalāi,* Patikam 1-2: VI 142.
33. Ibid., XVII 88.
34. Ibid., XXIV 161.
35. Ibid., Patikam 4, II 1-2.
36. Ibid., VI 136-7.
37. Ibid., VI 170.
38. Ibid., XIV 10-11.
39. Ibid., XXV 149.
40. Ibid., XIV 18.
41. Ibid., XIV 9-16.
42. Ibid., XIV 17-21; XXV 139-153.
43. Charles Eliot, *Hinduism and Buddhism,* Vol. II (London, 1921), p. 14.
44. *Maṇimēkalāi* XXVI 35-59, XXVII 125-45.
45. Ibid., XXVI 6.

24

Kurukullā, Tārā and Vajreśī in Śrīpura

R.N. MEHTA

INTRODUCTION

Śrīpura or Śrīnagara is described in the *Lalitopākhyāna*, an appendage to the *Brahmāṇḍa Purāṇa* (published by Motilal Banarasidass in 1973, edited by Acharya Jagadish Shastri). A perusal of the *Brahmaṇḍa Purāṇa* indicates that it is narrated by Vāyu. It is therefore related to the *Vāyu Purāṇa*. The available text of the *Vāyu Purāṇa* had Gayā-Māhātmya as its last chapter and hence like *Lalitopākhyāna*, it also is an addition to the text of the *Vāyu Purāṇa*.

It therefore seems very likely that the *Vāyu* was popular in Magadha, Bihar and in the neighbouring areas of the Maikal and Amarkantaka region. Due to the popularity of the *Vāyu*, it was used in the Gayā area for Gayā Māhātmya and in the Narmada area its core was used as the *Brahmāṇḍa Purāṇa*. Its popularity in the east and south up to Kanchi, led to the addition of, as well as development of, the Paraśurāma legend in the Amarakantaka region and *Lalitopākhyāna* in the Kanchi area.

These aspects of the Purāṇas require further work for their critical editions and analysis of their historico-archaeological contents for cultural and chronological appraisal. Here, the Śrīpura is examined for some of the dynamics of Goddess-worship as noted in the *Lalitopākhyāna* of the *Brahmāṇḍa Purāṇa*.

LALITOPĀKHYĀNA

The *Lalitopākhyāna* occupying Chapters 5 to 44 of the Upasaṃhāra-bhaga of the *Brahmāṇḍa Purāṇa* opens with a prayer to the goddess and the arrival of Agatsya who was on Tīrthayātrā, at Kanchi. There he offers his worship to Kāmākṣī and performs *tapas* that pleases

Viṣṇu, who presents himself in the Hayagrīva form. The dialogue between Agastya and Hayagrīva is the *Lalitopākhyāna.*

Lalitopākhyāna mainly described the exploits of Lalitā, the Śakti of Viṣṇu. In Mohinī Svarūpa Viṣṇu bewitched even Śiva. Lalitā, the Śakti of Viṣṇu, fought with Bhaṇḍāsura and destroyed the power of the Asuras. After the victory there is a description of Śrīpura or Śrīnagara with its divisions. The *Lalitopākhyāna* them deals with Kamākṣī and her worship.

KANCHI

Kanchi is noted in the beginning; it is noted again in Chapter 39 where Lalitā is identified as Kāmākṣī. In Adhyāya 40 again Daśaratha is made to travel from Ayodhya to Kanchi. These references that emphasize Kanchi and its Kāmākṣī Pīṭha indicate that *Lalitopākhyāna* is a Tīrthamāhātmya of Kāmākṣī Pīṭha of Kanchi. It is a famous Tīrtha and its *māhātmya* is natural. These aspects that are included in the *Brahmāṇḍa Purāṇa* would suggest that this addition in the *Brahmāṇḍa Purāṇa* took place at Kanchi, in the Śākta circles of Kamākṣī.

ŚRĪPŪRA

As already noted, the *Lalitopākhyāna* describes Śrīpura. In Adhyāyas 32-6, the details of Śrīpura with its population are given. They are summarized here.

Śrīpura is stationed on one of the four peaks of Meru. The three other peaks represent three worlds and Śrīpura occupies the fourth peak. The entire description notes a fortified town with a series of square forts that concentrate on the Cintāmaṇi Gṛha, abode of the deity Kāmākṣī and Kameśvara.

It is to be noted that the lines of square forts have large *gopuras* at cardinal points. Between the space enclosed within two consecutive fort lines, structures for deities, *vāpis*, etc., exist. A perusal of these lines suggests that the first seven lines were of metal. They were occupied by Mahākāla and different seasons beginning with *vasanta* and associated deities.

The other five lines, of precious stones, are occupied by Mantranātha, the chief deity of Mantra and the Siddhas, Cāraṇas, Gandharvas and devotees of the goddess.

The inner four lines are occupied by the Nāgas, devotees of the goddess and different gods along with the Digpālas. In the innermost line the Tāmrapaṇi flows and palm trees and noted.

The other three lines are occupied by Brahmā, Viṣṇu and Śiva. The place of Śiva is described as a thousand pillared hall. Within these, are three lines with Mano Vāpī, Buddhi Vāpī and Vimarśa Vāpī in them. The crossings of these Vāpīs are possible with the assistance of the chief navigators, Tārā, Vāruṇī and Kurukullā and their associates. These are followed by two lines of Sūryaśālā and Candraśālā. The latter is occupied by Somanātha Nakṣatras and Tārāśaktis. The other is a Śṛṅgāra Śālā with Śṛṅgāra Parikhā.

The last is the Cintāmaṇi-gṛha with Cakrarāya Mahālaya and Mahāpadma Aṭavī, where Mahādevī and Kāmeśvara perform the Yajña. There the Cakraratha, Giriratha and Kīriratha exist. Among them is the *binducakra* of Kamākṣī and Kāmeśvara.

This description is an idealized version of the typical Dravidian temple that develops after the eighth century AD.

TĀRĀ, KURUKULLĀ AND VAJREŚĪ

This description of Śrīpura is an idealised picture of universe including time, deities, and devotees. In this picture the reference to Tārā, Kurukullā and Vajreśī is of specific interest for this small note.

TĀRĀ

Tārā, as the descriptions in the *Lalitopākhyāna* indicates, is noted in two places. One of them is the Manovāpī and the other is the Candraśālā. Tārā is known as the wife of Brhaspati and the mother of Buddha in the Purāṇas. The other Tārās as deities are not important. On the whole the role of Tārā in the Purāṇas is not very important.

In Buddhist iconography, Tārā is an emanation of Amoghasiddhi, the Dhyānī Buddha representing *saṃskāra.* Her ten forms are noted. With Amoghasiddhi on her crown, she carries a rosary, book and other objects; so she is related to learning and hence like Tārā, the wife of Bṛhaspati, the teacher of the gods. Buddhist deity Tārā was popular at Tāraṅgā in north Gujarat where, her form, Dhanada Tārā is worshipped as Padmāvatī. This goddess, associated with learning and *saṃskāras,* becomes the navigator of Manovāpī that would represent the human mind. Significantly, this navigator of Manovāpī is not noted in the *Lalitāsaharasranāma,* an important Śākta text. This omission of Tārā could be explained as perhaps due to her importance in the Buddhist tradition and very minor role in Pauranic tradition. It is therefore highly probable that this important Buddhist deity was included in Śrīpura as the goddess controlling Manovāpī or mind in general, but was not given her due in later Śākta tradition.

Her role in Candraśālā is that of star. There many Tārās noticed in the night.

KURUKULLĀ

From Tārā, one of the powerful Buddhist deities Kurukullā emanates. She was a very popular deity associated with Amitābha as well as all the Dhyānī Buddhas. She was popular in eastern India and China. One of her images is worshipped at Tāraṅgā in north Gujarat. In the *Sādhanamālā,* out of her twenty *sādhanas,* she is noted as Tāraodbhāva or is associated with Tārā. It is a significant that some of her *sādhanas* were the works of Śabarapāda, Karuṇa Kavi, Sahajavimala, Kṛṣṇapāda, Indrabhūti who were active in the eighth-ninth and succeeding centuries. Kṛṣṇapāda was flourishing in the eleventh century and hence Kurukullā was well-known in these centuries. Her absence in the *Devī Māhātmya, Mahābhārata* and other Śākta works and her important postion in Buddhist worship indicates that she is a Buddhist deity adopted as a navigator of Vimarśavāpī in Śrīpura. Thus Tārā is the navigator of Manovāpī and Kurukullā, one of her emanations, is ascribed the role of the navigator of the Vimarśavāpī in Śrīpura. They are responsible for mental activities and thinking.

Kurukullā has a number of forms with two, four, six or eight arms. This deity of *vaśīkaraṇa* has Kāmadeva and Rati below her seat. She has mild and energetic forms. Her complexion is red or white. Her *śukla* or white form has ornaments of serpents of many colours, including blue and smoky ones. Śukla Kurukullā is worshipped for obtaining wisdom, poetic ability, and *vaśīkaraṇa* power. Her worship in Bhramarī-yoga includes *prāṇāyāma* and other yogic practices of *dhāraṇa,* etc. Her association with serpents and her power to remove poison are indicative of the characters suitable for her role in Vimarśa Vāpī in Śrīpura.

Kurukullā was well entrenched in Śākta worship as could be inferred from her references in *śloka* 144 of *Lalitāsaharsranāma.* In the commentary *Saubhāgya Bhāskara,* Vimarśa the Vāpī of Kurukullā is described as *Prakāśātmakasya parabrahmaṇaḥ svābhāviekāṃ sphuraṇaṃ, vimarśa ityucyate. Taduktaṃ saubhāgya sudhodaye svābhāvikīn sphuratā vimarśa rūpasya vidyāte śaktiḥ. Śaiva carācaraṃ akhilaṃ janayati jajadetadapi ca samharta iti. Sa eva rupaṃ śaktirasyāh, vimarśo vācaka sabdo va sa eva rupaṃ nirupakaṃ nirupyam cāsyāḥ. Taduktaṃ mātṛkā viveka vācakena vimarśena vinā kiṃvā prakāśyate. Vācyenāpi prakāśena vina kiṃvā vimarśyate. Tasmād-vimarśo visphuratau prakāśaṃ samapekśate. Prakāśa sacātmano jñāne vimarśam samapekśata iti* (*Saubhāgya Bhāskara*, p. 122).

This importance of *vimarśa* for *atmajñāna* would emphasise the worship of Kurukullā among the Śāktas. The comments of *Saubhāgya Bhāskara* on Kurukullā indicate '*Kurukullā khyā devī Śrīpure ahaṃkāra. Cittamaya prākāryormadhye vimarśa maya vāpyāmadikṛtvā taduktaṃ lalitāstava ratne vāpīṃ prakṛtya. Kuruvindo taraṇi nilayṃ kulācala spardhi kuclanamān madhyāṃ/ Kumkum viliptā gātrāṃ Kurukullāṃ manasi kurmabe śatatam' iti.* This commentary is based on the description of Kurukullā in *Lalitopākhyāna.* Here she is noted as

Athaḥ buddhimahāśalāntare mārutyojane
Ahaṃkāra mahāśālāḥ pūrvavadgopurānvitaḥ/ / 35.34
Tayostu śālayormadhye kakṣayābhurkhite mune/
Vimarśa vāpikā nama sauṣumṇāmṛtarūpiṇī/ /35.35
Tanmahāyoginām antarmano mārutauritam
Suṣumṇā daṇḍavivare jāgarti paramāmṛtam/ /35.36
Tadeva tasyāḥ salilam vāpikāyāstapodhaa/
Pūrvavattaṭa sopānpakṣi naukā hi taḥ smṛtaḥ / /35.37
Tatra Naukeśvari devī Kurukulle ti Viśrtā
Tamāla syāmalākāra syām-kañcuka dhāriṇī/ /35.38
Naukeśvarībhiranyabhissva samānā bhirāvṛtā
Ratnaritrakarā nityamullasanmadamānsalā / /35.39
Parito bhrāmyati mune Maṇinaukadiro rohiṇī/
Vāpīka payasāgdhā pūrvavat parikīrtitā/ /35.40

This description of Kurukullā indicates her identity with the Suṣumnā-nāḍī of Haṭhayoga. The identification is possibly based on Amitābha and Amoghasiddhi that represent *saṃjñā* and *saṃskāra* as well as her association with *yoga* and *vaśīkaraṇa.* Her white or red colour in her Buddhist form is altered to *śyāma.* Her power of *vaśīkaraṇa* or control and use of *yoga* in her worship are retained. Her association with serpents is probably utilized for her identification with Suṣumnā-nāḍī or serpent power. This power would help the devotee to move forward to the understanding of the Sūryaśālā, Candraśālā and even cross the Sṛṅgāraśālā and reach the Cintāmaṇigṛha of devī Kāmākṣī, the ultimate Śākta reality.

VAJREŚĪ

It is interesting to note that the names of three supreme deities are Kāmeśī, Vajreśī and Bhagamālā (37.21). While explaining the term *vajra saubhāgya,* Bhāskara observes: *vajra padasya brahma paratvāt paricchedakatena sambanadhena tadvaitva.* Thus *vajra* is equated with Advaita by the Śāktas.

It is significant that vajra is equated with *Śūnya,* and its deity is Vajradhara in the Buddhist pantheon. This fact suggests that Kāmākṣī, the highest power of the Śāktas, is also Vajreśī, the highest female part of Vajradhara of the Buddhists. It is thus likely that Vajreśī is also an adoption from the Buddhists.

CONCLUSION

The Purāṇas are works that deal with Sarga, Pratisarga, Manvantara, Vaṃśa and Vaṃśānucarita. Within this sphere, the Purāṇas have developed their activities on different lines, during long historical times. One is the periodical revision of an old text. In it sections were added or omitted as per requirement of time and place. This aspect of textual revision has to be properly analysed to understand spatio-temporal dimensions. It appears that the *Vāyu* and *Brahmāṇḍa Purāṇas* were popular in eastern India. A comparative analysis suggests that *Vāyu* was adopted by *Brahmāṇḍa* with its own addition of the *māhātmya* of Amarkaṇṭaka region and Kanchi.

While revising this Purāṇa, sections are added to meet the challanges of the given time by adoption and interpretation. In the present case Buddhist deities that were popular in the centuries following the eighth and possibly continuing upto the twelfth, were included in Śrīpura, at suitable places. The emphasis on the Nāthas, Siddhas, Haṭhayoga and such practices also points to this period and therefore suggests the probable date of *Lalitopākhyāna* as post-twelfth century. Further work to confirm or reject this suggestion is essential.

It is, obvious that not only was preservation of the Pauranic tradition a task of this branch of learning, but its texts went on being revised. So chronologically earlier and later data are found in them. Modern critical methods are essential to understand this aspect, with the help of archaeology.

The other method adopted by the Paurāṇikas is the writing of new Purāṇas as and when necessary. Their method is based on the use of old myths, narratives, etc., in their new compositious. They explain various aspects of the local practices of a place by these old stories. These compositions belong to different periods. For their appraisal Pauranic archaeology is essential.

Archaeological investigations have indicated a long tradition of about three thousand years for Śākta worship. In this long history there are many gaps that would require much inter-disciplinary efforts to understand the universe of Śākta worship in its manifold aspects, that has witnessed both continuity and change not only in our country, but also in other parts of the world.

REFERENCES

Shastri, Acharya Jagadish. *Brahmāṇḍa Purāṇa,* Delhi: Motilal Banarasidass, 1973.

Pansikar, W.L.S. *Lalitā Sahasranāma,* Delhi: Nag Publishers, Jawaharnagar.

Bhattacharya, B. *Indian Buddhist Iconography,* Clacutta: Firma K.L. Mukhopadhyaya, 1958.

Bhattacharya, B. 'Tantrika Culture among the Buddhist', in *Cultural Heritage of India,* IV, 360ff.

Bhattacharya, B. *Sādhanamālā,* Vol. II, G.O. Series, No. XLI, Baroda: Oriental Institute, 1928.

Vāyu Purāṇa, Anandāśrama edition, Poona.

Patil, D.R. *Cultural History from Vāyu Purāṇa,* Pune: Deccan College, 1946.

Mehta, R.N. *et al.* Tāraṅga , Padmāvatī, Siddhāyikā and Tārā, Kalā, *Journal of Indian Art History Congress,* Vol. I, 1995.

Kenoyer, J.M., T.D. Clark, J.N. Pal, and G.R. Sharma, 'An Upper Palaeolithic Shrine in India', *Antiquity,* Vol. LVII (1983), pp. 88-95.

Bagchi, P.C. 'Evolution of the Yantras' in *Cultural Heritage,* IV, 311ff.

Bagchi, P.C. 'The cult of the Buddhist Siddhācāryas', in *Cultural Heritage,* 373ff.

Sen, Sukumar. 'The Nātha Cult', in *Cultural Heritage,* IV, 260ff.

25

The Tantric Dance of *Dharma*: The Mask Dances at the Hemis Festival in Ladakh

MADHU KHANNA

In recent years there has been an attempt to give a wider frame of reference to the study of religion and religious expression in practice. Traditional cultures with ancient roots, both Hindu and Buddhist, have engaged themselves in expressions of religiosity through sacred dance, drama, music and ritual. So rich and diverse are these expressions that they tend to 'transcend the textual exegesis', that supports them. The creative religious expressions while speaking for themselves, are often a mirror image of philosophical notions and invariably construct a definite model of reality. This paper explores the tradition of sacred Mask Dances that take place every year at the Hemis monastery, during the Hemis festival in Ladakh and examines some of their coded meanings.

The mask dances of Ladakh are referred collectively as *Chams* Performance. These dances are an essential part of Tantric Vajrayāna tradition. They constitute an indispensable part of monastic and religious life of the people in Ladakh. The origin of the *Cham* dances goes back to the year AD 811 when the Guru Padmasambhava performed the Black-Hat tantric dance to banish evil spirits who were an obstacle to building the Samaye monastery in South-East of Lahsa. They are usually performed in *gompas* where monks follow the Tantric Vajrayāna teachings. *Chams* are performed with masks, and costumes of various meditative and protective dieties with solemn movements of legs and hands to the special music of drums, cymbals and wind-instruments. While there can be any number of meanings given to dance,[1] it is in the hidden codes of gestures and postures that one may look for a constructive interpretation. The *sādhana*-class of literature belonging to Vajrayāna Buddhism.[2] that flourished in Tibet and northern Himalayas includes performing arts, theatre and

Yogic dances with clear directions on visualization, posturing and attitude of the dancer. However, not all aspects of the performative tradition is committed to writing. A great many secrets of the tradition is orally transmitted, from generation to generation. While this paper records the Mask dances performed today[3], it will attempt to interpret these dances in the light of some significant categories of Vajrayāna Buddhsim. It is in the hidden codes of the gestures and postures of the maskers that one may find a constructive key of interpretation.

I

The Hemis monastery was established in AD 1620 by the then king Senge Namgayal. Hemis monastery lies in the foothills on the southside of the Indus approximately at a distance of 42 km from Leh, and is reached by a motorable road. Crossing the river at a cantilever bridge, the road skirts up towards the village of Chushod. Then it passes over to a green oasis in the middle of rugged mountains and high altitude desert plains, lined with Poplar and Willow trees, mani walls and chalk-white *chortens.* The spur of hills in the vicinity abound with terraced fields against the rugged upright pinnacles where the shimmering light of the sun plays with breathtaking beauty. As one nears the adjoining hills, the Hemis *gompa,* comes in view. Across the stillness of the wide expanse, the Hemis *gompa* stands upright built in Tibetan style, jutting out of the mountain top. Arriving at Hemis, one enters a large rectangular courtyard where the monastic dances take place (Fig. 1).

The Hemis monastery traces its intellectual lineage to the Nyingma or the Ancient tradition of the Vajrayāna school of Tantric Buddhism. The Tibetan Nyingma tradition is divided into several sects: (1) The Kargyu founded by Marpa (1012), (2) The Sakya, founded by Khom Kon Chok Yal Po (1034-1102), and (3) Gelug, founded by Je Tsong Kha pa (1357-1419). The Hemis monastery locates itself in the bKa-rgud-pa, or the Followers of the Transmitted Command. Their authoritative text are the *Mahāyoga* Tantras which expound the teaching of the esoteric inner Tantras as opposed to the exoteric ones. These works have a different flavour from the *sūtra* texts of early Buddhism. Buddhist works after the 11th century are known as the New Tradition. The Vajrayāna expounds a Tradition of Empowerment, wherein the goal of enlightenment is reached in a short period of time. In the inner esoteric Tantras, the *sādhanās*

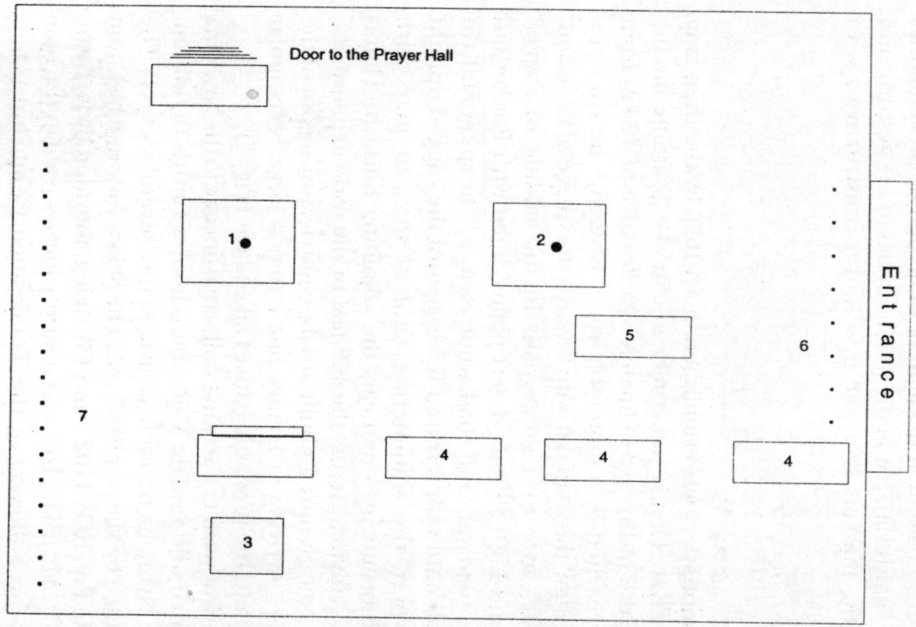

Fig. 1: The layout of the Performance Space. 1 and 2 Central altar with flagstaff. 3. Dais for head Lama. 4. Seats of the musicians and other Lamas. 5. Space for the sponsors. 6. Space where eight aspects of Padmasambhava receive worship. 7. Space where 16 forms of Katicham or Ḍākinīs sit during the worship of Padmasambhava.

expound the experience of oneness through simultaneous awareness of the true nature of Vajra body, speech and mind. The practices at the Hemis monastery are a direct lineal descent of the teachings expound in the *Mahāyoga* Tantra school, or the esoteric school of Vajrayāna. This school has an impressive lineage of teachers[4].

The Hemis festival takes place in the rectangular courtyard in front of the main door of the monastery. The space is wide and open save two raised square platforms, three feet high with a sacred pole in the centre. The platforms mark out the centre of the performance space, in front of the main door to the monastery. According to the Tibetan calendar, the great annual festivals held in the villages of Ladakh all take place in winter, with the exception of Thsechu held at Hemis in summer. This is one of the most important events of the valley, its chief feature being the presentation of a mask dance-drama for two days on stretch. From the time of Rgyalsras Rinpoche around the year 1730, the Hemis Festival has been observed year after year without break and has now become well known the world over.[5]

It is believed that guru Padmasambhava descends as a representative incarnate of all the Buddhas, to bestow grace and improve the conditions of the living. He does so on the tenth day of each month and all the tenth dates which come in a year or the most important of the tenth of Monkey year in a cycle where the *Thangka* of the guru is exhibited. However, each year, the Hemis Festival is observed on the fifth month. The purpose of sacred performance and the dances is to bestow good health, subjugate disease and conquer evil spirits. The festival commemorates the birthday of Guru Padmasambhava, the celebrated founder of the Lama tradition and the presiding authority of Tibetan Buddhism. According to the records in Sikkim, Padmasambhava came northward and convinced the Lamas of Tibet that he was sent to Tibet as an incarnation of Buddha. The festival both eulogises the great deeds of Padmasambhava and also reiterates the victory over evil for the protection of Buddha-*dharma*.

II

THE PERFORMANCE

Before the commencement the festival, the monk storekeeper decorate the *gompa* with *Thangka* paintings, flags, banners, etc. Out side in the courtyard, another group of monks prepare the dais where the head lama will be seated. The dais marks a sacred precinct where the head lama, musicians and the other lamas of the monastery will be seated. The most exacting ritual is the preparation of the seat of the head lama with a small finely carved table with ceremonial ritual ingredients.

While the welcome music is being played, the *Thangka*, nearly twenty feet in length made of pathwork textiles, with a portrait of Gyalsas Rinpoche, the initiator and founder of the Hemis monastery is unrolled, and hung against the facade of the monastery. All this takes place to the resounding music of trumpets, drums, cymbals, etc. Around 9.40 A.M. two adolescent monks blow conch-shells from the roof top of the *gompa.* The sound of the conch, blown from the roof of the Hemis monastery represents the voice of *dharma.* This is the first call for the monks and the visitors to get ready. The *Thunkur* is blown again twice. The second call is to march towards the *gompa* and the third, to gather in the assembly hall for morning prayers before starting the dance. While the lamas scurry around, a number of monks play welcome music in the courtyard. Tibetan ritual music played during *Chams* performance contains a variety of protean forms. Tibetans believe that religious music has its origin in the teachings of the Ḍākinis. Legend also holds that a lama named Takpo Dorjechang (1543-88), was transmitted that most complex and beautiful music the yang (*olbyangs*) through Ḍākinis. Within the ritual context, the main function of music as described by Chogyam Trungpa Rinpochey, is to act 'as an accompaniment to the general psychological process of the rite'.[6] Music is looked upon as a sacred offering to the deities. Aurally beautiful, it inhances the dance-drama by sustaining and lending the whole performance an orderly rhythmic element. The music that is played in monasteries is often catagorized in terms of the deity to whom the offerings are made. The musical offering are often suited to express the nature of the deity.

The music at Hemis consisted of chanting and recitation of texts and instrumental music played by monk musicians. The entire orchestra at Hemis consisted of many instruments (some in pairs:) (1) a *Damaru* or drum (2) two conches (*Thunkur*) (3), Panshaped drum (*Na*) (4) two long trumpets (*Dughchen*), (5) two pairs of large cymbals (*Bukjal*), (6) two reed instruments (*Rgya Gling*), (7) one hand bell (*Tilbu*), (8) two small cymbals (*Silmyan*). The long trumpets create sound that are said to create sound from the 'Womb of the earth and depth of Space'. It is believed that the sound of each instrument captivates and relates to a state of mind and consciousness. The reed instruments, the large trumpets and large cymbals relate to the peaceful deities, the short trumpets and the more 'shriller' cymbals correspond to the fearful deities. And the drums may be played for either deities. Deities are summoned and bid farewell with the sound of trumpets. The most compelling moment of the ritual music is when the dancer-deities are invited in the courtyard to perform. The resounding sound of cymbals, drums and the trumpets echo across the landscapes and lend an altered dimension to the whole performance.

A procession of monks walked in from the prayer hall into the courtyard led by two monks playing reed instruments (*rgya Gling*), two holding incense pots, and a lama holding a staff adorned with flags and banners. Suddenly the stillness in the monastery gets recharged by the resonances of the welcoming music. Then the lamas who were playing the instruments, walk near the dais and take their seats according to their status. After these preliminary preparations, the show gains momentum, and our attention shifted to the door of the prayer hall, wherefrom two Hatuks, masked figures with yellow cap, yellow silk robes holding a small stick covered with colourful ribbons on top, appear and came down the steps of the prayer hall. Their masks were benign and human. They mixed freely with the devotees and onlookers and played the role of a police-jester throughout the ceremony. Their task was to put the audience to order, bless them with their sacred stick and urge them to pay a small sum of money. They pounced on people, joked, laughed and held the crowds with their policing operations.

BINDING THE QUARTERS

While the fanfare is in full swing, the thirteen Black-Hat tantric dancers with large hats with wide round rims entered the scene. A stick about one-foot-high rose from the crown of the hat with an image of a skull. From the back of these hats coloured ribbons streamed down. Their robes were heavy and made of rich Chinese silk and brocade embroidery. They wore rich capes and aprons and a necklace with a skull emblem. The skulls are a potent symbol to remind the viewers of the impermanence and brevity of life. Stretching their right and left arms alternatively, advancing and retreating from the centre of the circle, they slowly danced their way round the courtyard, clock wise. The dance was slow, their posturing stately and was accompanied by the drone-like low pitch chanting and occasional beat of loud crashes made by the cymbals. Each dancer was given a few sprigs of dried sacred herb by a lama, and then they slowly made their way to the exit. The purpose of the tantric dance was to dispel evil forces and mark out the exterior limits of the performance space and 'bind' the quarters by their sacred movements. The number thirteen is identified with the thirteen *yugas* of the cosmos and thirteen rings of the *chorten*. The thirteen dancers were led by a lama holding decorated staff, two pipe players and two incense pot holders. At the close of their dance, a lama ran round the courtyard with a bowl of burning embers for purification of space and to sustain the 'aura of light' created by the tantric dancers.

DANCE HONOURING PADMASAMBHAVA

Sixteen males dressed as compassionate Ḍākinīs with metal masks enter the arena of the performance. Each of these dakinis held a *damaru* and a bell in their hands. They danced in slow steps around the sacred pole to the chant of cymbals and drums chanting in a low melodious voice the mantra of Padmasambhavā: *Om Vajra Guru Padma Siddhi Hum.* They chanted the mantra four times and they offer their benediction. Their task was to purify the scared space, the objects of worship and the lineage of teachers.

Then began the most spectacular aspect of the whole performance: the dance honouring the eight aspects of Padmasambhava. Now, the great guru Padmasambhava, in whose honour the festival is performed made a dramatic entry with his entourage. It was a royal entry. The guru Padmasambhava wore a golden mask with benign countenance, and a serene Buddha-like face found so often in the sculpture of SE Asia. The guru was led by a procession of musicians, some masked and otherwise, to the resounding sounds of music : two lamas held incense pots (*phoks*), two blew wind-pipes, two played long trumpets, and wear masks. They entered the arena in rows. Then followed guru Padmasambhava accompanied by a disciple who carried a parasol for the guru. Padmasambhava was accompanied by his seven personifications. It is interesting to observe that the bodily size of Padmasambhava was nearly one and a half times more than his other incarnations. Their details are given in Table 1.

TABLE 1: EIGHT ASPECTS OF GURU PADMASAMBHAVA

Name	*Colour of Mask*	*Attributes in hand*	*Aspect*
1. Padmavajra	Gold	Bell and Skull	Preached teachings to Dakinis
2. Padmasambhava	Blue	Vajra and Bell	Moved the wheel of *Dharma* Subjugated evil
3. Lolden Mchhog	Flesh-coloured	Damru and Incense	A great teacher
4. Padma Rgyalpo	Flesh-coloured	Damru and Incense	A great teacher
5. Niyama Odzer	Yellow	Sun symbol and trident	Showed Miracles
6. Shakiya Senge	Yellow	Bowl and meditational Mudra	Received teachings of *Mahāyoga* Tanta
7. Senge Dadogs	Blue-black	Vajra and Scorpain Mudra	Destruction of Heretics and their conversion
8. Dorje Tolod	Reddish Brown	Vajra and Iron	Subjugated all the evil spirits of Nepal, Tibet, and Bhutan and revealed the truth for the people.

DANCE OF THE *DHARMA*-GURDING DEITIES

After the guru Padmasambhava is propitiated, the performance focuses on another significant theme: the protection of *Buddha-dharma* and banishment of evil, so that *dharma* retains its unshakable strength at the face of destructive forces and obstacles that lie on its path. Hence the afternoon session began by, The Dance of the Protectors of *Dharma.* Twelve Dharmapālas who are especially assigned the task to protect the teachings of Buddha emerged wearing their colourful masks, and holding their respective weapons, as given in Table 2.

TABLE 2. DHARMA GUARDING DEITIES

	Name	*Colour of Masks*	*Attributes in Hand*
1.	Yab (Male)	Red	Spear and heart
2.	Yum (Female)	Black-brown	Tishud and heart
3.	Vajrasatva	Black	Flag and hammer
4.	Yama	Brown	Noose and chain
5.	Naga Demon	Black	Snake rope
6.	Demon	Black	Sword and rope
7.	Titan	Red	Rope
8.	Srinpo Giant	Blue-black	Stick and iron hook
9.	Brahma	White	Knife and arrow
10.	Mātrī-Kālī	Brown	Sword and bag of diseases
11-12.	Monkeys		

They danced in ecstasy to protect the teachings of Buddha. Then four monks enterd the courtyard and made liquid offerings of tea and rice grains. They are followed by four dancers wearing white masks representing graveyard ghouls with sunken cheeks, gaping mouths and protruding fanged teeth. They are the masters of the graveyard. Their task is to locate evil and carry those evil and demonic entities to higher deities who have the power to destroy them. Their bodies were covered with white cloth on which skulls and ribs are depicted by red streaks. They danced in ecstasy to protect the teachings of Buddha.

The four dances with orgre-type masked faces with a third eye on their foreheads entered the courtyard. They mouths were open with a protruding tongue curled upwards. Each of them held a weapon with which the demonic and evil forces can be combatted. The yellow masked figure held a strong rope; the red masked figure, an iron chain; the green masked figure, a bell and the white masked figure, a hooked knife. They danced for nearly ten minutes. Then symbolically conveyed the object of heir weapons. The evil spirits who pose a threat to *dharma*were caught by the 'hook', tied with the 'rope' rolled with the 'iron chain' and paralysed by the resounding sound of the bell which does not allow it to move any where. Another procession of dancers come down the steps. They are the four Herukas or the wrathful form of Buddhas. They danced to put an end to evil. Then came five more dancer-deities with grotesque masks, in red, white, yellow, green and brown. There was one among them who led, and wore a big devil mask, with curled tongue and tusks. Monks entered and held out a plate with offering which were sprinkled, the remainder was placed by the uncovered effigy made of dough. The monks left the scene. Then the leader with a demon mask, approached the effigy embodying *adhrama* and cut it into two. This signified the ultimate death of the evil spirit. After this they danced their way out. The monks removed the remenants of the figure.

In the final episode of the performance, five heros, (*saking*) who belong to the earth and five from the heavens, (*namking*) with masks appear amind the drum beats, demonstrating their triumph at the destruction of the enemy. The common people of Ladakh refer to them as the heros of the sky and earth. The colours of their masks were yellow, brown, red, green and blue. They performed a dance indicating that they have the power to drive away evil forces, whether they inhabit the sky, atmosphere or the earth. In the final act,the *Thangka* of the guru is rolled up to the resonance of music.

III

On the second day the first act of devotion consisted of preparation of the high altar and the seat for the incarnate lama. The altar was recreated as in the previous day. Seven cups with water, grains and butter *tormas* are kept in position. The ceremony began by unrolling of the *Thangka* of silk parch-work of the great Lama Rgyalsras Mipham Tsewang Rinpoche, the great teacher and guru who established this monastery.

As in the previous day, dancers wearing Black-Hats with long flowing robes enterd the performance arena. They were led by lamas playing instruments and two, Hatuks, who play the role of police-jesters. They mixed with the crowd and called for their concentrated attention. The Hatuks amused people with their gestures, miming acts, blessed them and then asked for money. The Black-Hat dancers, as before danced around the central post and set the sacred limits of the performing space. They carried dried barley sprigs. As they went go out they threw away the sprig all around. Then a young lama walked in and put a flat incense pan and fumigated the place of performance. After the dance, the stage was cleared.

THE WORSHIP OF RGYALPO PEHER

Then the monks assembled in the prayer hall to 'recreate' the altar of Rgyalpo Pehar, the protectress of Hemis monastery. The Rgyalpo's body was decorated with textiles, silk cloth, flags, streamers, ornaments, various weapons and a black mask. *Thangkas* of Avaloketshvar, goddess Tārā, the sages and Padmasambhava were hung around the alter. A long wooden altar with fine carving was placed infront of the shrine. Various offerings were placed in a row: cups full of water, uncooked rice, grain, eatables, tea-leaves, fruits, flowers, and butter-lamp, incense, chopa, torma etc. A skull-cup containing chang, drink made with formented barley, is placed in the centre with cups full of water. On the right side a raised altar was placed where the young incarnate lama witnessed the ceremony.

I was told that Rgyalpo Pehar is the Tibetan form of goddess Kālī, the protector deity of the monastery. This worship is performed solely for protection of the monastery, the people, the land, the animals and the ecology of the area. After the worship, a black caparisoned horse with embroidered silk and a black dog belonging to the monastery were brought in the courtyard and received worship. With this the morning sessions ended.

THE DANCE OF THE *DHARMA*-GUARDING DEITIES

The afternoon session began with the dance of Maha Dongchen, with a buffalo faced mask, and his entourage of the following masked figures: four Black-Hat Tantric dancers; four dancers with metal masks; four Pumets with masks with gaping mouths; four dancers with monks, robes with benign masked faces with staff and bowl in hand; four Piksy-faced dancers, unmasked with painted faces; four Figures wearing grotesque and ferocious brown, white red and green masks. They together formed the helpers and gate-guards of Dongchen. Their task is to put end to evil forces. They come in and danced together encircling the flag-staff. While the dancers performed their dance, two monks inscribed a triangle-*mandala* in blue with white and red outline. Another lama walked in with a plate with a sacrificial effigy made of dough concealed with a veil. The dish was placed in the centre of the *mandala* on which a mantra is also inscribed. Two lamas entered, one with a plate with ritual chalices and the other with the *samovar.* They stood by the *mandala.* The

Black-Hat dancers entered alongwith them and stood around the *mandala.*

Then began the most elaborate ritual dance of the day. The demonic Buffalo Masked figure emerged from the hall. He dances with his troupe with symbols of death and destruction. He was accompanied by eight dancers: two with white, two with yellow, two with green, two with red masks. The ten maskers with faces of blue, green, red, skin-colour and yellow were grotesque and leering. The gruesome group in succession danced around the *mandala.* Then four figures appeared carrying a bell and a *dorje* accompanied by two lamas, one carried a *samovar* the other, four holy cups in a tray. These two lamas made offerings of chang and grains of barley, to the four with demon-deity masks, who stood in front of the *mandala.* While the music played these four, emptied the cups on the ground and themselves chanted *mantras,* ringing their bells and swinging their *dorjes.* The ceremony of filling and emptying the cups was performed four times. The procession of demon-deity headed by horned masked deity, approached the sacrificial effigy of *adharma* and purified it with holy water from the plate left at the side. He then cut through the effigy. The effigy, representing evil forces lay mutilated. Four figures with graveyard ghoul masks come in to dispose the corpse. The four danced about and two of them standing on the *mandala* on which the plate was placed, rhythymically wiped away, all traces of the mystic triangle. The skeletal masked figures danceed about, becoming more joyfull of their victory over evil.

The final episode of the dance-drama displayed the interplay between the teacher and his disciples. Once the the effigy of *adharma* is slain by the demon-deity with a horned mask, all acts of reverence came to an end. The last item reminded the audience about the message of *dharma* which is passed through teacher-pupil lineage. An old figure with a mask of a laughing Buddha representing the teacher came trotting alongwith young boys with bare legs, short skirts, capes and smiling masked faces. They played, jumped about, laughed, boxed each other, and interacted with the public and made fun of each other, caricaturing acts of descipleship and worship. This was the last item of the performance and added greatly to the amusement of the audience.

The sun's rays slowly began to fade into the oblivion of the horizen. Four lamas rolled up the *Thangka* hung in the morning. While the resonances of the ritual music faded, the twilight engulfed the atmosphere and the performance space looked empty, bare and desolate.

INTERPRETATION

Creative forms of expression that emanate from gestures and posturing of the body are broadly called dance. However, the monastic dances are something else. The *Chams* performed at the Hemis festival, embody a host of implicit meanings. Firstly, there is no concept of a dancer as a person, the dancer is a empowered deity in the body of the human. The masks serve to energise and generate the character and personality of the deity chosen for the occasion. It is believed that the deity in some sense is present in the body of the dancer, while the performance is on. Seen from this perspective, the monk dancer is a dancer-deity, whose human character undergoes a significant transformation through the masking process. The use of masks while it veils the immediate and mundane reality, simultaneously reveals another dimension of the divine mythical beings and supersensable forces. The mask retains its significance as an image of transformation, whereby the dancer assumes the nature, posture and the very character of the deity. As Vajrayāna abounds in an extraordinary number of gods and goddesses, the masks vary in character in accordance to the episodal attributes of the performance. They can be broadly grouped into two types of characters: from the very benign to the malefic deities in the extreme. The dancer and the deity-power is throughout manifest in the performance. The shifting of the boundaries between the sacred and the mundane and the transformation of the players from ascetic monkhood to the plane of the deity, reflects certain meaningful categories of Vajrayāna Buddhism

The performance is characterized by nine dance movements, postures and gestures and each of these has to be performed by every dancer-deity. They are as follows:[9]

1. *Gesture of Power,* which enables the dancer-deity to raise from the Hinyana to the *Mahāyāna.*
2. *Gesture of Boldness,* which signifies that the deity can transform its physical, corporeal form to a particular end.
3. *Look of Terror,* which enables the dancer to symbolically destroy evil and anti-life forces.

4. *Mahāyāna Gaze,* which represents the glory and majesty of the deity.
5. *Look of Horizon,* represents attachments.
6. *Gesture of Readiness,* enables the dancer-deity to help humankind from the morass of the cycle of birth and death.
7. *Look of Compassion,* enables the dancer-deity to help all sentient beings.
8. *Look of Peace,* for bestowing calm and abiding nature.
9. *The Big Wonderful Gesture,* which enables the dancer-deity to attain the highest state of Śūnyatā during the performance.

The colour of masks also embody special attributes. Peaceful deities wear white masks; for merits, yellow masks are worn. The masks for the wrathful deities is represented by black; and for power, by red. It is difficult to state which is the most significant element of the mask dances at the Hemis festival, whether it is the beauty of the masks, the slow stirring chants of the *mantra* recitations, the lyrical and slow movement of the body, the representational or the interpretative motifs that underlies the performance. While all these elements converge into an integral whole to produce an intoxicating spell over the audience, one can discern multiple layers of meaning which are central to Buddhism in practice. The first is the Mahāyāna ideal of Bodhisattva represented by the life of Padmasambhava and his eight aspects. The second layer is illustrated by the role played by some overtly fierce, some more implicitly fierce deities in an encounter between adharmic or evil powers and the *dharma* guarding deities. The third layer is expressed through what constitutes meaning for the viewers. I shall take each one of them to illustrate the unchartered deep structures of the performance.

Padmasambhava represents but one great sage in the succession of enlightened beings in Buddhism upon whose life and spiritual experience the ideal of *Buddha-dharma,* depended and nurtured, and who, held the beacon of light to illumine the darkness of ignorance from Tibet down to the northern Himalayas. To the people of Ladakh he represents a second Buddha, an enlightened Bodhisattva who took the vow of seeking perfect awakening for the salvation of humankind. His whole life was engaged in assisting numberless beings on their way to enlightenment. During the performance, Padmasambhava is presented as the pure and perfected human form of Buddha—a divine personification and a cultural hero who is in some respects even greater than Buddha. As Padmasambhava personifies the totality of the secret doctrines of *Mahāyāna*, the performance knits together philosophical notions of value to the *Mahāyāna* devotees. In one sequence (ante) the *Trī-kāyas* or the Three Divine Bodies through which the Buddha-essence manifests itself, are praised over and over again. These are the Bodies of Truth (*Dharma-kāya*), The Divine Body of Perfect Endowment (*Sambhoga-kāya*), the Divine Body of Incarnation (*Nirmāṇā-kāya*), divinely pure human embodiment. These three together represent the united body of Bodhi-essence which sustains all existence and makes liberation possible. From the *Trī-kāyas* arises all and into it everything returns. In the *Trī-kāyas* exist 'all the Buddhas of all aeons'. To the devotees on the Mahāyānic path, the *Trī-kāyas* is their final refuge and goal. It is these very three bodies of Padmasambhava that receive reverence so that the devotees can be at-one-ment with the esoteric significance of the *Trī-kāyas*, essential for their deliverence. In this item of the mask dances one can discern how the dance-drama adopts the transmission of doctorines though a medium entirely their own.

It is also believed that Padmasambhava lives in his bodiless form and returns each year to Ladakh to liberate the people. He is a fully enlightened Bodhisattva who has mastered the ten stages of the *Dharma-meghabhūmi*, that correspond to the ten *pāramitās* or perfections; (1) generality, (2) morality, (3) patience, (4) vigour, (5) meditation (6) wisdom, (7) skilfulness in liberating means, (8) the aspiration for enlightenment and welfare of all beings, (9) strength and (10) knowledge. He had attained a level of awareness so perfect, that he is free from liberation. He can now choose freely, if and when and where he is to take birth. His indisputable and unquestionable authority is praised throughout the performance. The dances aim to bring out the need for continuous renewel and reaffirmation of the Bodhisattva ideal represented by the exemplary life of Padmasambhava.

Violence and disorder belongs to 'other' albeit outsiders. While the monks are forbidden to display anger to outsiders their masked dances are saturated with items that contain images of violence for the restoration of disorder, disharmony and falsehood. Thus several smaller episodal events in the dance such as the destruction of the sacrificial body of *adharma*, by the Faith guarding deities, invocation to Gyalpo Peher, the protector deity of the monastery and the role played by fierce masked dancers who invariably come and go in groups play a significant role in the performance. There are any number of wrathful deities. These personas play the role of guardian figures. These deities are a common feature of Tantric iconography. They carry weapons of destruction and with their dare-devil fierce appearance keep the forces of evil at bay. The encounter between *dharma* guarding deities and forces of *adharma* becomes apparent on both days of the performance (see Table 1). The effigy of sacrificial body of *adharma* is slain ceremoniously for the welfare and cohesiveness of society. The victory of *sad-dharma* over *adharma* is a *sine que non* of the performance, as compliance to *dharma* alone can wipe out the turbidities of beings.

The mask dance of the wrathful deities may serve other ends. The dance *macabre* of non human beings such as the masters of graveyard *(Turdag)* spontaneously produce mental images of impermanence and transience of life. The grotesque leering faces with sunken cheeks, fanged mouths, curled tongues express 'death's universal domain'. It is the experience of death that persuaded Buddha to abandon the fleeting life of senses. When I questioned Lama Tashi Rabgias on the meaning of the horrific masks, he said: 'At death they will reappear again. The person will not be afraid of them. Having seen these dances year after year, one begins to understand the fleeting nature of life and the real meaning of death'. The wrathful masks have the effect of arousing definate psychic states, whereby the hidden subconscious fear of impermanence and transience of life are brought to rest.

From the point of view of the audience, viewing the dances represents an aspiration for *dharma*, it is an act of self-purification and constitutes a positive act of repaying *kārmic* obligation and a means of self-transformation through accumulation of merit. While the esoteric content of *Mahāyāna* practice is known to the initiated monks, the monastic religion served the laity with effective religious means. For the lay Buddhist, popular religious means, like offering donations to monasteries, pious actions such as lighting lamps, spinning prayer-wheels, learning about the *kārmic* wheel of life through the image of the Wheel of Life, painted on the walls of the monastery, or simply watching the masked dance-dramas and ceremonies are a means for accumulating good karma. Outside the scope of ritual, the monastic masked dance can be seen to reflect a certain social process. Monastic Buddhism practiced at Hemis is not entirely divorced from the exoteric popular religion of the laity. While the tradition of esoteric meditation is the exclusive concern of the lamas, monastic festivals and masked dances and other sub-systems of religiosity bring together the monks and the laity. In the Hemis festival, for example, the lamas and the lay people meet for a common aim of accumulating merit and resisting evil. The festival is a transmitter of this basic truth on which the foundation of Buddhism is based. In all these respects, the performance through a series of mask-dances builds a model of reality conducive to the propagation of the Buddhist ideals and value-systems that sustain their religion. It is not out of place to describe the performance as a dance of *Dharma*, that reveals the essence of Buddhism in practice.

NOTES

1. On different interpretations on dance in anthropology see; Spencer, Paul. Ed. *Society and the Dance.* Cambridge, 1985, pp. 1-46.
2. See for instance, W.Y. Evans-Wentz, The Yogic Dance which Destroyeth Erroneous Belief, in *Tibetan Yoga And Secret Doctorines.* Oxford, 1958, pp. 301-34.
3. I am indebted to the Indira Gandhi National Center for the Arts, New Delhi for facilitating my research tour to Ladakh in June 1996 to record the Hemis Festival performed at the Hemis monastery in Ladakh. I record my gratitude to Lama Tsewang Rigzin, and Lama Tashi Rabgias for clarifying several details about the festival.
4. The lineage of teachers at the Hemis monastry: Vajradhara Buddha in Tantric Form, Tilopa, Naropa, Marpa, Milaraspa, Sgampopa, Thaltashapa, Lingrapa, Sages (names unknown), Rgod Eshangpa Mgonpo Rdor Rja (1191-1274), Stagshang Raspa (1590-1620), Founder of Hemis monastery, Rgyalsars Rinpoche (1730), Founder of the Hemis Festival. Vide Rigzin, Tsewang. *Hemis Fair,* Delhi, 1992, p. 38.
5. Op. cit. Rigzin, p. 39-40.
6. Quoted from, Newbery, Beatrice. Ocean of Sound, in *CHO YANG*: (*The Voice of Tibetan Religion and Culture* No. 5), Dharamshala, 1992, p. 24.
7. An outline exposition of the Hemis festival is dealt in several works. See Waddell L. Austine, *Tibetan Buddhism,* New York, 1992, rpt., pp. 516ff; Evans-Wentz, op. cit., pp. 289ff; Rigzin, Tsewang, op. cit.
8. For a complete account of Padmasambhava's life, See Book I, 'An Epitome of The Life and Teachings of Tibet's Great Guru Padmasambhava (According to the Biography by Yeshey Tshogyal)', in *The Tibetan Book of The Great Liberation,* Oxford, 1958, pp. 104-92, op. cit.
9. Personal communication from Henry Osmaston, vide forthcoming publication: Namgyal, Konchak *Recent Research in Ladakh* 6, (in press).

Plate 1: The *Thangka* adorning the facade of the Hemis monastry.

Plate 2: Masked figure of Guru Padmasambhava.

Plate 3: Masked performers dancing around the central post.
Hemis monastry.

26

Arapacana: A Mystic Buddhist Script

B. N. MUKHERJEE

A widely prevalent practice, followed until recently (and in certain areas still continuing) in parts of the Indian subcontinent is to teach a letter of an alphabet by citing along with it a sentence in the first letter of the first word of the character. Thus while teaching or learning the form and pronounciation of the letter *a* of the Bengali script the teacher and pupils recite, 'in the case of *a* an *ajagara* (a kind of snake) is approaching aggressively' or 'in the case of *ā*, I shall eat the *āma* (mango) after plucking it out of the tree'. The idea is to allow the student to draw the form of the letter to learn its pronounciation and also to know its use. This practice is bound to create more enthusiasm among infant students than just pronouncing the name of a letter and writing its form in tedious repetition

A similar method of teaching letters of the alphabet was probably followed in ancient India. However, sometimes it was used with an additional purpose. For getting a hymn or an important religious precept learnt by heart by new initiates or lay worshippers, each letter was used at the beginning of the first word of the text to be memorized. The *parivarta* or chapter on the *Lipisalasaṃdarśana* in the *Lalitavistara*, a Buddhist text of the first-second centuries AD, given an account of Siddhārtha's instructions to young novices of the Buddhist order on the *mātṛikā* (the alphabet, really Brāhmī). It is stated here that when the letter *a* was pronounced the correct expression of *anitya saṁsāra* ('transitory world') came forth; when the letter *ā* was pronounced the correct expression of *ātmaparahita* ('wholesome for oneself and others') came forth; when *i* was pronounced the correct expression of *indriyavikalya* ('dubiousness of senses') came forth when *ī* was pronounced, the correct expression of '*ītibahulaṁ jagat*', ('world abounding in distress') came forth;

when *u* was pronounced the correct expression of *upadrava-bahulaṁ jagat* ('world abounding in mischief') came forth; when *ū* was pronounced the correct expression of *ūnasattva* ('non-existence of anything') came forth. In this fashion each letter of the Brāhmī script was given an explanation conducive to Buddhism and its philosophy.[1] Through this method one could be taught the alphabet, pronunciation and the use of each character, as also religious tenets.

The Buddhists became gradually very efficient in using the alphabet for preaching the religion. For this they devised a sort of new syllabary. Several conjuncts were included in it. Generally the letter or conjuct occurring at the beginning of the head-word of the selected hymn of mystic value or philosophical tenet was one of the chosen characters of the syllabary. However, sometimes the second or third character of the head-word was used for the purpose. Thus in the *Pañcaviṁśati-sāhasrikā-Prajñāpāramitā* of about the third century the letter *ṇa* is followed by a precept having the first word as *raṇavigatatvāt.* Again, the conjuct *jña* appears in the same position before the head-word *sarva-jñānānu-labdhitvāt.*[2] Here the chosen letter is the second character of the first word and the selected conjuct is in the third position of the concerned head-word. The exact reason for these deviations from the norm is not known. However, we may guess that in order to avoid recurrence of the same letter or conjuct (if it was found to have occurred more than once as the first character of the head-words of the selected precepts) the second or third character was employed.

It may be claimed that after finalizing the hymns or precepts the first (or in certain cases another) character of the each head-word was enlisted to form an alphabet or rather a syllabary (consisting of mono-syllabic letters and conjuncts).

The list of characters and precepts appearing in the Chinese translation of the chapter called *Lipisalasaṁdarśana* of the *Lalitavistara,* by Dharmarakṣa in 308, is different from the above noted list in the same treatise written in hybrid Sanskrit.

In the Chinese translation the selected hymns and precepts (and aphorisms) are stated, but no separate list of the first or chosen character of their head-words is furnished.[3] J. Brough was of the opinion that perhaps the list of the syllabary had been devised after finalizing the texts and the order of appearance of the hymns, aphorisms and precepts.[4] We may guess that there had been no such list in the hybrid Sanskrit manuscripts of the *Lalitavistara* utilized by Dharmarakṣa for translating the work.

It appears that the Buddhists utilized an age old method of teaching an Indian alphabet (perhaps Brāhmī), causing the letter to be written and memorized along with a sentence having its first word or head-word beginning with that letter. The initial characters of the head-words of the hymns and precepts were arranged according to the normal order of the letters in the alphabet (Brāhmī). In this way religious tenets were taught to students (or novices in the Buddhist order) while ostensibly giving instruction on the forms and names of the letters. The chosen aphorisms, precepts and hymns could be remembered and recited conveniently following the order of the letters in the alphabet. Later, perhaps by about the second century, the list of aphrorisms, precepts and hymns was recast to make it more convenient for preaching the religion. It was then noticed that the initial characters of the head-words of the precepts, etc., in the list did not follow the order of letters in the alphabet (Brāhmī). The initial letters of the head-words of the first five precepts were found out to be *a, ra, pa, ca* and *na.* So the list, consisting of letters and conjuncts, came to be known as the Arapacana script.

Initially the recast list might not have had the characters in identical order everywere. But many of the letters or conjuncts appearing early in the list appear to have been common to all lists. It should also be noted that though the total number of the letters and conjuncts is generally taken as forty-two in the noticed lists, in other cases, the number is forty-one, or forty-three or forty-four.[5]

In this connection we can refer to the *Pañcaviṁśati-sāhasrikā-prajñāpāramitā.* Here the help of the Arapacana list has been utilised to teach the *dhāraṇī* or 'protective hymns' (having secretive power).[6] Such a use of hymns believed to have magical power can be found in the Vedic literature, especially in the *Atharava-veda.*[7] Many apparently unintelligible words or syllables were used in the Vedic rituals.[8] The continuity of this trend is noticeable in the Buddhist *dhāraṇīs.*[9]

In any case, the number of characters in the Arapacana list as given in the *Pañcaviṁśati-sāhasrikā-prajñāpāramitā* is forty-one. There are (1) *a;* (2) *repha;* (3) *pa;* (4) *ca;* (5) *na;* (6) *la;* (7) *da;* (8) *ba* (9) *ḍa;* (10) *sa;* (11) *va;* (12) *ta;* (13) *ya;* (14) *sta;* (15) *ka;* (16) *sa;* (17) *ma;* (18) *ga;* (19) *stha;* (20) *ja;* (21) *śva;* (22) *dha;* (23) *śa;* (24) *kha;* (25) *kṣa;* (26) *ta;* (27) *jña;* (28) *ha;* (29) *Cacha* (or *ścha?*); (30) *sma;* (31) *ddha;* (32) *sa;* (33) *dha;* (34) *ṭa;* (35) *ṇa;* (36) *pha;* (37) *ska;* (38) *ja;* (39) *ca;* (40) *ṭa;* and (41) *ḍha.*[10] In this list *ra* is obviously replaced by *repha* (which is a burring guttural sound of *ra*), since the first letter of the concerned head-word is *ra*.[11]

Certain examples may be cited illustrating the use of the letter and conjuncts for explaining religious precepts and rites.[12] (1) *Akāro mukhaḥ sarvadharānām-ādyanutpannatvāt* [The letter *a* is the principal of all religions because these are unproduced (*anutpanna*) in the beginning]; (2) *Repho mukhaḥ sarvadharmānāṁ rajo'pagatatvāt* (*Repha* or *ra* is the head of the all religions, because they are freed of darkening quality). (3) *Pakāro mukhaḥ sarvadharmānāṁ paramārtha-nirdeśāt* (The letter *pa* is the chief of all religions because of the expounding of the ultimate truth); (4) *Cakāro mukhaḥ sarva-dharmānāṁ cyavanopapattyanupalabdhitvāt* (the letter *Ca* is the head of all religions because of the non-perception of decease and rebirth); (5) *Nakāro mukhaḥ sarvadharmānāṁ nāmopagatatvāt* [the letter *na* is the chief of all religions because they are freed of name (or nameless)], etc.

In this syllabary the letters *ja* (nos. 20 and 38), *ta* (nos. 12 and 26) and *sa* (nos. 16 and 32) occur twice. Perhaps the intended pronunciation of the second *ja* or *ta* or *sa* was not the same as that of the first *ja* or *ta* or *sa*, respectively. For example, in north-western Prakrit the letter *ja* was often pronounced, under Iranian influence, as a voiced sibilant (like *z* of the Roman script as used for writing English). The dental *sa* was sometimes pronouncd like *z* or *jha*.[13]

Another example of the process of formulation of the syllabary can be noticed in a Kharoshti inscription, engraved on a rectangular slab of stone, on the other side of which appears a panel of sculpture Gandhāra style displaying Siddhārtha looking at his bride[14] (Fig. 1). This panel, found in the ruins of a stūpa at Takht-i-Bahi was obviously created for decorating it. So the inscriptions on the other side of the slab was not meant to seen by the public.[15] When we first published the inscription its import was not clear.[16] Recentaly Richard Salomon has guessed that a meaning may be found if the inscription is read downwards from the top and not from right to left (as is usually done in reading a Kharoshtī inscription).[17] If the inscription is deciphered in that manner, it can be divided into four columns (Fig. 2). The first column on the right can be read as *a, ra, pa, ca, na, la, da,* (and) *ba*. In the next column we can read *ba, bra,* (or *ḍra*), *iṁ, ma* (and) *pa*. In the third column one can notice *le, iṁ, da* (?) (and) *dhra* (?). The numerals 44, 11, 6 (and) 9 occur in the fourth column. Though Salomon read *a, ra, pa, ca, na, la* (and) *da* in the first column ke was not sure about the nature of the contents of the other columns.[18] But if the first column deals with the Arapacana script, the next two columns must also be related to it. However, the list found here does not tally completely with the list quoted above. So the inscribed list which may be palaeographically dated to the first-second century AD, may represent a particular stage in the evolution of the syllabary in question. The evolution was obviously dependent on the selection of hymns or precepts for the purpose. So it apears from this list that though the use of the Arapacana script might have commenced, an ideal list, acceptable universally, had not yet been prepared.

A point should be noted here. If the inscription was engraved on the reverse of the slab, which was never to be seen by the visitors to the stūpa, why was it engraved at all? This phenomenon probably betrays the devotees' faith in the mystic value of the script. By inscribing it anywhere one could gain merit. This hypothesis stands even if we concede that many of the donative records placed inside the stūpa were not meant to be read by outsiders. These perpetuated the name of the donor, the date and purpose of the pious act and the donor's desire for merit. Of these objectives, only the last is applicable to the inscription in question. The numerals in this record may indicate the specified sections of the stūpa where such a list might have been engraved (viz., in the sixth, ninth, eleventh and forty-fourth sections of the stūpa as determined by the architect).

Whether this explanation is acceptable or not, an idealized list of letters and conjuncts evolved by the third-fourth century AD. Their number was forty-two, though, as noted, above, some lists contained forty-one, forty-three or forty-four characters. The forty-two characteers may be listed as follows:[19] (1) *a*; (2) *ra*; (3) *pa*; (4) *ca*; (5) *na*; (6) *la*; (7) *da*; (8) *ba*; (9) *da*; (10) *sha*; (11) *va*; (12) *ta*; (13) *ya*; (14) *shta*; (15) *ka*; (16) *sa*: (17) *ma*; (18) *ga*; (19) *tha*; (20) *ja*; (21) *śva* (or *sva*); (22) *dha*; (23) *śa*: (24) *kha*; (25) *ksha*: (26) *sta*; (27) *jña*; (28) *rtha* (or *ha*, or *pha*, or *ita*); (29) *bha*; (30) *ca*; (31) *sma*: (32) *hva*; (33) *tsa* (or *sta*); (34) *gha*; (35) *ṭha*; (36) *ṇa*; (37) *pha*; (38) *ska*; (39) *ysa* (pronounced as *z* of the Roman script as used in the English language); (40) *ścha*; (41) *ṭa*; and (42) *ḍha* (or *sta*).

The Arapacana list is known to have been used in Mahāyāna Buddhist treatises like the *Lalitavistara*, the Gaṇḍavyūha section of the *Avataṁsaka-sūtra* and the texts of the Prajñāpāramitā class.[20] The relevant texts were composed in different periods from the third to the eighth centuries.[21] However, the evolution of the Arapacana might have started earlier. We have already referred to an early list of the first-second century.

The Mahāyāna may not have been the only inspiration behind the initiation of the formulation of the Arapacana list. Inspiration might have been received also from those Hīnayāna sects which favoured or approved of the growth of several Mahāyānic ideals in the first-second century.[22] We can here especially refer to the Sarvāstivāda and Dharmaguptaka sects.[23] It should be noted that the existence of the Arapacana list can be traced in the Chinese translation of the *Vinaya* of the Dharmaguptakas.[24]

Let us now tackle the question of fixing the area of the origin of the Arapacana list. Long ago Sylvain Lévi drew attention to the appearance of *ysa*, a conjunct in the Arapacana list, in the name of *Ysamotika*, the father of Caṣṭana, a satrapal ruler of western India in the first-second century AD.[25] This name occurs in coin legends and inscriptions in the Brāhmī script. Since the same conjunct is known to have been used regularly in writing Khotani Saka in the Brāhmī script, S. Konow located the origin of the Arapacana script in Khotan and observed that Caṣṭana might have come to India from Khotan.[26] But neither is there any independent evidence connecting Caṣṭana with Khotan, nor data suggesting the use of the Khotani Saka with the Brāhmī script in Khotan prior to the second half of the first millennium AD. However, the kingdom of Shan-shan near Khotan could have been familiar with Brāhmī by the third-fourth century, or a little earlier.[27] But here the Kharoshṭī script and a form of the Prakrit language were used officially during the third-fourth centuries.[28] An incomplete list of Arapacana, written in Kharoshṭī, has been unearthed in the Niya area within the limits of Shan-shan. Many of the letters and conjuncts from nos. 16 to 35 of the above noted ideal list are noticeable here. Only *jña* (no. 27) is replaced by *ña* (since *jña* changes into *ña* in Prakrit).[29]

It is noteworthy that the conjuct *ysa* does not appear in the incomplete list. Even if a complete list had been recovered from the area of Shan-shan, the occurrence of *ysa* therein was unlikely. In the local Kharoshṭī script the phonetic value of *ysa* (like *z* as used in the English language written in the Roman script) was expressed by adding a slanting stroke to the bottom of the letter *ja*.[30] In spite of this, we shall have to concede that in the southern part of the eastern side of Central Asia (i.e in the south-eastern sector of Xing Jiang of

China) the Arapacana list or script was current in the third-fourth century AD.

The process of preparation of the Arapacana list commenced earlier in the north-western section of the Indian subcontinent. In two Gandhāra panels two persons (Bodhisattva is one case and Viśvāmitra in the other) are shown writing on a slate.[31] Written on the slate of the first panel, now preserved in the Lahore Museum, R. Salomon found ... *ra(ṁ)pacaṇa ... (ba).*[32] But the correct reading is *Arapacana ... ba.* Here there is a little (inadvertently created) gap between *a* and *ra.* The inscription on the slate in the second panel has been deciphered by R. Salomon as *pacanalada- (ba) (ḍa).*[33] We can notice only ... *pacanala.* ... However, there is no doubt that both the inscriptions, datable to the first-second century, allude to the Arapacana list. So around this period the list was current in the north-west.

We should like to point out here that the conjunct *ysa* of the Arapacana list is not known to have ever been used in the Kharoshṭī records of the north-west. The sound of *z* (as used in the English language written in the Roman script) was expressed in that area by the letter *ja* (changeable into *ya* in Prakrit) (*cf. Azes = Aja* or *Aya*). So the process of preparation of the Arapacana list was not complete in the north-west.

On the other hand, the conjuct *ysa* was used in Brāhmī in the area of Mathura in about the first century AD, perhaps for writing foreign (Iranian) names or words. The name *Nāysa* can be seen engraved in Brāhmī on the long helmet of a head in stone unearthed in that locality. Palaeographically the inscription can be assigned to the first century.[34] (Fig. 3). *Nāysa* (*Nāza*) was probably the name of the person represented in stone. The long helmet, is known to have been used by the Śakas. At least the evidence of this inscribed sculpture proves that the users of the Brāhmī script in Mathurā were familiar with the conjunct *ysa.* So it may be guessed that the ideal or final list of the Arapacana script could have been completed in a Brāhmī using zone like Mathurā. It is well-known that the latter area was closely related, politically and culturally, with the north-west in the first and second centuries AD. The Sarvastivāda sect exerted considerable influence in Mathurā.[35]

Certain inferences can be drawn from the the above discussion. It appears that for making the form, sound and use of a letter well known to a student a sentence with the letter concerned in the beginning of its first word was taught. A sculpture of the Kushāṇa age, found in north India, displays the scene of an infant learning the vowels of the Brāhmī script. The same letter was written and read repeatedly. In the panel concerned the list of vowel letters appears four times (though none of them is complete) (Fig. 4).

The two main scripts mentioned in the list of scripts furnished by the *Lalitavistara* of the first-second century are Brāhmī and Kharoshṭi.[36] The list of letters, including *a, i, u, au,* etc., as given in the same section of the text, must refer to Brāhmī, since these are absent (or nearly absent) from the Kharoshṭī script used in the north-west.

In the list of Brāhmī letters furnished by the *Lalitavistara* each character is followed by a phrase or sentence with the character concerned in the beginning of its head-word. Here, however, each phrase or sentence has a religious import. Thus a religious garb was given to a popular and scientific method of teaching. The process of formulation of the list commenced in the first-second century AD in the north-west and in the Mathura area of north India.[37] In the early stage of development there were some differences between different lists, at least in the selection of certain characters in their (i.e. the lists) middle and the last parts. An ideal or idealized list was formulated by the third-fourth century and was named by its first five letters (*a, ra, pa, ca,* and *na*).

Arapacana is not an alphabet in the ordinary sense of the term. It may better be called a syllabary consisting of monosyllabic letters and conjuncts. It may be glorified by calling it a script.

As already stated, the list concerned is found in Mahāyāna Buddhist texts. But inspiration might have been received at the early stage of its formulation also from certain Hīnayāna sects like the Dharmaguptaka and Sarvāstivāda.[38] The task of preaching religious ideas in a ritualistic function would have been made easier by reciting the total list along with the sentences bearing religious import.[39]

The Arapacana list or script itself became an object of purity and respect through its use in religious ceremonies and texts. At least, in course of time it became the name of a special form of Mañjuśrī, the Buddhist deity of transcendental wisdom. Acoording to a description in the Buddhist *Sādhanamālā,* Arapacana Mañjuśrī carried a book (or manuscript) in one hand and a sword in the other.[40] Apparently the book represents knowledge while the sword is supposed to be useful for piercing or destroying ignorance (Fig. 5). Numerous representations of Arapacana Mañjuśrī or Sadyonubhava-Arapacana are known in a stone, metal and painting (illustrations in manuscripts).[41] The deity is quite popular in Tibet, Nepal and China. The letters *a, ra, pa, ca* and *na* are known to be uttered n secretive prayers to Bodhisattva Mañjuśrī.[42] Here the letters have magical or mystic power.

Thus the Arapacana syllabary or script or list evolved out of the process of using the alphabet for religious purposes. Its relligious sanctity and secretive power deified it and introduced it in the magical circle of Tantrayāna.[42] Through this line of argument we can trace the transformation of a script into a deity. In any case, the history of the Arapacana list represents and eternal Indian idea—script symbolizes knowledge, and knowledge is god.

NOTES

1. *Lalitavistara,* Ch 10 (ed. P.L. Vaidya, Darbhanga, 1958), pp. 88-9.
2. *Pañcaviṁśati-sāhasrikā-prajñāpāramitā,* ed. N. Datta (Calcutta, 1934), p. 212 (the chapter on *'Dhāraṇi-sambhāra'*). Dharmarakṣa translated this text in Chinese in AD 286 (ibid., introduction, p. 5)
3. *Bulletin of the School of Oriental and African Studies,* Vol. XL (1977), pp. 85 and 94. It should be noted here that the concerned hymns, aphorisms and precepts were translated and not transliterated into Chinese in the work of Dharmarakṣa. However, the head-words were transliterated in the Chinese rendering of the *Pañcaviṁśati-sāhasrikā-prajñāpāramitā* done by the same scholar in AD 286 (ibid., pp. 86 and 94).
4. Ibid., pp. 94-5.
5. *Journal of the American Oriental Society,* (hereafter *JAOS*), Vol. 110, no. 2 (1990), p. 256; N. Datta, op. cit., p. 212.
6. N. Datta, op. cit., p. 212.
7. M. Winternitz, *A History of Indian Literature* (Eng. tr.), Vol. I (Calcutta, 1927), pp. 109-10, 119, etc.
8. Ibid., p. 185.
9. Ibid., Vol. II, Calcutta, 1933, pp. 380-1.
10. N. Datta (ed.), op. cit., p. 212.
11. Ibid.
12. Ibid.
13. The name appearing in an inflected term as *Ajasa* in the Prakrit inscription on the reverse of several series of coins is expressed as *Azou* in the accompanying Greek legend. Another name occurs in different records as *Vāsishka, Bazeshka, Vajheshka,* etc.

14. J. Marshall, *Buddhist Art of Gandhāra* (Cambridge, 1961), pl. 27, no. 49.
15. The slab of stone bearing the inscription and the panel of sculpture is now in the British Museum (No. 1900-4-14, 13. BOM).
16. B.N. Mukherjee, 'An Enigmatic Kharoshṭī Inscription', *Journal of the Asiatic Society*, Vol. XXIX (1984), pp. 16-18.
17. *JAOS*, Vol. 110 (1990), p. 259.
18. Ibid., pp. 259-61.
19. Ibid., p. 256.
20. *JAOS*, 1990, p. 255; *Memorial Sylvain Lévi*, Paris, 1937, pp. 355-63; M. Winternitz, op. cit., Vol. II, pp. 313f, 325 and 380f.
21. *Acta Orientalia*, Vol. XII, p. 14. However, the Tibetan translation of the *Prajñāpāramitā* texts were done later than this period. Again a recension of the Arapacana list is found in the *Book of Zambasta,* written in the Khotani Saka language [R.E. Emmerick, *The Book of Zambasta* (London, 1968), pp. 120-1 and 454-5].
22. The evidence of numerous donative records and several Gandhāra sculptures of the early centuries AD from the north-west of the Indian subcontinent testify to this development.
23. The Dharmaguptakas originated from the Mahīśāsaka branch of the Sarvāstivāda sect.
24. *Taisho Tripiṭaka,* 1428, Ch. 2, 639a; E. Lamotte, *History of Indian Buddhism* (translated from the original in French into English by S. Webb-Boin) (Louvian-la-Neuve, 1988), p. 497; *Journal Asiatique,* S. XI, Vol. V, p. 440; *JAOS*, Vol. 110 (1990), p. 255. It has been claimed that the Arapacana list is found also in the *Mūlasarvāstivāda Vinaya* (*JAOS*, Vol. 110, 1990), p. 255. N. Datta was of the opinion that there had been not much difference between the *Vinayas* of Sarvāstivāda and Mūlasarvāstivāda sects (N. Datta, *Buddhist Sects of India*, reprint, 1977, p. 151).
25. *Journal Asiatique,* S.11, Vol. V, (1915), p. 191; 'Ysa', *Memorial Sylavin Lévi,* Paris, 1937, pp. 355f.
26. *Acta Orientalia,* 1933, Vol. XII, pp. 13-14.
27. B.N. Mukherjee, *India in Early Central Asia—A Survey of Indian Scripts, Languages and Literatures in Central Asia in the First Millennium AD* (New Delhi, 1996), p. 18.
28. Ibid., pp. 39f.
29. A.M. Boyer, E.J. Rapson and E. Senart, *Kharoshṭī Inscriptions Discovered by Sir Aurel Stein in Chinese Turkestan,* Vol. II (Oxford, 1927), p. 187, no. 512 (N. 24.6.2); *JAOS*, Vol. 110, no. 2 (1990), pp. 265-8 and Fig. 7.
30. B.N. Mukherjee, op. cit., pl. 4b.
31. *JAOS*, Vol. 110, no. 2 (1990), pp. 262-5; Figs. 3-6.
32. Ibid., p. 263.
33. Ibid., p. 255.

34. J. Rosenfield, *The Dynastic Arts of the Kushans* (Berkeley and Los Angeles, 1967), reproduction of sculpture numbers 4.
35. B.N. Mukherjee, *Mathurā and Its Society—The Śaka-Pahlava Phase,* (Calcutta, 1981), pp. 1f, 94f and 162f; E. Lamotte, op. cit., pp. 523 and 527.
36. P.L. Vaidya (ed.), op. cit., p. 88.
37. So we cannot believe, following R. Salomon and G. Fussman, that the Arapacana list originated and evolved only in the north-western section of the Indian subcontinent (*JAOS*, Vol. 110, no. 2 (1990), p. 256; G. Fussman, 'Upāya-Kauśalya: L'implantation du bouddisme au Gandhāra', *Bouddhisme et Cultures locales*, ed. G. Fussman and F. Fumimasa (Paris, 1994), p. 39.
38. E. Lamotte, op. cit., p. 497.
39. In this connection see the *Journal Asiatique*, S. XI, Vol. 5 (1915), pp. 401f.
40. B. Bhattacharyya, *The Indian Buddhist Iconography*, 2nd edn (Calcutta, 1958), p. 120; B. Bhattacharyya (ed.), *Sādhanamālā*, Vol. I (Baroda, 1925), p. 121.
41. B. Bhattacharyya, *The Indian Buddhist Iconography*, pp. 120f; S.K. Saraswati, *Tantrayāna Art—An Album* (Calcutta, 1977), pp. 20-1.
42. L.A. Waddell, *The Buddhism of Tibet of Lamaism*, 2nd edn, rpt (Cambridge, 1959), p. 181; A.K. Gordon, *The Iconography of Tibetan Lamaism* (New York, 1939), p. 68; E. Lamotte, op. cit., p. 498.
43. S.K. Saraswati, op cit., pp. 18f.
44. In this connection see also our article in the *Deśa* (a Bengali periodical), 14.8.96, pp. 103f.

Fig. 1: Arapacana by B.N. Mukherjee.

Fig. 2: Arapacana by B.N. Mukherjee.

Fig. 3: Arapacana by B.N. Mukherjee.

Fig. 4: Arapacana by B.N. Mukherjee.

Fig. 5: Arapacana by B.N. Mukherjee.

Index